HOW MONEY
BECAME
DANGEROUS

HOW MONEY BECAME DANGEROUS

THE INSIDE STORY OF OUR TURBULENT
RELATIONSHIP WITH MODERN FINANCE

CHRISTOPHER VARELAS
AND DAN STONE

ecco
An Imprint of HarperCollins*Publishers*

HarperCollins books may be purchased for educational, business, or sales promotional use. For information, please email the Special Markets Department at SPsales@harpercollins.com.

FIRST EDITION

Designed by Joy O'Meara

Library of Congress Cataloging-in-Publication Data has been applied for.

ISBN 978-0-06-268475-2

19 20 21 22 23 LSC 10 9 8 7 6 5 4 3 2 1

Dedicated to three generations of amazing women

Αθανασια

Jessica
Kimberly

Athanacia

CONTENTS

PROLOGUE: ZERO BALANCE

If you learn how money moves, you can understand how the world works.
—ANN RICHARDS, FORMER GOVERNOR OF TEXAS,
IN CONVERSATION, AS REPORTED BY A COLLEAGUE

The world of money used to be simple. A person might have both a checking and a savings account, a home mortgage and a car loan, and maybe some basic investments in the markets, like municipal bonds or shares in Sears, Roebuck or General Motors. But rarely were a person's finances more complex than that. Wall Street wasn't particularly controversial. The financial services industry didn't have a reputation for being impersonal, selfish, and reckless. Most of the time, it was seen as just another facet of a functioning and growing society.

That all started to change rapidly in the 1980s as our financial system became increasingly complicated, with each evolution moving the world of money further beyond the understanding of the general public. Wall Street began to feel like an adversary, an enigmatic and potentially dangerous force controlled by slippery bankers whom we didn't trust. After the mortgage crisis, collapse of banks, and Great Recession of

2008, our wariness boiled over into anger. The system no longer seemed to be working for the average person.

How did we get here? In just one generation, how did our financial system become so labyrinthine and loaded with peril as we became more disconnected from its workings?

Why do we care so little that the national debt is more than $20 trillion and growing? Why do we care so little that our government employee pension system is massively underfunded, with the gap growing wider each year? Why do we care so little that we have grossly insufficient funding for promised Social Security and healthcare benefits? Why do we care so little that student debt stands at $1.6 trillion, weighing down millions of graduates who can't find jobs worthy of their degrees and are incapable of repaying what they owe?

Is it really the case that we don't care about these looming crises, or is it that we feel shackled by our lack of understanding and connection? Whatever the reason, the result is the same. As the world of money continues to become a bigger and bigger part of our lives, we understand it less and less. Everyone talks about *sustainability* these days—in regard to the environment, or food, or economic matters, or cultural and social issues—but no one is talking about the sustainability of our financial system, despite the fact that it occupies such a prominent place in our human existence and future well-being. This is the most important discussion that we are not having.

If we stand by, remaining disengaged from the world of money, we are headed to a dangerous place. Regardless of your background or occupation, this will affect you in your lifetime, most assuredly altering your children's quality of life. It is imperative that we increase our knowledge and engagement with the financial world and change the current trajectory. Otherwise it will end badly for us all.

———

My first exposure to the financial world was in 1970 in the second grade, when Mr. Samson, the manager of Springfield Savings and Loan, came to speak to our class about banks. There was nothing exotic about

Mr. Samson; he wore a gray suit, red tie, and shiny grown-up shoes. He circled the room with a stack of booklets, passing one to each of us. On the cover, the logo of the bank was printed, along with a place for me to scrawl my name. I flipped through its pages of unfilled lines and boxes, each page backed by the ghosted portrait of a US president. As we inspected our booklets, Mr. Samson instructed us to pull out the dimes we'd been asked to bring to class. Mine had been burning a hole in my pocket all day.

"Those dimes," he said, "are your first deposit. If you bring in a dime every week, I'll come by on Fridays to collect them and give you a stamp for your book, then I'll deposit your money in the bank. While it's in the bank, your money will collect interest, which means we'll reward your account with a little bonus each month. And during the time your money is with us, we might use it for other purposes, such as loaning it out to people who are opening a new shop or buying a house. Any time you want to withdraw your money, you just come down to see us. But if you leave it alone and let it grow, after time, you'll have accumulated savings."

Our teacher told us to line up. At the table in the front of the room, Mr. Samson collected our dimes in a black leather bag and stamped the first pages of our books to verify our deposits.

"There are thirty weeks left in the school year," he said. "If you bring in your dime every week, you'll have saved three dollars by summer break."

We were floored by the prospect that we could someday possess that much money. Back at my desk, I quickly calculated how much I could save if I did this for three additional years, until the end of fifth grade. Three plus three plus three plus three. Whoa—I could have twelve dollars. From that day on, I brought in my dime every week, without fail, and assiduously filled my book with stamps.

My parents' experience with money wasn't much more complicated than what Mr. Samson taught us that day in second grade. Back then, in the late 1960s, when their friends paid off their mortgages, they would often throw a party at which they would burn their mortgage slips. Finance was simple enough that the common path for a family was to purchase a home, dutifully work to pay down the mortgage, then enjoy an easier retirement. That level of simplicity is almost unheard of today.

We spend so much time worrying about money now—almost around the clock—and I can't say that makes us better off. Yet on the flip side, there was a time not too long ago when we didn't have the many advantages the financial world now provides. For example, mortgages weren't widely available to the general public. If you wanted to buy a house, you had to save up the entire purchase price. So the increase in complexity in the financial world has also brought with it products that have made many people's lives better. Modern finance always seems a double-edged sword, which is why the universe of money has long intrigued me.

I got my first glimpse of the dangerous side of money in high school, when my family moved from Springfield, Massachusetts, to Orange County, California. My father had been offered a new job as CEO of a company that had been acquired in a leveraged buyout. I vividly recall him distraught at the dinner table, talking about how interest rates had skyrocketed, and as a result, he was forced to cut costs at his new company in order to service the debt. Cutting costs meant cutting jobs, and my father felt a heavy responsibility for his employees and concern for their families. At that young age, seeing the effect of those pressures on my father and his company, I had little understanding of leveraged buyouts and the movement of interest rates, yet I was filled with apprehension—what would happen to the people who lost their jobs due to the cutbacks? How did those larger, external economic factors force my father to make uncomfortable and unpopular decisions? It would take years before I could begin to understand these concepts and their impact on people's lives.

Ending up working in finance, however, surprised me at first, because I've never had the cutthroat personality for which Wall Street is notorious—I worked at Disneyland while studying liberal arts at Occidental College—nor have I ever developed a lust for fast cars, fancy watches, and vacation houses, the tokens of status and accomplishment that are the trophies of the banking world. I simply loved the work. And I've been lucky enough to have a role in or a ringside seat for many of the big financial moments over the past three decades. After college in the 1980s, I started as a corporate lending officer for Bank of America, loaning money to gold and diamond wholesalers in LA's jewelry district, then attended The Wharton School. I landed at Salomon Brothers in the 1990s, working my way from the trading floor through the investment bank until I served as the global head of Citi's TMT (technology, media, and telecom) group, head of the National Investment Bank and the regional offices, as well as Citi's first culture czar. After twenty years, I left Wall Street to cofound a private equity firm in Silicon Valley.

I was an unlikely person to end up in these positions. Both sides of my family were Greek immigrants from Sparta. We led a normal middle-class life. As a teenager, to save for college, I not only worked at Disneyland but a slew of other odd jobs, from pool cleaner to peanut vendor. I definitely was not on the career track for Wall Street, nor did I know that such a track existed. But, in ending up there, I found that my unorthodox background gave me a unique perspective as someone who has, at times, been an insider, an outsider, a participant, and a skeptical observer.

I'm not claiming to be the only person with such proximity to the big moments in finance over the past three decades, but it is not a large group, and I may be one of the few who thought to chronicle each event as it happened. I'm certainly the only one who started off his Wall Street career wearing a polka dot vest and bow tie at Disneyland.

This book, by telling true stories from the financial services industry— most of which have never been told before, or at least not from this particular vantage point—aims to highlight the changes over the past thirty-plus years that have made the world of money so complex and laden with risk. The moments and inflection points captured in this book changed the arc of how money moves. These stories will help one better understand how money has become dangerous at the personal, community, national, and global levels.

My accomplice and co-author, Dan Stone, is a finance outsider. A writer and editor, Dan also owns a small Main Street business. That juxtaposition of our backgrounds proved instrumental in our efforts to write this book for a broad audience—for both Wall Street and Main Street, for people who have spent their careers in the industry, as well as for people who have no previous knowledge of how the financial system works. This is not a book about capital ratios or Federal Reserve policy or dry, technical concepts; rather, it tries to get to the root forces that are impacting all of us and driving the financial services industry.

A note on terms: We use many phrases and names to describe the world of money—Wall Street, the banks, the financial services industry, modern money, the financial system, and so on. While each of those terms may carry its own shade of meaning, here we use them more or less interchangeably. The most accurate term to describe the subject of this book is *modern financial capitalism*, which captures the world of money most comprehensively, encompassing the movement of money through our public and private lives, the social trends around money, as well as the workings of Wall Street and the broader financial industry. This is a book not only about how the financial world has changed but also about how money has transformed us and the world in which we live.

You'll notice that the book's early stories, in particular, depict a male-heavy world. That was the reality of the financial services industry for a long time—and in many ways, it still is. The loudest-talking guy in the room, often praised as a Big Swinging Dick or a Master of the Universe, once dominated the day. Over the past few decades, the cultural sensitivity and awareness of the industry as a whole has dramatically shifted in tone. But even while Wall Street culture has evolved in terms of bravado, behavior, and personality, it has hardly become more accessible to women, particularly at the senior ranks. Clearly more needs to be done than simply a change in office etiquette. As our larger society continues to evolve toward a more democratic and balanced environment for women, hopefully we'll see that inclusiveness extend more robustly to the financial services industry.

In our contemporary discourse, there are defenders of Wall Street and there are condemners, with few in between. The defenders argue that Wall Street should be appreciated for providing our modern world with the opportunities and advantages that most of us enjoy, from the financing of bridges and public schools to the issuance of home mortgages and small business loans. For the defenders, Wall Street is undeniably a force for good. The condemners stand defiantly on the opposite end of the spectrum. To them, Wall Street has poison in its veins. They believe that its corruption and greed are solely responsible for the 2008 Great Recession and most of the evils visited upon a defenseless population. The system is irredeemable, they say, and needs to be torn down.

The chasm between these two groups is vast and growing. But could it be that the truth lies somewhere in the middle? Could Wall Street be both necessary and troubled, essential to a functioning society and yet increasingly difficult to understand and govern? I hope that this book does more than simply illuminate the recent changes in finance. I hope that it might also provide a framework for a constructive discussion between the disparate corners of our culture, so we can work toward creating the financial system on which a healthy society must rely, one that serves the interests of the people by supporting the basic necessities of life and the pursuit of dreams and aspirations. Our success and failure as a society are directly connected with how our financial system is constructed and managed.

By the time I reached high school in Orange County, I no longer brought dimes to class, but Mr. Samson's lesson had stuck with me, and I'd continued to save and deposit income from various jobs—mowing lawns, washing cars, cleaning the neighborhood pool each Saturday morning. As graduation neared, I found that I'd amassed two hundred dollars, which sat in a savings account accumulating interest. I left it alone until four years later, on the cusp of finishing college, when I was home visiting my parents. I was about to begin my first job postgraduation, working at Bank of America as a corporate lending officer, and I figured it would be a good idea to move my account from the regional Orange County bank to that of my new employer. As I entered the lobby, I could only imagine what my balance had become after four years of steady growth. A two-hundred-dollar savings account wasn't going to buy me a house or nice car, but I expected it might have swelled into a decent chunk of change.

After waiting in the teller line, I was directed to see a bank officer. I settled into a chair across the desk from him. "Name and account number?" he said without looking at me as he typed my information into his computer. It must have been 45 degrees in the bank; the air-conditioning was running full tilt.

"I'd like to withdraw my funds," I said, with a twinge of anticipation, or perhaps it was a shiver from the blast of cold air descending on us.

The man stared into his monitor. "That account," he said, with an excruciatingly long pause, "is empty."

"What? How could that be?"

He swiveled his head and regarded me over the top of his glasses. "There were no funds in the account. So it was closed."

"But I haven't touched that money for four years."

He studied his computer terminal again. "It looks as though a fee was initiated two years ago," he said, "of ten dollars per month, and eventually your balance was zeroed out by the service charges."

While it was only two hundred dollars, the loss of that money meant more to me than any other financial loss later in life, no matter the amount. I had done so much to save that money. To have it wiped out in such a callous, impersonal way made me start to question the institution that I had long trusted. The situation seemed unfair, but I didn't have enough knowledge or experience to articulate why that was so. I looked across the desk at this bank officer, unsure of what to say. And he didn't seem to have anything more to say to me. So I left, climbed into my old hand-me-down car, and drove away, thinking back on those halcyon days of saved dimes and neighborhood jobs, of the friendly smile of Mr. Samson and my naïve trust that the system cared, somehow, about my well-being.

1

FOOL'S GOLD

O Zeus, why is it you have given men clear ways of testing whether gold is counterfeit, but, when it comes to men, the body carries no stamp of nature for distinguishing bad from good?

—EURIPIDES, *MEDEA*

That's what I fucking said, 30 percent off the Rap sheet, Princess cut. It's a fucking beautiful stone. Like headlamps on a Rolls-Royce. Figure it out and call me back." Barry Kagasoff slammed down the phone and looked up from his desk, on which were stacked dozens of tiny sheer paper envelopes holding diamonds. With tweezers, he returned a stone to its envelope and pointed a thumb in my direction. "Who's this?" he asked my colleague, Mark.

"This is Chris Varelas. The new guy."

"Varelas," Barry said, not looking at me. "What is that, Latino?"

"No, it's Greek," I said. My voice sounded weak and distant, like it was coming to us from an adjoining room. I tugged at my lapel. My new suit felt hot and ill fitting.

I scanned the diamonds on his desk, the value of which represented far more money than I'd ever seen before. Barry's hair was slicked back, shoulder length, coal black. He looked like a gangster from a classic film—handsome and potentially charming, if only you weren't worried that at any moment he might stave in your skull with a baseball bat if you said the wrong thing. The sleeves of his dress shirt were rolled to the elbow. He wore no jewelry, which was surprising given his profession. An adjustable-arm lamp hovered over him, every bit of it covered in yellow Post-it notes scrawled with names, numbers, and codes that must have been diamond specs. The surface of his desk was littered with Post-its too, as if that few square feet of the office had been hit with a miniature windstorm.

"Greek, huh?" Barry's interrogation continued—where I'd grown up, how old I was, and where I'd previously worked that made me qualified to take over his account. The exchange wasn't going well.

He scowled. "Wait, what the fuck did you just say?"

I flinched. No one had ever said *fuck* to me in a business setting before. Disney was my first real job, and there hadn't been a lot of foul language in the Magic Kingdom. I shifted uneasily and glanced at Mark, who was subtly shaking his head in my direction, showing his disapproval and a touch of what might have been fear.

"Disneyland," I repeated.

"Disney-fucking-land." The word circled in the air like a bird of prey. "That's what I thought you said." Barry grinned at Mark. Not a happy grin. "Really?" he said to Mark. "I got fucking Mickey Mouse as my new loan officer?" The phone rang. Barry picked it up and barked "Kagasoff," then began negotiating another deal.

Mark and I waited through the call as Barry plucked Post-its and read off prices and descriptions of diamonds, while also scribbling new notes. Since it was my first day meeting him, I needed to establish myself as his lending officer. My initial goal was to get him to sign the documents I carried in the leather Bank of America folder tucked under my arm. While organizing my files at the bank earlier in the week, I noticed that Barry hadn't signed any paperwork regarding his line of credit. Not a single document, ever. From the day he had opened his wholesale diamond business several years before, the bank had loaned him millions of dollars on nothing more than a handshake. My bank bosses had decided that my taking over his account would provide a good opportunity to bring his files up to date, so here I was, with the documents ready to go. It should be easy. No big deal.

He hung up the phone.

"Mr. Kagasoff." I took a step forward and started to open the folder, but his eyes came up to meet mine so suddenly and fiercely that I froze. He looked at me as if I'd drawn a gun—and it wasn't surprising that firearms sprang to mind, since it was well known that Barry kept a full artillery at hand, including a sawed-off shotgun, an Uzi, a 9 mm tucked in the back of his belt, and a .45 mounted under his desk. I swallowed, pulling the papers slowly from the folder, inches at a time.

He regarded them with disgust from five feet away. "What the fuck is that?"

"Mr. Kagasoff, these are our standard loan documents. We noticed that our paperwork wasn't in order, and you had never signed—"

"Is this guy serious?" he asked Mark, who shrugged meekly.

"Sir," I tried again, "all our clients have signed these. They're very standard—"

"Listen, Mickey Mouse. You either trust me or you don't. Okay? You don't know shit from Shinola about how this business works. So put those away and get the fuck out of here."

Mark and I crossed the street to the bank in silence, papers unsigned.

Only days earlier, when the list of clients I was inheriting had been dropped on my desk, several co-workers gathered around to see who was included. "Ohhh! You got Barry!" they yelled. "He's gonna eat you alive!" I'd laughed it off then, but now I knew what they meant.

———

I was only twenty-two when I started at Bank of America in 1985, a job that would teach me more about the importance of character than probably anything else I could have done. I was a newly minted graduate of Occidental College and had just finished five years of summer and part-time employment at Disneyland. My role at the bank was to loan money and manage lines of credit for diamond and gold wholesalers in

Los Angeles's jewelry district. Theirs was a raw, bald-faced industry, built entirely on trust. As Barry taught me that first morning, you either take people at their word, or you don't. If I had landed in any other facet of the bank—lending to the trucking industry, for example, as I would later do—it might have taken me decades to gather the experience and insights that were thrust in my face from day one in the jewelry business.

When you were hired at Bank of America as a corporate lending officer, they tossed you into a yearlong training program, rotating you through various branches and positions, so you learned each job from the bottom up. This comprehensive approach provided a holistic under-standing of the bank's mission, as management believed you could do your job more effectively if you had a clear grasp of how the entire firm worked and where you fit into the big picture. To start, I fished envelopes out of ATMs and processed deposits. I then worked as a teller in the City of Industry. Later they moved me to South LA, where I learned con-sumer lending, which mostly involved issuing car loans to people who could barely afford them. After a few months, my commercial lending training rotation began at the International Jewelry Center on Hill Street. And then I got lucky: Dozens of employees jumped ship, all across Bank of America, scared off by the firm's exposure to several industries that were in crisis, and that exodus created a dearth of lending officers and an opening for me. At the time, the general consensus was that landing a job in commercial banking at B. of A. was a career for life. I was thrilled for the opportunity, but even in that excitement, I doubted that I would spend the rest of my working days there.

Among the new employees, I should have been at the bottom of the barrel after I completely blew the pretest meant to ascertain my background knowledge of banking and finance. I scored a 6 out of 100, which I was told was the lowest mark in bank history. But I guess if looked at from a certain angle, my score was at least statistically remark-able, since several of the questions were true-false or multiple choice. A drooling infant with a crayon could have gotten at least a third of the questions right. And yet, despite my abysmally low test score and lack of finance experience, the bank bosses at the Jewelry Center liked me—

probably because my Disneyland background made me seem fresh and incorruptible—so my training time was slashed from twelve months to only five, and the files of about seventy clients landed with a dull thud on my desk.

During the training program, the central concept presented to us was "the five *c*'s of credit," which guided our decisions on whether or not to loan someone money. They were *capital* (how much money and assets a potential borrower has), *capacity* (a borrower's ability to handle debt and expenses), *conditions* (the health of the market and industry), *collateral* (cash and assets to put up against the loan), and *character*. While the first four *c*'s were based on plenty of data that could be crunched and analyzed as needed, the fifth *c*, *character*, was in fact the one that mattered most, the one you could not disregard. Assessing character meant considering your client's work experience and background, credit history, trustworthiness, and integrity. Of course, character could be faked, as I would later experience firsthand, but right away I came to understand the importance of that fifth *c*.

At the bank, the standard practice among the lending officers was to stick to your desk and let the clients come to you. However, given my youth, inexperience, and short-lived training, I began walking the neighborhood each day to visit my clients on their own turf. The LA jewelry district surrounds Pershing Square, just blocks from downtown and Skid Row. By day, the neighborhood was frenzied and professional, the streets full of jewelers, foreign languages, negotiations, double-breasted suits, nervous couriers, and armored cars. By night, the area turned into a carnival of drugs, prostitutes, homeless people, and hustlers. An estimated fifty thousand people made their living in the handful of blocks that composed the jewelry district. The majority of these people were engaged in legitimate business, although most of the illicit financial activity in Los Angeles happened within a quarter mile of our Bank of America branch.

While walking a daily beat began as a self-imposed necessity, it soon became enjoyable. These guys were too interesting, entertaining, and unique *not* to visit. And since assessing character was the most important element of the job, spending time in their environment allowed me to get to know the jewelers in a deeper way than if we had met only at the bank. Each day, one of them would take me to lunch, and I'd hear unbelievable stories, crude jokes, dramatic arguments, and scraps of history about their Jewish and Armenian ancestors, from whom most of them had inherited their businesses and their industry savvy.

It's a historical fact that Jews and Armenians have long thrived at the top of the diamond and gold markets. The vast majority of gold dealers were ethnic Armenian, and almost all diamond guys were Jewish—both persecuted peoples who had learned to carry a universal currency wherever they were forced to relocate throughout the centuries. Diamond dealers would proudly tell me their family stories about nomadic Jews who would sew diamonds into the hems of their clothing so they could hide their worth as they crossed unfriendly borders.

My new fellow loan officers at Bank of America were mostly Mormons freshly graduated from Brigham Young University, and they were some of the nicest people you could find, with their water-cooler conversations and softball leagues. But the diamond and gold wholesalers populated a rough and fascinating world that I couldn't have imagined existed when I'd left Disneyland only months earlier.

———

Like most diamond wholesalers, Barry Kagasoff was born into it, and his family history was rich with persecution, long odds, and perseverance. Harry Kotlar, his grandfather, was a Polish Jew who narrowly evaded the death camps during WWII. Following the war, he fled Europe, came to Los Angeles, and fell in love with a woman named Helen, who had also emigrated from Poland. Her brother, who had previously been a diamond wholesaler in Israel, brought Harry into the business at the ground level, making him one of the original founders of the emerging wholesale diamond industry in LA. Harry and Helen got hitched and had three daughters, one of whom, Gloria, would become Barry's mother. Meanwhile, Barry's father, Nathan Kagasoff, was working as a gas station attendant in East LA. He was eighteen years old when he met Gloria. After they married, Nathan was also brought into the family trade, under the guidance of his new father-in-law.

Barry started working for his grandfather as a kid; he grew up in a powerful diamond-dealing family. When he was old enough to drive, he began splitting his days between school and work—school in the morning, then he'd head over to his grandfather's office for the afternoon. Barry's father, Nathan, took on a partner who helped him build up the largest diamond-wholesaling business on the West Coast. After Nathan's company multiplied in size, Barry shifted over to work for his father. But since Barry had been raised in an enterprising diamond family, it was only natural for him eventually to carve out his own wholesaling practice, which he did at age twenty-three. When I became his banker, my B. of A. branch in the International Jewelry Center was catty-corner from his office. Barry's father's office was upstairs. The diamond business was truly a family affair.

Barry and his father were put in charge of a membership organization called the Diamond Club, and they soon came to be considered the de facto bosses of the LA industry. If a new guy arrived in town, say from Israel or Belgium, and he wanted to open a line of credit and start his own business, the bankers would first consult with Barry and Nathan. The Kagasoffs might give the new guy a green light, or—if they thought he needed to prove himself first—they might suggest a trial period of six months; but whatever they recommended was followed to the letter. In their free time, they helped other wholesalers collect on delinquent accounts. Their reputations served as the muscle.

Barry's clients knew that he wouldn't bullshit them or try to squeeze them for extra money, that he was entirely fair in his dealings. I once watched him work with a customer who was looking for diamond earrings for his wife. They were arguing over what color grade would be appropriate. (Color is graded from D through Z, with the most expensive diamonds, which are colorless, graded D, E, or F.) This customer wanted to splurge on E or F color, but Barry told him, "You don't need to waste your money on that. Get the G color. Why the fuck would you want F color for earrings?"

"Because I want nice clarity," the customer said.

"Get the G," Barry said.

"No, but I want—"

"Listen to me," Barry said. "If anyone gets close enough to your wife's ear to know whether they're G or F color, you should take a crowbar to his fucking head."

Barry may not have been refined, but he was brutally honest. Leading a customer astray, stretching the truth to make a buck—those behaviors were anathema to Barry. For him, trust and reputation were everything. I heard him on the phone one afternoon, fired up at someone who had questioned his integrity. "Send the fucking diamond back to me right now," Barry said. "Just put it in the mail and send it back. I don't ever want to see you, and we will never do business again. If I do see you, I might beat the shit out of you."

———

There was another client I inherited, Nazareth Andonian, who had started his career by opening a small jewelry-repair shop with his brother, Vahe. Later they became gold wholesalers specializing in bracelets, necklaces, and watches. While Barry was a tough and intimidating presence in the diamond world, Nazareth was his opposite in the gold industry, an affable and affectionate charmer. He was a Lebanese Armenian from Beirut, a hardworking immigrant who had come to America in search of opportunity, not unlike my own Greek relatives. Nazareth dreamed of building up his own business and making a comfortable life for his wife, children, and extended family. I couldn't help but root for him.

Not long after I started working with Nazareth, his business, called Andonian Brothers, Inc., began to see enormous jumps in sales and revenue. His most popular products were gold nugget bracelets, gold rope chains, and big pendants depicting Jesus on an anchor, which sailors and young people loved. While Nazareth wasn't one of my top-five clients when I took over the account, he grew quickly and upgraded to bigger offices—*much* bigger offices—on the third floor of a building located a few blocks from the Jewelry Center. I was surprised by all the empty space when I first visited. "Nazareth, this is huge. How are you going to fill this?"

"We are growing fast, and I don't want to have to move again."

"You could fit half of Los Angeles in here, Nazareth."

He laughed loudly and squeezed my shoulder. "It's nice, no?"

Nazareth exuded warmth and humor. This was the mid-1980s, and everyone was calling each other "babe"—as in, "Jimmy, babe, I need those projections like five minutes ago"; "Florence, babe, do me a favor and pull the Corvette around front"; "Mitch, babe, you're an asshole." Nazareth had his own charming malaprop version of this slang: In his thick Lebanese accent, he would call me "Baby Chris." "Hey, Baby Chris, how are you? You get good boogie action this weekend?" Nazareth had a voracious appetite—for sex, money, cars, success. He was a man of the decade, and he wanted it all. He had a mistress on the side, whom he talked about openly, and later he would tell me about call girls he flew in from Atlanta on weekends. "Baby Chris, you want to meet Saturday? I am bringing in girls from Atlanta for good boogie action. You come have some?" He never stopped with the offers, no matter how many times I turned him down. Meeting someone like Nazareth—someone who engaged the services of prostitutes and spoke about it so freely, someone so funny and charming and odd, someone whose background I could barely imagine—was an entirely new experience for me.

I accepted an invitation for dinner at Nazareth's house one night. The table was packed with boisterous relatives, several generations of Andonians. His wife cooked traditional Lebanese food, and Nazareth toured me around, showing off the preposterous remodel of his bedroom, which featured circular walls, blinds that transformed into a mirror when you closed them, and a round rotating bed.

After dinner, he took me for a drive in his new yellow Lotus out on the empty Glendale Freeway. We accelerated to 80, then 100. I glanced sideways at Nazareth, whose face was lit red by the glow of the instrument panel. He slid the car into fifth gear as his lips curled into a demonic grin. "Here we go," he whispered. The needle passed 140, and I pressed my feet hard against the floorboard. I couldn't help but envision a sudden deer or pothole and wonder how we could survive at that velocity. But soon the ride was over, and we were downshifting back into Nazareth's neighborhood, and when his house came into view, we laughed with the exhilaration of survivors.

———

I was surprised that, even with Nazareth's impressive success, he was utterly clueless about how the lending system worked. He knew he needed to borrow to fund growth, but that seemed to be the extent of his comprehension. Since most businesses—gold and diamond wholesalers included—don't have sufficient capital to fund inventory purchases, they need to borrow through a line of credit in order to carry products for sale. Each year, a client's line of credit must be reviewed and renewed.

Commercial lending has been and still is the engine that fuels the growth of American business—not the large public companies, but small- and medium-sized businesses that compose most of the commercial activity and jobs in America. On a national scale, the commercial lending market is massive. With an outstanding balance of higher than $2 trillion today, commercial lending is more than twice as large as credit card debt.

With a client like Nazareth, whose business was doing so well, I boosted his line of credit as much as I could when it came time for his review. Yet since I was still fairly fresh on the job, I screwed up that first year and forgot one final simple step. It was a minor clerical error, but because of my oversight, Nazareth got a notice in the mail saying that his line had matured and the balance was due immediately. He came into the bank looking pale.

"Baby Chris, we gotta talk." There was an anxiety in his voice that I'd never heard before.

"Naz, how are you?"

"Not very good."

"What's going on?"

He sat down. "This weekend I was having boogie action with Rosa.

But I'm not thinking, *Oh, this is great boogie action.* Instead I'm thinking, *How am I going to pay Baby Chris the money I owe him, 'cause I don't have it.*" He handed me the notice he got in the mail. He was genuinely concerned. And I was concerned too—about the idea of him thinking of *me* while he was with Rosa.

I looked at the notice and recognized my oversight right away, but I didn't want to appear incompetent, so I said, "Nazareth, I'll tell you what. The last thing I want to do is mess up your boogie action. Don't pay me now—take another year. I'll get this sorted out for you." I set the paper on the corner of my desk.

"Thank you, Baby Chris, thank you," he said, leaning forward and patting my hand. "I thank you. Rosa thanks you. You are the best, Baby Chris."

The fact was, I'd done everything to renew his credit—completed the required financial analysis by hand on the yellow paper spreadsheet, created the support documents, gotten the bank manager and regional credit administrator to sign off—but I had forgotten a final detail: to peek my head into the back office and tell them that the renewal for Nazareth had gone through so they could enter it into their systems. And here I'd gone and upset poor Nazareth's weekend, ruined his boogie action.

My first year as a lending officer at Bank of America was the last year that the yellow paper spreadsheet was used for credit analysis. The shift from the paper spreadsheet to a computer spreadsheet may not sound like much, but it was a pivotal moment in the history of finance. With the yellow paper spreadsheet, you would complete a detailed analysis of the borrower's financial profile, filling it out by hand using a pencil, eraser, and calculator. Before writing anything down, you would carefully consider the most likely scenario for the future of that business. There was a lot of initial thought put into what the assumptions should be because if you changed an assumption or made a mistake, you had to start over.

With the change to the computer spreadsheet, you could skip the thinking stage and jump straight to inputting numbers and running various scenarios via the computer program. If you didn't like the outputs and conclusions, you could tinker with the assumptions until you got the result you wanted, since the program would automatically add and adjust as you made changes.

Any new tool can have both positive and negative impacts. The computer spreadsheet was no exception, facilitating a transformation in action and thought that would provide the framework to engineer the modern financial world, for better or worse.

With the yellow paper spreadsheet, your primary question while working on any financial analysis was, *What is the most likely outcome?* This encouraged and rewarded analysis that was right down the middle of possible outcomes. *If I can map only one outcome*, the thinking went, *then it should be the most probable.* Being constrained to a single outcome served as a safeguard against inputting aggressive assumptions and acting on inappropriate incentives.

But when the computer spreadsheet arrived in the mid-1980s, its tactical power provided a way to manipulate data and map infinite permutations of possible outcomes. The question was no longer, *What is most likely?* The question was now, *What is possible?* That change in mentality unleashed the energy and drive of the finance industry to create products and strategies that have altered our lives in countless ways. Capital was made more available and efficient as we came to understand the boundaries and limits of how much and where a business or individual could use additional debt or equity to support growth and expansion. New products were created to support specific needs, ranging from insurance to investment advisory to risk management. The door was opened to a whole new world, with the only limitation being your own ability to identify a need or even imagine a new one and then create the product or service to satisfy that demand.

But with those advantages also came a Pandora's box of new challenges. The computer spreadsheet not only allowed for the manipulation of the microanalysis of a business, person, or product, but also for the mapping of product usage at the macro level. It is one thing to manipulate the projections of a single business or person with the goal of lending that entity more money than it may be able to service. That evolution alone has troubling implications, but then the ability to execute analysis at the macro level facilitated the bundling of individual products to create new instruments that were centered around scale, scope, and diversification.

Once computer analytics were taken to a macro level, everything started to become unduly complicated, to the point that many of the people creating and analyzing the data would have a hard time explaining what it all meant and what future consequences it might bring. Suddenly you could crank out a hundred-page analysis that crunched every possible number in every possible way. Such analyses impressed the bosses and clients, but the priorities within the bigger picture became obscured. When the analytical objective became single-mindedly focused on building complicated models to support a complex new financial product with minimal to no consideration as to how it fit into the bigger financial system, that created sensitive, dangerous situations that were more susceptible to unforeseen changes or errors.

The mortgage market is perhaps the clearest and most widely appreciated example of the possibilities unleashed by the computer spreadsheet. The technology allowed home mortgages—including many risky ones—to be packaged and grouped into new products (a practice referred to as "securitization"), which spreadsheet analysis determined could yield good returns by packaging enough of them together and appropriately pricing the risk. The safety was in size and number, the argument went, and that not enough of the loans would go bad to hurt returns. Mortgages were sliced, diced, and bundled to be sold to public investors, and this was done on a massive and highly complex scale.

This concept, as we later learned, became disastrous. But there was initially a positive aspect to packaging mortgages into new products: The construction and sale of these bundled mortgages freed up banks' capital, allowing them to make more loans to individuals wishing to finance a home purchase. This made the dream of home ownership possible for more people.

If the story had stopped there, it would most likely have had a happy ending. Indeed, it has been said that every bad idea on Wall Street started as a good idea. But, in time, it all turned tragic, as the computer spread-sheet allowed us—or even encouraged us—without any governance other than our own character, to manipulate and push that initial good idea be-yond the boundaries of acceptable risk.

The second and arguably more troubling change ushered in by the computer spreadsheet was the removal of character from the financial services world. Character doesn't have a column in a computer spread-sheet. The process of cleansing character from the financial system be-gan with the disintermediation of the bank lending officer, who was essentially replaced by computer analytics. The importance of assess-ing character diminished, insofar as character meant anything more than paying bills in a timely manner. We eventually reached a point at which the fifth *c* of credit, *character*, was replaced with a single mea-surement called "credit worthiness." In the case of the individual, that was often reduced to a single number with the creation of the FICO score—a number that told a credit provider everything about an indi-vidual's credit worthiness that he or she wanted to know in deciding whether or not to approve a loan. Except that it didn't. Someone could be a terrible person—lying, cheating, mean, and reckless—but if he paid his bills on time and settled all debts, or did whatever the algo-rithm rated as positive behavior, then credit would be available to him. Conversely, someone could be Mother Teresa, but if there was a single black mark on her credit history, nothing could be done to secure her a loan.

Sacrificing local knowledge for the sake of scale and efficiency meant that little hope remained for a good person with no credit, nor forgiveness for someone who was late or missed a payment because of an unfortunate family emergency or other anomalous event. Local bank managers—the George Baileys of the world—had been relegated to a nostalgic scrap heap of people who relied on quaint and old-fashioned means to assess risk, means that were, for good or ill, influenced by the biases of emotion and subjective parameters, such as likability and manners. Throughout our financial system and arguably much of our culture, we've stopped relying on our gut and our eyes and our human connections, and we've handed over the decisions to computers and algorithms.

Removing character assessment from the equation has stripped away much of the humanity from the financial world. We've ended up with a system of evaluation that encourages only those behaviors that can be quantified, which diminishes the importance of qualities that are less easily measured—trust, loyalty, resilience, and judgment. If we allow those character traits to be tossed aside, how can we expect them to grow and thrive in us and in our communities? Whether or not we pay our bills on time is an important factor, sure, but whether or not we will take extraordinary steps to honor our obligations seems to be a more crucial question and one well beyond the understanding of a computer spread-sheet or algorithm.

And yet, replacing human character assessment with unbiased computer-based analytics is not entirely a bad thing. In addition to argu-ably being more accurate, computer-generated analysis and algorithms can support and implement financial practices that are less prone to rac-ism, sexism, and other prejudices. There was a time when a person of color was hard-pressed to find a banker who would lend him or her the capital to buy a house or start a business. That has drastically improved; while there's still a long way to go, the path we've forged is thanks in part to the objective analytics provided by the computer spreadsheet. So the issue is not whether computer analysis is better or worse than human analysis. The issue is that if we fail to measure character, then it only follows that character will become less prevalent, not just in the financial services industry but throughout society. It may not seem that way now, but historically the world of money had been the one place that assessed and rewarded good character and punished bad character.

———

Barry Kagasoff had started to soften to me in small ways, and eventu-ally his office became a stop on my daily rounds. I felt that I was inching closer to getting him to sign the documents that every other client had signed. Even though I'd already filled out his yellow paper spreadsheet, there were some questions that only he could answer.

"Look, Barry," I started. "I've done some analysis."

"Some what?"

"Some credit analysis."

"Fuck your credit analysis."

"Come on, Barry."

"Why would you do credit analysis on me? Are you telling me there's a possibility that my credit isn't good?"

It's funny to realize now that, to Barry, I must have seemed like some strange invasive species—a new generation of loan officer, creeping in with a fancy yellow paper spreadsheet to threaten the old-school culture of my-handshake-is-my-word—while only one year later, that paper spreadsheet would be obliterated by the move to computers.

Finally he helped me complete the credit analysis. There were several things I had a hard time making sense of. For example, when other diamond wholesalers closed a deal, they would typically be paid within six months, but it was different with Barry. His accounts would be settled immediately. "People pay me." That's the only answer he gave when I asked him about it.

"But, Barry, the industry average is 180 days, and yours is close to *zero days.*"

"People pay me."

I was beginning to understand the value of a tough reputation in the diamond industry, but despite Barry's intimidating personality, it didn't take long to recognize that he was good to his core, a man who had built his reputation through honesty and integrity. Over time, he became someone I could call for advice about any loan I was considering making. The diamond wholesaler community is small enough that everyone knows everyone else. While loan losses are higher in the jewelry industry than most other sectors, I never once had a loan that defaulted—I actually won an award for that—and my secret was that I would call up Barry and ask, "Is this guy's money good?" If Barry said, "Yeah, this guy will sell his daughter to pay you back," then I made the loan. If Barry said,

"Don't do it. He's a fucking liar and a cheat," then I didn't. Barry became my credit guy, my diamond *consigliere*—better than any spreadsheet.

———

George and Richard Elmassian were brothers who owned a gold whole-saling business that specialized in charms. I would visit them on my client rounds each day, and George and I quickly became very close. They were Armenian émigrés from West Africa who had decided to go into gold after abandoning their first plan, of opening an auto body shop. While George was even-keeled, cordial, and honest, his brother Richard was wild, emotional, and a great storyteller and jokester.

Richard had seemingly endless reserves of energy. He apparently donated enough money to the police department in the city of Bell—a nasty, corrupt town south of LA—to score a weekend job as a volunteer officer. While he was only five feet tall, if that, they matched him up with a six-foot-eight partner, and the wisecrack around the station was that by averaging their heights, they cleared the minimum requirement. Richard liked having a side job that allowed him to play the tough guy and oc-casionally smack the hell out of people.

George and Richard's gold business was growing steadily, and even-tually it became the number-one charm manufacturer and wholesaler in the country. Like many in their trade, Richard had a deeply competitive streak. "How big is Nazareth's line of credit?" he would ask me. "Our line better be bigger than his."

Nazareth's daily cash deposits at the bank had grown massive—often exceeding a million dollars. One month he cleared $60 million. Richard had heard rumors about this. "He's doing something bad," Richard told me. "I'm sure of it. No one deals in that much cash."

I broached the subject with Nazareth. "How are you growing so quickly, Naz? We've never seen this much cash coming in."

"Baby Chris, it's beautiful. I decided I'm also going to be a gold dis-tributor, selling to other wholesalers. Come have a look at this."

Nazareth led me into the vast back room of his office and lifted a sheet to reveal a knee-high stack of gold bars, worth an unfathomable amount of money. "Look," he said in a dreamlike voice, placing a hand on my shoulder. "Can you believe there is so much gold?"

I was shocked to learn this, but if you gathered together all the known gold reserves in the world—all the gold mined throughout history—it would reach only a third of the way up the Washington Monument. So Nazareth's stack of bullion must have registered as a noteworthy percentage of the world's supply.

Being a gold distributor was a high-cash business, he explained, which justified his daily deliveries of increasingly huge sums of money. In the movies, a million dollars fits conveniently into a briefcase. But in real life, a single briefcase isn't going to cut it. So here came Nazareth and his brother and dad with loaded duffels and brown paper grocery bags, cash spilling out onto the carpet as they trudged through the lobby of the bank. We had to hire four additional tellers simply to handle Nazareth's deposits, and we charged him for the extra staffing, to which he agreed without complaint.

Nazareth was so charismatic and easy to like that it was nothing but heartening to see his success. If Richard or anyone at the bank expressed concern over the bags of money he brought in, I was quick to defend Nazareth. He had shown me the evidence: He was building a legitimate business, amassing his fortune through hard work, realizing the 1980s' American Dream.

———

I picked the worst possible weekend to take my girlfriend, Laurie, to Las Vegas—Labor Day, which was also when the Jerry Lewis telethon took place. The city was packed. Laurie also worked at Bank of America, in consumer lending in the Valley. Neither of us had been to Vegas before, besides passing through on college road trips, and we weren't anticipating the mob scene we encountered. No vacancies at any hotel on the Strip. We must have tried them all. The woman at the Tropicana reservations desk actually snickered when I admitted that we didn't have accommodations booked. Her expression said, *This clown really thinks he can waltz in here and land a room?* We were out of options and distraught, and I was embarrassed and more than a little frustrated. This was 1986. Las Vegas wasn't quite the global hot spot that it is today, but still, I'd botched the planning, and now Laurie and I were stuck far from home, driving back and forth on the Strip with nowhere to go.

The last hotel to try was Caesars Palace. There was a reason I'd been avoiding it. That very morning, sitting in Nazareth's office, he said, "Baby Chris, what are you doing this weekend?"

"I'm taking Laurie to Las Vegas."

He clapped once. "You're going to Vegas? Yes! I love Vegas."

I nodded. Of course he loved Vegas.

"You should stay at Caesars Palace," he said, while writing himself a note beside the telephone. "Tell them Nazareth sent you."

"Oh, that's okay, Naz. Thank you, but I already have accommodations figured out."

"Where are you staying?"

I hesitated, unsure how to answer. I didn't want to lie.

"Go to Caesars," he said. "Let me arrange it."

"No, no, no. Thank you. I have it taken care of." I tried not to appear ungrateful, and I was careful to mask my skepticism over whether Nazareth really had such access to the top hotel in Vegas. He smiled knowingly and patted my shoulder.

Mentioning his name in a Las Vegas hotel was a ridiculous proposition. *Nazareth who?* they'd say, and laugh me out of town. I wasn't interested in another dose of humiliation.

But later that night, we walked up to the Caesars front desk smiling, hoping to be given a room the old-fashioned way.

"Hi," we said in unison, trying to win over the crisply professional receptionist.

She looked up from her computer screen. "Welcome to Caesars. May I help you?"

"Yeah, um." I looked at Laurie, and she looked hopefully—maybe desperately—back at me. "Do you have any rooms available?"

"I'm sorry, sir, but we're completely full."

"Nothing at all?" Laurie asked. "Not even a broom closet?"

The receptionist just shook her head. "I'm sorry," she said. "It's a very busy weekend."

Laurie's shoulders slumped with disappointment, and she tugged on my sleeve, pulling me a few steps away from the desk.

"Ask her," she whispered. Sure, I knew what Laurie meant—we had joked about Nazareth's offer on the way to Vegas, but it felt too outrageous to try. "Chris, it's our only shot. Otherwise we're heading home or staying outside of town."

I looked over my shoulder at the receptionist, who had turned her attention to sorting papers. *What the hell*, I thought. If anything, it would be something to laugh about later. I stepped back up to the counter, feeling like a character in an old movie as I leaned across and whispered, "Nazareth sent me."

The receptionist's eyebrows went up, and her lips curled into something resembling a smile. "Just one moment, sir."

She disappeared behind a wall, and soon I was shaking hands with a hotel manager. He had a firm grip and already knew my name, and within minutes he was unlocking the door of the penthouse and holding it open for us. It was the biggest residential room I'd ever seen, and I wanted to throw a baseball across it, just to see if I could reach the other side. Laurie dropped her bag and rushed in, while I stood dumbfounded next to the manager.

He rhapsodized about the many things available to us at the hotel. After a while, I was hardly listening, as the whole situation seemed so preposterous. "Sir," he said, waking me from my stupor and making an offer that both shocked and scared me at a level that would be seldom matched in all my later years of deal making on Wall Street, "would a $50,000 line of credit be sufficient?"

"What?" I turned to him.

"Would $50,000 be acceptable to start?"

"Oh, that's okay," I said. "I hit the ATM this morning."

I didn't intend that to be funny, but fortunately he took it as a joke, laughing loud and deep and even bending at the waist a little, as if my humor were almost too much to bear. I laughed with him to hide my naïveté. The truth was that he was offering me two and a half times my annual salary with which to have fun in the casino.

Laurie's voice reached us from a mile away: "Chris, there's a mirror on the ceiling in here! You gotta see this!" I debated whether to tip our host one or two dollars, then fished a five from my wallet and proudly held it out, but he waved it away and exited the room walking backward, telling me to call his personal number if we needed anything at all.

We couldn't gamble at Caesars that weekend—as the hospitality staff would follow us around to make sure we had what we wanted, and if they saw us playing nickel slots our cover would be blown—so we slipped across the street to the seedy, low-stakes Casino Royale, where the two-dollar blackjack and dollar craps tables were permeated with the scent of stale sandwiches.

Back in our penthouse, it was a luxurious couple of days. I was grateful to Nazareth for taking care of us, although I couldn't help but wonder—while soaking in the massive Jacuzzi or drinking complimentary champagne, looking out over the gaudy lights of Vegas—*Who is this guy?* Nazareth must have been a major high roller to be able to arrange all this with a simple phone call. I hadn't even spoken his last name at reception—just "Nazareth sent me"—and now here we were in what had to be one of the nicest hotel rooms in the city, if not the world. I didn't know anyone else in the jewelry industry who had the level of wealth or clout to be able to pull this off. Nazareth had become far more successful—and more willing to revel in that success—than I'd imagined.

When we left, I insisted on paying for the room. It didn't feel right to let Nazareth cover the cost, and besides, bank policy prohibited us from accepting gifts valued at more than $100 from clients. At reception, they weren't sure how to handle charging me, as apparently that sort of room didn't have a price. They finally settled on $130 a night. I dug for my wallet. Ironically, Bank of America, my own employer, had rejected my application for a credit card, claiming that I didn't yet have enough of a credit history to qualify. Sure, I had signing authority to issue hundreds of thousands of dollars in corporate loans and to receive millions in cash deposits from Nazareth, but they couldn't trust me with a credit card. I counted out the twenties and slid them across the reception counter, and Laurie and I headed home.

———

Security was a serious concern in the jewelry industry. The offices of wholesalers were never located on the ground level. For visitors to gain access, they would take the elevator up, ring a hallway buzzer that was monitored by cameras, then be admitted to the "man-trap" room, where a receptionist behind bulletproof glass would determine whether it was safe to buzz them through into the office. Most jewelers were armed, and many—including Barry and his father, Nathan—had what they called a hotline between their offices, which allowed them to call each other for immediate backup in the case of aggressive behavior or a robbery attempt. If someone was messing with Nathan Kagasoff, whose office was in a perilous location near the elevator, Barry could burst in with an Uzi and spray the place down. Luckily he never had to do that.

Despite the security and firepower, robberies and muggings were an increasingly common problem on the neighborhood streets—especially targeting, as Barry described, "men in suits carrying briefcases and wearing yarmulkes"—but no one ever touched Barry. That was partly because he was too smart to walk down the street with a briefcase full of cash or diamonds, but also because he was feared and respected.

Robberies in the jewelry industry were often staged, ploys to rip off insurance companies and other jewelers whose inventory was lost in the hustle. "There were many fake robberies," Barry said. "In fact, it got to a point where unless somebody got beaten badly or shot, I for one didn't believe that it was a robbery. Then there was a guy—I forget his name—who legitimately had a robbery and did get shot, but still, as soon as he got back, he paid off everybody anyway [for their losses in the robbery], because he was the real deal. Eventually he got killed somewhere, if I remember right."

When these fake robberies happened, other wholesalers often suffered large losses if they had stones on consignment that disappeared in the staged theft, which was a common occurrence. In one particular situation, Barry lost about $80,000 when a crooked wholesaler fled Los Angeles. A few years later, the guy wanted to slip back into town to attend his mother's funeral, so he called Barry first to settle his debt and make sure they were square. "It was all insurance fraud," Barry said. "If somebody owed me money and something happened, they made sure I was taken care of. Yeah, it's hard to swallow that I got taken care of because they were in fear, while everybody else had to go down swinging with it. You've got an illusion, that I'm allowing you to manifest, that I'm nine foot two, three hundred pounds, and the earth shakes when I walk and talk. I was a legend in my own mind, and I was a legend in everybody else's mind too."

One such staged robbery was the Pfefferman scandal of 1983, in which a father and son who were diamond wholesalers arranged to have themselves robbed, then they skipped town with the insurance money. The situation, while damaging for many, created an opportunity for me: Our bank branch lost enough on the Pfefferman heist that it became a central reason for the reshuffling of our lending department—all the loan officers were moved out to work in other sectors—which paved the way for me and a pack of Brigham Young graduates to land jobs. My bosses at the bank used to joke that they needed to fill the jeweler lending department with honest people, so they hired a bunch of Mormons and a guy from Disneyland.

———

Day by day, Nazareth continued to burst through the bank doors with more and bigger bags of cash, and the ever competitive Elmassian brothers, George and Richard, kept warning me about the illegal activity that they were sure was behind Nazareth's ascent. To be fair, George didn't say much about it. Richard was the more overtly aggressive of the brothers, and he had used some of his connections through his weekend vice cop gig to manufacture law enforcement interest in Nazareth's business. He convinced his superiors to take the accusations seriously, and they in turn contacted the DEA. Richard claimed that I had told him Nazareth was engaged in suspicious activity, most likely money laundering. This couldn't have been further from the truth. I had continued to defend Nazareth whenever anyone questioned his success.

Nevertheless, one afternoon I got a call from Richard. The DEA was at his office, and they wanted to speak with me. I knew what it was about before I walked through the door.

A big, square-jawed DEA agent sat off to one side listening while Richard asked me questions, putting on a bit of a show, as if we were in an episode of *Hill Street Blues*. George wasn't around. "Where do you think Nazareth Andonian's cash comes from? What does he tell you the source is? How much cash does he bring to the bank each day? When you visit his office, do you see any interesting people passing through?"

I answered each question honestly, since I felt there was nothing to hide. Yet it all sounded a bit suspect as I said it out loud, and I started to get nervous. I knew that I hadn't done anything wrong. Every time Nazareth came in with a large deposit, I accepted the money and completed the form required for deposits greater than $10,000, which was filed with our central office, and then reported to the appropriate authorities in the federal government. I did my job exactly as trained. Sure, Richard had told me wild stories about Nazareth, but I was certain those were simply tall tales meant to sling some mud at a rival gold dealer who was seeing great success. No one doubted that Nazareth loved money and all its associated indulgences, admittedly with more enthusiasm than most people, but he was too nice a guy, too caring, smart, and ambitious to get involved in criminal activity that might ruin him. While the DEA meeting was unsettling, I still believed in Nazareth.

Later that day, I stopped by his office and sat down in a chair in front of his desk. Nazareth was standing up facing in the other direction, looking at a document over near the filing cabinets.

"Hey, Baby Chris! How are you?" He smiled over his shoulder and kept flipping through the pages.

"Hi, Naz. I'm fine."

"Dinner on Thursday?"

"Yeah, okay." I paused for a minute, but there was no way to hold back. Nazareth was a friend; he should know. "I feel like I have to tell you this," I said. "But I'm sure it's nothing to worry about. I was questioned this morning with a DEA agent present, asking about your deposits."

He swung around to face me. His smiling eyes narrowed and darkened as he started walking toward me, setting the papers on his desk. "What did you tell them?" he asked in a tight, low voice. "What were the questions? What did you say?" A dose of adrenaline shot through me. My cheerful, compassionate friend had transformed in an instant into someone who felt dangerous and unpredictable, a side of him I'd never seen. And right at that moment—it took all of five seconds—the truth was clear: *This guy is laundering money, and I was too stupid to realize it.*

Nazareth was leaning over my chair. All his warmth was gone. I knew I had to keep my wits about me and stay calm. Without mentioning that Richard had been involved, I recounted the DEA interview and repeated that I was sure he didn't have anything to worry about, but every part of me wanted to get out of there as quickly as possible without seeming frightened or concerned. Once we'd exhausted the conversation, I walked back to the bank and sat at my desk, staring blankly at a smattering of documents until quitting time. Thankfully he hadn't asked me more pointed questions about how the DEA meeting had come about—I had stepped into his office without preparing any sort of cover story, since I had been quite sure, up until that moment, of Nazareth's innocence. The next morning, after a sleepless night, I told my supervisors what had happened.

After commuting for a year from my folks' house in Orange County, I lucked into an apartment in Santa Monica, thanks to an old classmate from Occidental. My mother wasn't hot on the idea, as she couldn't understand why I would waste money on rent when our house was a mere hour's drive from work in light traffic, but I was more than ready to be in my own place. I commuted in my hand-me-down '78 Caprice Classic each morning, listening to punk and New Wave on KROQ. Traffic was always terrible. I probably could have walked the fifteen miles just as quickly. Twice I was pulled over for reading the newspaper while driving.

On the first day of October 1987, I was inching along the 10 freeway, thinking about my talk with the branch manager from the previous day. Word had come down from the regional office that Bank of America planned to pull back substantially from loaning money to jewelers. The institution wanted to limit its exposure to what was seen as a high-risk industry. So my managers told me to figure out which ten accounts I should keep of my seventy or so, and we would cut the others loose.

This wasn't an easy decision, and really the whole thing was sour news. My clients were family-owned mom-and-pop businesses—the essence of Main Street—and their operations relied heavily on the ability to borrow money from the bank. I hated to think of turning them away.

Barry was the client I most wanted to keep, but the bank wouldn't see it that way, since he never borrowed from his line of credit for more than a week. He didn't need us as much as other clients did. But I needed Barry and his unvarnished, honest counsel. There was no simple way to explain that to my superiors. His conservative practices should have been an advantage, but in this case they worked against him. I would have to spin an argument that Barry was so esteemed in the industry and such a pillar of LA's diamond community that it would be a mistake to let him go. That wasn't untrue, but I didn't know if it would be convincing enough to the suits up in the regional office, who were completely removed from the on-the-ground action. Ironically, it was my bank training that had taught me to value character above all else, and now the bank was disconnecting itself from that fundamental concept. I mentally ranked my other clients in order of importance so I could make my case when I got to work. Since I'd already told my supervisors that the DEA might be investigating Nazareth, they seemed eager to sever ties with him, which of course was fine with me. I'd fight to keep Barry and George and make concessions on the others.

The highway traffic patterns shifted, and I was able to get my speed above thirty—and then my axle must have snapped because the Chevy was all over the road. I fought to regain control as I slowed down, countersteering against the swerves. The cars around me were a mess too. It seemed as though everyone was in the same predicament. When

I finally came to rest among a sea of cars, still in our lanes but stopped at odd angles, it became obvious what had happened—we had been caught in an earthquake. We all sat at our wheels for a couple of minutes. No one ahead was moving, so we finally emerged from our cars and walked around to compare notes. I had never noticed that the 10 freeway was elevated above the city. We wondered if we should abandon our cars and hike to safer ground, but there was no easy way off. An ominous tower of smoke rose in the sky on the south end of downtown. We waited it out, and eventually the cars ahead started to creep, and we filed off the highway at the next exit.

I got to work late that morning and learned that it had been a 5.9-magnitude quake that shook for twenty seconds, with an epicenter in the area of Whittier Narrows, a dozen miles east. Eight people were killed, and damages were later tallied at a few hundred million dollars. I'd felt plenty of earthquakes before that day, but there was something particularly unnerving about that October morning, when so many things in my life seemed to be cracking at the foundation. One minute I was coasting on the freeway, air-drumming to Billy Idol's "Mony Mony," windows down, thinking about the day ahead; and the next minute I was wandering over the tarmac with a bunch of strangers, concerned that the ground might fall away under our feet. It felt too metaphorical for my comfort.

In the wake of the bank's shift away from the jewelry industry, I was able to keep most of the customers I wanted, although it wasn't easy. They pushed back on Barry, but I won in the end. Nazareth had been a much more attractive client to them, until it became clear his activities may have been less than forthright. I found it ironic that it would have been easier to keep Nazareth, even though he had a dark side to him, than Barry, who had strong, proven character. Despite my training, I started to doubt how much the bank truly cared about character.

My commute was even worse for the next many weeks, due to construction and repairs on the 10. But still I climbed into the Caprice Classic each morning, buckled my seatbelt, and turned up the radio, mumbling along to the new R.E.M. song that was everywhere that winter. "That's great, it starts with an earthquake," Michael Stipe sang, as if he knew exactly what was happening in my life. "It's the end of the world as we know it. It's the end of the world as we know it. It's the end of the world as we know it, and I feel fine."

———

Vernon, the trucking and meatpacking capital of Southern California, has got to be the ugliest town in America. Despite its proximity to downtown LA and the fact that two of the busiest freeways in the state intersect there, a recent census reported that barely more than a hundred people actually live in Vernon—it's all pollution, cement, noise, and industry.

When the bank pulled back from the diamond industry, I myself departed. I was offered a promotion to move to the Vernon branch and take on bigger accounts, and I accepted without hesitation. So I left behind my days of visiting with colorful clients, gazing at gold and diamonds, lingering over two-hour lunches and fancy dinners. The glitter and glitz of the jewelry industry gave way to the grimy, smelly wasteland of Vernon, a place where you often dined on something called "chili size," a hamburger patty dropped into a bowl of chili. For the truckers, that was a big lunch out. Although I missed seeing my clients in the jewelry district, it was in many ways a welcome change. I knew I hadn't done anything wrong, but simply being that close to Nazareth's criminal activity was enough to keep me up at night, running back through various conversations and scenarios. Nazareth, meanwhile, switched his accounts over to Wells Fargo.

When I arrived in Vernon, there were no clients to visit—they were all rolling around the country in eighteen-wheelers and stopping into the bank only every few months—so I spent a lot of time at the office chatting with my new colleagues. Many of the senior guys were scooping up stock as prices dropped, seeing the market correction as a good buy opportunity, and they expressed surprise that I'd never bought stock before. Even after I reminded them that, at age twenty-four, I had zero investment experience and very little in the way of savings, they kept after me about it until I finally agreed to acquire some.

More than any other company, Bank of America was the one I knew best, since that was my employer, so I called a broker and placed an order for a hundred shares of B. of A. stock. For me, this was no small purchase. The date was Friday, October 16, 1987. I headed into the weekend excited at having made my first investment, but that thrill quickly turned to anxiety when the markets reopened on Monday, October 19, and the biggest single-day crash in Wall Street history took place, nearly double the largest one-day percentage drop during the Great Depression. It would become known as Black Monday.

Panic ensued. And in a market crash, panic leads to selloffs, which lead to steeper stock price declines and further panic. One fascinating thing about Black Monday, besides the sheer scale of the disaster, was the cause. For the first time, a crash was brought about by nonhuman factors—it was triggered by computers. In those early days of technology's entrance into finance, when we were still learning to replace the yellow paper spreadsheet with the computer spreadsheet, a company named LOR had come up with the notion of "portfolio insurance," designed to guard against big losses in institutional portfolios. This was achieved through a set of computer algorithms that would automatically trigger sales if certain things happened in the market, and then it would automatically trigger buys once the market readjusted. But the algorithms backfired on Black Monday as the computer-generated selloffs far outpaced the traders' limited human capacity to keep up, resulting in more algorithmic sells, and so on. The computer algorithm had not accounted for a situation in which there were no buyers, pushing the sell bid lower and lower in search of a price that would clear the market, which soon was in freefall.

Within a couple of days of Black Monday, I joined the panic and sold off my Bank of America shares, deciding that I could afford only so much pain. My first investment had been a loss, and I felt foolish. I wavered between self-castigation and open condemnation of the system that had taken my hard-earned dollars. Was my market ignorance to blame? Was it the fault of the system? Something beyond fundamentals had driven the stock price volatility. I didn't know the answers to these questions and wasn't sure I ever would. I couldn't understand at the time that I'd been a very small participant in the grand entrance of computers onto the public financial markets stage.

———

After my move to Vernon, I would return to the jewelry district from time to time to visit Barry and George. If I needed a gift for a girlfriend or my mother, it was a good excuse to head back to the neighborhood and spend an hour with my old friends. I never again visited Nazareth. Richard told me in confidence that the case against Nazareth was building steadily, that the Feds had cameras on his offices and had taped him counting millions of dollars with the help of prostitutes, then having sex with the women on piles of money. I was starting to believe it, although I wished it weren't true.

I lasted about a year in Vernon. It wasn't the chili size that did me in, and I enjoyed the company of the truckers, even if they weren't as entertaining as the jewelers. I simply knew that I wasn't interested in building a career in corporate lending, so it seemed right to move on. I applied to The Wharton School, which was the doorstep to Wall Street and felt like the center of the universe at that time.

During my first year at Wharton, I was watching the national news with my roommate one evening, and there he was on TV—Nazareth Andonian, being led away in handcuffs. By that point I didn't doubt that he was into some bad stuff, but I had no idea of the scale. I tracked down a copy of the *LA Times* and later found an article in *Businessweek*, which included even more details about the developing case.

Nazareth had been taken down in the biggest money laundering operation in US history. On the morning of February 22, 1989, federal agents surrounded the few blocks that made up the jewelry district. Within a couple of hours, roughly forty people—along with documents, money-counting machines, gold, $30 million in currency, every related item—had been packed into a fleet of trucks and whisked away. It was as if a stage set had been dismantled at top speed, the floor swept, the lights extinguished. By the next day, business in the neighborhood returned to normal, and you would never have known that any of it had happened.

The case went to trial the following year. Phones, pagers, and cars had been bugged. Tracking devices were used. The Feds had rented rooms all around Nazareth's office, using fake jewelry store names, so they could headquarter their surveillance on-site. Tiny cameras were installed throughout the building, and the DEA had figured out how to tap into the Andonians' own security system, allowing them to watch live feeds of everything going on inside Nazareth's office during their thirteen-month sting investigation. They called the case Operation Polar Cap.

Nazareth had been laundering money for Pablo Escobar's Medellín drug cartel, the biggest and baddest Colombian exporter of cocaine. In an elaborate scheme that involved scores of operatives in several US cities—primarily New York, Los Angeles, and Atlanta (which explained the imported prostitutes)—boxes of loose cash, labeled "gold scrap," would be shipped to Andonian Brothers, and Nazareth would count the money, often with the help of prostitutes. Government affidavits described how so much currency began flowing through Nazareth's office that his counters would simply toss any bill smaller than a twenty against the wall; it wasn't worth their time. Once the money was added up, Nazareth would sift his percentage off the top, then drag the rest into the bank to deposit through me. After that, the funds would be wire-transferred enough times to sever the connection between the source and destination, and the profits would end up back in the hands of the Medellín cartel. The system was so efficient—such an ungodly amount of cleaned money cycled back to the Colombians, more than $1.2 billion—that the drug lords affectionately named the laundry *La Mina*, "the mine." Nazareth covered his tracks by pretending to have entered the gold distribution business. The massive stack of bullion he showed me was most likely gold-painted lead. Most of his receipts were fabricated.

The trial lasted longer than any in the history of the Los Angeles federal courthouse. Nazareth and his brother, Vahe, were each convicted on twenty-five felony counts of money laundering and one count of conspiracy. They were given sentences of 505 years without parole, the harshest ever doled out up to that point. The Andonian brothers are currently incarcerated in a federal prison in California northwest of Reno, Nevada. There was another LA jeweler caught up in the Medellín laundering activity and convicted of similar crimes, but he's already been released. The word on the street is that the Andonians had crappier lawyers, and because of that they'll almost certainly die behind bars.

––––––

By the time of the bust, Nazareth had no remaining relationship with Bank of America, so most of the trial proceedings and resulting press highlighted Wells Fargo rather than my former employer. From where I was at Wharton, I knew I wouldn't be called to testify in the trial, as the camera footage and other evidence provided irrefutable proof of his guilt, and I was far enough removed at that point. I also didn't worry about being implicated in any way. Sure, I had indirectly been one of many who helped clean hundreds of millions of dollars of drug money for the Colombians, but I had been entirely forthcoming with the DEA, hadn't broken a single law, and had been unaware of what was happening until I'd confronted Nazareth. I'd been duped. In retrospect, I should have heeded the warning signs that Nazareth's character might not be as solid as I had first thought. Yet I'd remained oblivious, perhaps willfully so. I was a wide-eyed tourist in a foreign land. Who was I to cast judgments over the rituals and customs of the locals?

The natural thing to wonder is whether I felt used by Nazareth, hurt that our friendship had been a sham and almost everything he had told me was a lie. I broke bread with his family, drove 140 in his yellow Lotus, was his reluctant but grateful guest in Vegas, talked with him for who knows how many hours. But I didn't feel slighted—he never asked me to bend a rule or do anything outside of my legal job description. Nazareth had taken advantage of the system, and, yes, I was part of that system; but in a way, he had kept me protected from anything that might have been destructive. Maybe it was my Disneyland background, or my fresh twenty-two-year-old face, or that I always turned down his offers to have boogie action with Atlanta prostitutes—or, most likely, that in order for the whole thing to work, he needed me, his bank connection, to remain oblivious and innocent—but either way, he kept me out of it. And although I had wrongly believed that Nazareth was honest in terms of business, I always knew he wasn't a saint. He was a frenetic and scatterbrained guy who kept a mistress and had a thing for hookers with Southern accents. I didn't have the highest view of his integrity. But I'd never known anyone like him before, and I was captivated. Since I was so young, I was still trying to assess where Nazareth fit in the circle of man. At the time, I didn't know to what extent he was an outlier. I was still learning how each person's behavior mattered in assessing business character.

Now that I'm older and feel as though I've encountered the full range of human character, I do feel some sympathy for Nazareth. I can so easily imagine that day when he set out from Beirut with a vision for what his life could be. He arrived in America to try to make it in the world, coming from a place where survival was the first, second, and third most important thing. How does someone's morality change when moving from struggle to opportunity? I think of Nazareth as an amoral guy with a decent heart who wanted a better life and wanted to succeed, and, through the lens of inexperience and ambition, he was presented with an offer that didn't seem terribly risky: Take this money, deposit it, and keep some for yourself. It was a situation that you might easily rationalize your way into if you were in his position.

Once I read about the case, I remembered a story he'd told me over dinner one night, which at the time was amusing. He had gone on vacation with his family to Bora Bora, and it rained hard for three days. Nazareth was so feisty, so active and spirited, that it drove him nuts to be trapped in his luxury hut as rain fell on the palm fronds, unable to get outside or do any work. He was a man who couldn't sit still for five minutes at a time. "It was complete torture for me," he said. "It felt like being in jail."

———

So I left the jewelry and trucking industries behind for Wharton and Wall Street, not foreseeing that I was throwing myself headlong into a world in which I would meet many Nazareths, a world of handshakes and cross-purposes, charm and deceit, ambition and rationalized immoral behavior. I couldn't have imagined then that I would come into such close proximity to many people throughout my career, often well-known public figures, who would fall from grace in one spectacular catastrophe or another.

Thankfully, my job at Bank of America didn't ruin me. I didn't leave with an inability to trust people, but I never again went into a situation wanting to trust someone to the point that it blinded me. In that job, I learned things about honesty and character that have been priceless in every other part of my career. It goes back to the first day of training and the five *c*'s of credit: *capital, capacity, conditions, collateral,* and *character.* As a lending officer—and as with most things in life—the single difference between making a good or bad loan or decision is your ability to assess character.

I was fortunate to have begun my career in the jewelry industry, where character is the most important aspect of the game. Often the people who look and feel the most honest are not. They're simply selling the perception of honesty. Diamonds have their own set of four *c*'s, as anyone who has purchased an engagement ring knows: *cut, clarity, carat,* and *color.* But that fifth unspoken *c*—*character*—also matters in buying a diamond. You want to trust the person selling you the rock, as it's the most asymmetrical deal you'll ever do, in which you have no information and they have it all. A salesperson can be masterful at smiling and putting you at ease and selling you whatever he or she wants, yet because buying a diamond is a rare and special occasion, with little or no opportunity to build a relationship of trust through repeat business, you want to believe in the salesperson's quality of character.

It's an industry of extremes: The people who survive long-term are honest; the crooks might also survive, if only short-term; and everyone in between fails. A scary guy like Barry—who says "fuck" every other word and puts you back on your heels—probably wouldn't be the sort of person you'd associate with honesty. You might look elsewhere to do your business. Yet in the case of Barry, integrity and reputation were everything. Barry wasn't only selling diamonds, he was dealing in trust. It may have come in an unorthodox package, at least to my sheltered sensibilities, but his character was solid and unshakeable.

Barry still has a diamond wholesale business today, even if the internet has taken most of the action away from the locally based wholesalers and dealers. "It used to be a small net of diamond dealers that grew only from *family*," he said, "but then it expanded out. I closed my office. Now I don't have to go fucking downtown anymore—excuse me—to that sewer world." Barry is not passing down the business to any of his children. "Those days are over. The internet basically ruined everybody as far as loyalty and trust and me knowing you and you knowing my suppliers. I don't want that life for them."

An unlikely pair, Barry and I have remained friends over the thirty years since I was his Bank of America lending officer. I've brought my wife and daughter to meet him. I've sent colleagues and friends to him for diamonds hundreds of times. We talk on the phone frequently, and he calls me every year on my birthday. Barry has mellowed with age, for sure, but not like a fine wine—more like a vintage scotch: still high proof, still infused with smoke and fire, but with the edges smoothed a bit.

2

WELCOME TO THE JUNGLE

The tree that would grow to heaven must send its roots to hell.
—FRIEDRICH NIETZSCHE

The first time I set foot on the infamous Salomon Brothers trading floor, at One New York Plaza, perched on the southern tip of Manhattan, it felt like a scene of chaos—but controlled chaos, as though I were watching a flock of starlings fly in wild but strangely organized formations. Across two open stories, traders worked at rows of long countertops that were alive with thousands of blinking lights and telephones, burning cigarettes and steaming coffee, flashing screens and tickers. Nothing seemed to be at rest. Chairs spun and arms waved as a sea of traders shouted into their phones and at one another. They spoke phrases that made no sense to me—it was English, I was pretty certain, but after that I was lost. "The tens just ticked up two bips. . . . Spreads are widening. . . . I need color on that last trade."

When you looked more closely, these weren't starlings. These were predators. The scent of the hunt—sweat and testosterone—was so thick in the air that you couldn't help but feel like prey. Even though it was my first day on the job, I was already imagining how my time at Salomon would end. I held still, sensing that any sudden movement might alert the salivating lions that a lamb was in their midst. I remained undetected for the moment, as traders whirled around the room in an aggressive choreography of deal making.

Weeks earlier, when I was offered a position as a 1989 summer associate—essentially a paid internship between the first and second years of business school, which came with no promise of a job offer but had the vibe of a three-month-long audition—it had seemed like an adventure and life experience I couldn't turn down. My Spartan mother had instilled in me the willingness to place myself in uncomfortable situations in the interest of growth and learning. But as I walked onto the trading floor that June morning, I felt that I had made a fatal error. Michael Lewis would later write in *Liar's Poker*, his seminal exposé of Wall Street trading, that on his first day at Salomon Brothers he felt like he was going to collect lottery winnings rather than to work. I felt like I was going to a firing squad.

My classmates at The Wharton School had portrayed the fixed income department at Salomon Brothers as the wildest, most Darwinian job in the world. This investment bank, founded in 1910, was indeed the lions' den of the Wall Street jungle, the top of the financial food chain. And somehow here I was—fresh out of Disneyland and commercial lending, an Orange County kid with a liberal arts degree. I hadn't even known what an investment bank was just one year earlier. My friend and Wharton classmate Ben Giess was also coming to work at Salomon for the summer, but he was headed for the much more civilized and sophisticated investment banking department. "I don't picture you on the trading floor," he said. "Are you sure that's a good idea?" Other classmates were similarly concerned. Clearly they didn't think I had the toughness to survive in fixed income at Salomon. And I would be the first to admit that they were probably right, although I accepted the offer anyway.

Sales and trading were the two main types of jobs that made up the fixed income department. The salespeople bought and sold bonds on behalf of their clients and customers, who included other investment and commercial banks, as well as large institutional investment firms such as Fidelity and PIMCO. Salespeople spent almost all of their time on the phone. The traders managed the inventory. They were charged with keeping the firm's balance sheet loaded with the assets that the salespeople needed for their clients. So the salespeople represented the demand and the traders the supply, similar to the sales and manufacturing departments of any company—one can't exist without the other.

While I was studying the room on my first day, a trading assistant touched my forearm, snapping me to attention, and directed me to a conference room. There was a short orientation planned for us, the six summer associates, with the head of recruiting—a woman we had met during the interview process and who had made us our offers. She explained that the summer was to be "a simulation of reality," meaning that it would be largely unstructured and unguided. It was up to us to make our way on the floor. We should find a folding chair and some double headsets and then request permission to unfold our chair beside traders and salespeople from various departments and listen in on their phone conversations.

Her pep talk continued with some special encouragement: It was unlikely that more than one or two of us would get a full-time offer at the end of the internship; everyone else would be out of luck. In theory, all of us *might* get offers, but the firm was content in making no offers if none of us deserved one. "Perception is reality," she said. "Think of yourself as a stock with a moving ticker on your forehead that represents your value. Every time you open your mouth, your stock price goes up or down depending on whether you say something smart or something stupid." I wondered what my starting price might be, but I was wise enough not to ask. It couldn't be good.

She left us with one last directive: "Be sure to introduce yourself to Penn King sooner rather than later." With that, we were dismissed from orientation, with no further guidance on the identity of Penn King or where we might find a folding chair or double headset.

We shuffled back onto the trading floor, staying close together for safety. I thought I spotted a chair off in the distance, leaning against the far wall, but it seemed undignified to make a sprint for it.

The youngest of the six summer associates was a muscular Latino undergrad named Victor, a rising junior from Wesleyan. He was part of the Sponsors for Educational Opportunity program, which had the mission of increasing diversity on Wall Street. Moments after we stepped back onto the trading floor, Victor broke off and asked someone where he could find Penn King, and we all watched with awe and a touch of concern as this intrepid twenty-year-old walked up and introduced himself. "Mr. King, I'm Victor, one of the new summer associates." Penn King was tall, blond, and—we soon learned—a legendary government bond salesman whose reputation extended far beyond Wall Street. The author Tom Wolfe had shadowed King, using him as the model for "Master of the Universe" Sherman McCoy in his bestselling novel *The Bonfire of the Vanities*.

Penn King peered down at Victor, smiled graciously, and offered a hand to shake. We observed them from a distance, trying to hide our envy, while Victor confidently asked if he could sit in an empty chair not far from King. It wasn't even a folding chair; it was the real deal, armrests and all. Victor sat down and let out a satisfied breath of air. He tilted the chair back a little and couldn't help but grin at his quick success. *This kid is good*, we thought, *very good, and he isn't even an MBA.*

Victor had just settled in when the phone in front of him lit up. (Phones on the floor didn't ring; they lit up and blinked until answered.) The traders nearby gave Victor the nod that it was okay to answer. He picked it up and said, "Salomon."

"Victor, get me Joe."

"May I ask who is calling?"

"Wake the fuck up, Victor!" Penn King stood behind him, holding a phone receiver like a seal club.

"What?" Victor nearly jumped out of his seat.

"Tell me, Victor," King snarled, "who in this place knows your fucking name other than the one person you've just met? Who else *could* be calling?"

Victor looked cautiously over his shoulder at his tall, blond assassin. Before King slammed his phone down into its cradle, he gave Victor one final Salomon welcome: "If you don't get your shit together quick, kid, you won't make it through the first day."

Victor spent the rest of the week in a state of mild shock. There was a saying at Salomon Brothers that no matter who you were, no matter how successful you had been, there was a bullet flying around with your name on it, and it was only a matter of time before it found you and brought your employment at the firm to an abrupt and inglorious end. Victor's wasn't a mortal wound, but he had definitely been grazed by a warning shot.

One of my fellow summer associates, Bo, was a proud graduate of The Citadel, the military college in Charleston, South Carolina. He had a slight Southern drawl and fiddled with his Citadel ring incessantly, as if he didn't want to risk forgetting, nor let anyone else forget, that he had graduated from that esteemed institution. Bo suggested we plot survival strategy at a nearby bar, a place he'd probably learned about from a fellow Citadel alum. The South Street Seaport was a touristy outdoor retail district on an old dock not far from the Salomon headquarters.

"Are you sure this is smart?" asked Ron as we walked along the water. He was another summer associate who had been an IBM salesman and looked the part, with his carefully combed hair, white dress shirt, and solid blue suit and tie.

"Nope," Bo said with a grin. "But if we're gonna be traders, we need to start acting like it."

While going for beers in the middle of my first day didn't seem like the smartest career move, I looked forward to the prospect of camaraderie and solidarity with the other summers, as well as anything that would delay having to drag a folding chair across the trading floor, begging to be let in on a desk's activity. We drank a couple of rounds—looking out over the East River and Brooklyn Bridge, as a few towering historic ships bobbed against the dock—and discussed tactics for dodging the bullets. Slurping the foam off his second beer, Ron surprised us by suggesting that we hang out at the South Street Seaport all summer, only showing up at the end of each day to wave goodbye. "Come on, guys!" He raised his pint and a little slopped over the brim. "No one will notice!" It was a tempting proposition.

———

Landing a summer associate internship with Salomon had been a surprise to me. My best guess as to how I made it through to the final round of interviews was that they interpreted my vague, uninformed answers as casual indifference to wanting the job. The head recruiter, the same woman who would later run our orientation, said, "People seem to like you, but we're worried that you don't have that salesman killer instinct."

"Okay." I shrugged, surrendering to my fate.

"But wait," she said. Apparently the less I appeared to want it, the more desirable I became. "Let's put you in one last interview with O'Leary, the head of fixed income sales. If you can convince him that you can sell, then you've got the spot."

She led me down the hall to the open door of O'Leary's office.

"Come on in," he yelled, waving me into a seat facing him. "Listen, Mr. Varelas, despite all the glitz around working on Wall Street, we're really just salesmen. And we need to make sure you can sell. For years now, I've always asked people in these interviews to sell me something."

"All right," I said. "What do you want me to sell you?" I scanned his desk for a pencil. It's always the pencil.

He wheeled his chair across the hard plastic floor mat and raised his arms. "Sell me this chair."

I looked it over from where I sat, as O'Leary animatedly rolled around in front of me. It was a standard high-end office chair.

"Well," I said, "you seem to like the fact that the chair rolls."

He squinted at me sideways, wondering if I was being a wiseass. "Yeah, I love the fact that it rolls. So what?"

"What about that is pleasing to you? Is it the smoothness of the roll? Is it the flexibility? Do you prefer wheels that always spin, or do you like wheels that can lock in place?"

He peered over the side of the chair at its base, as if seeing it for the first time. "What do you mean, lock in place?"

"Well," I said, lacing my fingers together, "we have a feature that lets you flip a lever to lock the wheels, so the chair isn't rolling when you don't want it to."

"Oh, I definitely want that."

"Okay. In that case, you need polyurethane casters, rather than plastic. That'll give you the sort of movement you like, but stability when you want it." He smiled broadly. I continued detailing the different sorts of wheel and caster choices—the materials, stems, optional features. I even named a couple of top caster producers, just for kicks. "We'll get you all set up, Mr. O'Leary. No problem."

When I was done, he exploded in laughter. "Varelas! I don't know how you made that shit up, but that's the best answer I've ever heard."

"Thank you, sir."

"Now I need to get a new chair."

What I didn't mention was that my dad's company made wheels and casters—for anything that rolled, from gurneys to Dumpsters to supermarket carts to high-end office chairs. I had helped him out during many summer months of my youth and picked up just enough knowledge to dazzle O'Leary, who of course was convinced that I was a master bullshitter. I didn't tell him the truth until many years later.

Salomon Brothers was founded in 1910 by Arthur, Herbert, and Percy Salomon. They broke away from the business of their father, Ferdinand, because he refused to open his firm on the Sabbath, even though the markets operated for a half day on Saturday mornings back then. The three brothers carved out a place for their firm by selling federal Liberty Bonds during World War I to help fund the war effort. The government bond market was new and growing, and Salomon Brothers came to rule it.

As middleman between the investing public and the government, Salomon performed an essential and important function—much like the role Barry Kagasoff served in the diamond industry. If someone wanted an engagement ring, he didn't call the mines in South Africa; he went to see Barry and other dealers like him, who created the market that helped get the assets from the source to the customer. In the case of bonds, when a government or corporate entity had to borrow capital, it needed someone, typically an investment bank, to issue that debt and later provide a secondary market for it. That's where Salomon came in. The government bond market—and Salomon's role as middleman—was necessary to allow the government to raise the capital needed to fund its mandate, and it was beneficial for the general public to have that done at the lowest and most efficient cost.

Salomon Brothers weathered the crash of 1929 and the Great Depression by remaining cautious and bearish. Most other firms didn't fare so well. The government bond market grew significantly during and after World War II, and Salomon Brothers remained at the top. Later it expanded its operations under the leadership of the family's heir, Billy Salomon, when he took over as managing partner in the 1960s. The firm broadened its focus to include research, block trading, and underwriting. By the end of the '60s—six decades after its inception as a modest discount house—Salomon had grown to join the ranks of Lehman Brothers, Blyth, and Merrill Lynch in what became known on Wall Street as the "Fearsome Foursome."

From the beginning—and up until 1981—Salomon Brothers was a private partnership rather than a public corporation. When renowned municipal bond trader Dale Horowitz began at Salomon in 1955, his starting salary was a modest $55 per week. Even the partners—whose ranks he would later join—had strict limits on their compensation. They were allowed to take out extra cash only for emergency situations or charity, while the majority of their pay cycled back into the firm and provided the means by which Salomon Brothers could grow. The outsized risks and bonuses for which Wall Street has become known today didn't exist under the partnership because the partners had a personal stake in the success of the firm. Their own money was on the line.

Dale remembered his unglamorous start in the business: "In the old days, none of the Wall Street firms had any capital, so everybody would borrow overnight from the banks to carry their inventory, and then they would repay the loan in the morning, and then the next day borrow again. You would pledge the bonds and stocks you had in your office—there was a great big safe in this building—and every afternoon at five o'clock, you would push these carts around Wall Street, a box that had wheels on it, delivering securities to banks. Then the next morning at eight o'clock, somebody went to the bank, put your securities in the box, and wheeled them back to the office.

"So for the first week, I was a runner, pushing the cart around Wall Street. When you brought in the securities in the evening, they gave you a check for $5 million, or whatever it was, because otherwise you couldn't open your business since you wouldn't have the capital. I was paired with a clerk who did this regularly, and he showed me where to go and so on. He went up to a window, and they gave him a check for $5 million. I'll never forget it. Who had ever seen a check for $5 million?"

Across Wall Street, partnerships were coming to an end. Salomon was one of the first, transitioning to a public corporation in 1981. This move from privately owned to publicly owned changed everything and—directly or indirectly—was the source of much of the volatility and abuse of the financial system that was to follow. It instilled a new Wild West culture at Salomon Brothers, ushering in an every-man-for-himself atmosphere, in which individual employees made colossal gambles for the possibility of lucrative payouts. The central reason for this massive shift in risk was that Salomon traders had essentially started playing with house money, the balance sheet of the public company, rather than using their own personal capital. Not using their own money led to higher risk tolerance and larger losses when things didn't go right.

Investment banks went public for multiple reasons. A primary reason was access to the capital needed to scale the business in response to customer demand for bigger financings and underwritings. Globalization and the creation of mega-international corporations demanded financial institutions that could underwrite larger and larger debt and equity issuances, as well as institutions that could support those issuances with trading and analysis on a level that a traditional partnership could not. Another reason was greed. Going public allowed for the partners to cash in, selling their ownership stakes for huge valuations, something previous partners were never allowed to do. And so one generation of partners was able to capitalize on the decades of work done by previous partners in building a successful firm.

Once public, there were no longer partners with skin in the game. Instead there were employees looking to maximize annual compensation. In an attempt to lure and retain the best talent, investment banks were forced to alter compensation structures to allow large performance-based bonuses for top traders and bankers. That also meant that, for the first time, those employees could make piles of cash and actually keep it for themselves, so the incentive to take large risks was further heightened. A common phrase on the Street described the new culture: "Heads I win; tails the firm loses." A few of the major investment banks, such as Salomon and Goldman Sachs, built up assets and liabilities approaching a trillion dollars. Backed by such deep pockets, the activities of a single trader could make or lose hundreds of millions and sometimes billions of dollars for his or her firm.

No bigger collection of risk takers existed anywhere on the planet or in history than on the trading floor at Salomon. Previously, the traders had simply managed the warehouse and made sure there was enough inventory on hand; but once they tapped into the firm's capital and were given the balance sheet to play with, they began making monumental bets on things like the direction of interest rates, the price of oil, and the strength of the US dollar. If something had price volatility and existed within a large enough market, these traders might take a position that could have a real impact on the firm, on the market in which they traded, and, in some cases, on the larger financial climate.

———

A beam of sunlight hit my face, and I woke up with a desert mouth and what felt like a horn impaled in my right temple. I opened an eye and quickly regretted it. Dozens of rainbows arched over an angry pink sea. Waves of white ruffles and lace rolled at my feet. From all corners, armies of wide-eyed miniature girls grinned at me. They were very happy and very awake. I threw a pillow, hoping to take a few of them out. Above my head, adrift in that terrible pink sea, was a smiling unicorn, most likely the one that attacked me in the night. I felt bad.

My digs were in a brownstone on the Upper West Side, owned by a

Columbia professor traveling for the summer. The guys who arranged the summer sublet had allowed me in as a late addition, and only the little girl's bedroom was left. The night before, I had stayed up late with my housemate Ben after our first day as summer associates. He'd been an accomplished beer drinker as an undergrad at Dartmouth, and I should have known better than to match pints with him as I recapped the horrors of day one on the trading floor. Meanwhile, he gushed about his much gentler environment across the street in Salomon's investment banking department. He mentioned an attractive twenty-one-year-old Frenchwoman named Laurence Borde, one of his fellow summer associates who had impressed everyone with her charm and intelligence. The more we drank, the more her name sounded like "Larry Bird." Of course, as a native of Massachusetts, I was a big Celtics fan.

At some point in the night, I must have crawled to my pink room, and now, in the awful morning light, the brightly colored, cheerful décor felt particularly insulting. I sat up and swung my legs over the side of the tiny bed, nodded a *good morning* to the unicorn, and shuffled hunchback to the door. The slanted ceiling was too low for me to stand up straight. I was a giant in a dollhouse.

While it seemed that the entire Wharton student body was in New York for summer internships, the guys who landed our brownstone were law students from the University of Virginia who Ben knew from his days at Deerfield and Dartmouth. One of them worked such long hours that, even though we'd lived under the same roof for three months, I didn't meet him until we threw an end-of-the-summer house party. Despite the special indignity of sleeping in a little girl's room—after enduring humiliations all day on the trading floor—the house was a welcome refuge from the intensity of Salomon.

Ben often worked through the night in investment banking, preparing presentations for the following morning, while my action on the trading floor happened during the day, when the markets were open. Many dawns I passed him on the stairs—him just getting home and me setting off for another day on the floor. But many other nights when we both were at the house, we sat together for hours discussing our experiences over beers, and the beautiful Larry Bird often joined us. "Don't waste your time," Ben warned me after I first met her. "You've got no chance." And he was right, but she and I became close friends.

Around the time of my summer internship in the late 1980s—nearly a decade after Salomon Brothers switched from a partnership to a public corporation—a sole government bond trader nearly put the firm out of business. Paul Mozer, the trader, was at the center of a scandal that would become legendary in the financial services world, as he tampered with federal securities auctions and lied to the US government, forever changing Salomon Brothers and the government bond market.

Paul William Mozer was born on Shakespeare's birthday in 1955, one of eight children of a New York City labor lawyer. Mozer had aspirations to become a drummer in a rock band and even enrolled at Berklee College of Music but dropped out when he realized he didn't have enough talent; he then went on to study economics and management. (Yet his love for music endured: He always kept a photo of Jimi Hendrix taped to the side of his desk.) Mozer was hired by Salomon's Chicago office at age twenty-four. In the summer of 1983, he was reposted to the government bond desk in New York. It was a good decade for government securities—interest rates were dropping, so the US Treasury was issuing more and more debt—and Mozer's new department was a distinguished one, since government bonds was the market upon which Salomon Brothers had been established decades earlier.

When the US government needed to issue debt, it would hold auctions and sell billions of dollars of Treasury bonds to approved buyers, who would in turn sell the bonds to other financial firms, as well as private clients. The government issued new securities almost weekly, and Salomon Brothers was usually the most aggressive and prolific bidder.

By the end of the 1980s, Mozer had risen to the head of Salomon's government bond desk. At the time, a single Salomon bond trader might move more in dollar volume of US Treasury securities per day than the value of all collective shares of equity traded on the New York Stock Exchange. In 1990, the US bond market had a value of more than $7.5 trillion—dwarfing most other markets. As the largest, safest, and most stable asset class in the entire global financial system, these bonds were indispensable financial instruments to every investment bank, commercial bank, insurance company, and money manager—pretty much every firm in the financial world of any material size. Mozer and his traders at Salomon Brothers understood that high demand, so they mastered the art of the squeeze—dominating certain auctions by purchasing the majority of bonds on offer, then sitting back to wait for the other investment banks to come begging.

Competing investment banks began to complain. Mozer in particular was so skilled at scooping up a mass volume of Treasury bonds that rival firms accused him of cornering the market and having the power to impact pricing, as in a monopoly. The Feds took heed of the complaints, and eventually they set 35 percent as the maximum that one investment bank could buy at each auction. This limit became known on the Street as "the Mozer rule."

Many at Salomon considered the newly imposed limit unfair and arbitrary, since, after all, in order to win an auction, you had to be the top bidder, which in this case meant offering the government the lowest interest rate. Getting a low interest rate was a good thing for the US Treasury and therefore a good thing for taxpayers, since the interest on the auctioned securities was paid for with tax dollars—a lower interest rate meant fewer tax dollars used. But the Feds' concern was that the massive, liquid, US government market was being artificially influenced by the actions of a few aggressive Salomon traders, with Paul Mozer chief among them. Public officials could not allow such an important market to be corrupted and damaged.

Tensions heated up between Mozer and the US Treasury. He had little respect for the federal officials who operated the auctions. Twice in late 1990, Mozer ignored the new 35 percent limit. Treasury officials warned him not to do it again, but Mozer was so incensed by the new restrictions that he turned to criticizing the Treasury in public, making comments that the media quoted with relish. Treasury officials weren't happy about the negative publicity, and they suggested to Salomon's top brass that they address the problem.

The Salomon bosses called on their chief municipal bond executive, Dale Horowitz, asking him to persuade Mozer to tone down the rhetoric and make nice with the Treasury. Horowitz had a good relationship with Bob Glauber, an undersecretary of the Treasury for domestic finance, and he figured he could broker a peace between Glauber and Mozer, easing the tensions between the firm and the government. Horowitz set up a breakfast meeting, at which Mozer would be expected to apologize to Glauber. Horowitz recalled: "I say to Paul Mozer, 'Look, this is not a question of what you think; this is a question of our business. You've got to apologize to this guy.' So we go to breakfast. We sit there—we have juice, we have cereal or whatever it is, we're drinking coffee—and Mozer still hasn't said a word of apology. Finally we're almost finished with breakfast, and I say, 'Paul, don't you have something to say?' 'Oh yeah, yeah,' he says, and he makes the weakest apology you could have ever heard."

The Treasury responded by tightening the rules even further, making it illegal for a single firm even to *bid* for more than 35 percent, let alone purchase 35 percent of an auction. Mozer secretly refined his approach, buying the maximum percentage allowed of a US Treasury auction, then illegally placing bids under the guise of his customers' accounts in order to buy significantly more of the auction. He got away with it for a while, until a few Salomon customers noticed that their names had been used to buy government securities, even though they couldn't recall having approved the purchases—not too dissimilar to the 2016 Wells Fargo scandal in which accounts were opened under customers' names without their knowledge in order to meet quotas.

In April 1991, Mozer confessed to his mentor, famed trader John Meriwether, that he had messed with a securities auction. Meriwether brought the bad news to Salomon's legendary CEO John Gutfreund (pronounced "good friend"), who shared it only with the firm's president, Tom Strauss, and general counsel, Don Feuerstein. Normally, if a violation of this magnitude were uncovered, senior management would call an emergency board meeting and immediately self-report to the Securities and Exchange Commission to save the firm and their own skin, hanging the violator out to dry. That's what Gutfreund, as the chairman and CEO, should have done. And he should have alerted the rest of Salomon's executive management team that they had a potentially huge problem on their hands. But he didn't. Instead, Gutfreund agreed to keep the discussion in-house and behind closed doors, involving only those few people.

What the top brass didn't know at the time was that Mozer hadn't tampered with only one auction; he had tampered with several. In some auctions he had amassed more than 90 percent of the bonds on offer—and this was in the face of a 35 percent limit imposed by federal mandate. Since the bosses weren't aware that the problem was so grave, they simply slapped Mozer's wrist and made him promise not to do it again, then they sent him on his way—back to the head of the government securities desk—with the unsupervised authority, more or less, to continue bidding on bond auctions on behalf of the firm.

———

John Gutfreund joined Salomon Brothers in 1953 in an entry-level position, and a few decades later he was crowned "the King of Wall Street" by *Fortune* magazine. It was an unexpected career path for twenty-three-year-old John—he had grown up in the suburbs of New York City as the son of a butcher who had found success as a meat wholesaler and distributor. John didn't take up the butcher's apron; instead he studied English at Oberlin College with aspirations to become a literature professor. He joined the army in 1951 and fought in Korea, and when he got out, he was offered a job by one of his father's golfing buddies—Billy Salomon.

John accepted a position as a trainee in the statistical department and quickly climbed the ranks, through the municipal bond department and onto the trading floor, where he became known as a talented trader. He also developed a reputation for being frugal. "When I made

John heir-apparent," Billy Salomon told the *New York Times* in 1988, "he was the most conservative person in the partnership, no question. If you turned in an expense account, and you had taken a client to Caravelle for dinner or something, John would ask you if it was really necessary. I thought that was a good example for the boys." In 1978, Gutfreund took over as CEO. Three years later, he led Salomon Brothers' transition from private partnership to public corporation, much to the displeasure of Billy Salomon, who had expected Gutfreund to protect the partnership.

Gutfreund cut a recognizable figure on the Street, a portly man with a round head and big glasses. He married a former Pan Am flight attendant, Susan, who became a fixture in the gossip and society papers for throwing lavish parties and spending fantastic sums of money on houses, shopping trips, antiques, and high fashion. She organized a sixtieth birthday party for her unsmiling husband, renting the Musée Carnavalet in Paris, and she bought a pair of seats on the Concorde to fly her favorite baker and his cake over from New York. This sort of showy extravagance was entirely counter to the personality of her husband, who smoked cigars, hung out with bond traders, and was as foulmouthed as any of them. *Women's Wear Daily* dubbed the couple "Social Susie" and "Solemn John."

Although Gutfreund had an office, he rarely used it. He preferred to be in the action. So he kept a desk out on the trading floor, and it was my good luck to be stationed next to him—and not far from another Salomon Brothers powerhouse, John Meriwether—after the head of recruiting decided the summer associates needed home locations when not observing a specific trader.

I knew of Gutfreund's famous advice to rookie traders—to wake up each morning "ready to bite the ass off a bear"—and I was eager for him to toss some similar scraps of wisdom my way, but he never spoke to me that summer except once, when he handed me an annual report he had finished reading and said I should check it out. I thanked him and enthusiastically dove into my directive from senior command, only to find that the report was written in German, a language I didn't know. I glanced at

Gutfreund, hoping to find him smiling good-naturedly at the prank, but he had already turned away.

Meanwhile, my supervisor had given me an assignment to document the terms of all past issuances in the high-yield bond market. I wasn't yet sure what that meant, but I gladly accepted the assignment, as it allowed me to interact with a few of the high-yield traders. One asked me what crime I had committed to be stationed in the DMZ, referencing the demilitarized zone between the hostile forces of Gutfreund and Meriwether.

I smiled at him naïvely. "I think it's a great opportunity to sit next to Gutfreund. I get to hear lots of cool stuff. And he seems like a nice guy."

The trader shook his head and walked away, calling over his shoulder, "You're probably safe. I don't see him wasting a bullet on a pissant like you. You're way too low on the scrotum pole."

And he was right. While Salomon seemed to operate in a sort of Darwinian chaos, there was in fact an unspoken rule that everyone followed: You only went after someone at or near your own level. "Lions don't hunt squirrels," they would say. The senior guys could make jokes at the expense of the young guys, haze and humiliate them in the name of edification and entertainment, but it was considered cowardly to take out someone who was much lower than you. My protection was my inferior status.

There was another refreshing observation that came to light that summer of 1989: Nothing mattered other than talent. I had expected a trading floor brimming with Ivy-educated, white, virile, heterosexual males who had vanquished their competitors to reach this pinnacle of Wall Street. And while those guys did of course exist in each firm, Salomon was much more diverse. I was surprised by the number of female salespeople and by the number of traders with no college education. Ethnicity and sexual orientation didn't seem to matter. Weight and attractiveness were overlooked. What mattered were intelligence, drive, and the ability to make money by moving financial securities. While much of Wall Street existed as the sort of boys' club for which the industry was notorious, Salomon's absence of bureaucracy and structure had created the purest of meritocracies. It could, at times, be crude, sexist, and brutal, but talent ultimately ruled.

———

As such, the fact that I was a Wharton student gave me no special advantage—my time on the trading floor was not going well. I didn't have a single great day the entire first half of the summer. I couldn't bear to think what stock price was flashing on my forehead. My assigned mentor, whom I secretly nicknamed Tor—short for *Tormentor*—wanted nothing to do with me. He seemed to take it as an insult from management that they made him babysit a green and worthless MBA student who was suspected of slacking off work to drink beers at the Seaport.

But eventually I had a real desk and was given the task of answering phones. I would stare at the bank of lights, waiting for one to blink, then answer as politely as possible.

"Good afternoon, Salomon Brothers, Chris Varelas. How may I help you?"

The third time I answered this way, I was talking into my empty hand, as the phone had been ripped away from me. I turned to see Tor glaring down with a look of utter disgust.

"What is that shit?" he asked. "You answer 'Salomon' and 'Salomon' only. If possible, keep it to two syllables: 'Saul-man.' Let me hear you say it."

I practiced saying "Saul-man" while others watched.

I'm sure I looked and sounded like a fool; I certainly felt like one. Learning the right way to answer the phone took me longer than it should have. The Salomon culture, in which efficiency trumped manners, was a shock to my Disneyland-trained sensibilities. I was accustomed to the way Walt Disney and my mother valued etiquette, but here on Wall Street, politeness was a market imperfection that could not be afforded in the breakneck pursuit of profits.

Later that night, on the phone with my mom, I asked her thoughts on the matter. To be honest, etiquette was the least of my concerns with Wall Street culture, but it felt like a safe subject to test out with my mom, even though I knew what she'd say. She had always believed that acting civilly to one's fellow man was an essential tenet of basic human decency.

"What do you mean, no time for 'good afternoon'?" she said. "That sounds like a crazy place."

"But, Mom, this is a fast-paced world in which every second matters. People don't have time for those sorts of niceties."

"Christokimou," my mom said, her Greek nickname for me, which meant *my little Chris*, "you must always make the time to be courteous. It is what separates us from the animals. Maybe you should get out of there. Remember, if you live with the cross-eyed, you become cross-eyed."

The cross-eyed saying was one I had heard hundreds of times as a kid, most often when I was running with a crowd of which she didn't approve. While I agreed with her point, I also felt that an outsider could never understand the Salomon culture without experiencing it firsthand. But part of me wondered if I was simply making excuses.

————

Why did Paul Mozer tamper with the Treasury auctions, putting the entire firm at risk? He wasn't the sort of guy from whom anyone expected such destructive and unethical behavior. He was a short man with a quiet disposition, yet he was fiercely competitive—particularly with himself, both as an amateur tennis player and in his Wall Street career. Mozer was one of eight children, so perhaps his competitive nature was to blame for his actions, and he was simply hotheaded and trying to ridicule the Treasury, even if it would ultimately be at his own expense. He was too smart to think that he might actually get away with it.

Or perhaps Mozer's actions were a result of Salomon's freewheeling culture, which espoused the belief that it's better to beg forgiveness than to ask permission—he may have imagined that he would be pardoned and possibly even rewarded for maximizing profits and exposing this weakness in the system. Or there might have been another factor, dating back to Mozer's transfer to the government bond desk in 1983 and his history with John Meriwether.

Meriwether was one of the most powerful people at the firm, vice chairman of the board and the head of the high-stakes proprietary trading operation. While most salesmen and traders worked for the clients and collected commissions on those deals, Meriwether and his proprietary traders used the firm's own capital to take positions on behalf of the firm. They were operating on a much larger scale than other traders; essentially, Salomon became its own biggest customer. The most often used analogy was that of a Vegas casino: The basic commission trading for clients resembled a sea of slot machines, steadily accruing profits, coin by coin; proprietary trading, however, was similar to the "whale" gambling alone at a blackjack table, betting a giant stack on every hand. The success or failure of that whale determined the profitability of the casino; the slot machines didn't move the needle much. If Meriwether bet right, Salomon Brothers had a great quarter. If not, Salomon had a bad quarter, regardless of sales and trading revenues. While the client-and-commission operation was necessary in order to create and maintain the firm's trillion-dollar balance sheet, the biggest action by far was happening with Meriwether's proprietary trading.

Meriwether lobbied successfully for a change to the pay structure in the late 1980s, marching into Gutfreund's office and arguing that since his team was making many times more money for the firm than anyone else, their compensation should reflect that profitability. Gutfreund acquiesced, and, with the knowledge of only two of the other nine members of the executive committee, he allowed Meriwether's team to collect bonuses of 15 percent of what they made for the firm, while other departments split a much more modest bonus pool. This had never been done before, and it would have far-reaching implications. When the other departments eventually found out, they of course demanded the same pay structure. That established the slippery slope of compensation being set by personal performance, with limited correlation to how well the overall firm did that year.

"Under the partnership," Horowitz recalled, "if your department performed better than others, you would get paid more, but you didn't get paid excessively, because it was believed that everything that was done was a firm-wide effort, which came from the ethic of the partnership. If you wanted to buy a fancy car, for example, and you went to Billy Salomon and said, 'Can I have some money from my capital account? I really want to buy this car,' he'd laugh at you. 'First,' he'd say, 'we're keeping the money in the partnership. And second, we don't want our partners living like that.'"

But the transition to a public corporation gave Meriwether the opportunity to instill an "eat-what-you-kill" bonus structure, as he fiercely protected his crew of mathematicians and former Ivy League professors who became his arbitrage specialists. Before Paul Mozer was moved to the government securities desk, he had been part of Meriwether's team, so while the proprietary traders' personal bank accounts were bursting at the seams over the decade, Mozer began to feel as if he'd been cast out and left behind. The new bonus structure for Meriwether's guys was kept secret for a time, but when they started reeling in eight-figure comp, word quickly spread. Mozer's bonus in the government securities department in 1990 reached almost $5 million—certainly nothing to scoff at—but he must have felt slighted when he heard that Larry Hilibrand, one of his former comrades on Meriwether's team, had cleared $23 million. It's easy to see how Mozer's rancor might have led him astray.

"At the time of the breakfast," Horowitz said, recalling the failed meeting with Mozer and the Treasury official, "we had no idea that he was already hiding stuff. Of all the people to cheat and lie to, you messed around with the United States government? I mean, greed is greed. There's just no way to get around it. And greed was the ultimate result of becoming a corporation, because it became other people's money, and that was the end of it."

———

Time frames on the trading floor were measured in seconds. Markets would react so quickly that you needed to have prebaked your moves before numbers were released or news hit. To stay sharp, traders would play a game called "What if," challenging one another on what to buy or sell if something major happened in the world, usually a catastrophe. One trader would pose a question, and the others would shout responses.

Tor was up with a question: "What do you do if Tokyo gets wiped out by a nuclear reactor meltdown?"

The traders began yelling out answers: "Short the yen; buy the dollar!" (*Short* was trader-talk for "sell.")

"Yeah, obviously." That answer got negative points for its lack of imagination, even though it was a revelation to me, as I was only beginning to learn how to analyze world events through a financial lens.

"Go long US and German automakers, given that their major competition just got taken out." (*Long* was trader-talk for "buy.")

"I'm shorting Disney," one trader called out from several desks away, "since half their customers just got blown up."

I couldn't help but nod at that one—and wished I had thought of it.

Early every Monday morning, we had a firm-wide meeting to discuss the economic data that would be released that week—something came out nearly every day that would affect the movement of the markets. Hundreds of traders gathered in the huge auditorium at One New York Plaza to discuss, for example, the new employment figures that would be released on Friday at 8:30 A.M. All the senior guys would sit up front, while experts from various departments, such as the syndicate desk, the government desk, and the foreign exchange desk, would parade across the stage to present the consensus around Wall Street regarding what the numbers would mean for their market. Then the traders would head back to their desks to debate what positions to take and why.

On Friday, as the time approached for release of the employment figures, discussion among the traders heated up. I watched from the sidelines as a trader said, "If the number's high, I think yields will go up because it's gonna signify inflationary pressure, and the Fed would likely raise rates." Another guy shouted, "Bullshit! Yields will go *down* because it's gonna signify growth, and I don't think there's enough employment here to worry yet about wages being increased due to inflationary pressure." Then they started quibbling about what might happen if the employment number came out lower than expected—and just as before, there were traders ready to argue opposite outcomes of the same news.

It was 8:28. The number would be released in two minutes. Bo appeared next to me with wide eyes. "What are they saying here?" he asked, taking the empty seat beside mine.

"I have no idea. It's like a different language. Some are saying yields will go up or down if the employment number is high, and they're saying the same thing if it's low. It seems like they're just guessing."

"You're in the wrong place, brother." He glanced over his shoulder and scooted closer. "I just heard that Meriwether's boys are betting on the number being high, and they're taking a friggin' huge position on the thirty-year. Like, *huge*."

"How does Meriwether know it'll be high? None of these guys seem to agree what the number will be or how it'll affect the markets."

"Because he's John friggin' Meriwether, that's how." Bo patronizingly patted me on the back.

"But what'll happen if he's wrong?"

Bo laughed and shook his head. He didn't answer.

In the final minute, all the salesmen were on the phone with their top clients, while the traders were at the ready to buy or sell. Bo studied the traders and absently played with his Citadel ring. The room quieted in the final seconds—like the countdown to New Year's—then the number hit, and there was a burst of energy, conversation, excitement, and fear. I looked over at Bo. He was leaning forward in his chair, his mouth slightly open, taking it all in, as the traders shouted and gestured. He seemed to love everything about the scene, while I felt like I was observing some exotic, indecipherable pageant.

I wasn't privy to whether Meriwether was right or wrong that morning. But it didn't really matter. His genius was based on a simple concept: that the market would eventually normalize. When spreads were wide, he would bet that they would tighten; when spreads were historically tight, he would bet that they would widen. And because he had Salomon's huge balance sheet at his disposal, he had enough money to wait until he was ultimately right.

The British economist John Maynard Keynes is often credited with saying: "The market can remain irrational longer than you can remain solvent." Backed by Salomon's coffers and a good deal of luck, Meriwether disproved that statement—for a time. After he left Salomon, he formed a hedge fund, Long-Term Capital Management. There he made bets using the same theory, but it didn't work, since his models (undoubtedly built on a computer spreadsheet) were flawed, and his bets turned out to be bigger than his new balance sheet could support. This quickly led to catastrophe, and since Long-Term Capital was doing business with so many large Wall Street firms, its failure put the whole industry at risk. More than a dozen banks had to join forces and cobble together a bailout to limit the damage in the larger global financial markets. Long-Term Capital Management collapsed after only four years, a spectacular disaster that tainted Meriwether's legacy and lost him and others enormous sums of money.

———

Why John Gutfreund chose not to report Paul Mozer's violation when he first learned of it is still a mystery, and Gutfreund took his secret to the grave in 2016. People close to the situation said that he simply didn't think it was that big of a deal. Others claimed that he eventually understood the gravity of the offense, but he played it cool to try to appear innocent or ignorant. Some, including Salomon's assistant general counsel, Zachary Snow, suggested that John Meriwether had persuaded Gutfreund to keep quiet, as Meriwether still felt guilty about allowing Mozer to be removed from his team, so he fought to protect him.

When Mozer got caught by the Feds in July 1991 for once again intentionally surpassing the 35 percent limit imposed on securities auctions, Treasury officials finally became aware of the scope of his violations. The government opened an investigation, while Salomon performed its own internal inquiry. Gutfreund, Strauss, and Meriwether quickly discovered that, despite Mozer's promises, he had continued to game the securities auctions, including having cornered 87 percent of an auction in May. That particular move by Mozer forced a squeeze that caused other firms to lose more than $100 million, and it even sent some smaller firms into bankruptcy. Gutfreund was finally obliged to report the violations to

Salomon's other senior executives, to the board of directors, and to federal authorities, yet he held back so many crucial details—including the fact that he had known of the offenses since April—that he essentially sealed his own doom.

Maybe Gutfreund had chosen not to report the violation because of his ego. He was a butcher's son and English major who had risen to the pinnacle of Wall Street, and he likely felt untouchable. When he finally spoke to his top executives about the matter in a closed-door meeting, he said to them, "I'm not apologizing for anything to anybody. Apologies don't mean shit. What happened, happened."

When the story hit the papers, most people didn't expect Salomon Brothers to survive. The federal government would simply put the firm out of business. Gutfreund called his close friend Warren Buffett, the famous billionaire who had invested $700 million in Salomon Brothers a few years earlier and who sat on the firm's board. Buffett was appalled at Mozer's actions and disappointed that Gutfreund hadn't handled the situation with more integrity. Yet he recognized that if Salomon were to survive, the firm would need to stand on the reputation of someone trusted and respected, and there was no one better than Buffett. If Salomon went down, Buffett knew, that might not only have a devastating impact on global markets, but it would also leave a stain on his own stellar reputation by his being associated with a corrupt failure. So Buffett agreed to step in as interim chairman.

After forty years with the firm, Gutfreund submitted his resignation. Meriwether, as vice chairman, was also out, along with president Tom Strauss, for knowing of Mozer's offenses and keeping his mouth shut. Heads had to roll. These men who had brought Salomon into the modern era, for better or worse—shepherding the transition from partnership to corporation—were now casualties of the culture they had fostered and championed. Billy Salomon, who no longer had a day-to-day role in the firm but was still the elder statesman emeritus, told *Businessweek*: "I'd be very happy to have my name removed from the door."

Paul Mozer was fired on August 17, 1991. When his criminal trial was finally over, he pleaded guilty to two felony counts related to placing false auction bids in the names of Salomon customers. A civil lawsuit that followed allegedly found that he had tampered with at least seven separate auctions and that his false bids had totaled $13.5 billion. In a settlement he agreed to a lifetime ban from the securities industry. His additional punishment was remarkably light—four months in a minimum-security prison and a fine of $1.1 million, which was just a drop of the downpour of money made as a result of the auction tampering. He went to prison in January 1993 and would be back home soon after the dirty snowbank melted on the sidewalk outside Salomon Brothers.

All summer long, Wall Street banks hosted cocktail receptions for summer associates from elsewhere in order to give them exposure to their firms. These occurred most weeknights. Sometimes we would stop at one on our way to somewhere else, and, while they were usually pretty dull, at least we could count on starting our Manhattan evenings with a free buzz. My housemate Ben was rarely able to join, since his investment banking gig required regular late nights and all-nighters, but when the Morgan Stanley reception came around, nothing could have held him back. It was Ben's dream to work there someday. While Salomon was at the zenith of sales and trading, Morgan Stanley was generally considered the top of the investment banking world.

I had nothing to do that night, so I went along. Ben was pretty anxious about the event, but I couldn't have cared less about Morgan Stanley. In fact, I had ridiculously called the firm "Stanley Morgan" during my first couple of weeks in New York, thinking it was the name of the founder, until an amused trader humiliated me with a public correction. The party was held at the Rainbow Room, the swanky establishment perched sixty-five stories above Rockefeller Plaza. If anything, I figured, the hors d'oeuvres would be decent.

As soon as the elevators spit us out into the dazzling ballroom—complete with a jazz band, crystal chandeliers, and ornate flower arrangements—Ben scooted off to schmooze with Morgan Stanley's investment banking kingpins, leaving me to wander along the banks of windows overlooking Central Park, uptown, and the rivers and boroughs beyond. It was the most startling view I'd ever seen.

"Looks small from up here, doesn't it? Like a diorama."

I turned to find a young woman beside me. She had shoulder-length brown hair with bangs and wore square glasses.

"It hardly looks real," I said.

She thrust out a hand and introduced herself as Jane, a summer associate in sales at Paine Webber. She had a pleasant, easy smile.

"Nice to meet you, Jane." I took her hand and gave it a squeeze, introducing myself.

When she heard where I worked, her eyebrows shot up. It was a reaction I'd gotten used to seeing that summer.

"Salomon Brothers," she repeated. "Dang."

Any time you told someone that you worked in fixed income at Salomon, you were immediately perceived as a badass and possibly a little dangerous.

Jane and I spoke for a while apart from the crowd, then mingled with a few senior Morgan Stanley bankers before abandoning the reception for a classic Midtown establishment, the Monkey Bar, beneath the Hotel Elysée. I'd heard stories about this place being a clubhouse for Manhattan literati and music luminaries decades ago, and I'd always wanted to check it out. On the way in, I mentioned to Jane that Tennessee Williams had died in a suite upstairs, bizarrely choking to death on the cap of an eyedropper.

"Who?" she said, teetering against me.

"Some writer." I should have known better than to bring up literature with a Wall Streeter. She could talk circles around me about any financial concept on the planet, but an appreciation of the arts was a scarcity in the world of banking.

The Monkey Bar was surprisingly bright and more run-down than I expected, but it had an old-school New York charm, with worn wooden floors, leather booths, red-and-white checkered tablecloths, brass wall sconces, and faded murals of monkeys playing cards and drinking booze.

The hotel upstairs was nicknamed the Hotel Easy Lay, due to its history as a popular setting for extramarital affairs. The Monkey Bar was one of those places where you could feel the residue from forgotten moments of cultural history and illicit conversations that had unfolded in its deep red booths.

We ordered beers and found stools at the end of the bar, affording us some privacy but also an angle to observe the crowd, which for the most part was older and conservatively dressed. Jane and I had gone through the basics of where we were from, where we studied, et cetera, and now she was analyzing recent financial news that was well beyond my experience and understanding.

"What do you think will happen with the CPI tomorrow?" she asked.

"Tomorrow? Hard to say." I was lost. "What do *you* think?"

"I think it'll be high. But inflation doesn't seem to be an issue. The Fed will likely lower interest rates, which is going to be expansionary, so therefore bond prices should be going up and yields coming down." Clearly, Jane had done her homework.

"Yeah." I gulped down half my pint. "That seems to be the conventional wisdom."

She squinted and cocked her head. "Go on," she said.

"It wouldn't be the first time, right?" I continued improvising. "But you never know, do you? I wouldn't be surprised if the exact opposite happened."

A slow smile broke over her face, and I thought she was about to call me out for having no clue what I was talking about. But instead she sweetly placed a hand on my knee. I felt a wave of relief and electricity. She hadn't outed me as a fake quite yet.

I finished my beer and signaled for another round. The voice of the woman who ran Salomon's recruiting echoed back to me, from that first day of orientation: "Perception is reality." How true, I thought, knowing that it was the mystique of the Salomon trader that enticed Jane, rather than the liberal arts book nerd and former Disneyland employee who sat before her. Perception and reality are tricky that way, sometimes unexpectedly leading you to win the favor of an attractive, anonymous young woman. I looked at her hand, delicate and shadowed in the glow of the bar, still resting on my knee. What a strange new world.

"Tell me something crazy." She leaned in conspiratorially. "I wanna hear a wild story from the notorious Salomon Brothers trading floor."

"Hmm, let's see."

"Something juicy."

"Okay, I got one." I was starting to enjoy playing the part in which Jane had cast me. "This happened today, actually. I was on the equity trading floor when they pulled off a big move on a stock. I can't say which company, so let's call it Company X. It was pretty intense."

She leaned even closer. "Yeah?"

I doubted from the beginning of the story whether I should be telling it and hoped that omitting the company's name might protect me a bit. Not that there was anything illegal about what had happened, but hearing myself describe it, the whole thing started to sound shady.

The equity traders didn't get a whole lot of respect within the Salomon hierarchy, particularly compared to the bond traders. So to flex their muscles, they orchestrated a tricky maneuver that could bring in a windfall of profits, but only if several things happened in just the right way.

To begin, they quietly bought a bunch of Company X stock. Then one of the traders picked up his phone and put out a whisper that Salomon had a big need for Company X shares in order to cover a short position. That, of course, was a falsehood, since Salomon had accumulated Company X with the sole purpose of pulling off this play. The whisper spread rapidly, as they expected it would, and other firms scrambled to buy up as much Company X stock as they could get in an attempt to put a squeeze on Salomon—if they had what Salomon needed, making the supply scarce, they could charge a premium for the assets (very similar to what Mozer did with government bonds). The team pulling off the play crowded around a Quotron watching the price of Company X creep up and up as the buying frenzy continued. They were waiting for just the right moment to pull the plug. Timing was key in these stock manipulations: If you pulled out too early, you left profits on the table; if you waited too long, the thing might fall apart. The traders anxiously looked over their shoulders at the senior equity trader orchestrating the maneuver. "Not yet," he said quietly. "Not yet." Then, after another jump in price, he finally barked, "Dump it." The traders dove at their phones and furiously started offloading the pile of Company X stock before their sell orders put too much downward pressure on the stock price, but they had to execute it in a way that didn't expose their play. The sale took all of six minutes, and when the last trader slammed down his phone, they all leapt to their feet and cheered. They'd made a quick and handsome profit, and their blood was pumping.

Jane listened with her mouth slightly agape, her hand tense on my knee. I milked the story too, for all the drama I could pack in. When I was done, she stood up, folded her jacket over her arm, and took my hand without saying a word. Less than half an hour later, we climbed the stairs of my brownstone, pushed open the door to my room, and flicked on the light. I flinched, as I hadn't prepared her for the explosion of pink, the lace and ruffles, the unicorns and dolls. Surely she would see me as the impostor I was. But she turned with a big grin on her face. "You Salomon boys," she said, "are out of your minds."

———

The squeeze the equity traders pulled off that day was nothing new. That sort of speculation—gambling on and manipulating stocks—has been going on in one form or another as long as the markets have existed. Before regulations were put in place to curb some of the dirtier practices, one popular way to make a quick buck was through the forming of a stock pool, in which a group of powerful investors would gather their resources, find a co-conspirator on the floor of the Exchange, and create false excitement around a certain stock in order to drive up the price. The general public would be the sucker on the other end of the heist, unwittingly buying up shares of the stock as its value increased. Then the stock pool would move to liquidate its position, and the members would head off with a tidy profit that they snatched from the pockets of the public as the stock price plummeted back to earth.

Stock pools were so common in the 1920s that the public eventually learned of the practice. Not only did people not object, they joined right in. They seemed to savor the challenge, feeling certain that they could make a buck if they could expertly navigate the market's wild fluctuations, but that rarely worked out, since they had so much less information than the traders who were manipulating the game. Some stock pools included members as lofty as Charles Schwab, Walter Chrysler, a Rockefeller, some top government officials, and the heads of major banks. But despite their acceptance by both the public and the titans of finance, not everyone agreed that the practice was ethical. In 1927, a Harvard professor named William Zebina Ripley published a book titled *Main Street and Wall Street* that considered stock manipulations in the market: "The first duty is to face the fact that there is something the matter. . . . I am conscious that things are not right. The house is not falling down—no fear of that! But there are queer little noises about, as of rats in the wall, or of borers in the timbers."

Yet these stock manipulations probably don't represent the first major instance of Main Street being overtly harmed by the actions of Wall Street. Arguably, that honor goes to Paul Mozer and his government auction scandal. With scams like the stock pools, Wall Street had slapped and cheated Main Street investors for decades, but what Mozer did in the early 1990s was more widely and deeply damaging: He corrupted a massive and essential market, corroding the public's confidence in the system. Never before had a large Wall Street firm fundamentally threatened an institution as important to Main Street as the government bond market. The Mozer scandal was a natural outcome of Salomon's shift from partnership to corporation. It proved what could happen when risk became disconnected from accountability.

It would be easy at this point—looking at guys like Mozer and Gutfreund—to conclude that everyone on Wall Street was corrupt and greedy. But that's not an accurate view. More than 99 percent of everything that I saw take place at Salomon each day was legal, ethical, and aboveboard. Most of the firm's eight thousand employees were decent people. Unsurprisingly, the abuses seemed most prevalent by those at the top, who both had the most power to wield and faced less and less accountability.

Would Mozer have done what he did under a partnership? Or, more to the point, *could* he have? The partnership had been built on a culture of togetherness and shared accountability, so people would self-monitor and make sure that others didn't take unnecessary risks. Those controls evaporated after the move to a public corporation, and then you could have one bad apple like Mozer—one among thousands of employees—take actions that could destroy the entire firm.

Warren Buffett understood the harm done to Salomon by Mozer and the difficult job he had of regaining the trust of the public and government. Although the Feds were accepting of Buffett's willingness to step in as interim chairman of Salomon Brothers, the transition was far from smooth. There was a tornado of criminal charges and fines still whirling, and every time the Feds levied a fresh punishment against Salomon, to make an example of the firm, the stock price fell even further. The government banned Salomon from bidding in auctions on behalf of clients—but not from continuing to bid for its own account. Yet that restriction, along with general public disgust, caused customers to flee from Salomon in droves. During the worst of it, Salomon's balance sheet was dropping by a billion dollars a day.

Buffett made bold statements to Congress about the ways in which he promised to clean up Salomon's Wild West culture and restore virtue to the firm. In his testimony, he described his leadership vision: "Lose money for the firm, and I will be understanding. Lose a shred of reputation for the firm, and I will be ruthless." Meanwhile, he sent a memo to all eight thousand employees—which included his home phone number—instructing them to report any illegal or unethical behavior directly to him. He took out a full-page ad in the *Wall Street Journal*, an open letter to Salomon shareholders that promised big changes to the firm's controls and culture. He could have sent the letter directly to shareholders, of course, but he wanted to make a public display of it. Buffett understood that restoring the trust of the people and government was the only thing that might save Salomon Brothers.

It took a while, but eventually clients began to return, and the stock started to recover. Buffett stepped down from his position in the spring of 1992, a year after Mozer first admitted his wrongdoings to John Meriwether.

In many ways, the scandal was unsurprising. When looked at with the benefit of time and perspective, it's easy to see the full arc that led from the early golden days of Salomon's partnership to Warren Buffett testifying before Congress, pleading to save the firm. Salomon Brothers had once been a company in which partners used their own dollars to finance their positions and underwrite securities. Then the world got bigger, and the firm needed more money to stay relevant, so it became a public corporation, and its balance sheet multiplied. At the same time, the senior people figured, *Why don't we start making money for our own account, betting the firm's capital?* So here came Meriwether and his band of proprietary traders. They started making outsized returns and eventually demanded to be compensated for the value they were adding. Management was obliged to agree. And then others wanted a piece as well, so they were inspired to push the limits even further, feeling as though they needed to become individual engines of profit rather than members of a team. The partnership was over, and the ethics and controls that accompanied that partnership had fallen by the wayside. It became every man for himself. From the forming of the public corporation in 1981 to Mozer almost demolishing the firm in 1991, it was a decade of increasing self-interested greed. And the firm never quite recovered.

Accountability kept diminishing, even as the need for it grew with the increasing size and complexity of Wall Street and the markets it served. The seeds of the 2008 financial crisis had been planted and would germinate less than a generation later, as the same thing would happen on a much broader scale, throwing Wall Street and Main Street into chaos.

———

When I returned from a coffee run one day, I spotted the young intern Victor with his feet up on a desk, eating Chinese food with Penn King. They looked like fraternity brothers exchanging off-color banter, laughing and poking fun at each other. But in fact, they were celebrating a trade that Victor had executed under King's tutelage, something unheard of by a summer associate. Just then, over the loudspeaker, known on the floor as the squawk box, a voice announced: "Victor the Sphincter with another million bonds!"

Good for Victor, I thought. He'd even earned a disparaging nickname. That kid had really come into his own.

It was a surprise to no one when I concluded that fixed income trading wasn't the best fit for me. Split-second decision making based on macro events was exhilarating to watch, but it struck me as random guesswork or, at best, a game of trying to predict others' reactions to events rather than the direct impact of the event itself. And I didn't welcome the prospect of betting millions or billions of dollars of the firm's money on whether the thirty-year US Treasury bond might move up or down a few basis points because of some seemingly unrelated economic indicator. It was a fascinating, entertaining, and terrifying place, but I knew my skills—whatever they were—would be put to better use elsewhere.

There was another thing nagging at me that summer of 1989: I didn't feel that I was adding any value—not only to the firm, a fact that no one would dispute, but overall, as a person in society. It wasn't as though I was about to run out and join the Peace Corps, but I wanted to feel that I was a functioning member of society and not just a cog in a money machine. I watched these traders, whirling around in their starling flock of madness, and I wondered if there was ultimately anything *good* about what they were doing. The majority of them had pursued the profession in order to chase excitement and make a lot of money. For most of them, their motivation started and ended right there.

But over time, my understanding deepened, and I came to recognize the complex, historical ways in which those bond traders were actually part of something essential and beneficial, no matter their motivation for coming into the profession. The bond market began as a way for governments and municipalities to borrow money to build roads and schools, to fund war efforts, to create and maintain the infrastructures through which our communities functioned. By 2018, the US bond market had swelled to more than $41 trillion, up from less than $8 trillion in 1990. The government needed someone to operate the system for it, managing the issuances of bonds and distributing them to buyers and other dealers, creating a vibrant and efficient market. That's where the financial institutions came into the picture. They created the market—making the transactions possible, thereby helping to facilitate growth. They were the necessary oil that allowed the machine to function. The secondary market, which the financial institutions also created and maintained, was equally important: If people decided they didn't want to own their government bonds anymore, they could go to Salomon or another investment bank to sell them. The more efficient and robust the market was, the easier it became for investors to access, which made the borrowing cost cheaper, requiring fewer tax dollars to cover interest payments.

So I found that these thousands of traders and salespeople, who are tiny but crucial pieces of the big machine—many of whom seem crazy or competitive or greedy beyond measure—are in fact adding value and contributing to society, even if only as a byproduct of their actions, because the market itself is essential to a thriving and growing society.

But with the move from partnership to public company and the separation of balance sheet from accountability, the financial system forced new questions: What is the new standard for good, and what is our own responsibility to act with integrity? Given human nature, should we be expected to be good, if no longer constrained by the threat of losing one's own capital? What are the new parameters and guardrails for encouraging and monitoring behavior? Maximizing one's long-term best interest would seem to require that bad behaviors be kept in check; but considering the lure of giant bonuses, the temptation to take financial and reputational risk became greater in the shift away from traditional partnerships.

—

My first summer blazed on, and August finally arrived, which meant it was time for Salomon's recruitment cocktail party. While most of the gatherings arranged by other firms were fairly staid, the Salomon Brothers party was of course the exception.

When I walked into the bar rented for the event, I saw a trader standing on top of the bar with a mini basketball, surrounded by men shouting and waving money. The trader was taking odds on whether he could nail the Pop-A-Shot from long range, and the bets were in the thousands. To my left, a dozen salespeople and summer associates were circled up throwing back shots of liquor. Their table was strewn with empty glasses and tipped-over beer bottles.

Larry Bird met me just inside the door on her way out, looking terrific in one of her many colorful Chanel suits.

"Leaving the party so soon?" I asked.

"Yes," she said. "Back to work. I have a presentation due in the morning."

"How's the party?" I scanned the circus.

"Typical Salomon. O'Leary is hanging out in the women's loo."

"What?" I asked. A mini basketball flew over our heads and scores of traders cheered.

"O'Leary," she said flatly, as if reporting nothing out of the ordinary. "He's in the women's bathroom." A guy I recognized as a respected managing director passed by at that moment, wearing his tie around his head like Rambo's bandanna.

"What the hell is he doing in there?"

"No idea," she said. "But I've got to go."

I spotted a trader slumped on the floor in the corner, passed out against the cigarette machine. "Well, maybe you're lucky to be getting out of here."

As she stepped away, she gave me a weary look.

A few minutes later, I was shouldering up to the bar for a beer when O'Leary appeared nearby. I heard a trader ask him why he'd been in the ladies' room.

"Listen," he said. "I was told to focus on recruiting more women. And goddamnit, that's where the women are."

"How'd it go?" the trader asked with a grin.

"Great!" O'Leary yelled. "They're all on board!" And the two men doubled over laughing.

Summer was coming to an end. I would soon return to Wharton for my second and final year at the institution that was credited with being the intellectual foundation for justifying Wall Street's value and mission. And after walking across the coals of the trading floor for a few months, I wasn't sure how I felt about it.

I sipped my beer and looked for Ben, but I couldn't find him. I looked for the other summers too, for anyone I knew or could talk to, but everyone was a stranger. They didn't even seem to be talking to one another—they drank, they hollered, they gambled. I stood in the corner of a room crammed with people beside whom I had spent the past few months working, and somehow they were nameless to me, a blur of revelers at an out-of-control party that must have felt as though it would never end. It would never be last call in their world; the lights would never be turned up; they were sure of it. They waved fistfuls of cash, making improbable bets just for the hell of it, risking huge sums on the off chance that maybe, just maybe, one of those Pop-A-Shots would lift off, arch across the barroom as they all raised their faces to the heavens, spilling their manhattans, tracking the flying orange globe that would miraculously miss the light fixtures and ceiling beams, get lost for a second in the darkest stretch, then reappear and finally drop through the tiny hoop, while the backboard exploded with golden flashbulbs and the red sirens of victory . . .

And there it is, fortunes won and lost on an impossible shot, and the room erupts, and rounds of drinks are ordered while the next trader climbs on top of the bar and toes the line and takes the ball and—with the eternal confidence of the young and wealthy—lets it fly.

3

MILK AND BALLOONS

Nostalgia ain't what it used to be.

—PETER DE VRIES

Working in the Café Orleans at Disneyland is not your typical starter job on the path to Wall Street. But that's how it happened for me. The summer I finished high school in 1981, I landed a position as a "hostess" (that's what the offer sheet read), after my name had been mistaken for a woman's during the application process. I loved the job— crossing Main Street, USA, at the beginning of a shift, as excited guests flooded into the park, meeting people from all over the world, orbiting around the hostess stand with my co-workers, being part of a beloved and storied institution—and I continued working summers and holidays as I attended Occidental College to study economics and philosophy. Then on June 8, 1984, during my fourth summer at the park, the nation's most famous Main Street collided with Wall Street in a way that would both rattle Disney and change the arc of modern business. I didn't know it at the time, but it would also be an important catalyst for moving me toward a career in the financial services industry.

That morning, some portentous and confusing news appeared in the papers. A corporate raider named Saul Steinberg was targeting Walt

Disney Productions in a hostile takeover. None of us knew what it meant, as we had never heard the terms "corporate raider" and "hostile takeover" before—the same was true for most Americans—yet I was fascinated by the news and gleaned what I could from the papers and TV reports. I learned that, while Disney hadn't been for sale, there was a process by which a well-funded investor could buy up enough stock in a publicly traded company that he would gain some measure of influence over the firm's board of directors. At that point, with the support of the board, he could make a move to eliminate the senior executives, install his own people, and essentially take over the company. Then he would institute changes, which might include breaking up the company and selling off pieces, almost always in the interest of increasing profits and stuffing his and his supporters' pockets.

Later that afternoon, I sat at a table in the break room with a hostess named Terry, an energetic Cal State student whom we affectionately called by her initials, T.C., which to us stood for "Totally Clueless." Another hostess joined us—Grace, a beautiful and demure young woman whose missionary parents had raised her in Japan. She could make our polyester red-and-white polka dot costume seem like the most glamorous fashion choice imaginable. Grace sipped from a mug of tea and started to talk about Saul Steinberg and his move against Disney. I liked the fact that she was following the news and appeared to understand it. That wasn't the case with many of the seasonal employees, who cared about what was happening far less than the full-time career employees.

A busser named Matt plopped into a seat beside us and started unwrapping his lunch. T.C. was scooting the components of a fruit salad around her plate with a fork. "How can this guy even buy it?" she asked.

"Yeah," said Matt, through a mouthful of bologna sandwich. "Isn't Disneyland owned by the government, like a state park?"

Grace covered her mouth and quietly giggled. Although she was six feet tall, dirty blond, and on the surface looked more American than anyone in the room, her upbringing in Japan had instilled in her an elegant and reserved manner. "I do not think Disney is owned by the government," she said.

"Right," I said, "it's just like sports teams. Owned by individuals."

In response, Matt took an enormous but thoughtful bite of his bologna sandwich.

Grace recounted what she'd read about Steinberg and his interest in Disney.

"That's weird," T.C. said, poking at a chunk of pineapple.

"Totally," Matt said. "Who is this dude?"

"No, I mean the pineapple," T.C. said. "Look at the color. It got stained by the blueberries."

Matt laughed, then abruptly quieted down as Snow White and Alice in Wonderland entered the break room and settled together at the Fantasyland table.

A deep voice spoke from behind us: "How do you two know so much about it?" I turned in my chair to find an astronaut pulling a burrito from the microwave.

"I don't know that much," I said. "Just what's been in the papers. Grace knows more than I do."

"No, Chris is the one studying economics," Grace said, winking at me. I felt my face flush under her attention. We hadn't discussed hostile takeovers in class at Occidental, so I really only knew what was in the press.

The astronaut dropped heavily into a chair at the Tomorrowland table. "I know one thing," he said. "This spaceship is changing course." I admired his ability to stay in character, even on break.

T.C. pushed her plate away and drew a piece of gum from her purse, a little slice of contraband that was forbidden throughout the park. "But, guys, are we gonna lose our jobs? I can't lose my job before the end of the summer. I have to buy books for the fall semester. This guy better wait until September."

Matt pointed at T.C.'s abandoned fruit salad. "Are you gonna eat that?"

Little did we know how right the astronaut was. With Steinberg going after a legendary, beloved institution, his move against Disney was being portrayed by the media as an assault on the American Dream, on our cherished memories and our childhoods. There were new things brewing on Wall Street in the mid-1980s, entire markets that were born seemingly overnight. Hostile takeovers and corporate raiders were about to have their decade in the spotlight. No one could have predicted the massive shift in public awareness and opinion, as well as corporate strategy, that Steinberg's battle with Disney would ignite.

Walt Disney gets well-deserved credit for his creative genius, but his most enduring contribution to American business may be revolutionizing customer service. For Walt, nothing was more important than the guest experience. Visitors to Disneyland don't notice most elements of the customer service, which is of course the point. For example, trashcans are carefully arranged every twenty-seven paces throughout the park, which Disney learned through exhaustive research is the average distance a visitor will carry a piece of garbage before getting rid of it. A *New York Times Magazine* reporter, in awe of Disneyland's sanitation staff, wrote in 1965: "It is calculated that a discarded cigarette butt will lie dormant for no longer than 25 seconds before it is pounced upon." That caliber of service, and the thousands of employee smiles that greet guests each day, are the backbone of the famous Disney Magic.

While most people think of Disneyland as an innately creative place, that's not quite accurate. The structure and work environment for a majority of employees are profoundly rigid and formulaic. Five years of working at the Café Orleans, and I remained the only male host. One would think that, after the policy had been broken, hiring procedures would change. But Disney wasn't a company that embraced or allowed for change. There were rules for everything—dress code, hair length, jewelry, the way guests were spoken to, every element of job performance. Individual expression was discouraged; no deviations from the formula were tolerated. You did nothing unless it was explicitly permitted, and suggestions for improvements were not invited. Just smile, we were told, and play your assigned role in creating the happiest place on Earth. These strict standards contributed both to Disney's enduring success, and, you could argue, to its later decline, as its utter unwillingness to adapt and evolve would make the company vulnerable in changing times.

Walter Elias Disney was a self-made man. Born in Chicago in 1901, he got his start drawing cartoons and short animations for a movie theater in Kansas City in the early 1920s. Although his initial success was moderate and local, he was confident enough to strike out for Hollywood, where, with his older brother Roy, he formed the Disney Brothers Cartoon Studio in 1923.

This, of course, became Walt Disney Productions, which by midcentury had grown into one of the largest film studios in history. In 1955, the brothers opened Disneyland as an embodiment of the family values and American Dream espoused in the studio's classic films. One example of Walt's commitment to these founding principles was to insist that the prices of milk and balloons be kept low. He believed that all kids who visited the park deserved a balloon—no matter how few coins they had in their pockets—and that every child should get a glass of milk.

There is a common perception of Walt as a mustachioed grandfatherly figure, the sweet and gentle man who conjured to life such adored characters as Bambi and Goofy. And while that portrait of him is not untrue, what is also true is that he was a ruthlessly ambitious entrepreneur with an eye on aggressive expansion—from films and amusement parks to hotels and real estate. Perhaps the best proof of Walt's entrepreneurial business savvy was in expanding his empire to include Disney World in Florida, done in large part to exploit the real estate opportunities created by the huge crowds that would visit the park—from accommodations to restaurants to transportation—opportunities on which he failed to capitalize when first building Disneyland in Anaheim, California. Before publicly announcing his intention to open Disney World, the plans were kept secret, known internally as Project X. Walt's team created multiple front companies through which it funneled the purchase of more than twenty thousand acres. If the owners of this worthless Florida swampland had known that their property would soon be transformed into an entertainment mecca, the real estate prices would have skyrocketed. Many locals later claimed to have been hoodwinked into selling.

One can't help but savor the irony that Walt, an idol of wholesome entertainment, was also a fierce businessman and foulmouthed chain-smoker. In 1958 he told the *Wall Street Journal*: "I suppose my formula might be: Dream, diversify, and never miss an angle." He was a compli-cated man, a true American.

———

The unwillingness of Walt Disney Productions to evolve and adapt had made it an attractive target for Saul Steinberg. During Walt's lifetime, he had tirelessly explored new areas of business, entertainment, and commerce—including laying the groundwork for Disney World, which opened a few years after his death, and Epcot Center, the nation's first private billion-dollar development project. But like many powerful men, he had also collected a stable of admiring protégés, and he left them the reins of the company when he died of lung cancer in 1966.

These successors were happy to coast by on Disney's longtime reputa-tion as the quintessential purveyor of safe, family-friendly entertainment. The valuable film archives languished in a vault, with public screenings of the classics, such as *Pinocchio*, *Snow White*, and *Dumbo*, only every seven years. The movie studio's profits dwindled, one disappointing release after another, as fewer young people came out to see its films, until finally in 1983 the studio saw its first ever loss, of $33.3 million. The core fans of yesteryear, now teenagers—who had been raised on a steady diet of Disney entertainment—wouldn't be caught dead at a Disney film by the 1980s. The brand had lost its allure, and the management team running the company either didn't realize this cultural shift had taken place, or they didn't have the determination and imagination to respond to it. Walt Disney Productions was simply living off its history. And when companies stop innovating—no matter who they are—they become weak, which is often reflected in a falling share price. Enter the corporate raiders.

Saul Steinberg, in the spring of 1984, sat in his Manhattan office with the declining fortunes of Disney spread out before him. In April and May, he began buying up shares of Disney stock until he had accumulated enough for the company's executives to notice and become concerned. A corporate chess match ensued. With the public still unaware that a great American institution was under threat, both sides geared up for battle.

The Disney executives asked themselves, "What would Walt do?" This was not an uncommon question. In any debate involving Disney policy, the assumed answer to that question would be the decider, from the prices of milk and balloons to who should direct the next major studio film. And of course it's unsurprising that the memory of a dead man, no matter how great, might lead to conservative policies and stasis. In this case, it was easy to argue that Walt would have protected the company from outsiders; he would have taken care of his own people; he would have fought tooth and nail against these Wall Street raiders who cared only about making a buck and not about what Walt had started building with paper and pencil six decades earlier in Kansas City.

But on the other side of the conflict, it was difficult not to admire the shrewdness of Steinberg's interest. Walt Disney Productions was rife with opportunity, especially when viewed by investors who weren't constrained by tradition, the historical enemy of change. That same question—"What would Walt do?"—could have been invoked for Steinberg's cause just as easily. Walt cared about profits, so he would have stirred things up, forced management to become more efficient, and kept moving forward into new territory. Walt would never have sat idly by and allowed his empire to stagnate.

Ultimately, Walt embodied the spirit of both sides. He represented the paradox of how Main Street and Wall Street could coexist within one person and within one nation. Perhaps his greatness rested in his ability to balance those two forces, a singular talent that allowed him to create a truly special institution. But now, eighteen years after his death, each of those forces battled for control.

Once the attempted takeover was publicly announced on June 8, 1984, the action moved quickly. The options available to Disney management dwindled, until finally they were forced to accept one solution they had pledged to avoid—offering greenmail to Steinberg, essentially paying him to leave them alone. On June 10, only forty-eight hours after Steinberg's intentions were officially announced to the public, Disney began negotiations to buy Steinberg's stock back from him at a premium, and they closed the deal the next day. Steinberg and his investors collected $325.5 million in total, with his own team making a quick profit of more than $50 million.

The public and press were outraged and vilified the greed of the corporate raiders. Yet hostile takeovers, which were becoming an increasingly common acquisition tactic, often worked this way. Steinberg, through his ability to gather support to pose a credible threat to Disney, needed only to buy enough stock to scare the company, and he could enjoy a huge payday.

The fallout at Disney was swift. While the Steinberg threat had been thwarted, what would stop other raiders from going after what was still a poorly managed, underperforming company? Within seven weeks, the board of directors had dismantled the management team and voted to install Michael Eisner at the helm of the company. Eisner, who had been president and CEO of the movie studio at Paramount Pictures, promptly implemented several changes. Disney's film archives were dusted off and released on videocassette. Admission prices at the theme parks were increased, as Eisner rightly predicted that demand would remain stable even at a much higher entrance fee. Disney stores were opened across the globe to sell merchandise and inject the brand back into popular culture. And finally, Eisner, with his exceptional Hollywood background and connections, brought in talented filmmakers to work on new releases, which resulted in several blockbuster movies that appealed to a broader audience. Touchstone Pictures—a Disney sub-brand focused on films for adult audiences—soon produced a string of box office hits under Eisner, including *The Color of Money*, *Ruthless People*, *Down and Out in Beverly Hills*, and *Good Morning, Vietnam*. Disney stock was on the rise. And so were the prices of milk and balloons.

Five years later, when I was a student at The Wharton School, the memories of watching Steinberg's hostile takeover attempt at close range lingered. One of my courses was a basic finance class in which we discussed the rise of takeovers and raiders. In a striking irony, the class was held in Steinberg-Dietrich Hall, which was largely paid for by the piles of cash that Saul Steinberg had made by raiding companies like Walt Disney Productions. I was probably the least knowledgeable of anyone in the room, with my Orange County and Occidental College background. The majority of the students were Deerfield, Andover, and Exeter kids who had attended Ivy League colleges and knew about Wall Street from the moment they left their mothers' wombs. Wharton was on their to-do list long before I even knew one was expected to have a to-do list.

One day, the class session centered on hostile takeovers, particularly Steinberg's move against Disney, and the professor unpacked a concept that seemed unassailable to the other students but was completely counter to my experience. When Michael Eisner took control of Walt Disney Productions, the professor argued, the changes that he put into effect were responsible for saving the company. And so Steinberg, as the aggressor, was ultimately to thank for forcing management teams either to produce positive financial results or be replaced.

I bristled at the notion that Steinberg should be thanked for anything. It was hard to justify the turmoil and disruption his actions had caused.

"You could argue," the professor said to the class, "that once Eisner took over, his improvements were somewhat obvious. As Disney was such an undermanaged asset, perhaps any smart MBA student could have done the same. Or maybe I'm giving you all too much credit." There was a bit of laughter from the rows of desks. "Yet," he continued, "Steinberg's attack on the company is what forced the turnaround. Under the old Disney, no one on the management team would have introduced those ideas, but Steinberg's shake-up, in a sense, gave Disney a license for transformational change."

I couldn't keep my mouth shut. "That's not how it seemed from Main Street."

The professor smiled. "You visited during that time?"

"I worked there."

"How fantastic!" He clapped. "We have an insider in our midst. Please tell us, Mr. Varelas, how did it seem on Main Street?"

"Well, people were worried about their jobs. It was hard to understand what was happening and why, but I can promise you that no one thought Saul Steinberg was a good guy who had the best interests of the company and employees in mind."

"That doesn't matter," said Tucker, swiveling in his seat to face me. He was the alpha-male WASP in our class, a wealthy prep-school kid who had already worked for a few years on Wall Street before coming to Wharton. "Those raiders—guys like Steinberg—are recharging American business by being the catalysts for change. And they do it simply by saying, 'You managers can't let things go to hell, or we'll come after you.'"

The professor didn't interject, so I responded. "But what was Steinberg's motivation? He didn't care about Disney. His intention wasn't to 'recharge' the company."

Tucker laughed condescendingly. "You're missing the point, Varelas. His motivation doesn't matter. The results matter. Did people keep their jobs? Does the company still exist? Is it doing better? Yes, yes, and yes. That's all thanks to Saul Steinberg. Disney was dead without him."

"Maybe it was struggling," I said meekly, "but it wasn't dead."

"Whatever," Tucker said, disposing of me and the conversation with a wave of his hand.

———

When I first came to Wharton, I expected that I would be sailing into an ocean of possibilities for where my life and career might lead. But now in my second and final year, a few months after finishing my summer associate internship on the Salomon trading floor, I realized that my options could hardly fill a puddle.

Even though I'd gone to Salomon's summer program to work on the trading floor, they'd allowed me to spend my last couple of weeks in the investment banking department. Only then had I made an impression, so that's from where my job offer had come. I was fairly certain I would accept it—until I got interest from Drexel Burnham Lambert. A dozen or so years prior, Drexel had been a mere shrub in the towering forest of Wall Street firms, but that all began to change in the 1970s after Drexel lured a brilliant young Wharton student, Michael Milken, to join its ranks.

At Wharton, Milken had noticed a simple market inefficiency— companies with lower credit ratings couldn't effectively get financing. These weren't necessarily bad companies; many of them were simply companies that had taken on too much debt, enough to threaten solvency, but they were still likely to survive and pay back their borrowings. Milken recognized that if someone were to focus on the outcasts that most of Wall Street didn't want to touch, then the higher fees from issuing and trading those bonds, which were considered riskier, could bring great profits.

That was the idea that Milken brought to Drexel and, through the 1970s, put into practice, forging an explosively powerful market around these high-yield bonds, commonly called junk bonds. Drexel became a major player on Wall Street, as Milken parlayed his junk bonds into supporting another booming market—mergers and acquisitions. His ability to access capital from the new market he created grew so deep and his connections so vast that he developed the ability to rapidly assemble armies of corporate raiders who could target any struggling company, no matter the size, backed by his junk bond war chest. That was how Saul Steinberg got the firepower to go after Disney. Drexel Burnham Lambert—which earned the nickname on Wall Street of Drain-'em Burn-'em & Lambast-'em—became the go-to investment bank and facilitator for these hostile takeovers on the strength of Milken's high-yield bond market. Milken himself became a Wall Street celebrity, coronated as the Junk Bond King.

Michael Milken had grown up in the San Fernando Valley outside of Los Angeles. The son of an accountant, he was exposed to numbers and finance at an early age. He was tirelessly ambitious, the definition of a workaholic—even in high school, he slept only three or four hours a night. He played on the basketball team and also served as head cheer-leader (imagine the costume changes at timeouts), and he picked up shifts at a local diner for extra cash. In his spare time, he trained himself as an amateur magician.

Milken's co-workers at Drexel knew he was smart from the moment he arrived as a summer intern in 1969, but he was so difficult to work with that he was relegated to the back office for a time. "He was *terribly* arrogant," a former colleague remarked. "And he didn't have the facility to shroud his ability, couldn't keep it from being threatening and abrasive. . . . He would assume he had conquered the problem and go forward. He was useless in a committee, in any situation that called for a group decision. He only cared about bringing the truth. If Mike hadn't gone into the securities business, he could have led a religious revival movement."

Once Drexel uncaged Milken from the back office, put him on special projects, and cautiously began allowing him more and more capital to work with, he created an entirely new asset class, multiplying those funds with paranormal results. Soon it seemed that he was indeed leading a religious revival movement. Converts and followers flocked to him, as Milken became the financial prophet that drove Drexel's revenue, culture, and operations. In the emergence of hostile takeovers and corporate raiders to the forefront of the American business landscape, Milken was the messiah.

After his early success, he informed his bosses at Drexel Burnham Lambert that he would be assembling his own small trading department and moving west to his hometown of Los Angeles, a highly unconventional headquarters for a large financial institution. His operations grew vast, and then all came tumbling down. By the time I interviewed for a job there, Milken had been driven out of Drexel and indicted on ninety-eight counts of racketeering, fraud, and insider trading, and the firm was facing its own slew of related criminal charges (investigated and prosecuted by US Attorney for the Southern District of New York, Rudy Giuliani). But despite these problems, Drexel was still doing surprisingly well. It had the reputation of a hot firm in distress, like a celebrity just after a sex-tape scandal: Everyone was talking about it, and the perceptions were simultaneously provocative and alarming.

———

I joined my Wharton roommate, Paul Hynek, at Abner's for cheesesteaks one night, just after returning from my interview at Drexel's Los Angeles headquarters. Paul was a brilliant eccentric, a multilinguist, and the son of a famous astrophysicist and ufologist, J. Allen Hynek. Paul was much more focused on the entrepreneurial aspects of the Wharton education, while he openly disparaged the finance offerings for which the school was world famous. He probably arrived at Wharton with less knowledge of accounting than anyone in the history of the school, but he definitely graduated with that distinction. He openly shared his disgust of people who worked in finance and had come up with his own lexicon to describe them. "You have consultant leeches," he told me, "venture capitalist bog dwellers, and investment banker polecats. Investment bankers are jackasses. They don't do anything. They just pirate. I mean, this is a little bit tongue-in-cheek, but yeah, they're Type A assholes only interested in money."

Since I was uncertain of how I felt about my visit to Drexel, Paul was the perfect person to discuss it with, as he would no doubt throw some daggers at Milken and the firm. It was good to have a friend at Wharton who was skeptical of everything involving the finance industry.

Drexel had put me up at the Four Seasons in Beverly Hills with the other candidates and organized a dinner for us to meet people from the firm. During our one full day there, we interviewed with various executives and were toured around the glass offices. My assigned host was named Grace, a Wharton alumna and very impressive young woman who had already reached VP status even though she appeared to be no older than I was.

On the flight out I had read *The Predators' Ball*, a new book by Connie Bruck about Milken and Drexel's forging of the junk bond market. One particularly juicy story described an annual four-day conference that Milken and his boys would throw in Beverly Hills, inviting

1,500 of their top clients—investors, corporate raiders, and CEOs. The conference—named the Predators' Ball by Milken and his partners—included presentations, extravagant dinners, performances by the likes of Frank Sinatra and Diana Ross, and on one of the nights each year, an exclusive cocktail party for the most powerful guests. This party was held in swanky Bungalow 8 of the Beverly Hills Hotel, and there the financial moguls in attendance would be rewarded for their loyalty with hand-selected escorts.

Grace must have been aware of the dark side of her firm, at least from staff rumors, if not from Bruck's book. While she was touring me around the office, I wanted to ask her what the female investment bankers were doing during the Bungalow 8 parties. I wondered if knowledge of those activities had tainted Grace's feelings about the firm. If it had, she wasn't about to reveal that to me. "There's a reason KKR chose us to get RJR done," she said as we crossed the trading floor, rattling off yet another pair of three-letter acronyms that made no sense to me. We stopped beside Milken's famous X-shaped desk, which still stood at the dead center of the trading floor as if marking the location of buried treasure, even though he was no longer with the firm. Grace must have figured that I knew about the desk. She placed a hand on its surface and said, "Drexel Burnham Lambert is now about much more than Michael Milken. We're the only firm that can effectively distribute high-yield offerings. We still have the database, the knowledge, the customers, and the clients." She was selling it hard.

Paul finished his cheesesteak, listening to the story without saying much, then wiped his mouth and stood up. We crossed to the trashcans, and he tilted his tray into one, letting the remains of his late-night meal slide off. "Fucking polecats," he said.

———

Of my two job offers on the table, I felt pretty certain that I'd accept the Salomon job, but I was still intrigued by Drexel's energy and its LA location, so I hadn't yet turned it down. Part of my hesitation was because of Mark Albert, my main contact at Drexel, who had been so intelligent, warm, open, and encouraging during our meetings and over several phone conversations that I almost wanted to take the job just so I could work with him. We spoke on February 13, 1990, and Mark presented both sides of the argument for and against Drexel.

I remembered the date because during the previous week, Drexel had reported losses of $40 million on its 1989 revenues of $4.1 billion. Mark addressed the news head-on. He didn't seem to be trying to spin me a tale or hide anything. He explained that he wasn't concerned—Drexel was putting together a line of credit from other banks—and he repeated all the reasons why Drexel was the best choice and how I was sure to be working on big, exciting deals. I half wondered why he was so keen to convince me. I'd gotten offers from only two firms, so I knew I wasn't in high demand and almost certainly wasn't the best candidate for Drexel, but they seemed eager for me to say yes. Were they having a hard time hiring, so they were lowering their standards and being overly aggressive? A note of exhaustion had crept into Mark's pitch, as if he only partly believed what he was saying.

"That all sounds great, Mark—and thank you for the kind words—but I'm actually leaning toward Salomon."

"Really?" he said. "But Drexel is still the center of the investment banking universe. No one is doing bigger deals. No one is making more money than our guys. Don't you want a piece of that?" I could overhear a loudspeaker announcement from his end, a woman's voice telling people not to remove any documents from the firm.

"What was that, Mark?"

"I'm not sure what's happening, to tell you the truth. Let me get back to you when I know more."

"Is everything okay there?"

"Yeah, yeah." He paused a beat. "I don't know."

I heard the muffled sounds of people yelling on his end, along with another loudspeaker announcement that I couldn't make out except for the phrase "will be prosecuted."

"Listen, Chris, I have to go." The noise in the receiver rose to a crescendo. "Think it over, and we'll talk soon."

The line went dead.

The newspapers carried the story the next day. Unable to get other banks to finance them, Drexel had defaulted on loans totaling $100 million and had filed for Chapter 11 bankruptcy protection. Despite the fact that Drexel had created the financial product that transformed American business, the firm was folding. Witnessing its downfall taught me something I would learn again and again in my career: Just because you develop a great product, or even a great business, and make a lot of money, that doesn't mean survival is guaranteed. Drexel Burnham Lambert became an ink smudge in the history books.

———

Gradually, almost imperceptibly, I started coming around to agreeing with my classmates about the value of corporate raiders and hostile takeovers. That shift of belief concerned me. Was I simply being reprogrammed by Wharton, this expensive country club for Wall Street disciples? Was this an education or a brainwashing? I feared I was losing touch with my West Coast/Main Street roots, but another part of me wondered if this was simply what it meant to grow up: coming to the realization that these issues, about which I had been so certain, were more nuanced and complicated than I had realized. The world was not black and white, despite what my youthful idealism had me believe.

I'd been flirting with the idea that Michael Milken had possibly done more to revamp American business for the better than anyone by introducing a way to go after underperforming management. This forcing function—management being held accountable for profits—would make America competitive in the 1990s and beyond. Milken's junk bonds later provided the financial vehicle for the rise of the telecom industry, the cable industry, and, one could argue, the technology world. Without junk bonds, none of these industries would have been created as swiftly and successfully as they were.

"Milken is one of the most brilliant people I know," Mark Albert told me years later. "Okay, he's a convicted felon, but he changed the United States of America, and how people do business, by funding entrepreneurs and businesses that could not get traditional funding from banks, by creating markets that really didn't exist, by creating the buy-side before he had the sell-side, since he knew there was always a sell-side. It was really Mike's vision and philosophy that we all bought into and we were huge proponents of. It was the liberalization of capital—we felt like it shouldn't just be the triple-A-rated companies that have access to capital. It should be the entrepreneurs who want to build something. We were in it for them as much as for us."

It took me years to understand and fully agree with Mark and my Wharton classmates, and as much as I hated to acquiesce on this point when I was still a student, it became difficult to deny that Milken had contributed invaluably to our national and global economies by forging his high-yield bond market.

———

Before the 1980s—for many centuries—the financial services industry had operated behind the scenes, a necessary but mostly invisible industry. The job of a banker wasn't much more glamorous than that of a merchant or blacksmith, and you could argue that it required less initial training. Even as recently as the 1970s, there were few traders at Salomon Brothers—the biggest firm of the time—who had so much as a college education, let alone an MBA. Of course, a special sort of talent, intelligence, and drive were necessary to succeed in the job, but those who made their names on the trading floor were unknown outside of their small world. It wasn't until the '80s that all this changed.

Late in the decade, trends in entertainment reflected the public's increasing awareness of and interest in Wall Street. The film *Working Girl* (1988), nominated for multiple Academy Awards, was set in the M&A department of a Wall Street investment bank. Another popular example was Michael J. Fox's character on the sitcom *Family Ties*—the briefcase-carrying, suit-wearing, Wall Street–crazy high school student, Alex P. Keaton. His ambition was to attend an Ivy League school, work as an investment banker, and make a fortune. Wall Street accepted and embraced the public's new definition of the financial world, never imagining that such a reputation would become problematic years later. The 1987 film *Wall Street* signified more than career highlights for Oliver Stone and Michael Douglas, who won an Oscar for his role. It also illuminated a massive shift in American culture and consciousness. That an Oscar would be awarded for the portrayal of a corporate raider would have been unimaginable only a few years prior, as most Americans still didn't know the ins and outs of the financial industry. Our obsession in the '80s with the accumulation of wealth swelled in concert with Wall Street's emergence from the shadows. As a result of that emergence, the financial services industry became an end in itself over the next three decades. For better or worse, it became the star of the show, rather than the hidden operator of the lights and curtain.

Steinberg's attack on Disney in 1984 was one of the first moments in which the *greed-is-good* Wall Street culture of the '80s stepped into the public spotlight. Because Disney was a beloved institution, this threat to its existence was major national news, and it provided a swift education for many Americans in this previously unfamiliar world. Wall Street became such a forceful presence in the national consciousness that, only three years later, Oliver Stone didn't hesitate to infuse his film with terms like "golden parachutes" and lines like "There is no nobility in poverty." He knew that his audience would get it; they would be right there with him.

In the enduring favorite *Pretty Woman* (1990), Richard Gere portrays Edward Lewis, a corporate raider who comes to Los Angeles to execute a hostile takeover of a struggling shipping company. While in town, he meets Vivian, a prostitute with a heart of gold played by Julia Roberts, and purchases a week's worth of her companionship. It's an old cliché, of course, but the ruthless businessman falls for the vivacious, disgraced, yet unexpectedly sweet girl and is utterly changed by the encounter. He decides to rescue her from her terrible profession, and in the end—to complete Edward's personal transformation—he abandons his plans for the hostile takeover, deciding instead to preserve and help manage the failing company. The implication here is that Edward's affection for Vivian has inspired him to be a better person. We are supposed to interpret this as a victory for love and morals. The movie closes with Edward's white limousine parting a flock of pigeons as he rolls up to Vivian's tenement building, waving a bouquet of red roses from the sunroof.

During my last semester at Wharton, while back home visiting my parents for spring break, I headed up to Westwood to catch *Pretty Woman*, which was a big hit at the time. I met up with three old Occidental buddies. Bruce had been my roommate in Santa Monica when I was working at Bank of America. He'd also been an econ major at Occidental, then landed a job with NASA's Jet Propulsion Laboratory. Ty was working on his PhD in atmospheric chemistry, studying under Dr. Frank Sherwood Rowland, whose research on ozone depletion would later earn him a Nobel Prize. The third friend, Tom, had also been an Occidental econ major and now worked at Grainger selling business equipment.

After the film we decided to stop by a favorite Santa Monica haunt, the Fox Inn, a German beer hall across from our old apartment. We hadn't been back in a couple of years. There were no TVs at the Fox, and no pretension—just picnic tables, a piano, and cheap drinks. The place was presided over by an internationally celebrated beer-guzzler named Bill "the Fox" Foster. He was the reason there was often a line of patrons down the sidewalk waiting to get in. He could lift a pint, drain it, and set it back down faster than most people could get the glass to their lips. The Fox could drink a forty-ounce pitcher of beer in 3.5 seconds. It didn't seem possible, but it was true. He'd performed the feat several times on television, and we saw him do it many nights at his pub, to great applause. "Tipping a pitcher in 3.5 is too fast for most people," the Fox said. "They don't believe it. They thought they didn't see me do it. So they'd say: 'Hey, would you do that again?' So I'd do it. But after two pitchers, it's all over. All over the floor, all over my clothes . . ." The other reason people flocked to the Fox Inn was to sing along with the dirty songs the host played on piano—bawdy barroom tunes, sea shanties, and classic numbers rewritten for maximum filth. The place was an institution.

We talked about *Pretty Woman* during the ten-minute drive down Wilshire to the Fox Inn. I'd come away with mixed feelings, and I expected that Bruce and Tom might feel the same since they were fellow econ majors, but I was mistaken. Sure, Julia Roberts's character was charming and sexy, and it was fun seeing Richard Gere portray a guy who populated a world I'd recently thought about so much, but I found the film's resolution—when Gere decides to join the failing company to "build ships together, great big ships," rather than to follow through with his takeover—to be stupidly romantic and unrealistic.

"So Gere's character," Bruce said, pulling his old BMW into traffic, "he's a corporate raider. Is that what you're gonna be, Chris?"

"No," I said. "I would either be on the financing side, representing a guy like Gere's character, helping him raise the money for the takeover; or I'd be running defense for the guy who owns the shipping company."

Ty rolled down his window. He always got to ride shotgun since he was six foot six. "Like the movie *Wall Street*? That's the sort of thing you'll be doing?"

"Not really," I said. "I'm much more *Working Girl.*" That got a good round of laughs. "*Working Girl* is about M&A, mergers and acquisitions, which is what I'm gonna do, while *Wall Street* is about sales and trading and corporate raiders." As is often the case, Hollywood movies probably did more than anything else to formulate public perception and disseminate a limited understanding of the financial services industry—even for smart people like my friends in the car.

"Come on, Chris," Bruce said, "you go to Wharton to become one of those people who thinks it's great to raid companies. Wharton exists to help you guys justify and defend the shitty things Wall Street does."

"That's not true," I said, then wondered if it was. "At least I don't think so."

"Then tell me this," Ty said. "Gere did a good thing at the end, saving the shipping company, right?"

"No!" I responded more forcefully than I'd intended. "That was absolute bullshit. The shipping company was struggling, so it *should* have been taken over, or at least forced to perform. Gere's character wouldn't decide to *join* it. Never in a million years. That was Hollywood garbage."

"But it's a good, honest company, as far as we know," Bruce said, scowling in the rearview at someone who'd honked behind us. "It's a family-run business. And Gere had the means to save it. Why is that a bad thing?"

I leaned into the gap between the front seats. "Because those raiders—guys like Gere's character—are at the forefront of recharging American business by being the catalysts for change."

"Jesus," Tom muttered beside me.

I ignored him, slapping the center armrest as I made my point. "And they do that by saying, 'You managers can't, you know, let things go to hell, or we'll come after you.' He should have raided the company. Change is progress."

"All right, dude, take it easy," Bruce said. "It's just a movie."

"Sorry," I said. "Hey, do you guys remember when Julia Roberts is sitting on the table in her bathrobe, and she tips the breakfast plate, and Gere is reading the newspaper?"

"Yeah, of course," Ty said.

"Did you notice the Salomon Brothers ad on the back of the *Wall Street Journal* that Gere was holding? That's the firm where I just landed a job."

"Why in hell," Tom said, "would we be looking at what Richard Gere was reading when Julia Roberts is sitting on the table in a bathrobe?"

I shrugged. "I thought it was pretty cool."

Bruce pulled up to the corner of 26th and Wilshire, stopping in front of the Fox Inn. No line outside. No lights on, either.

"What the hell is this?" Tom said as we stepped out of the car. There was a CLOSED sign and a short note affixed to the front door. Thanks for the patronage, the memories, et cetera. The Fox Inn was no more. Shut down, sold, soon to be something else. We tried to peer through the windows, but all was dark.

"Goddamn," Ty said. "It's gone."

"But why?" I said. "This place was legendary."

We looked both ways along Wilshire, as the lights shifted green, yellow, red, green, and the anonymous cars rolled by. A gas station on one corner. A chain convenience store on another. Some dull shops up the way. Fast food. Not much.

Bruce stepped up beside me. "Change is progress. Right, working girl?" They liked giving me a hard time, but none of it felt mean-spirited. "Come on." Bruce put his arm around my shoulder. "Let's find another place to get you a crappy drink before Wall Street swallows you up."

———

On the twenty-fifth anniversary of *Pretty Woman* in 2015, screenwriter J. F. Lawton's original script was released, revealing a much different tone and vision than what became the final film we all know. In the original script, Richard Gere's character, Edward, doesn't save the shipping company but instead follows through and raids it, and he even begins planning his next target: "North American Steel." In that script, Vivian is a crack addict. Remember the scene when Edward bursts into the penthouse bathroom, certain that she is doing drugs, only to find her flossing her teeth? Well, in the original script, there's no dental floss to be found, just drugs. In his final scene with Vivian, rather than the limousine-and-roses schmaltz, Edward throws her from his car, and as she weeps on the sidewalk, he crushes an envelope of money into her palm, then drives away. Her final words to him are: "Go to hell! I hate you! I hate your money! I hate it!" When Julia Roberts read the original script, she called it "a really dark and depressing, horrible, terrible story about two horrible people."

It's an amusing coincidence that Touchstone Pictures, the adult-focused brand of Disney, was the studio that produced *Pretty Woman*, and this was only a handful of years after the Saul Steinberg attack. It would be convenient to suggest that this story—featuring a corporate raider who flies from Manhattan to Southern California in order to perform a hostile takeover of a classic old business—may have hit a little too close to home for Disney, and that the vast changes to the plot and characters may have been intended as a stab at Steinberg and his kind, as the film was transformed into a modern-day morality tale about a raider who sees the evil of his ways and is "rescued" from being a bad person. But more likely Disney just wanted a happy ending. And ironically, the fact that Disney was still around to produce *Pretty*

Woman may have been because Steinberg's takeover attempt had forced the company to become more profitable and efficient.

The product that Walt was selling was nostalgia, a brand built on a bygone era, an homage to late-nineteenth-century small-town America. Disneyland was billed as "the happiest place on Earth." But as the decades burned on into the 1980s, that definition of happiness became stale and outdated. What happens when a place is no longer "happy"? Or, as in the case of Disney, when it stops producing a brand of happiness that people want?

Those in control nearly always resist making the required changes to adapt to the evolving definition of happiness. Or they don't know how to adjust to it. So an outside agent is often required to force that change. For Walt Disney Productions, that agent was the corporate raider. The resulting disruption from such change is seldom pleasant. To the incumbent managers—and to the other employees whose futures are now uncertain—the disruptors are the bad guys. But the changes that they bring about can be necessary for the survival of the company.

Before the corporate raiders of the '80s, the mission statements of most companies were focused on *creating the best product* or *providing the best service*. Then corporate raiders forced management teams to prioritize share price above all else. *Maximizing shareholder value* became the new mantra. In making management decisions, those in charge had only to ask if the decision would increase the company's share price, with the most direct means being an increase in profits; if it did, then the decision was easy to justify.

Increasing profits is not a bad thing, of course; it's a vital objective for any company. The model of maximizing shareholder value gave us a clear and concise North Star for making difficult management decisions. It would transform business by focusing action in a way that made the managing of global enterprises efficient and effective like no framework the business world had ever seen before, creating incredible growth, jobs, and opportunities for a globalizing world.

Yet with such disruption, there's always the risk that the changes in response to that disruption go too far. In that shift from focusing on creating the best product to maximizing shareholder value, something important was lost. Business became much more impersonal and antiseptic. We ourselves no longer had to fire Bob or Sue. Now it could be blamed on an RIF—a "reduction in force," the acronym itself distancing us from having to face the fact that Bob and Sue were people with families who depended on these jobs. There was now less latitude to take into account considerations beyond profitability. The phrases *It's nothing personal* and *It's just business* became common justifications for any action that may have previously been viewed as ruthless and cold. The loss of the personal broke all implied social contracts between employer and employee and between company and consumer. Management decision making was reduced to a cost-benefit analysis of risk and return.

Today, if you open up the financial section of any major publication, you'll discover that an incredible change has taken place in the public perception of corporate raiders. Gone are the days when the media painted them as scoundrels. They aren't even called corporate raiders anymore, but rather *activist investors*. And in general, they're viewed as good guys because they keep management teams honest and motivated. I recently attended a San Francisco Giants baseball game, and who threw out the first pitch? Our former-hero-turned-prison-inmate, Michael Milken. The crowd set down their hot dogs and beers and applauded him warmly. After serving two years in prison on multiple felony convictions, he had reinvented himself as a philanthropist, and even his once infamous history as the Junk Bond King was now celebrated. Except that nowadays, no one says *junk bond*. The accepted term is *high-yield bond*. So Michael Milken is again a hero, *junk bonds* are *high-yield bonds*, and *corporate raiders* have become *activist investors*. This signals a major evolution in American business, from the time of Steinberg's attack on Disney through to the current day.

While these activist investors can certainly bring about positive results, one unfortunate consequence is that management teams have become laser-focused on the bottom line—and, in particular, the short-term bottom line—often at the expense of investing in and creating the best product three or five years from now. They don't really have a choice, since the climate in which they operate demands that they deliver strong short-term results. That approach doesn't seem to be the way to build the happiest place on Earth. So how do we find a middle ground, a place where managers don't become complacent but are also not frightened into worrying only about today's profit at the expense of tomorrow's happiness for customers, employees, and shareholders? Is it possible to restore the balance?

Today there is a lot of discussion and pressure to expand the mission of public companies to encompass more than only profit and maximizing shareholder value. One example is the B Corp, which certifies that a for-profit entity is voluntarily trying to do well by doing good, meeting higher standards of transparency, accountability, and performance. While the notion that "profit" should incorporate more than just bottom-line results and instead flow from a broader social purpose has begun to resonate with many both inside and outside the business community, the concept has had difficulty gaining traction with any entity that can't afford to compromise its competitive position. We remain embedded in a system in which consistently profitable financial performance is vital to survival and sustainability.

Despite these efforts for a broader corporate mandate, the facts suggest that the general investing public is completely content with the shareholder maximization model. So content, in fact, that they have relinquished any desire or ability to influence management teams or hold them accountable. A majority of the investment in publicly traded securities is now done through passive exchange-traded funds (ETFs)—a vehicle invented more than twenty-five years ago in which one can buy a diversified portfolio to get market or sector returns as cheaply as possible.

While ETFs may have given the common investor cheap access to public market returns, they have also served to separate them from the companies in which they are invested and therefore the need or ability to assess the management teams. Investors have no doubt become comfortable with abdicating this responsibility because of the universal acceptance of the shareholder maximization model. The public now trusts that a management team will undoubtedly focus on profit and shareholder returns. That trust encourages shareholders to "rent" public equities, as it is often described, serving their broader investment objectives with little to no desire for the responsibilities that come with ownership. A significant majority of both ownership and trading volume is now passive or based on computer-driven trading algorithms, which leaves very few shareholders in the position of being watchdogs of accountability. Most of that responsibility is in the hands of the activist investors. Once considered bad guys, now they have become the conscience and protectors of our public markets.

In the closing scene of *Pretty Woman*'s abandoned original script, Vivian is on a Greyhound bus with her roommate and best friend, Kit, who is also a prostitute. Edward had just left Vivian in a ruined heap on the sidewalk, and now the young women have hit the road to blow some of the money Vivian made that week as Edward's escort. What would be the most ironic place they could go? Disneyland. Kit asks if she can have a balloon when they get there: "You know, the one with the ears." Vivian is exhausted, blank-faced, dejected. "You can have a balloon," she says. "One with the ears." And the film fades out. It was a wicked idea for an ending, yet also poignant in its clashing of two diverging branches of 1980s Main Street—the traditional, almost puritanical idyll of old America, as manifested in Disneyland, being invaded by the country's lost, corrupted youth, in the form of two crack-addicted prostitutes. But looked at another way, it might have also been a very touching dénouement for the film. During her week with Edward, Vivian had flirted with the false romantic hope that her life might turn around, but those hopes were crushed, and she was left on the side of the road. Where can a girl turn to reclaim some semblance of purity and goodness and innocent joy? Why, to the happiest place on Earth, of course.

At the Café Orleans, a single hostess was assigned to be the cashier for each shift, and most of us didn't want the gig because it meant sitting in a corner of the restaurant settling checks and making change for the waitstaff, so there was essentially no guest interaction and much less of the employee camaraderie that got you through a shift. You were also responsible for doing a lot of mathematical calculations to ensure that the drawer came out correctly.

I didn't really mind the job, dull as it was, so I spent hours sitting at the antique register, and I would daydream—about the cutest girls (like Grace, who had never dated anyone we'd met), about our intramural sports teams, and about more efficient ways to organize tables and other parts of the restaurant. I even figured out ten ways to steal money without getting caught. Of course I never would have done it, and just to demonstrate the depth of my loyalty, I wrote up the list and presented it to my managers. It would have been so easy to skim cash out of their system that I knew they would want to make the necessary corrections to protect the company.

The managers looked over my list. "We don't believe this," they said. "Show us."

So I did, explaining that since the register kept no record of transactions, a cashier could decide not to ring up a ticket, or they could close out the session but keep taking checks; and I demonstrated eight other simple ways to rip the company off.

"Okay, great," one manager said. "Don't show this to anyone."

I nodded, excited to have helped bring about improvements, but then he folded up my list and said, "We don't want to mess with the system. It's done this way for a reason."

I must have looked surprised or upset because the other manager said in a consoling tone, "These hostesses aren't really the type that could pull this off, Chris, so don't worry about it."

There was nothing I could do but let the matter drop.

When I was the cashier on closing shifts, it would require staying late to compute the entire day's sales, then delivering the money and gross receipts to Cash Control, located behind Space Mountain. New Orleans Square was at the opposite corner of the park, so the walk to Cash Control took about ten minutes if you kept up a steady clip. Some of the most memorable moments of my five years at Disneyland were those peaceful late-night walks through the park with all the lights glittering and the music playing. The guests and employees had gone home, and the cleaning crews usually hadn't arrived by then, yet everything was kept turned on twenty-four hours a day, whether the crowds were there to enjoy the spectacle or not. It felt as if the lights and music were on for me alone. If the hour was late enough, I would see the maintenance guys at Frontierland repainting the back wall of the shooting range. They did this every night of the year, slapping color over the BB dents from that day's marksmen to create the illusion of a fresh start the next morning. On some nights, I'd detour past Snow White's Grotto where the song "I'm Wishing" would drift up from the well ("I'm wishing for the one I love to find me . . . today . . ."). And I would sometimes stop off at the Tomorrowland arcade to play whatever video games I wanted.

One night, on my way to a session of pinball and Zaxxon, I was passing the Plaza Inn restaurant on Main Street and saw a female employee sitting on a rail, crying. I went over to her, partly out of concern, but also curiosity. I had strolled alone through the park, and now the only other person around was a dark-haired young woman in a pink-and-white prairie dress, the costume of the Plaza Inn, quietly weeping here in the happiest place on Earth.

I walked up to her and spoke in a gentle voice. "Are you okay?"

She turned away, gesturing to be left alone. "Yeah, I'm fine."

"Is there anything I can do to help?"

"No, thank you," she said, her shoulders shaking almost imperceptibly.

"Well, I'm happy to talk," I said.

I had a lot of experience discussing relationships and other personal concerns with the hostesses at the Café Orleans, so I felt like I could be of help. But she didn't speak another word. She simply faced the opposite direction until I left.

I made my drop at Cash Control, then went to wardrobe and changed out of my uniform, trading it for a fresh one, which I hung in my locker. All the while I was thinking of the young woman in the prairie dress, wondering who she was and why she was crying. I wished I could have helped her.

Now in my street clothes, I went back to the Plaza Inn, but she was no longer sitting on the rail. Maybe I was under the sway of the classic Disney tropes of the damsel in distress and the knight in shining armor—so perhaps my motivation wasn't entirely selfless. I poked my head through the border shrubs and scanned the patio, then approached the front windows and peered into the vacant restaurant, startled for a second by my own reflection, as my street clothes looked so entirely out of place. I bore no resemblance to a knight whatsoever. I walked back to Main Street, hoping I might find the young woman, but she was gone.

Not another soul in sight. Melodies blew in on the cross-breeze from a few directions and combined for a momentary cacophony, like a merry-go-round on the fritz, then the sounds drifted away. The lights blazed on empty pavement, on the rows of trees pruned shorter and shorter as they progressed up the street, on the fronts of buildings of likewise diminishing height, meant to create a spatial illusion to make Main Street appear longer. The magic of the place dissipated for a moment. It all felt wrong, forced, even a little ominous. I saw Disneyland at that moment for what it was—a carefully orchestrated, profit-motivated business, not a Magic Kingdom that existed solely to spread happiness. I turned around and left through the guest entrance, rounding the towering outer walls to the employee lot, where I found my car alone in the far corner and drove home.

———

"Oh my god, you guys, I'm totally freaking out."

Whenever anything unusual happened, T.C. freaked out. We were gathered in the hostess area during a rare lull in the action, discussing the vague news we had all heard about the coming "reorganization"— changes to the Café Orleans that had been ordered by Michael Eisner and his new team. A fellow hostess, Cathy Conway, had gotten the inside scoop from an assistant manager. He told her that our restaurant would soon be converted to cafeteria-style service, in which customers would queue up at a long counter and cobble together their own meals from a variety of options. We imagined chafing dishes under pillars of steam and heat lamps, like a middle school lunchroom or a Sizzler.

"Seriously, like, somebody pinch me," T.C. whispered fiercely. "Why would they do that?"

Grace leaned in. "I'm guessing it would save a lot of money. Streamline things. They could serve more people."

"But what about us?" T.C. said, a little too loudly. "What about the hostesses? The waitresses? The busboys? What about this place?" She reached to Cathy for a hug. "I love this place." T.C. had a point. The Café Orleans staff was remarkably close and unjaded. Employees from other sections of the park envied what we had, from our enduring friendships to our offsite parties at the bowling alley to our softball and canoe teams in Disney's intramural league. Thinking back on those times later in life and knowing that restaurant employees rarely get through their shifts without healthy doses of cynicism and irony, I almost distrust my memory. But that was our unique situation—we cared for one another, we cared for the Café Orleans, and we cared for the larger institution, Walt Disney Productions.

We looked around the room and out toward the patio, admiring the nuanced choreography of a smoothly run restaurant—the servers and bussers gliding across the floor in a kind of service tango, the clink of flatware and the buzz of satisfied diners, the kitchen pushing out orders on time, water glasses and iced teas all filled, tables cleared and reset as soon as they were free. Most of us had worked together for at least a few years, and we did our jobs well. Picturing a long buffet line and the cavalcade of a cafeteria was depressing, to say the least. Something important would be sacrificed, something intangible, something human.

But were we the only ones who would notice and be troubled by the change? This sort of reorganization wasn't uncommon when management focused on efficiency. Yet, over time, it seemed that the customer-service religion that Disney founded would fall by the wayside; the streamlining of the Café Orleans felt like one small step toward that decline.

Grace turned away to greet a foursome of incoming guests. Then she walked down the line of people waiting for tables, as we often did, making sure everyone was happy. There was a party of Japanese guests speaking in their native tongue. Grace slipped into their conversation in fluent Japanese, and they responded naturally to her for a moment before the shock registered that this tall, stunning woman in red-and-white polka dots could speak Japanese as well as they could. The guests' voices rose together in surprise, a reaction the rest of us had enjoyed many times.

It was my fifth summer and the final season at Disneyland for Grace, Cathy, Matt, T.C., and me. From the time we'd met, we had always asked one another the half joke: "What's your *real* job going to be?" I'd just graduated from Occidental and would soon begin working as a corporate lender to jewelers. Grace was off to become a flight attendant, assigned to the transpacific routes between Southern California and Asia. Cathy Conway would be a dental hygienist. Matt decided to trade his polka dots for head-to-toe brown as a UPS delivery driver. And T.C. had gotten engaged to a rich guy, so she would soon start her life as a pampered housewife. Our time at Disneyland was coming to an end, and we knew it. We shouldn't have been worried about the reorganization of the café. And yet we felt as though we had a personal stake in this place.

By that summer of 1985, Eisner had been in charge for almost a year, and on the surface, it didn't seem that much had changed since he took over, besides increased prices for almost everything. But there was definitely apprehension among the ranks. When you're dealing with a company that is founded on the bedrock of America and centered on long-standing tradition, change is seen as a scary thing. There was a general sense that Walt Disney Productions was becoming a *business*, and some of the staff weren't sure how they felt about that, despite the fact that since Steinberg's takeover attempt, profits were up. But, we wondered, at the expense of what? Steinberg clearly hadn't given a damn about the company, or its history, or Walt's vision. Cast as the perfect Disney villain, he was simply hunting the almighty dollar. And now, from what we could tell, the new management seemed more focused on profit than guest experience.

Our final summer was waning, and there we stood, covered in polka dots and impossibly young. The sun had set, and you could just see a faint smattering of stars overhead. "It's 9:29," T.C. called to us, and we gathered in the doorway to the patio as the café lights dimmed—Matt, Cathy, Grace, T.C., and me, there in a line, our shoulders almost touching—and then that familiar voice came over the speaker, the voice that was projected each night throughout the park at the same time. It was Walt's opening-day speech from 1955: "To all who come to this happy place: Welcome. Disneyland is your land. Here age relives fond memories of the past, and here youth may savor the challenge and promise of the future. . . ." My eyes wandered over the imagined buffet counter, picturing lines of guests ladling food onto plates.

The voice continued: "Disneyland is dedicated to the ideals, the dreams, and the hard facts that have created America, with the hope that it will be a source of joy and inspiration to all the world." *The hard facts. The hard facts that have created America.* Even though I'd heard that speech hundreds of times before, I'd never noticed the mention of *hard facts.* What was Walt getting at? I wondered. What pain or difficulties or sacrifices or unpopular decisions compose the hard facts that built this place, this kingdom, this country? Had Walt Disney himself predicted that hard facts would ultimately catch up to the empire he had built? Was he speaking to us from the grave, an opening-day prophecy that we ourselves would have to face future hard facts?

It didn't matter—or maybe it did, but for then I let it go. I still had those people and that café on a July night, if only for another moment.

The first fireworks spread out in the sky above us, and we all gazed up at that ephemeral beauty, those flashes of color and fire that can last only seconds, but will repeat tomorrow, and the day after, and next summer, and for years—hopefully—whether we are there to see them or not.

4

CONQUISTADORS OF THE SKY

America is all about speed. Hot, nasty, badass speed.
—ELEANOR ROOSEVELT, AS ATTRIBUTED IN THE FILM *TALLADEGA NIGHTS*

It used to be that if I wanted to kill *you*, sir"—the speaker leveled a finger at a member of his audience and wandered from the podium with a handheld mic—"I'd have to blow up the entire banquet room." He waved his arm in a big arc, decimating the banquet hall and its half a dozen round tables of institutional investors and analysts, men and women in business attire who laughed over their chickens cordon bleu. "In order to kill *this one gentleman*, you would all be sacrificed." Jim Roche, a senior executive at Northrop and former US naval captain, was the speaker. He wove through the rapt audience. "Then the technology of warfare improved, but still I would have to blow up his whole *table*, wiping him out along with nine other folks." The people at the table pulled comic faces, and an investor across from the condemned gentleman put his hands to his throat and stuck out his tongue, miming death, which got a chuckle from the crowd. "Then the technology got even better, and I could kill this gentleman and only the two people on either side of him. But now"—he had been moving through the room slowly, and at this point he arrived directly behind the condemned gentleman, putting a hand on his shoulder as he continued—"now the technology has gotten *so precise* that not only can I eliminate this gentleman *alone*, but it is expected—it is *demanded*—that no other casualties will occur."

He walked back to the podium through the crowd, the only sound in the room the clinking of flatware. "Operation Desert Storm," he continued, "changed everything. We sent fifty thousand body bags to the Middle East to prepare for American casualties, but we lost very few soldiers—many of them from friendly fire. That changed the whole expectation around warfare. Now we believe we can fight a war without casualties."

This particular luncheon was in a hotel banquet room in Manhattan, the fourth stop on the road show. The purpose of these events was to schmooze and tell the story of the company, to show off some of the more impressive weapons, gadgets, and technologies, and hopefully stir up enough excitement and interest that the investors would drive up the share price. Usually one of the senior members of the Salomon Brothers deal team would step to the podium at the beginning of lunch to introduce our speaker for the hour—and sometimes my fellow Salomon associate Petros Kitsos would serve as MC, which impressed me, as we were both junior bankers. I was only a couple of years into the job at Salomon, on one of my first big accounts, so my role in the road show was fairly minor. I would welcome investors and mingle, then we would all mix in with the guests at the circular tables and dig into yet another cordon bleu or prime rib or broiled salmon. I buttered my roll and turned to a woman from Fidelity sitting next to me. She was carefully squeezing a lemon wedge into her iced tea. "So," I said with a pleasant smile, "had you heard about Northrop's JDAM-guided bombs before today?"

On the surface, Salomon's investment banking department existed in an entirely different realm from the trading floor. In investment banking, there was at least the patina of civility, with three-piece business suits, glass offices rather than a loud open floor, and *Fortune* 500 clients who were buying professional advice. But a similar aggressiveness and underlying tension were still palpable. Much like the trading floor, it was a freewheeling culture with fierce competitiveness and its share of memorable characters.

One of those characters, who arrived fresh and green from Kalamazoo, Michigan, was Michael Soenen. He may have been the only person I encountered at Salomon who was less prepared for a Wall Street career than I'd been.

Mike was the eldest of four siblings, raised in the suburbs of Detroit. His mother, Colleen, worked as a dental hygienist, and his father, Don, designed engines for Ford. After their fourth child arrived, the family needed more income, so Don started managing dive bars at night, getting home at two in the morning, then heading off to Ford when the sun came up. He eventually bought his own bar, then a bigger one, finally owning and operating a 1,500-capacity music venue. As a kid, Mike would hang out at the venue in an oversized burgundy security jacket, watching from the front row or the balcony as acts like Tina Turner, Harry Chapin, Hall & Oates, the Police, and Linda Ronstadt played for the people of Canton, Michigan. On weekend mornings, he would sneak onto the stage and try out the bands' instruments, which were often still there from the night before, then he'd help his dad count the money and make the bank drop. "John Cougar Mellencamp almost died in our bar," Mike recalled. "That was our big moment. It was a New Year's Eve gig and John Cougar was singing, and his guitarist did one of those spin-arounds, hitting him square in the head with the end of the guitar, and knocked him out cold on New Year's Eve."

After high school, Mike packed off for Kalamazoo College, a couple of hours west, to study economics. When he finished his coursework in 1992, he landed an internship in Japan with a tier-three auto supplier, but after half a year or so living abroad, he'd grown bored with the work and was certain that it wasn't going to be the right career path for him, so he returned to Kalamazoo with no plan for what was next. Wall Street seemed like a good idea.

"Everyone knew you could make money there," Mike said. "My high school, Detroit Catholic Central, had this book you could buy that would show each graduate and where he worked. So I bought it on a long shot and went through every freaking page, looking for a connection—what are the Wall Street firms and who worked at them, right? There were the Michalik twins from my high school, these two perfectly good-looking people, perfect this, perfect that, went to Ivy League schools, captain of the football team, that whole thing, like right out of central casting. One of them worked at Salomon. He'd been three years ahead of me and never heard of me, but our school was pretty loyal. So I mailed him a letter, and the guy called me. 'Well, since you went to my high school, I guess I'll try to get you an interview.'"

With that glowing endorsement, Mike arrived at Salomon Brothers for his interview. He had the distinct advantage of applying off-cycle—during the time he'd been in Japan, Salomon's M&A group was exploding and urgently needed more junior-level support—so Mike didn't have to face the usual fierce competition of interviewing against a bunch of hungry Ivy League candidates. Still, it was no warm and breezy process.

"I must have done thirteen interviews over the two days. And you can tell they don't care about you. You're trying to get a gig as an analyst"—which is the lowest rank in an investment bank—"so it's annoying that anyone even needs to interview an analyst to begin with. You're in for five minutes, and then you're out. They just had to check the box to say they did it. My final interview was with David Wittig."

Wittig had become notorious on Wall Street when he appeared on the cover of *Fortune* magazine in 1986, arrogantly holding a cigar under the header WALL STREET'S OVERPAID YOUNG STARS. The article went on to talk about how much money he made, a topic of conversation that was very taboo on Wall Street at the time. Over the seven years since the *Fortune* cover, he'd risen to the top of Salomon's M&A group. He was the quintessential aspiring Master of the Universe of 1980s Wall Street—pompous, smug, brimming with bravado—not quite suave enough for a place in *The Bonfire of the Vanities*, but he seemed to be auditioning for the part. Mike Soenen—just flown in from Kalamazoo, carrying an empty briefcase from meeting to meeting to keep up appearances—had never heard of David Wittig.

Mike settled down in a chair facing the big desk, and Wittig slid an open binder across it to Mike. "Do you know what this is?" he asked.

Mike leaned forward. Columns of letters and numbers that looked like codes, alongside other columns with names of companies. "I don't think so," he said. "What is it?"

"Tail numbers."

Mike had never heard of tail numbers. He didn't know that all the corporate jets that shuttled the titans of industry to and from New York could be identified by these tail numbers, which would reveal who was in town doing potentially important business. He sat there trying to figure out if he could even fake it. "Right," he said. "Tail numbers."

"Are you willing to sit out at Teterboro and watch every corporate jet that flies in and out of here and tell me who is coming and going?"

Mike raised his eyes from the binder back up to Wittig to make sure it wasn't a joke. Mike didn't know what a tail number was, and he had never heard of Teterboro. He couldn't have guessed if Teterboro was within a thousand miles of New York.

"Sure," he said.

"You're willing to do that?" Wittig said.

Mike answered with what he hoped sounded like nonchalant confidence. "Yeah, yeah, yeah. I can do that."

"Okay," Wittig said. "What time does the *Wall Street Journal* get printed?"

"What do you mean?"

"What time do the hard copies come off the press and the bad smudged ones go into the Dumpster?"

"I don't know," Mike said.

"They go in at three thirty in the morning. And you know why you need to know that? Because you're going to crawl through that Dumpster, you're going to find the paper, and you're going to summarize the headlines for me before I wake up." Wittig paused and looked at Mike. "That's what it'll take to be successful. Are you willing to do that?"

Mike nodded, as if he were agreeing to a completely reasonable directive. He was desperate for a job. "I didn't know if Wittig was trying to scare me off," he recalled later, "or if any of what he said was true. And it turned out none of it was true—I was never asked to do any of that stuff. Anyway, Wittig was the guy who ultimately looked at me and said, 'I think you've got what it takes.' I didn't know anything about Wall Street. I really couldn't have told you the difference between a stockbroker and an investment banker. So Salomon gave me an offer."

———

I was a couple of years into my job at Salomon, still a lowly associate, when I was put on the Northrop account. Northrop was an aerospace and defense company that was best known for creating the B-2 or Stealth Bomber, as well as other weapons and warplanes. Salomon's role was to provide Northrop with financing and strategic advice—whatever banking services it needed. Since the aerospace and defense industry was seeing a lot of consolidation in the mid-1990s, the core of our relationship was to provide guidance on all things M&A: whether to acquire other companies and if so, which ones; how to react to overtures made by others; and whether to sell the company.

The aerospace industry was highly secretive. To avoid conflicts of interest and to protect confidentiality, each bank partnered with one of the major aerospace firms. Salomon, for example, represented Northrop, while Bear Stearns was the banker for Martin Marietta. Goldman Sachs was the one firm that seemed to skirt this system, ending up advising one side or the other on nearly every aerospace deal. My first exposure to high-level negotiations was between my boss, Michael Carr, and Gene "Tiger" Sykes from Goldman. They were discussing a potential deal involving Northrop and another aerospace firm, McDonnell Douglas, which Tiger Sykes represented. The deal wasn't ultimately consummated, but it was memorable for me, as I'd never before witnessed a detailed M&A negotiation—the back-and-forth, the parrying of positions and objectives, terms and strategic leverage, and the fact that every word was so well managed and thoughtful. I didn't fully understand what Carr and Tiger Sykes were saying, but I remember thinking, *Man, I want to learn to talk like that.*

As we worked on several other Northrop deals over time, Tiger Sykes always seemed to show up on the other side of the table. He was a legend on the Street—very put together, good looking, and he never appeared to be trying too hard. He was supposedly one of the youngest people ever to make partner at Goldman. And even with all that, he couldn't have been nicer or more respectful to me, despite my junior status at Salomon Brothers.

When Northrop began friendly merger talks with a similar aerospace firm called Grumman, once again, Tiger Sykes was there at the table, representing the other side. Both companies had been founded by aviators between the World Wars; their shared focus on military aircraft made them a natural fit. Discussions between the two companies had been going along well enough, but then the lines of communication dried up. Northrop's CEO, Kent Kresa, put in several unreturned calls to his counterpart at Grumman, Renso Caporali, whose secretary often claimed that the boss was skiing.

Silence is never a good sign in M&A. We feared the worst as we tried to get in touch with our Goldman contacts, eager for any indication that the deal was still moving forward. But nothing. Silence, in this case, probably meant that someone had gotten in Grumman's ear and planted doubts—either convincing them to back out or cut a deal with someone else, or they could simply be making us sweat in order to get a better price. Silence is always the toughest tactic to respond to in a negotiation. We quickly set up a meeting at Northrop's LA offices to discuss next moves.

The meeting would be led by Salomon's head of M&A, Eduardo Mestre. He was born in Cuba, and his family had fled the communist regime for Argentina when he was young. He was sent to the States to study, along with a couple of siblings, and he never left, eventually making his way to Wall Street and Salomon Brothers, then climbing the ranks to managing director and the top of the investment bank. He rose early each morning to exercise before work, was lean and well dressed. And he was tough on everyone, no matter his or her seniority, yet he was a good person from whom to learn. Eduardo would ask us before every meeting what was unique and special about our presentation and how it was different from the ten other banker books that would be offered by our competition.

Around this time, back home in Anaheim, my mom was diagnosed with brain cancer and began treatment. Taking any opportunity to see her and my dad, I flew out to Los Angeles early for the meeting at Northrop. I worked from Salomon's LA office, driving down to Anaheim as often as possible for dinner or a visit. There were lots of quiet nights on airplanes and in hotel rooms, and, over many weeks, I slowly made my way through Tolstoy's *War and Peace*, reading for a while each night before bed. It seemed a perverse sort of self-punishment to lug a 1,300-page novel back and forth across the country, but it was the perfect companion for this moment in my life.

Eduardo was also out in LA early, working on a deal with Sony. The rest of the team was scheduled to come out on the first flight that day. They would bring along the presentation books that the junior people had been pulling all-nighters to prepare. But a heavy fog rolled in at JFK, and the flight was canceled.

Eduardo and I met at Salomon's LA office to brainstorm a solution. We knew that we needed to convince Northrop to be assertive if it wanted to stay alive. This, we understood, was against the firm's nature.

"Goddamnit," Eduardo said. "There's no way to get a copy of the presentation?"

"Not in time," I said, watching him pace, simultaneously thinking through the problem and losing his temper. I tried to lighten the mood. "This probably won't help," I said, "but I noticed a fortune cookie hanging in someone's cubicle that seems to sum up our situation."

"What the fuck are you talking about? Fortune cookie?"

Someone had blown up the fortune on a Xerox. I'd borrowed it and made myself a copy, thinking Eduardo might find it amusing, considering Northrop's concern over Grumman's silence. "Yeah, check it out."

Eduardo took the sheet from me and read it a few times, then dropped it on the table. "All right, let's go in with that."

"Go in with it?"

He answered as if his patience had already been fully tapped. "Yeah, the fucking fortune cookie. Make a bunch of copies. We'll go in with the fortune cookie."

An hour later, we walked into the room with a dozen copies of a single sheet of paper in the center of which was the image of the fortune, flanked by smiley faces. It was the sole document we had for our big meeting with Northrop, in which we would try to convince them to change the way they'd been doing business since their founding in 1939. Northrop was at a major crossroads—whatever decision management arrived at could make or break the company. I thought it was crazy to head into a meeting of this magnitude with only a fortune-cookie platitude, but I was cautiously excited to see where Eduardo would go with it. Even though he was often a hardass, he was always provocative and could become a silver-tongued charmer the moment he got in front of a client.

As I passed the photocopies around, Eduardo set the stage. "Gentlemen, none of us is comfortable with Grumman's silence, which almost certainly signals that our deal with them is in jeopardy." A few Northrop executives flipped the page over, looking for the rest of our data and analysis. There was a bit of whispering. Eduardo spoke from the head of the table. "Yes, yes, this is from a fortune cookie. But there's a relevant message here. I, for one, am not content with being shut out of this deal." He picked up his copy of the fortune and read it aloud: "Discontent is the first step in the progress of a man or a nation." Eduardo looked around the room, meeting the eyes of each person.

"Gentlemen," he continued, "I could have come in here with a bunch of numbers and projections. I could have shown you all the analysis in the world, but that would only have obscured our focus on what's truly important, which is this: When things don't go our way, what are we going to do about it? Do we throw in the towel, or is this simply the first step in our progress toward something greater? Does Northrop want to be the acquirer, or do you want to be the acquired? Do you want your name to stay on the door, as it has for more than half a century?" He lowered his voice for this next part. "Northrop is one of the nation's great companies. Does it have a future? That is for you to decide." Eduardo raised the sheet of paper above his head and shook it. "This, gentlemen, is what's important here. Leverage your discontent into something meaningful."

For a few seconds, the only sound was the eerie crinkle of the paper as Eduardo shook it, then he continued with his pitch.

"The numbers, the analysis, accretion and dilution—it all works. Don't worry about those details. What you need to decide"—he set the fortune on the table—"is what sort of future you want for Northrop."

An hour later, I was racing down the Northrop hallway trying to keep up with Eduardo's long stride. "That was amazing!" I said. "You just walked into the room with nothing more than a fortune cookie and convinced Northrop to go hostile."

"Yeah, it was pretty damn good," Eduardo said without enthusiasm, pressing the elevator button. "But you know the sad part?"

"What's the sad part?"

"No one was there to see it."

"What?" I said. "I was there."

He shrugged and frowned.

"I'll tell everyone what a great job you did," I said.

"Yeah, but that's not the same. It won't mean anything coming from you."

I spent a lot of time reflecting back on that meeting, and what I wondered was this: Would we have been better off if the New York fog had lifted and the books had made it to the meeting? Our team had spent dozens of hours building incredibly detailed and precise models of various acquisition scenarios—not dissimilar from the levels of precision that had become expected of Northrop itself. By the time of this deal in 1994, that sort of precision had become expected of Wall Street too, that each factor could be analyzed with extreme accuracy to assess whether or not the deal was worthy. If the books had arrived, we would have devoted most of our focus to poring over their hundred pages, dissecting the accretion-dilution analysis, valuation, effect on competition, et cetera. We'd have been mired in the weeds of smaller details. Would we have spent enough time on the big-picture strategy? Probably not. Yet since the books didn't make it, we spent 100 percent of our time on the big picture, which proved that, in the end, all the analysis in the world wasn't as important as understanding and defining the guiding vision.

Even though we knew then that more time should be allocated to thoughtful analysis around long-term strategy, it was unthinkable to have walked into that Northrop meeting with just the fortune cookie. We all felt the pull of precision, the idea that if one could measure it, then one must be on the path to the right answer. But you can only be as accurate as your grasp on the known correct value, and precision does not guarantee accuracy. Finance is so much more art than science, a knack for choosing the best course with limited information in the face of an uncertain future.

Years later, when I was a more senior banker, I would often show up at meetings without a presentation. We had done all the analysis to help form the advice we were going to offer, but I didn't feel compelled to show up with that large bound book full of numbers and charts. In fact, I believed it to be a hindrance. Almost unanimously, clients commented on how refreshing and productive it was to have, as they often put it, "a conversation about what matters." One client even told his board that he hired us specifically because we didn't show up with a presentation.

As for Eduardo, I did my best to tell everyone at the office about his amazing performance at Northrop, which soon became famous as the "Fortune Cookie Meeting." But Eduardo only shrugged when I told him how impressed everyone was. Instead, he took the opportunity to describe a personal philosophy to me. "I divide the world up into three groups of people," he said. "Horses, birds, and muffins. The horses get shit done. Birds hop around and seem busy, but they don't actually do anything. And muffins just sit there taking up space."

I stood staring at him.

"I have a feeling about you," he said—which seemed promising—but then, "I definitely have you in the muffin category."

I didn't reply. He walked away.

———

After a few more interminably long days of silence from Grumman, our fears were realized on March 7, 1994, when we picked up the *Wall Street Journal* to find that a larger competitor, Martin Marietta, had made an offer to Grumman, and very quickly the two sides had agreed to terms, leaving Northrop holding a wilted carnation at the edge of the gymnasium. It was a shitty way to find out we'd been dumped. We figured Goldman Sachs had persuaded Grumman not to take Northrop seriously, possibly because of Tiger Sykes's earlier experience negotiating with us on the failed McDonnell Douglas deal. Newspaper reports suggested that Grumman was attracted to Martin Marietta because of its broader business base. Martin Marietta was essentially an electronics company that installed radars and sensor systems into military ships and helicopters, while also producing missiles and spacecraft and related items.

These aerospace companies, no matter their particular focus, were nourished by a steady feast of expensive US military defense contracts. But just a year earlier, in 1993, there had been a major summit known as "The Last Supper," at which senior officials from the Department of Defense broke bread with about fifteen CEOs of the big aerospace and defense companies. The Lexington Institute described the meeting in an article: "The story, as recounted by Norm Augustine, then chief executive of Martin Marietta, is that then-Secretary of Defense Les Aspin told the assembled titans of industry that with the fall of the Soviet Union and planned decreases in defense spending that there would not be enough money for all of them to survive. Consequently, Aspin announced, they needed to merge." Aspin's warning had been the catalyst for Northrop's urgency to join forces with Grumman or to find other big deals that would keep it from being swallowed up by a larger competitor.

Many of the top executives at the big companies—Martin Marietta, Lockheed, Boeing, Grumman, and Northrop—were themselves ex-military. The industry operated under a sort of gentlemen's code of conduct. The CEOs were members of a secret club called the Conquistadores del Cielo, which held its inaugural meeting back in 1937 on an Arizona dude ranch and had convened twice annually in the decades since—each year they would gather in New York and also throw a weekend ranch party in the West, where the guys dressed up in cowboy costumes and competed in a tournament of games that featured knife throwing, bronco riding, hunting, poker, trapshooting, and pétanque, a French version of bocce. The members, which included senior executives from commercial airlines, aerospace, and parts manufacturers, developed an elaborate initiation ritual with horses, Spanish conquistador costumes, torches, and fireworks. They even had an official drinking song, which contained the lyrics:

We're Conquistadores, gay Conquistadores,
We're birds of a very fine feather!
We're happy amigos no matter where he goes,
The One, Two, and Three goes, we're always together.

On these weekends, the executives would sometimes engage in private discussions of business deals, which was forbidden by the rules of the Securities and Exchange Commission. Eventually the SEC tried to shut down the group, yet underground meetings are still said to take place today, typically on golf courses or lavish Wyoming ranches.

Despite the fact that Northrop often led off its annual strategic review with the line: "Once again, ladies and gentlemen, we believe in the future of war"—and despite the fact that the aerospace and defense industries produced the tools and vehicles of warfare, and that the companies themselves were run very much like extensions of the military—these executives weren't comfortable waging financial warfare on one another. Protocol and etiquette were cornerstones of their business relations—as if extreme decorum were required to counterbalance the gruesome reality of the killing machines they designed and manufactured. Once Grumman announced its deal with Martin Marietta, we reminded Northrop that it had to make a difficult decision—that the time was over to stand passively by; they must get aggressive, even if that disrupted the niceties that the aerospace and defense industries had long practiced.

Investment banking at Salomon Brothers was governed under a classic hierarchy. The junior people were worked to the bone, and they needed to hustle and scrap to earn the respect and attention of the senior bankers. They were expected to sweat and bleed and meet every demand, no matter how unreasonable the request and how brutal the hours. It was common to juggle a few projects at the same time, each with a different deal team. There was never time to plan ahead for future client meetings or presentations. Everything was in crisis mode, all the time. The senior bankers would give you loose guidance at the end of the day, tell you what analysis they wanted to see, and you would work through the night to achieve those results. You often had an early morning deadline for a client presentation to be made the next day—leaving you just enough time to bind twenty copies of the presentation book, go home to shower and change, and make the flight to wherever in the world your meeting was.

For traders, everything happened at top speed and during the day, when the markets were open, the action driven by macro factors. But investment banking work usually happened in the middle of the night, the pace frenzied and then languid and then frenzied again, the action driven by microanalysis and the sleep-deprived deliberations of college grads with little to no Wall Street experience. While thousands of other kids their age were out on the town in New York, acting young and stupid, here were these analysts and associates working in a conference room in a skyscraper at three in the morning, masquerading as financial conquistadors, formulating recommendations that could affect the reputation of the firm and the fate of the corporations they advised.

The worst feeling was when, in the middle of the night, the numbers didn't compute as you needed them to, or they didn't support the arguments the senior bankers expected to make at the client meeting later that day. That would leave you with two bad choices. You could change the thesis of the presentation to match the numbers, or you could fudge the numbers to fit the thesis. A third option—worse still—was to wake your managing director with a phone call. That was never smart. So you would usually alter a revenue assumption here and a margin assumption there, just enough so that none of the changes seemed too aggressive but in total-ity got you to the profitability and earnings growth needed to justify the deal. *Where is the line*, you would wonder briefly, *between subjective business judgment and manipulation of data?* Then you'd yawn and look at the clock and reply, *Who gives a shit?*

Often, no matter how careful you tried to be, sheer exhaustion would lead to errors that weren't caught until it was too late. Sometimes it was due to what we called the F9 mistake. Back then, computers were very slow, so you didn't want to wait for the spreadsheet program to recalcu-late automatically every time you made a change. You would instead turn off that feature, but then you needed to be careful to remember to hit F9 at the end, which would trigger the recalculation of data throughout the model. There were always stories about analysts who made a bunch of changes and then forgot to hit F9, printing the books with faulty num-bers. They might realize during the client presentation, or perhaps after the meeting, that the wrong data had been utilized. The models were so complicated that usually no one would notice, but people were mak-ing big decisions based on erroneous information. How many deals were done, we wondered, or people laid off because some sleep-deprived ana-lyst got a model wrong? *Steve forgot to hit F9; ten thousand people got fired.*

Sure, everything would have been better if the analysis were done at least a day earlier, so the team could have time to debate the best ad-vice for the client, but that wasn't a luxury afforded in the modern age of banking. As complexity increased, along with the tools and products to manage that complexity, the time set aside to analyze and formulate strategy dropped dramatically. We would lament that the emergence of FedEx required the presentation be in front of the client the next morn-ing. Every Wall Street analyst from the 1990s has tales about the absurd race of meeting each day's FedEx deadline. Then once the fax machine was created, deadlines went from *tomorrow* to *as soon as you can.* "Fax it over," your client would request, "then let's hop on the phone to discuss." With the advent of voicemail, you were already thirty minutes late by the time you got back to your desk and heard a client's message. Email and cell phones hurled us into a relentless on-call world with no ability to hide or delay. Distance and boundaries were obliterated. Technological advances were a great boon for efficiency and convenience, but those developments also brought increased complexity, higher expectations of analytical precision, and accelerated time frames—ingredients that didn't usually promote prudent decision making and optimal outcomes.

There's no doubt that speed has created real value in many ways. Whether through the dynamic availability and pricing of an Uber ride or through efficient price discovery that allows for the narrowing of bid–ask spreads in the trading world, speed has opened doors to new products, while facilitating innovation in traditional business lines. But speed has permeated corners of the financial world in which it doesn't seem to benefit any parties involved. Speed is not the friend of any financial challenge that requires analytical or strategic deliberation. The Roman orator Cicero understood this more than two millennia ago, when he said, "It is not by muscle, speed, or physical dexterity that great things are achieved, but by reflection, force of character, and judgment." Speed only begets more speed, serving to accelerate the processes of decision making in order to remain competitive with others who are now operating under the same constraints. The financial world moved from one in which you did the analysis, debated the options, and made an informed decision to one in which you first asked, *How much time do we have? What's the deadline?* Then you determined what could be done within that time frame. It was no longer an option to let information marinate and then consider the implications of that information. Time became the dominant consideration and variable in decision making throughout the financial system.

———

On my very first deal team, we were trying to find acquisition targets for an important financier. Before coming to Wall Street, I would have called him a *corporate raider* rather than a *financier*, but the terminology softened when someone became a client who might hire you for a lucrative job. I was barely more experienced than an intern at that point, and, lucky for me, we had a crack analyst on the team who didn't seem bothered by having a novice shackled to him. His name was Papa; he was from Senegal, in his second of a two-year analyst program.

As we pored over potential takeover targets for our client, I would know when it was three in the morning because that was the time of Papa's nightly call with his family, for which he would conference in relatives in London and Africa, with Salomon footing the exorbitant bill. Papa would put them all on speakerphone so he could continue with his computer work while listening to the family updates.

When I completed each company profile, I would run it by Papa to assess it as a potential target, which was known as "spreading" the company.

Papa would mute the call while we went through the summary of the business, both operational and financial data.

He would first ask, "Does it make the cut?"

"Maybe," I said. "If recent profitability isn't a deal breaker."

Meanwhile, Papa's mother would be warning his sister or cousin about the perils of dating. "These boys in London," she said, "they are not the same as boys in Senegal."

"But, Mom," one sister argued, "David seems nice."

"He is just doing what it takes," the mother said. "These British boys may be willing to put in the time, but it always ends the same. Tell her, Papa."

Papa quickly reached across the spread papers and unmuted the phone. "Not all guys are terrible," he said. "What about me, Mom?"

I imagined similar conversations occurring thousands of times each day, all over the world, as families were broken apart by the search for better lives, jobs, and education.

"Papa," I asked one night, "don't these calls cost a ton?"

"Probably. I think it gets lost in the utility bill. I've been doing this for months, and nobody has said anything yet."

"But what do you think will happen if you get found out?"

He pointed to a brown cardboard box in the corner. "If someone comes to me and says, 'Papa, we need to discuss your phone bill,' I will simply put up my hand and say, 'Stop. You don't need to go any further.' Then I'll sweep all my personal belongings into the box, walk out of the building, and they will never see me again." He made a sweeping gesture with his arm, as if he'd internally played out the moment many times before.

"So you would risk your job for these phone calls?"

He shrugged. During our time together, I came to understand why he would risk it. As excited as I was by the work, I sensed that Papa's survival was likely dependent on the nightly phone calls. Ours was a stressful and solitary lifestyle. Those intercontinental calls preserved him, kept him connected to something real and personal. Plus the extreme hours and isolation to which the job subjected him created feelings of bitterness and resentment, and taking something back from the firm seemed justified, given they were taking so much from him.

Working on that first deal team was exhilarating. When our project was over, I stepped into an elevator at the end of the day, where a senior member of my team was standing with his jacket folded over his forearm, holding his briefcase, headed home. "Hi, Bob," I said, smiling, expecting that we would rehash the project and pat each other on the back for all our hard work. But he didn't speak a word in reply. He wouldn't even look at me. We rode silently to the ground floor, and he walked off without acknowledging that we had ever met, let alone that I had sacrificed the previous six nights while logging more than a hundred hours. Right then I understood: *These people don't actually care about me or anyone else beyond what it takes to get the work done.* It was a sobering realization.

Because of the demands of the job, it wasn't possible to maintain friendships outside the office. I tried, but after breaking plans enough times, people stopped calling, and I didn't want to be the unreliable friend who constantly canceled, so I stopped calling them too. It seemed that my colleagues at the bank were mostly in the same predicament—we had the temporary camaraderie of our deal teams, and then maybe we had family somewhere, which in my case was three thousand miles away and in Papa's was across the globe.

———

Salomon Brothers had a position called the analyst staffer—which was assigned to me as the third-year associate. My duty was to pair the analysts, ranging from meek and doe-eyed to seasoned but jaded, with appropriate deal teams. It was classic matchmaking, taking several factors into account—personalities, experience, strengths and weaknesses, areas of expertise, prior relationships, schedule. In order to do the job well, I had to satisfy the needs and desires of both the senior people and the analysts, aiming to make everyone happy and productive—or, during busy times, making everyone equally unhappy. Impartiality and equitableness were the armor of the analyst staffer.

Many people viewed it as a power position because you'd have a lot of resources under your control. But not me. I considered it a serious and often painful responsibility. The heaviest burden was choosing whose weekends and vacations to ruin. I hated when on Friday afternoon I'd get requests for analysts to work over the weekend, and then I had to decide whom to assign. "I'm sorry," I'd tell the condemned. "Whatever you had planned, it's dead." I tried to spread evenly the blowing up of people's private time, so everyone felt some of the pain, but no one felt more than his or her share. In many ways, the analyst staffers were the only ones who cared about the survival and contentment of the analysts. Wall Street isn't a place that peddles in compassion. It's too fast paced and cutthroat for feelings, but I tried at least to be fair as an analyst staffer, even though I was often forced to make unfortunate choices.

When Mike Soenen arrived at Salomon Brothers, the M&A group was so overwhelmed and in need of help that four days into his month-long training program, they yanked him out to put him on a deal team. "We'll train you by fire," they told him, in quintessential Salomon Brothers fashion. As the analyst staffer, I felt an obligation to protect Mike, especially since I could see how ill equipped he was for the job. I was worried he might not survive for longer than a couple of weeks. I staffed him on his first deal team, hoping I was placing him in a good situation, even though I couldn't do much to guard him from potential perils. He would have to be thrown into the flames.

Mike's first assignment was with Barbara Heffernan, a very smart managing director, tough, intimidating, yet known for being just and reasonable. The client was a young Mexican entrepreneur, Bernardo

Dominguez. He was interested in buying Westin Hotels, but no one could tell how serious he was.

Barbara told Mike to do the analysis and determine if it was a good deal. She asked Mike for a DCF (a discounted cash-flow analysis), but Mike didn't know what that was. She wanted comps and an engagement letter, and Mike was likewise stumped. She presumed that he knew what he was doing.

Despite Mike's total ignorance, he did understand the importance of making a good impression this early in his time at Salomon, so he dove in hard, barely sleeping for three days. When he was done, he thought he might have created the *Mona Lisa* of finance. He had nailed it, he was certain.

Barbara invited Mike into her office. His work lay on the desk in front of her. "Listen," she said, "I have a question." Mike smiled, eager for Barbara's help in fine-tuning his analysis. "I need to know whether you're stupid, lazy, or both."

Mike was stunned. He stalled for time, with no idea how to respond, yet he figured he'd better come out with something. He thought he knew the right answer.

"Before you speak," she said, "I want you to think long and hard about your answer."

That paralyzed Mike. He sat thinking, *Shit, is this one of those weird Wall Street mindfucks?*

After a long delay, Barbara continued. "Fine, let me give you the answer. Don't say lazy, because I won't be able to do much about that. Say stupid. I can fix stupid."

Mike had been awake for most of three days. He knew that whatever was wrong with the analysis on Barbara's desk wasn't due to lack of effort. "Stupid it is," he said.

Mike continued to work on the deal with the young Mexican entrepreneur, but ultimately there wasn't enough capital to get it done. In the eleventh hour, another large hotel group wanted to join the bid for Westin to help push the deal over the line.

Barbara called to inform Mike she was away skiing for the weekend and needed him to run the meeting. That Saturday, he found himself welcoming the CEO, CFO, head of business development, and other senior executives from the hotel group, who had just arrived from London on a private jet. They met in a conference room on the thirty-third floor. Mike—brand new to the firm and to Wall Street—was the only Salomon representative in attendance.

They settled at the table, and one of the senior executives asked, "What do we think the deal terms should be?"

Mike nodded knowingly. "Deal terms. Right. Let's figure out what we're gonna do." He was completely lost from the first question.

They had brought some documents to discuss and asked Mike if someone could make copies.

"No problem!" he said with a bit too much enthusiasm. "I'll get my assistant to do these." A minute later, Mike was running the copies when the machine jammed. He yanked the toner cartridge out, and ink sprayed across his shirt. Another junior analyst, Tom Purcell, sat in his cubicle nearby. "Hey, Tom," Mike said breathlessly, "I have this deal going and now I've got toner all over me because I just told them my assistant was running the goddamn copies but it was really me. These guys are gonna figure out I'm just an analyst. I need your shirt." Tom obliged, and soon Mike strolled back into the meeting with a stack of copies and wearing a different color shirt than when he had left the room only moments before.

Unsurprisingly, the meeting didn't turn out well.

Only on Wall Street, and only at Salomon Brothers, would a green twenty-five-year-old be placed across the table from the CEO of a major hotel group, running a deal. "The executives should have walked right out," Mike said later, "but you were seen as legitimate because you were at Salomon Brothers, so they were probably like, 'Wow, this must be one of their young hot guns.' They didn't know I was from Kalamazoo and had trouble even working a goddamn copier."

If Goldman Sachs and Morgan Stanley existed on one end of the Wall Street spectrum of pedigree and sophistication, Salomon Brothers occupied the far other end. When Goldman made a hire, the firm placed value on alma mater and family name, history and connections. Salomon didn't give a shit where you came from, as long as you were tough enough to survive and were willing to work hard. Where's Kalamazoo? Who cares?

"At Salomon Brothers," Mike said, "there were more blue-collar guys who kind of muscled their way in. So the guys at the top would say, 'Just to be clear, we're going to torture you. I'm gonna ask you a question about tail numbers, just to see how you react. I'm going to tell you you're stupid, just to see how you react. And if you handle that moderately easily, we'll let you run a deal.'" Before the Westin deal fell apart, Mike led the people at the table to an agreement on price and terms. The deal didn't stick, but Barbara was pleased with his effort. "There was the sense that she hadn't seen the whole thing as a write-off," Mike said, "that I wasn't just guaranteed to fail. Sure, it was a long shot, but Salomon Brothers was built on long shots. Almost everybody who got to the top was a long shot one way or another."

———

Around this time, my younger sister, Lea, arrived as a summer associate at Salomon Brothers. One of the final events of the summer, which I myself had participated in three years prior, was the golf outing held at Oyster Bay on Long Island.

Lea's day was a disaster from the outset. The plan was to meet at the office, and then the summer associates would board a bus for Oyster Bay. Lea, who had never golfed besides Putt-Putt on Cape Cod, showed up in her newly purchased golf outfit. "What are you doing?" her supervisor asked incredulously, shaming her in front of a roomful of colleagues. "It's inappropriate for you to be wearing this at the office." They had expected her to show up in business attire, then change into her country club clothes after half an hour.

Once they reached the links, foursomes were assembled, each consisting of two summer associates and two managing directors. For the summer associates, walking the course with the senior bankers for a few hours provided a great chance for them to get to know you. If you were an experienced golfer, this could be an opportunity to distinguish yourself and impress the people who would ultimately decide if you'd be getting a job offer. If you weren't a good golfer, you would need to impress them in other ways—humor, charisma, storytelling, courage, whatever you had.

David Wittig, the notoriously arrogant head of M&A and once the tormentor of Mike Soenen, strutted onto the course and yelled out: "We need a summer associate over here. Who's the worst golfer?" Knowing she'd never golfed, a few people pointed at my sister, so she ended up with Wittig and another managing director in a threesome.

All through the course, Wittig and the other MD gave my sister pointers and lessons, but Lea wasn't going to master the game on a single outing. She felt that they were annoyed with her slow, erratic play. They finally reached the eighteenth green, the last group to come in. A handful of MDs and summers who had finished gathered around the green to heckle everyone else as they approached. It was a pretty intimidating scene for the summer associates—a rowdy crew of peers and bankers, critiquing and hazing them and generally acting like arrogant buffoons.

Once they had finished the hole and were still on the green, Wittig— never one to squander an audience—told a story about a summer associate from the previous year whose ball lay a foot from the cup, and, just to mess with him, Wittig said, "Are you willing to bet your future on this putt? If you make it, I guarantee you a job offer. Miss it, and we never want to see you again." The guy had to accept the challenge, but he got so nervous in front of the crowd that he managed to rim the shot, drawing the ridicule of everyone present.

Lea, standing near Wittig on the green as he told this story, said, "Can I get the same deal?" She dropped her ball, fifteen feet from the pin. Wittig and the other MD laughed in surprise, expecting that Lea was joking, but she didn't so much as smile.

"Yeah, sure," Wittig said. It was no easy putt.

Lea leaned down to scope the pitch like a seasoned golfer, then she stepped up, gripped the putter, and hit the ball toward the cup. Utter silence as the ball rolled across the green and into the hole.

I wasn't an MD and so wasn't senior enough to golf with the summer associates, but I showed up for the after-party. Everyone was talking about her putt, stopping by to hear her recount it and to shake her hand. "Congrats on being the first person to get an offer," she was told several times. A lot of people slapped me on the back and said, "Your sister's got bigger balls than you do."

A few weeks afterward, Lea got her offer. (And, incidentally, so had the kid who muffed his shot the summer before.) Lea had understood that it didn't really matter if she made the putt or not—the act of proving that she had the guts and confidence to take the risk meant that she would win either way. That was exactly the sort of behavior Salomon Brothers championed.

———

Eduardo's fortune-cookie pitch had been effective in helping convince Northrop to launch a hostile bid on Grumman, which put Martin Marietta's agreement with Grumman into peril. This enraged Martin Marietta's chairman, Norman Augustine, an aggressive businessman and former Pentagon official. "The attack by Northrop," Augustine announced in a statement, "degrades the entire character of the rational consolidation taking place within the United States' national security industrial base." He declared that he was "deeply disappointed that Northrop has chosen to launch a hostile attack that seeks to disrupt an agreement between Martin Marietta and Grumman for a friendly consolidation." Augustine pledged that his firm would respond.

Martin Marietta's purchase price of Grumman had been set at $55 per share. The bid our team put together for Northrop was $5 higher, at $60 per share, or $2 billion total (a figure that seemed huge at the time but actually approximated the cost of building a single B-2 bomber). Kent Kresa, the chairman of Northrop, engaged in a PR battle with Augustine. Kresa argued that he was not trying to disrupt an agreement but that Northrop had no choice but to make the bid, since Northrop's own negotiations with Grumman had been previously cut off by Martin Marietta.

Then speculation hit the press that Martin Marietta might turn its financial missiles toward Northrop in order to squash Northrop's moves on Grumman. *Newsday* published a piece about the rumor under the title: "Is Hunter Hunted?" If true, it would be a classic attack-the-attacker approach. The Northrop board quickly blamed us for putting them in play. If the board members had known that this move would place them in the crosshairs, they said, they wouldn't have done it.

The battle had developed very quickly, beginning as soon as Martin Marietta first broadcast its deal with Grumman on March 7, 1994, and Northrop responded by announcing a hostile bid on Grumman three days later. By March 17, Kresa was forced to reply to possible takeover attempts against Northrop: "We've said this repeatedly: We're not expecting any offers. We're not encouraging any offers. If there was an offer, obviously we'd have to consider it." Kresa, not allowed under corporate law to deter an offer publicly, said only that the terms would need to be "enormously attractive." A couple of weeks prior, Northrop had been carrying on business as usual, chugging dependably along, constructing weapons and warplanes, marching reliably into the future. And now, quite suddenly, it had launched a hostile on a major competitor and was consequently now itself the rumored takeover target of an even bigger competitor.

Aerospace and defense companies are often under contract to build weapons for the government, which might require years of work by large teams of people. Confidentiality can be a matter of national security. Northrop approached every relationship, including its work with us, under that same sheen of paranoiac secrecy. All the bankers who worked on the deal were asked to sign personal confidentiality agreements, which we had never done for any other client. When we met at Northrop's LA headquarters, we had to show our IDs every time we entered the building, a level of security that was highly uncommon at the time. And the meetings nearly always occurred on Saturdays, so we could come and go without anyone catching wind of what we were working on. This meant we'd have to take the red-eye back to New York, arriving Sunday morning after a sleepless night, then work all day to prepare for a Monday conference call. The hours were especially brutal during that deal.

A secret fax machine was housed in a locked closet at Salomon Brothers, and only Eduardo Mestre's assistant, Fran, had access to the key. If you had a fax to send to Northrop, you had to request the key from Fran, call Northrop to warn them that something was coming, and then, once you got the green light, you would fax the document from the closet at Salomon to the fax machine in another closet at Northrop, which was protected by a key-code combination lock.

After Grumman shared its nonpublic information with Northrop, there was significant due diligence to be done and other details to sort through. We darted back and forth from Northrop's offices in LA, to Grumman's in Long Island, to our Manhattan home base. Despite the fanatical secrecy, some details of the deal leaked to the press and ended up in the newspapers. Michael Carr, Salomon's MD who was the lead on our team, met with Kent Kresa to discuss next steps on the deal, and he brought up the leaks.

"Kent," Carr said, "you've got to talk to your team about security and plugging up this leak. It's not gonna do any of us any good."

Kresa adjusted his glasses and spoke in a calm, measured tone. "Let me tell you something," he said. "When we created the B-2 Stealth Bomber program, the largest contract in the history of the world, we had ten thousand people working on it for more than ten years, and there wasn't a single leak. Not one. Eight people know the details of this deal we're working on. Half of them work at your firm. Where do you think the leak is?"

To Northrop's relief, the counterattack from Martin Marietta never came. On March 29, Grumman stated that it wanted best and final bids from both companies and was putting it to an auction. Martin Marietta and Northrop had two days to respond.

A year or so into his time at Salomon, Mike Soenen met a woman. Let's call her Lisa.

Carrying on a relationship was no easy task on Wall Street. The hours of the job didn't agree with romance and courtship, and there weren't the convenient tools of communication that we have today. In order to date someone, you had to plan ahead, and with such a demanding work schedule, that sort of planning was often impossible. Against these odds, at a bar after work one night, Mike connected with Lisa, a broker at Prudential who was impressed with his job at Salomon. "We dated for about six months, which was enough time that it was clear to me, a kid from Kalamazoo, Michigan, that I had a New York girlfriend. It was clear enough that I mentioned it to my parents, that I was seeing a girl who worked for this firm called Prudential, which sounded very big to me."

It was an exciting time for Mike—Manhattan, new job, new girlfriend, good paycheck. Then he arrived at the office one day to find a message on his voicemail from an unknown woman. She was crying. "I know who you are," the message said. "I've spoken with her. You should know that we're together. She's the love of my life, and that's not going to change"—the woman was sobbing now—"and there's nothing you can do about it." The message continued. It was very heartfelt, very sad. She had returned home from a trip and found something in the apartment that belonged to Mike, confronted her girlfriend, and the whole story poured out. Mike had known that Lisa had a roommate, but he'd never met her and had no idea that their relationship extended beyond sharing an apartment. She was conveniently never around when he visited their flat. "The best thing is for you to just stop right now," her message pleaded. "Please do not contact her."

In the early 1990s, especially in a culture as conservative as the financial industry, bisexuality was far from common. It was especially foreign to Mike. "Even the *idea* that somebody was bisexual—none of this stuff ever occurred to me. I'm from Kalamazoo. What the fuck do I know?" Mike adored Lisa—enough that he'd told all of us at work about her—so for him it wasn't merely a fling, and of course he hadn't meant to hurt this unknown woman. At a loss for what to do, he canvassed his buddies in the surrounding cubes.

The technology had just been introduced that allowed someone to forward a voice message to another person or group, so Mike sent the woman's message to his five cubemates, asking for guidance. They listened to it and briefly discussed potential responses, then they broke for lunch without reaching a consensus.

When Mike returned to the thirty-third floor after lunch and crossed the room to his work area, a dozen or so smirking heads popped up from surrounding cubicles and snatched looks at him. One guy, whom Mike had never spoken to, barked out, "There he is." Mike arrived at his desk as Fran, Eduardo Mestre's assistant, walked by and said, "Wow, Mike, I didn't know you had it in you." He sat down and privately assessed the situation. *Jesus*, he thought, *everyone knows*.

But Mike had no idea of the size of it. By the end of the day, the entire firm had heard the message. Then it leapt to other firms. "I'm going to say by forty-eight hours tops," Mike said, "it was all over Wall Street. Because, unbeknownst to me, one guy could forward it to somebody, but then he could forward it outside the firm. And people were like, 'You got to hear this.' It was my first lesson in something going viral. You have a good story about a jilted bisexual lover? It freakin' cascaded."

This, of course, happened pre-internet, pre–cell phones, pre–social media. Even the phrase *going viral* didn't exist yet—that came along a few years later with the arrival of widespread internet. Before voicemail technology, stories were told over a meal or a cup of coffee or by the water cooler. The new voicemail-forwarding technology allowed many more people to share directly in the experience, to listen to the actual voice of the aggrieved lover, rather than receiving the story secondhand. And so people were able to feel that they were part of it in a way they hadn't before. By the next day, nearly everyone on Wall Street was talking about the voice message. There were rumors that Howard Stern had played it on his radio show and debated what Mike should do—which, if true, meant that the message had leapt from Wall Street to the worlds of cab drivers and construction workers and a broad cross section of New Yorkers. Big-shot managing directors from the Salomon trading floor, who had never deigned to set foot in the investment banking department before that day, descended to the thirty-third floor to find Mike. "I'd like to shake your hand," they said. "You know what you have to do, right?" Everyone came with the same advice.

"Yeah," Mike said, resigned to his fate. "I gotta try for the threeway."

"Atta boy."

Mike played phone tag with the aggrieved lover for two days; they left messages on each other's machine and finally set up a time to talk by phone. Thursday at four o'clock, he would pitch the threesome to this woman whom he'd never met. Meanwhile, his Salomon colleagues—and, by extension, all of Wall Street and much of New York—followed each turn in the story as if it were a celebrity tabloid romance. "Everybody knows about the call," Mike said, "and so five minutes before it's supposed to take place, people start migrating down to the conference room." Many in the M&A group and others from the investment bank had asked to listen in. Mike didn't want to make a spectacle of it, but he was very junior, and the pressure was overwhelming. A muted speakerphone was set up in a conference room where the gathered masses could eavesdrop while Mike made his pitch from the phone in his cubicle. "Before the call, I was feeling good. Everybody had me pumped up. Little did I know, they didn't really give a shit. They just wanted to see something interesting, right? I had a million reasons why not to make the call. But I also understood that there was no downside. At Salomon, I would get credit just for swinging for it."

Mike sat at his desk, deep breath, and he dialed the number. "So everybody's in the conference room, and I get her on the phone. And I just start selling my heart out. 'Maybe if we all get together and talk it out. Seems like we all like each other—I like her; she likes me; you seem nice.' I was trying not to go to the obvious, right? I wasn't pitching a threeway; I was pitching a let's-get-together-and-talk-and-maybe-there's-something-here, right? I get totally and completely shut out for fifteen minutes, across the board. Basically, every end road was *grenade, grenade, grenade.* Then there was a sensitive moment and she said, 'You have no idea how much this has hurt me. And I'm not sure I could physically stand seeing you.' So I said, 'I didn't mean to hurt you. I didn't know you *existed.* But if we just could get together to discuss it.' And it was a hardcore *no.* So anyway, I hung up in defeat in front of the entire floor."

The show was over. People emptied out of the conference room and headed back to their desks. "But in true Salomon Brothers fashion," Mike said, "everybody was like, *Great job. That's just what we expected of you in a moment of uncertainty, when you could have totally wimped out.* Suddenly, the little kid from Kalamazoo—I had stature. Wall Street was chattering; partners were interested. I had the balls to get on the phone and go make the big pitch. It put me on the radar. Everybody was aware of it. That gave me table stakes for being part of a conversation."

When Mike tells the story today, he's remorseful for having allowed the hurt feelings of the aggrieved lover to become entertainment for his co-workers, but at the time, he couldn't have anticipated the reaction, and he felt that he didn't have much of a choice. None of us did. The rogue wave of viral sentiment was rolling, and we were all powerless against it. Any one of us could have spoken out against a scene that was fundamentally heartless and insensitive. We could have said, *This is unacceptable; it's not happening,* and hung up the phone; but that sort of awareness and sensitivity didn't exist in that day, let alone in an industry not known for those qualities. In fact, our thought processes were quite the opposite. Because we'd heard the voicemail ourselves, we felt that the story was our story, which gave us the right to participate in watching it unfold. The events had happened so quickly and unexpectedly that there hadn't been time to process their possible implications. Thus began our training in dealing with the new world of speed and viral communication.

The aggrieved lover story paralleled Northrop's circumstances in many ways. Mike had been contentedly dating his girlfriend, then the other woman stepped in and told him to beat it, and he had to be convinced to be assertive and suggest a threesome, rather than slinking off passively into the background. Mike was the sweet kid from Kalamazoo who never would have had the gall to pitch the threesome until Wall Street got its hands on him. He would have been disappointed and hurt, left with no choice but to move on. Likewise, Northrop had been making overtures to Grumman, then Martin Marietta shut it down, so Northrop had to be convinced to be assertive, rather than slinking off passively into the background. Conceptually, Northrop was interested in going hostile, but since it existed in a genteel industry, and since aggressiveness wasn't yet in the firm's nature, Wall Street was needed to validate this departure from protocol.

———

Mike's romantic debacle may have been one of the first things ever to go viral, and it was certainly our introduction to the idea that something *could* go viral. Increased speed of information flow, combined with the ability for that information to go viral, created pressure to make quick decisions with limited information and time to evaluate the consequences. Soon everyone felt the need to get access to the same information at top speed, or else they would be at a distinct disadvantage. As the nature of communication in the financial world evolved, there was now an ever-present fear of being out of the loop, of being left behind.

With advances in technology and the new religion of speed, it became an accepted practice to engage in investment strategies disconnected from fundamental value drivers, such as potential long-term growth and value. An investor owned a security for only as long as the information available made owning it seem like a good investment. This had a massive and unforeseen result—the rise and acceptance of speculation (which is an investment made with limited or incomplete information and the possibility of material loss). Trades and deals had once been carefully measured, but with the increases in speed—both in the access to markets as well as to information—speculation itself felt more worthy of consideration as a legitimate financial practice.

Once it became accepted, if not required, to make fast decisions based on as little as a single new fact and how that would influence prices, that became the new game. Investors who could best analyze the real-time implications of a fact set were heavily rewarded. This also paved the way for the emergence of hedge funds, a fancy name for a relatively exclusive partnership known for engaging in aggressive and risky investment strategies. Investment horizons were shortened to mere seconds. What not too long before would have been viewed as speculation or even gambling was elevated to the status of prudent investing. Old-time value investors could take solace only in the belief that they would be right in time. Unfortunately for them and, arguably, for investors, that time stubbornly has not come, having been supplanted by volatile short-term price reactions to every bit of new information. Long-term value investing became the privilege of only those who could afford to be patient or stubborn.

Many hedge funds (and later quant funds) canonized speed as a central tenet of their business models. Given a window measured in split seconds, a trader had to move extremely quickly and put his or her faith in computers and algorithms to take advantage of opportunities. It became popular to trade securities utilizing investment strategies that weren't based on fundamental metrics, such as profit and cash flow. Instead, momentum plays became acceptable strategies, and no one seemed concerned that many trades had become divorced from the underlying assets themselves. Prices were now reflective of the constraints of time and speed, more than any other factor having to do with traditional assessments of value. The squeezing of time had disconnected prices from reality.

———

Managing and refining one's personal image was another way this desire to control information and perception was manifested. Through the 1980s and into the '90s, the persona of the "investment banker" became firmly rooted in the public consciousness—spurred on by men real and imagined, like David Wittig and Gordon Gekko; bolstered by books like *The Bonfire of the Vanities* and *Barbarians at the Gate*; lionized in the public imagination by their portrayal in films, such as the iconic scene from *American Psycho* where a bunch of Wall Streeters are sitting around in a conference room trying to one-up one another with the design and quality of their business cards, and the stakes seem murderously high. Through those two decades, a growing majority of bankers came to dress and play the part. The way that one looked, moved, and spoke had become an indicator of status. You wanted to be known as a Big Swinging Dick or, better yet, a Master of the Universe. Nothing could top that.

The quintessential Salomon banker—the cliché that everyone conjured in their minds when they heard the name of the firm—had long been the loud, uncivilized trader with a lingering hangover and mustard stains on his shirt. But Wall Street's new obsession with optics and perception had even pervaded the crass, vulgar Salomon Brothers, forcing a turn toward sophistication and image consciousness.

I, meanwhile, remained oblivious to these pressures. One day while working on the Northrop deal, Michael Carr, the managing director on the team, told me I was lucky that I could just be myself.

"What do you mean?" I asked.

"You don't have to try to create a separate persona. Your thing seems to work." Carr looked like a magazine ad for Wall Street—impeccably dressed, hair always in place, megawatt smile, seemingly born in a suit and tie.

I gazed at him, mystified, and said, "I didn't know it was an option to create a separate persona," to which Carr laughed and turned away.

During the time we were prepping to do diligence on Grumman, both Eduardo Mestre and Carr, our two senior bankers on the team, were unavailable due to consequential family events, so I was sent to run a big meeting scheduled at Northrop's headquarters in LA. Eduardo made it clear that he wasn't happy about putting me in charge, but he didn't have another option.

I worked with the Northrop deal team to create revenue and cash-flow projections on Grumman and on the prospective combined company. While this sort of thing was typically an exercise in educated forecasting, the assumptions came a bit more easily in the aerospace and defense industries, since most of a company's activity revolved around publicly shared US military contracts. Eduardo wasn't aware of that advantage, so he was impressed when word got back to him that the meeting had gone well—and he was impressed again weeks later when my projections were revealed to be remarkably accurate.

When he returned to the office from his leave, Eduardo came over to my cubicle and said, "Good job, Varelas. I need to create a new category for you."

"Okay."

"You're a horse disguising yourself as a muffin."

In spite of myself, I thanked him.

After Grumman put it to an auction, we had two days to come up with our best and final offer. This was an unwelcome development in the deal, since we had already submitted the highest offer, so essentially Grumman was forcing us to bid against ourselves. If we didn't increase our offer, we would be at risk of losing the deal to Martin Marietta, and we had no idea what they would bid. Kent Kresa took to the press to deride the rules of the auction, claiming that they favored Martin Marietta and perpetuated "the unlevel playing field." But to no avail. Our bid was coming due.

Our strategy was to build an offer that included a contingency that we would top any bid by Martin Marietta by up to $2, capped at a certain amount. We structured the offer and got it in on the March 31 deadline; the next day, Grumman contacted us to make it official that we had won. Martin Marietta had left their price at $55 per share, and we agreed to raise ours to $62 to get the deal done. Grumman's board voted unanimously to approve it. The news would be made public after the weekend, giving both firms a few days to finalize the merger agreement. The deal officially closed on April 5, 1994, forming a new combined company called the Northrop Grumman Corporation.

Two weeks after the acquisition was announced, the annual gathering of the Conquistadores del Cielo was held. One of my Salomon colleagues who also worked on the merger, Petros Kitsos, talked to Northrop's Kent Kresa about what it was like to face the other Conquistadores after having launched a hostile and thwarted Martin Marietta bid for Grumman. "Kent had to decide if he was going to go to the ranch and be apologetic," Petros said, "or he could blame the whole thing on Goldman Sachs and Bear Stearns [the bankers for Grumman and Martin Marietta, respectively] and say, 'Look, we are industrialists. They are just service people.

They're looking for a fee, and we're looking to restructure the industry.' He went through the whole mental analysis, but he didn't feel he had to explain his intentions or provide justification." Kresa knew he had acquired the weapon of reputation as someone who should not be messed with.

———

A few months later, in early July 1994, I got a phone call from my father to say that my mom didn't have much time left. She had been battling brain cancer for two years, and—strong as she was—the battle was nearing its end. I hate to admit that one of my first thoughts was how much time I could take off without alienating my deal teams. It wasn't that I didn't want to be with her in Orange County—it was the only thing I wanted—but Wall Street culture had a very limited capacity for empathy and flexibility in such situations. There was no clear protocol for time off, but it was generally accepted that there were only a few sorts of life events that warranted so much as a brief absence from the office—weddings, honeymoons, and family funerals. Even the birth of a child allowed the father to miss only a day of work, and stories of new mothers returning to the office less than a week after leaving the maternity ward were commonplace. When mourning the loss of a parent and tending to the obligatory ceremonies, the unspoken expectation was that roughly a week was the appropriate length of time.

With a sense of guilt and insecurity, I left New York and flew to California. I hated that I felt this way. As I expected from my father's call, when I arrived my mom wasn't doing well. By then she was in hospice care in Anaheim, drifting in and out of consciousness. When she was awake, she was distant. I had recently finished reading *War and Peace*, in which I encountered one of the most realistic death scenes I'd ever read. When people are dying, they often pull away, almost like a transition. It feels very cold and disconcerting, and if I hadn't read that novel, I don't think I would have been able to understand what was happening. I would have felt as though my mom didn't care about my father, my sister, and me, as we stood huddled around her bed.

She had been a proud American. Although she had been born

and raised in Sparta, Greece, she spent her last several decades in the United States. She fiercely defended her adopted country against anyone who spoke negatively about it, and she was tough on immigrants whom she felt didn't work hard enough. To her, that was unacceptable. This was partly because she had come from a nation as troubled as Greece, where the economy was terrible and the government was loaded with corruption. She would often remind us, "You don't realize how good you have it."

She died on the evening of the Fourth of July, and from where we gathered around as she drew her final breath, we could hear the muffled detonations of the Disneyland fireworks a few miles away. Thirteen years before, to the day, I had begun my career as a Disneyland host, and now here was another formative moment heralded in by Disney's fireworks on Independence Day.

I stayed the rest of the week in Orange County before heading back to New York. At LAX, I drifted through the terminal, a sea of anonymous faces passing by. Every age and shape and color, here at this crossroads—we were nowhere, yet we were travelers coming from someplace and going someplace else, all of us suspended in the bardo.

I was excited to return to the job—it was the beginning of my fifth year, and very little of the thrill had worn off—but part of me dreaded having to endure the forced condolences of my colleagues. My mom had been my tireless advocate, urging me to work hard, yet scolding me for working too hard. She'd always had my back. She was the person I called when I needed a conversation that didn't involve revenue projections, when I needed to be reminded that my world was bigger than the current deal team and client. And now she was gone.

An ethereal voice spoke from above, echoing through the terminal, telling me to find my departure gate. I did so and then sank into a seat on the margins of the crowd, facing the windows, watching the heat and fumes radiate off the tarmac, the little puddles of mirage here and there, cut through by jets maneuvering around the runway as sluggishly and awkwardly as elephants in captivity.

So many of the classic Disney movies are touched off by the loss or absence of a parent: *Bambi*, *Cinderella*, *Peter Pan*, *Beauty and the Beast*, *Tarzan*, *The Little Mermaid*, *The Lion King*, and others. I dug out a pen and scrawled a list on the back of my ticket jacket.

Up to that point, my career had essentially consisted of following commands from superiors and clients. With seniority would come a much wider array of moral and ethical considerations. What part would I play in the dramas to come, I wondered, and how would I face those challenges? The passengers around me started to congregate into lines, and finally I joined them. A man in a crisp, patterned vest scanned my ticket. "Welcome aboard, Mr. Varelas."

"Thanks," I said, managing a weak smile. Thirty years old, exhausted, motherless, I shouldered my bag and walked down the jetway, boarding a flight toward the skyscrapers of the financial world and an uncertain future.

5

MODERN ART

Several dozen factory workers gathered on the third floor of a New Jersey plant. Some had goggles pushed up on their foreheads. Some were holding gloves. A few shifted from foot to foot, clearly tired. The weekend was almost here, and it had been a long, shitty few days. Word came down from management on Monday that their company had been bought, and none of them knew what this might mean for their jobs. These were union guys, and a number of them had been through similar fiascos before. Would they be downsized? Made redundant? Would the factory close and production move overseas?

They studied the rich California guy as he stepped forward to address the group—a blue dress shirt oddly untucked, khaki pants, loafers, rounded eyeglasses, a wave of silver hair, a West Coast tan. He looked as out of place in their factory as they would look at a White House banquet for the French prime minister. Who was this outsider who now owned their company? Rumor was that he had arrived on a private jet that afternoon and then marched in with a security detail and fired the company's president, vice president, and four or five other top executives. Not that the union workers felt much sympathy for the bosses, but there seemed to be a bloodlust in the air that made everyone edgy.

"I'm Dick Heckmann, the CEO of U.S. Filter," the rich guy said. "And I know some of you are nervous about the changes. Some of you are maybe even pissed off. But do me a favor: Before you jump to conclusions, listen to Coach."

Dick Heckmann stepped back, and then—miracle of miracles—Lou Holtz came forward. The legend! One of the greatest football coaches of all time, there on their factory floor! Where the hell had he come from? Some bewildered but enthusiastic applause and a few hoots rippled through the room.

"Some of you may know me," Coach Holtz said and then began recounting his years at Notre Dame and other football programs before retiring in 1996. He was funny. He looked them in the eye. Right away the union workers began to relax and engage with Coach, as his humility and self-deprecating humor disarmed them.

Coach recognized their concern over the acquisition, and he respected it. He described his childhood in West Virginia—born in a cellar, shared a one-room house with his sister and parents, never sure if there would be enough food to eat. He understood struggle. He understood the men and women standing before him. But why, he asked them, do you want to live your life fighting?

"I think it's wrong to be bitter," Coach Holtz said, pacing back and forth in front of the workers. "We've all had injustices done—by society, by a spouse. But you know what? Don't go through life where you're being bitter, where you pass away and your spouse has to hire six pallbearers because you don't have friends. Just do the right thing! I think it's right to have an excellent, positive attitude. See, ladies and gentlemen, enjoy life. Have fun. You're gonna have difficulties because that's part of life. But if you have fun doing something, people are gonna have fun being around. Every day when I walked out on the football field, I said, 'Boy, what a great day to work,' and I meant it. Don't let other people control your attitude."

Coach went on to tell a bunch of football stories, with the union workers hanging on every word. He described his confidence in Dick

Heckmann, the California guy standing behind him, and in U.S. Filter, the company that now owned this plant, and Coach talked about his faith, about integrity, teamwork, living a life full of love and hard work. These ideas had never been voiced on the factory floor. Love was never mentioned, unless it was *I love pepperoni pizza* or *I love my new lawnmower.* But Coach said things like, "There's a statue of me at Notre Dame. I guess they needed a place for the pigeons to land. But if you go look at it, just look at three words on the pedestal: Trust. Commitment. Love. Those are the three rules I had for my children and my team." By the time Coach was finished, many of the big tough guys in the room were swiping at tears.

Coach said he'd be happy to stick around and sign autographs if anybody wanted one. And then Heckmann, the Californian, stepped forward and brought the meeting to a close with a final directive: "Look, I want you guys to go home for the weekend and think about what Coach said. If you're not willing to sign on, then have the balls to not show up, because if you show up and I hear one word about the way it used to be done or how you feel sorry for the guys we fired, I will fire you on the spot, end of story. We're not going to put up with it."

Later at dinner, Holtz said to Heckmann, "Geez, nice going. I wonder if anybody's going to show up."

Monday morning arrived, and everybody reported to work. Heckmann recalled: "Half of them were wearing Notre Dame hats, Notre Dame sweaters. It's New Jersey, so they weren't going to say, 'Okay, Boss, I'm with you; I pledge my allegiance,' but they were going to send a signal that they got me. And it turned out to be a great plant. That's what Coach Holtz did—every time we made an acquisition, he would go in and spend a couple of days. These are people who work in plants; when they go home to their cul-de-sac and they barbecue with their friends, none of their friends have ever listened to Lou Holtz or had a chance to shake his hand. They don't get a chance to do that. So you just made your guy the king of the neighborhood, and incredible loyalty flows from that."

Dick Heckmann had developed a close friendship with Holtz, and when he retired from coaching at Notre Dame, Dick suggested that he keep himself busy by working for U.S. Filter. Whenever the company executed a major acquisition, Coach would come out and give his speech. Damian Georgino, the chief legal officer for U.S. Filter, remembered some of the stories Holtz would tell the often apprehensive new employees: "I think it was on Notre Dame's '88 team," Georgino said, "there was a left guard at practice who was just dogging him. So Coach says, 'You're out of there.' And so the second-string guy goes to take his place, and Coach says, 'No, you're out of there too.' They say, 'Why are you doing that? We can't play without a left guard.' He goes, 'Well, you're playing without a left guard now.' So they started to run the plays. The quarterback's getting creamed; the running backs are getting creamed; the kids are just all beat up. Coach says, 'Do another one. Do another one. Look what happens when you just take one person out. And that's what I want you to think about on every play. I want you to be the best team player that you can be. Know your role, know your job, and know what you're supposed to be doing every time.'"

When a company gets acquired, the toughest challenge is to build trust between the workers and new ownership. "And so what do you get with Coach?" Georgino said. "The ultimate trust guy. So he went around on all the major transactions. He was the first person after Dick who would talk."

———

Dick Heckmann was the man at the helm of U.S. Filter, a commercial water-treatment company that, during the 1990s, grew from nothing into a powerhouse by aggressively acquiring scores of smaller companies and assets. In the banking industry, this sort of company is known as a *roll-up*, a reference to the tactic of buying several companies in the same sector and rolling them up into one huge company. To succeed in building a roll-up as massive as U.S. Filter would become, one must have rare powers of persuasion, an excess of self-regard, and a talent for storytelling. Dick Heckmann had those qualities in spades. And it's not a bad idea to have a ringer like Lou Holtz to help convert the skeptics when necessary.

I've heard people describe Dick as a visionary, a brilliant entrepreneur ahead of his time. He understood water to be a precious and increasingly valuable resource at a time when nobody was thinking about it that way. And he could spin a yarn like no one else. More than once, I also heard him described as an egotistical bullshit artist who had no problem twisting facts if it helped him expand his empire. Some called him the best salesman alive. Some called him a ruthless narcissist. The Father of Water. An irrepressible charmer. An insatiable demagogue. Poseidon. The truth was that Dick embodied all of these contradictions.

He was enterprising even as a kid. Dick was born in St. Louis, and moved a lot throughout his childhood because of his father's job with GE. "High school in Des Moines," he recalled in an interview with Jeff Bailey, "I was bagging groceries and delivering newspapers. College in Hawaii, I sold Fuller brushes door to door. I didn't graduate. I went to Vietnam in '65 and was assigned to the 33rd Air Rescue Squadron. When I came back in '66, I wasn't in any mood to go back to school. I got a job selling insurance." From there, Dick parlayed his military experience into making rescue beacons for downed airplanes. When that company failed, due to a lack of expertise in how to run a business, Dick borrowed the capital to acquire a company that made surgical implants and prosthetic limbs. By aggressive management on both the revenue and cost sides of the operations, he made a small fortune selling it off in 1977, and at thirty-three years old he "retired to Sun Valley, Idaho, to ski."

But he was far too restless for the life of a ski bum. He served two years in the Small Business Administration under President Jimmy Carter, despite their very different politics. He bought a hotel and a taxi service in Sun Valley and was elected town mayor. (He earned 124 votes of the 204 people who turned out at the polls.) But halfway through his four-year term, he resigned over accusations that the taxi and hotel businesses were creating conflicts of interest with his elected office.

Meanwhile, he'd had some luck playing the market. That sparked the next phase of his career—as a stockbroker. He relocated to Palm Springs and took on clients, one of whom was Verne Winchell, the founder of Winchell's Donuts and CEO of Denny's. Verne mentioned to Dick that his neighbor owned a struggling water company in nearby Whittier and suggested they take a look at it.

Dick seemed to have the audacity, the ego, and the appetite to pursue every vaguely interesting opportunity that crossed his path. He called Greg Smith, his brokerage firm's head of research, to ask for financial profiles of water businesses in which to invest. Greg sounded doubtful but agreed to look into it.

When he called back, he said, "Dick, there aren't any."

"What do you mean?" Dick asked.

"Unbelievably," Greg said, "unless you want to buy a water utility, there is no way to buy the water business. None. Zero."

Dick mulled it over. "So I'm thinking, it's the biggest product on the planet Earth. Nothing grows without it—no human, no plant, no animal grows without it. There can be no cities without it, no expansion without it. It's the base of everything we eat and drink and use. There is no more important thing in the world than water, and you can't invest in it? Nobody was thinking about it at the time. Nobody."

Dick and Verne put some money into the struggling company, which had the unfortunate name American Toxxic Control. (Dick likes to say: "It wasn't controlling it—it was causing it.") The company tanked even further, but that didn't deter Dick and Verne. They drove to Whittier to see American Toxxic Control in person and meet the CEO. "I just fell in love with it," Dick said. "But I thought the guy running it was a complete idiot and a huckster." So, with Verne's help, Dick bought it. He changed the name to U.S. Filter, aiming for something that sounded iconic and successful, a name that they would be forced to grow into, and he quickly set to work turning the company around and building it up through acquisitions.

"It was a really simple thing to me," Dick said. "I understand water. And I understand it's important. And because I was a stockbroker, I can tell you who the major steel company is, the biggest car company, the biggest toy company, the biggest bio company, the biggest fucking drug company. You can live without all that shit. Five days without water, and you're a dead duck. Who's the biggest water company? In 1989, if you believed that water was going to be an ever more important factor in your life and the life of your business and your city and your state, there was no way for you to make that money. How can it possibly be that the market was so inefficient that it missed it?"

———

My desk phone rang just before noon. "Chris Varelas."

"My life sucks."

I knew only one person who started phone calls that way—Mark Davis, a Salomon coverage banker out in Los Angeles. A former college baseball player, he always had a funny story to tell about the pitfalls of day-to-day life. "What's happening this time?" I asked.

"My wife wants to move the pool."

"The swimming pool? Is it an aboveground?"

"Fuck no," he shouted. "It's a goddamn pool in the ground, and she decided she wants to move it to the other side of the yard. Better sun or some shit."

"How do you move a pool?"

"V, that's the fucking question of the year. She thinks you can just pick the pool up and move it. I keep trying to explain that you have to fill in the old pool and dig a new one. It's not a simple thing. It's expensive. She doesn't give a fuck. 'Just shut up and move it,' she says. Anyway, how are you?"

"Great. I'm not moving any pools."

"Count your blessings. So listen, I spoke with Caesar." Caesar Sweitzer was another coverage banker, based in New York. I'd always liked both him and Mark, but we rarely had a chance to work together, since we focused on different sectors. "We've got a proposition for you. It's a little sensitive." The volume of Mark's voice dropped considerably during that last sentence and was replaced by a lot of background office noise and faint sirens in the distance. He said something I didn't catch.

"Are you still there, Mark?"

"Yeah," he said, back at full volume, "I'm here, V. Sorry, this is a little sensitive."

"I understand. Shoot." I switched the phone to my other ear.

"You're from Orange County, right?" He was speaking in a harsh whisper, and I could barely make out what he was saying.

"Did you say Orange County? Yeah, I'm from there."

"Good, good. Are you a preservative?" Someone started cackling in the background.

"What's that, Mark? Preservative?"

"*Con*-servative, V. *Con*."

I was fairly sure he'd said "conservative." The sirens on his end had gotten louder, and it sounded like someone at his office was badly singing opera for an impatient audience.

"What's going on over there, Mark? I can't hear you too great."

Long hiss, then Mark's voice returned: "V, you there? Can you hear me? We need an M&A guy on the U.S. Filter account."

U.S. Filter . . . I recalled what little I knew about the water company— growing quickly through acquisitions, a boisterous CEO, that was about it. Maybe Mark had said *conservationist*? They could be trying to tap water resources in a protected area of Orange County. But why would they want my opinion? I was an M&A guy.

"Did you say 'conservationist'?" I asked, raising my voice against the static.

Mark responded with something that sounded like, "Right—lurp."

"Sure," I said. "I like hiking and that sort of thing. I've never exactly identified as a conservationist, but yeah, I guess I am." The sirens grew louder, as if Mark's building were on fire. "Why do you ask?"

"Hiking? What the fuck are you talking about, V?" The cackler cranked back up, making Mark even harder to hear. "I'm furious about the deluge. Are you gay?"

"Sorry, what?" I pressed the phone into my ear. "You're not coming through clearly. Will you repeat that?"

"Can you hear me, V? Are you gay?"

"Am I *gay*?"

"Yeah. We need a guy—" Long stretch of noise, like the wrong radio frequency.

"I don't know if you can hear me"—I was nearly shouting into the receiver at this point—*"and I'm not sure what you're asking, but I'm not gay."*

The line went dead.

I set down the phone and looked up to find several people around the office staring at me. "Bad connection," I said with a shrug, as they turned away.

I later caught up with Mark and Caesar and got some clarity. "We think you'd be a good fit for this account," Mark explained, "and I was just doing my diligence to see if there was anything we didn't know about." Dick Heckmann was a known ultraconservative. Caesar and Mark were aware that I'd spent my teenage years in Orange County—known for its large population of conservative, wealthy Libertarians—so they figured that would provide a welcome association for Heckmann.

"That should be easy," I said. "One mention of working at Disneyland and we should be okay."

I liked Mark and Caesar, and despite the fact that I was more than busy running the technology M&A effort as the dotcom industry continued to explode, working with those guys on U.S. Filter sounded like a fun side project. So I found myself on a plane for Palm Springs, headed out to present some acquisition ideas.

———

Andy Seidel had the longest tongue anyone had ever seen. The great thing about Andy was that, even though he was COO of what was fast becoming a massive and successful water company, he had no problem showing his tongue. Dick Heckmann never tired of insisting that Andy roll it out for the amusement of others.

Dick was like the rowdy and unpredictable yet affable president of the frat house. He loved to remind everyone of the unglamorous start to Andy's career. "His job out of Wharton was to make the license-plate manufacturing more efficient at Sing Sing Prison. How would you like that job? Anything is an upgrade from there. He called me from a pay phone outside of Sing Sing, and I convinced him to come and meet me. I loved Andy from the beginning." It was actually Soledad State Prison in California, where Andy was working for a consulting company that helped improve the prisoner furniture-manufacturing process—a bit less dramatic than making license plates at Sing Sing, but Dick had a flair for the theatrical.

Andy flew to Sun Valley to meet Dick and discuss a job. "We go to dinner," Andy recalled, "and he's walking through the room saying hello to Nancy Kerrigan and Arnold Schwarzenegger. He didn't introduce me to them. But it was like he knew them as best friends. And I remember that was my first impression: *This guy knows everybody.*"

When Dick acquired the struggling American Toxxic Control with visions of building it into an empire, he began assembling a small team of senior executives to help him. In one of my first meetings with him, he mentioned the names of some of his staff, and nearly all of them were familiar. "Wait," I said. "Did these guys go to Wharton?"

"Yeah," Dick said.

"Have you seen Andy Seidel's tongue?"

"His tongue?" Dick grinned. "I can't say I have."

"When you get back to the office, ask him to show you."

"Don't tell me you're another Wharton graduate," Dick said.

"I went to school with all your guys."

"How about that?" Dick was impressed, even though a Wharton diploma was as common as an Asprey briefcase in the world of business and finance.

"He was one of these guys who had degree envy," Andy said. "Instead of introducing me as 'Andy Seidel, the COO,' he would introduce me as 'Andy Seidel, undergraduate Penn engineer with a Wharton MBA, smartest guy I know.' He was very status-conscious. He would make those kinds of comments, but he was very respectful internally, and I was always flattered by the way that he would introduce us to people."

Among U.S. Filter's group of Wharton MBAs, Andy served as the main yin to Dick's yang. While Dick was the sizzle, Andy was the substance; Dick was volatility, Andy was stability—and that sort of counterbalance was crucial for success. When meeting with prospective investors or Wall Street analysts, Dick would dazzle them with stories and grand visions for his water empire, then Andy would walk them through the data and explain how it all actually worked.

"Dick would say the pithy things," Andy recalled, "make everybody laugh and feel good, and then we would come in to talk technology and calm everybody down, so they would know it's not just this comedian in front of them; it's some real technology. I was always brought in to add realism. I was recently looking at some of my notes from when I prepared for analyst meetings, and I noticed mine were all very technical: 'Here's the EBITDA growth; here's the organic growth.' That was my role."

Dick became legendary for his performances on road shows—the tours on which CEOs pitch their story to potential investors. He enjoyed the spotlight. "Wayne Huizenga had Blockbuster hotter than a motherfucker," Dick recalled. "And that was the same time we were hot. Wayne and I would follow each other at analysts' conferences. I mean, we'd have people hanging out the doors, sitting on the floor in front of us, down the sides in the aisles. At Raymond James they'd always schedule us one after another; nobody would leave because they were both great stories. You know, his Blockbuster story was fabulous—until Netflix."

But there was no Netflix coming to disrupt U.S. Filter's tightening grasp on the water industry. With Wall Street's love for Dick and his captivating story, U.S. Filter was expanding rapidly.

I sometimes attended those same conferences, meeting with one client or another, and whenever I saw Dick's name on the schedule, I would try to shift meetings in order to catch his presentation. He had no shortage of evangelical zeal for water. Like an itinerant preacher, he would travel the country to spread the good word, meeting with various funds—Fidelity, Wellington, pension funds, institutional investors of all types, basically anyone who might buy large blocks of equity. He would talk with any investor who would listen, proselytizing to the equity markets about why U.S. Filter was going to create long-term value.

Whether Dick was speaking to a big crowd or dining with Wall Street bankers, he enchanted his audiences with water stories:

"Look at that table. Everything on it is our product. Everything on the table. I mean, this is really simple. You can't live without us."

"When Minnesota flushes, Iowa drinks it, because it's coming down the Mississippi. The great thing about our product is that every single person who's using water, and every manufacturer of products, is generating wastewater. Once you use it and send it down the pipe, whatever you washed or cleaned or whatever you did, it's in the water. So now why don't you let us fix your water?"

"Water is fucking simple. We've been treating it since the Egyptians. Nothing will ever be found in water that we don't know about and that hasn't been found before."

"The majority of the planet's freshwater is trapped in the polar ice caps. There's not another drop on this Earth more than when it formed or will be here when it blows up. This is a closed-loop system. Everything you drink is somebody else's wastewater by definition. Ultimately we'll have a pipe that goes right from the toilet to the tap. Yeah, sure, you'll have to cool it down. . . ." The audience would roar with laughter.

Once an investor asked him, "What's your strategic plan? Where do you see taking U.S. Filter?" And Dick replied: "I stamp out strategic planning wherever I find it in this company. We gotta be opportunistic, flexible. Our mission is to become the biggest water company in the world. That's our strategic plan."

Dick pitched his story again and again—followed by Andy and his team providing the technical and financial substance—and together they converted skeptical investors into true believers, which kept the stock price soaring, allowing U.S. Filter to keep acquiring smaller companies, rolling up the industry. Andy said: "U.S. Filter was a roll-up in a very fragmented industry. At a high level in the United States, you have eighty thousand municipalities that treat water, then you have tens of thousands of industrial users who use different levels of treated water—they either do wastewater treatment prior to discharge into a stream, or they're generating very high-purity water in the case of the semiconductor industry. So your two generic customer bases are municipal and industrial, hugely fragmented. It was very expensive to work with lots of companies who could serve all these needs. U.S. Filter was the first company that came along with this vision of building an integrated service and technology platform where we could go to Intel and say, 'We'll sell you not only the high-purity water for making semiconductor chips, but we'll also sell you a system to treat your wastewater prior to discharge, and guess what, we'll service it.' And so U.S. Filter really changed the way the water industry works."

They struck lucrative deals with numerous big companies such as Starbucks, devising a system that would make the local tap water taste the same at every franchise location on the planet, so they could swear by the consistency of their Skinny Hazelnut Frappuccinos, whether it was ordered in Brooklyn or Beaumont. Similar relationships were set up with Budweiser and Miller breweries and with the Johnson Wax factory. With all these companies, the central ingredient in their products was water; U.S. Filter could ensure that their water would always be identical in every production facility. Dick bought a huge stake in the water rights to the Colorado River, one of the most important sources for California's agriculture and for the metropolitan areas of Los Angeles and San Diego. (His pitch to his investors was that, with these water rights, they would be able to "turn profits on and off, as needed, like a fucking faucet.") Additionally, they worked with scientists to devise a wildly ambitious plan to desalinate and clean up the heavily polluted Salton Sea, with visions of restoring the area as a tourist destination. There was no opportunity too bold or outrageous for U.S. Filter to pursue. Through a combination of nerve and voraciousness, Dick Heckmann was on his way to building the largest water empire the world had ever seen.

———

Then something curious happened: The company started running out of targets. U.S. Filter had taken over so many smaller companies—an astonishing 250-plus acquisitions in less than a decade, including 22 acquisitions during its busiest single quarter, which calculated to roughly 2 per week—that there wasn't much left to roll up and tuck under its umbrella. If U.S. Filter's growth slowed down, however, its stock would get hammered. It was up against a formidable menace—the tyranny of quarterly earnings expectations.

Here's how it works: Through regular quarterly phone calls or meetings, a company discusses its financial outlook with Wall Street equity analysts so those analysts can report earnings estimates. The company is essentially making a sales pitch, trying to impress the analysts with an outlook as convincingly optimistic as possible, then each analyst puts out a rating—a *buy*, a *neutral*, or a *sell*—along with a stock price target. The analysts say, "Here's what we think this company's earnings are going to be for the upcoming quarter and year." The public market investment community will then form a consensus view from all the analysts' projections, and that'll be the expected earnings for the company.

When the earnings actually come in, the stock price will go up or down based on two things: first, how the company did in relation to the expectations; and second, what the revised earnings and growth projections are for the next quarter. In order to keep its stock price soaring, a company consistently has to beat the estimate for the current quarter and raise the estimate for the next quarter—beating and raising, beating and raising, beating and raising.

U.S. Filter understood that plateauing or slowing its growth was not an option. A flame of panic flickered through the company, an urgency to figure out how to maintain its pace of expansion. All of a sudden, after so many years of success, U.S. Filter seemed to be always at risk of missing a quarter, but with a blend of luck and determination, it somehow kept the whole thing moving down the tracks.

One quarter, the company was saved from the train wreck by a literal train wreck. "We had a plant in Whittier," Dick said, "where we manufactured this huge water-treatment product to go on a Marathon oil rig in the Gulf. They were in a hurry, and we got it all done, but it was so big that it couldn't move through LA except between midnight and four in the morning, so it wouldn't hold up traffic. It was on a special truck that Marathon had made. So they pull out of the plant at midnight. Ten minutes down the street they high-center it on a railroad track, and a Union Pacific train hit it going fifty miles an hour. Splattered this shit everywhere. The driver luckily saw it coming and got out of the cab before the train hit it."

This could have been a tragedy for U.S. Filter, having its expensive, newly built equipment destroyed by a speeding train. It could have missed its quarter based on this event alone. But once the water-treatment equipment had rolled out of the plant, the responsibility sat squarely on the shoulders of Marathon Oil.

"And so," Andy said, "our finance department basically says, 'That's not bad news; that's fucking great news.' They had insurance, and Marathon asked us to build another one exactly the same, because they couldn't float this platform without this piece of equipment. So not only did we get the insurance payment, but we also got an order accelerated for a replacement, so we could take all the inventory in the shop, charge it to the job, take earnings on the project—and that's all legal."

"So we did it and had a great quarter," Dick said. "Nick Memmo [an executive VP at Filter] is in Boston and sees the numbers. He calls and says, 'How did you engineer that train wreck?' It made the year. It was just crazy shit."

When they couldn't rely on train wrecks, the management team had to keep meeting Wall Street expectations through even more creative and bold acquisition ideas. Dick set his sights on Culligan, the legendary company known to thirsty housewives and every office worker who has gossiped around a water cooler. Culligan specialized in water bottling, softening, and filtration. "The Culligan Man"—depicted in commercials as a handsome, old-school delivery guy—was an American icon. In the world of water, Culligan's name recognition made it a sexy asset, but it was an audacious acquisition target for Dick and U.S. Filter, partly because of its size, and also because U.S. Filter had always planted its flag in the industrial and commercial spaces, and now it would be making a leap into the unfamiliar territories of consumer and residential.

But Dick, armed with a new idea, was like a mighty and unpredictable weather system, and indeed working with him resembled tornado chasing. I often felt as though we were meteorologists in a van, racing along the freeways with camcorders and clipboards, trying to follow Dick's capricious impulses. His attention could switch directions on a dime. There was an exciting intensity about the way he did business, but it could also prove destructive.

For one thing, he usually insisted on doing his own deal negotiating, striding alone into highly sensitive meetings to haggle over price and terms. It was seldom a good practice to send in the CEO without his M&A experts, legal counsel, and analysts, but Dick's outsized personality didn't leave much room for discussion.

That was what happened with the Culligan meeting. We met at Culligan's lawyers' offices in New York to discuss the transaction, and Dick demanded that he meet alone with Marc Rowan from Apollo, the private-equity firm that owned Culligan. Before the meeting, Caesar Sweitzer, Mark Davis, and I cornered Dick in our conference room, with the help of Filter's chief legal officer, Damian Georgino, and we all begged Dick not to pay more than $54 per share. He smirked as he reached for the door handle.

"Dick," Caesar repeated with some urgency. Dick turned and looked him in the eye. "I recognize that if you'd always listened to me, U.S. Filter would still be a tiny, worthless company, because I would have talked you out of every deal, and I know you want Culligan, but we need to stay firm at fifty-four. Promise me you will walk away if they demand more. Okay?" No reply. "Okay?"

"Fine, fine," Dick said with a dismissive wave. "Fifty-four. Got it."

As soon as Dick left the room, we started betting on how far over $54 he would go. The consensus was that he might go all the way to $56 per share, but we sincerely hoped he wouldn't. Damian leaned back in a rolling chair and looked out the window. As Filter's legal counsel, he had to worry about the details of the contract, and he was always concerned about price when Dick went into a negotiation. At most companies, the legal counsel would have attended every important meeting, but by then Damian was used to Dick shutting everyone out of the room. My role, as the M&A advisor, was to determine what companies U.S. Filter should target for acquisition and the best tactics to acquire them, as well as to oversee the analysis that determined the valuation of the target company—concluding, in this case, that we shouldn't pay more than approximately $54 per share. Finally, I would typically handle the negotiations at the table. As the coverage bankers, Caesar and Mark would handle the client relations, advising Dick on how best to raise money and fund his operations. They had worked with Dick on countless acquisitions, and most of those deals had made Caesar and Mark somewhat anxious, but on Culligan the stakes were drastically higher. A per-share increase of each dollar would translate into a giant leap in the perceived price U.S. Filter had to pay to get the deal done.

So we waited in our conference room like nervous friends in a maternity ward, hoping everything would go all right and there would soon be occasion to light cigars. We weren't worried about the baby being born—we expected there would be a deal—we just didn't want the baby to be ugly.

After half an hour, Dick burst through the double doors of the conference room with a big shit-eating grin on his face.

"Don't hate me." That was the first thing he said.

We let out a collective groan.

We already knew what he'd done, but Caesar asked anyway, wanting to know the degree of the problem. "Why would we hate you, Dick?"

"Sixty." Dick had gone over by $6 per share, which, in the full scope of the deal, added up to a price increase of well over $100 million, which was not insignificant given a deal size of roughly $1.5 billion.

Our pleasure at acquiring such a huge asset for U.S. Filter was dampened by the outrageous price.

Dick expected to have been met with more enthusiasm. "Come on, guys," he said, smiling, trying to soothe our worries but also unable to mask his excitement over closing the deal. "I know I paid more than you wanted, but it's *worth* it. This is Culligan, and now we own it! We're going to be fine."

Mark's hands covered his face as he spoke. "This is not good."

"I don't think I can get this through our fairness committee meeting," Caesar muttered.

"Look," Dick said, starting to sound defensive, "I'm not some idiot. The deal is accretive to earnings. Do the math, okay? Our earnings are going up."

Mark raised his head. "Yeah, that might be true this year and *maybe* next year, but in the future—"

"Mark," Dick said, squeezing his shoulder. "I'll worry about the future in the future. We're fine, okay? Let's go get steaks."

Andy Seidel wasn't present at negotiations, but he didn't hesitate to describe why he thought the Culligan deal, and others like it, signaled trouble for U.S. Filter. "The law of large numbers was catching up to us, and we just couldn't grow the business to meet expectations. And what that necessitated was doing the next biggest deal to set up accounting reserves, and there weren't any big deals to do anymore, so we started doing crazy-ass things." By this point, U.S. Filter was buying whatever companies it could, simply to keep ahead of the demands of quarterly earnings expectations. "Culligan really didn't fit with our core pursuit. We also bought a company called Kinetics, which had nothing to do with what we did. So we were having to stretch ourselves into bigger and bigger deals so we could look like we were growing organically. Analysts loved organic growth, because *anyone* could just buy companies. Every roll-up company eventually runs into this problem."

Dick also understood the challenge. "These roll-up strategies," he told the *New York Times*, "run into trouble when they run out of things to roll up."

———

In closing Culligan, Dick believed the deal would ultimately be a win. Yes, he paid more than we advised, more than the determined value of the company. But the determined value wasn't nearly as important, in this case, as having the guts to take the risk, step up, and go for it—a familiar motif in business and finance.

"It was simple," Dick recalled, "but none of the bankers thought about it. There was only one company in the United States at the time that could have blocked me or run the prices up or competed with me—and it was Culligan. I got them out of the game. I didn't fucking care what it cost; everything else was going to be cheap because there wasn't any other buyer. And it was a great brand."

Whatever way you looked at it, Culligan was a hell of an acquisition. But once the dust had settled, we found ourselves in the same difficult corner: Consistent growth was becoming impossible, as the sea of potential acquisition targets dried up.

We needed to find a buyer and get out while the company was still riding high, which meant selling U.S. Filter before it hit the wall of slowing growth. Dick resisted with everything he had. He had built U.S. Filter from the scraps of American Toxxic Control into a kingdom over which he held dominion. He didn't want to give it up. But there was simply no way to keep meeting Wall Street's unforgiving earnings expectations. Our insistence finally struck home, and Dick agreed to explore a sale of the company.

In building U.S. Filter, Dick had been in the business of selling hope, peddling an abstract idea that a powerful industry could be created around water, that he was the guy to do it, and that this was the right time. Like all visionaries, he was imagining a future that hadn't yet arrived. The investing world, which loves to finance hope, backed the vision. Dick had the talent and willpower to pull it off—with the help of his gifted team—meeting expectations quarter after quarter and steering enormous growth. So that initial seed of an idea became a reality. But then at some point he was confronted with the inevitability that it couldn't be sustained, that he was going to fall short. Wall Street's quarterly earnings expectations were too impossibly demanding to satisfy forever. Eventually Filter would miss a quarter, and when it did, the bottom would fall out. Dick—the great salesman—needed to find one last believer. He went from selling the vision of U.S. Filter to millions of people to selling it to one man. And that one man was Jean-Marie Messier.

In the French business world, Jean-Marie Messier was king. He was a handsome and well-dressed jetsetter who kept a $17.5 million apartment in Manhattan. His company owned the flagship restaurant of chef Alain Ducasse, one of the most glamorous spots in Paris, where Messier regularly held business meetings over long, luxurious meals in the private dining rooms. At age thirty-nine, Messier had ascended to the top role at Vivendi, a huge French multinational conglomerate focused on entertainment, telecom, and utilities. He introduced a lot of bold ideas for how to diversify and grow the company.

Like Dick, Messier was an ambitious entrepreneur who would sometimes let his appetite rule over his better judgment. Like Dick, he overflowed with charisma and grand visions. But there were fundamental differences between the two men as well. Messier had studied at the best schools and risen to the pinnacle of the French business world at a very young age. He had refined tastes and an impeccable wardrobe. His company, Vivendi, was almost a century and a half old, founded in 1853 by imperial decree of Napoleon III. Dick, on the other hand, was a self-made man. He had dropped out of school and then catapulted himself to success by sheer will, inventing his own history when necessary, erecting his empire from the rubble of a struggling company. Messier was the embodiment of the old republic of France; Dick was pure USA. Despite these differences, they hit it off splendidly and started meeting to explore the possibility of Vivendi acquiring U.S. Filter.

Vivendi's business model resembled a three-legged stool: entertainment, telecom, and utilities. Its entertainment leg was centered on a recent acquisition of Seagram's, which came packaged up with Universal Studios and Music Group. Vivendi's telecom leg boasted an arsenal of valuable assets. But the third leg of the stool, its water and waste division, was weaker. This had once been the core of its business—it had started a century and a half earlier as a water company called Compagnie Générale des Eaux—and so Messier was searching for a key acquisition that would bolster the company's utilities leg. U.S. Filter could be just the thing, and it would also give the French a stronger foothold across the Atlantic. Messier wanted it. He was a big-picture guy, always thinking ahead to how these various elements of Vivendi could harmonize into something truly great.

"You look out this window and see the Eiffel Tower," Dick recalled of Vivendi's board meetings, "and the Arc is one block away, and Alain Ducasse would prepare lunch, with everybody waiting on us wearing tuxedos. So the Seagram's guys come in, with Stacey Snider and Ron Meyer from Universal Studios; and then Jimmy Iovine, the music guy, comes in in fucking leather pants, hat on backward. There's the SFR cell phone company and Canal+, which is the HBO of Europe. They do this dog-and-pony show, which they were really good at. All these things were supposed to come together. Messier had this convergence idea—that Universal would teach Canal+ how to make decent movies and then we'd stream it all through the cell phones. It was brilliant. He was just five years early. Everything he said would happen has happened. Everything."

"That's why he bought Bertelsmann," Andy Seidel said, "the German publishing company, and Universal Studios—to get a corner on content. He'd talk about how people would be able to read books and watch movies on their cell phones. But at the time, cell phones were these little piece-of-shit Nokia things, and we're all like, *Oh my god. This guy's a fucking nut.* But he was right on the fucking money. It's crazy how on the money he was, and how we would just roll in the aisles, tears pouring down our faces, laughing at the idea that you would watch a movie on a cell phone. Messier was a true visionary. He was just way too early."

———

In late 1998, I started jetting back and forth to Paris with Dick, working on the deal. Up to that point, I knew that U.S. Filter had been equal parts creative and aggressive about meeting its quarterly earnings expectations, but as someone outside the company, I wasn't entirely aware of how desperate the struggle had become to maintain such ambitious growth. Dick would never let on that the ship was at risk of sinking. "Like all great entrepreneurs," Andy said, "he believed there was a better day around the corner. He was an eternal optimist."

U.S. Filter's value wasn't quite what it seemed to Wall Street analysts, and there was one main reason for that—a totally legal accounting practice called *pooling*, which since 2001 is no longer allowed. "Pooling was phenomenal," Dick said. When he describes the old days, he leans in and speaks with the animated zeal of a pro athlete recounting a championship run. "You could never have done what I did without pooling. And that's why it's never been done again. In today's environment, when you acquire a company, you have to merge the financials together as they stand at the date that you close the deal. So you add their assets to your assets and their liabilities to your liabilities. And if there's some bad news in there, then it comes out, because there is no choice.

"In pooling, there were six or seven tests that you had to meet [such as the requirement to use mostly company stock rather than cash or debt to effectuate the acquisition], and if you met every one of them, you would put the companies together as if they had always been together. So you go back and restate from your first day of operations, as if you had owned the company you acquired for all of that time, which makes it impossible to compare." This allowed companies, during the accounting process of an acquisition, to hide anything negative, essentially resetting their numbers to tell whatever story they chose. "If you wanted to make sure that your next couple of quarters were going to be good, you could reserve in against bad debt, so you're reserving all of this stuff. And they couldn't tell whether that was your accrual or the other company's accrual. The other thing they couldn't tell was what your internal growth was. You're just growing by acquisition, but you could say, 'No, we're growing internally 4 percent a year.' 'How can you prove that?' 'Well, we just know we are.' So pooling gave you the ability to essentially say anything you wanted to say about your business." In essence, pooling allowed a company to reserve a bunch of money that it could access as needed to achieve whatever quarterly financial results it desired.

Hearing pooling described now, it sounds shady. There was a lot of smoke and mirrors. But it's important to note that there was nothing illegal about the practice at the time if it was done correctly. In fact, pooling was a method of accounting for mergers and acquisitions that was initially instituted to provide a financial picture of greater clarity and relevance to investors. There were companies that abused it—such as WorldCom, Waste Management, and Enron—and they were taken down for subverting accounting laws. U.S. Filter took full advantage of the opportunities afforded by pooling, but it never overstepped the legal bounds.

"It was one of the great games of hide the bean," Dick said. "The

bean is there; you just can't find it. That's how General Electric had—
what was it?—thirty quarters in a row of increased earnings. They did
an acquisition every quarter, and they pooled it. So it was a great way in
the '90s to build some of these big companies."

U.S. Filter's 250-plus acquisitions frequently allowed the firm to reset its accounting and paint whatever financial picture was desired. And,
once started, it couldn't stop. It was like eating spicy salsa: As long as you
keep shoveling in chip after chip of the hot stuff, your tongue won't burn.
You might sweat a little, but you can survive the heat and even enjoy it,
as long as you keep it coming.

The problem with pooling, of course, was that when the acquisition
targets began to dry up, sooner or later it would become impossible to
keep meeting earnings expectations because there was no longer a way
to reset your accounting and hide the bean. The truth about a company's
value would surface, and one missed quarter could kill the stock price.
That was precisely the danger that U.S. Filter was facing when, one
night in Manhattan, we pulled up in front of a restaurant in a stretch
limo, and Dick told everyone but me and Rod Garra, our lawyer on the
Vivendi deal, to go wait inside. Dick asked the driver to circle the block
until further notice. Then, after a quiet, tense moment, he turned to Rod
and me and said, "We're not going to hit our quarter."

Neither of us responded right away.

Dick continued, finally letting it all topple out: "Next quarter we've
only got so many acquisitions to make and I'm looking out a year and
our growth rate's going to plummet and there's nothing I can do about it
because we've got the law of large numbers and I don't know where the
fuck the stock goes but it ain't going to stay at twenty-six and a half."

He stopped, took a breath, and looked at us as the limo continued
rolling around the block.

At this sensitive moment in the negotiations with Vivendi, if U.S.
Filter wasn't going to meet its quarterly expectations, the deal would be
at risk. Success depended on the ability to sustain Vivendi's confidence
in U.S. Filter's value until the acquisition was finalized. A new urgency
washed over me. Dick had been dragging his feet on closing the deal,

unwilling to give up his passion and sell the business he had built from nothing, but now there could be no more delays.

When I was sure that he was done talking, I reached inside my jacket for my pen and leaned across the seat and handed it to Dick without a word. He held the pen in his palm for a moment, then laughed. The message was clear: *Sign the fucking papers.*

Soon after, we were in a boardroom in the CBS Building in New York, with about fifteen people on our side of the table facing roughly the same number on Vivendi's side. We discussed and debated the details, but after an hour or more we were still at an impasse, and Dick was clearly growing frustrated with the tedious legal and financial due diligence process. He addressed Messier across the table and asked if he wanted to join him downstairs for dinner.

The bankers and lawyers on both sides got up screaming. "You can't go alone! We have to go with you! It's a multibillion-dollar public deal!"

Dick looked at Messier and said, "I don't know about you, but nobody tells me who I have dinner with. Do you want to go have a bite?"

"Oui," Messier said, "I do."

Dick and Messier left all of us upstairs staring at one another, while the lawyers fumed.

Downstairs, the waiter asked if they'd like a bottle of wine. Dick pointed to an item on the wine list. "We'd like a bottle of Opus One," he said.

As the waiter was opening the bottle, Messier asked, "Why did you order *that* wine?"

"Because it is the collaboration of your greatest winery and ours, Rothschild and Mondavi. They came together to make a great bottle of wine, and I think we should come together to make a great bottle of water."

Dick and Messier tapped glasses and agreed to a deal right there at dinner.

"Let's go!" Dick yelled toward the cockpit. "Let's get the fuck out of here!" We were in Paris tying up the final strings of the deal. Dick was in high spirits and already on his second appletini in the fifteen minutes since we boarded Filter's corporate jet for the flight back to the States. (Dick had insisted that the deal include an agreement that Vivendi would pay all expenses for his jet, and somehow they consented.) "*Six billion dollars* in an all-cash deal. Are you fucking kidding me? We'll be shitting French francs out the exhaust pipe the whole way home!" The plane accelerated for takeoff.

After the deal closed, Vivendi combined U.S. Filter with its water and waste departments, and, as part of the agreement, Dick took a seat on the Vivendi board of directors. Once Vivendi realized that it had overpaid for U.S. Filter, of course that created some tension. But when asked about it later, Dick, like most manically optimistic visionaries, couldn't recall a single combative moment between him and Messier— only the positive memories remained—but the story we all heard was that Messier confronted Dick after the full scope of the deal came to light, saying, "I thought we were partners and friends."

Dick replied, "At that time, Jean-Marie, we were on opposite sides of the table." Eventually, they did become friends and have helped each other out on numerous occasions over the years.

Despite Dick's elation at closing the deal, he was, in a sense, giving up on his dream. He always viewed U.S. Filter as a great asset, and so he never saw Messier as a sucker. Dick begrudgingly relinquished the company. The interminable challenge of meeting Wall Street's earnings expectations every quarter proved exhausting and, in the end, impossible. Such is the complicated relationship between Wall Street and the visionary entrepreneur—Wall Street loves to finance hope and an exciting story, but then it suffocates the entrepreneur with an avalanche of unreasonable expectations. So Dick escaped just before he was crushed, but he always believed Filter was a great company and would continue to be one.

Andy Seidel, who stepped in as CEO of U.S. Filter, saw it differently. Andy was saddled with most of the fallout after the French realized that the full state of affairs hadn't been revealed during negotiations, even though the French had full ability to scrutinize U.S.

Filter's projections during months of due diligence on the company. "Dick's hubris got us to this point where it's fourth down and fifty, and we had to complete a pass," Andy later said. "And we ran into the greater fool at exactly the right time, and that's what made the deal break. Let's say that we didn't find Vivendi. What would've happened? It would've been a disaster." So Andy had a mess on his hands, but he did a great job running the company and quickly earned the respect of Vivendi's senior management.

In business, so much of success and failure comes down to timing. Dick's was impeccable. He built a water empire at the perfect moment when all the stars were aligned around him—he launched it at the right time, when no one else was looking at water as a potentially profitable industry; he built the company up through pooling acquisitions, just before pooling was no longer allowed; the markets were booming during Filter's ascension; and once the demands of quarterly earnings expectations weighed too heavily on the company, he exited like Indiana Jones sprinting out of a collapsing temple.

Jean-Marie Messier, on the other hand, was undoubtedly a visionary, but he failed because of horrible timing. If he had brought his bold ideas together five years later—for a global media empire in which Hollywood and French culture would converge, distributed through mobile streaming—once the technology and consumer habits had caught up with his prophetic understanding of the future, he might have been hailed as a sort of French Steve Jobs. Yet he was too early, and he also ran face-first into the dotcom crash. So instead of being a hero, Messier became a cautionary tale, a symbol of corporate excess and recklessness. It wasn't the Filter acquisition alone that ruined him, but that was certainly one more bad domino to topple against him, eventually leading to his fall from grace. Once the favorite son of France, Messier was forced to resign, charged with share-price manipulation, fraud, and abuse of company funds. On appeal, his sentence was reduced from three years in prison to a suspended sentence of ten months and a fine of $70,000. After his downfall, Messier quietly rebuilt his life. He now works as a business consultant.

So why does one guy nail the timing, while another ends in bankruptcy or handcuffs? Is it chance? Is it talent? Is it pragmatism combined with foresight? Is there an instinct for when to throw in the towel? Was Messier really the greater fool, or was he just unlucky?

While several events and missteps ultimately led to Messier's ruin, Dick's explanation is much simpler. Dick was friends with Richard Grasso, who ran the New York Stock Exchange, and Dick helped Messier get a seat on the NYSE board. Immediately after the terrorist attacks on September 11, 2001, the markets were plummeting, and Grasso was desperate to avoid an all-out panic. "Grasso called all of the CEOs of the major companies that were listed on the Exchange," Dick recalled, "and Vivendi was one of them, and he said, 'I need you to be there when I open the Exchange to buy stock, because if you're not there to buy stock, this thing is going into the tank.' Messier is such a good guy and he's such an emotional guy that that resonated with him. He went into the bank market in Paris and borrowed $5 billion and bought in his stock at between $60 and $70 a share. And then it went to $14, and he couldn't pay the debt back, and that's when he got in trouble in France. He borrowed the money, and he didn't have board approval because it was happening in real time. But he did it for all of the right reasons. If it hadn't been for 9/11, he would have been a hero."

Dick takes the credit for getting Vivendi listed on the NYSE, which had been a dream of Messier's. And in order to get it done, the accounting rules for Europe and America needed to be standardized, which meant effectively getting rid of pooling in the United States. "I was the guy that killed pooling in order to get Vivendi listed," Dick said, seemingly unaware of the beautiful circular irony of it: Dick killed pooling to help Vivendi, and yet Dick's opportunistic use of pooling had facilitated the rise and ultimate acquisition of U.S. Filter by Vivendi.

Pooling had allowed companies like U.S. Filter and GE to go many, many quarters in a row beating and raising expectations. But today, years after the death of pooling, the markets continue to believe and demand that steep, consistent growth can be maintained over an extended period of time, even though companies no longer have the tools to beat and raise, quarter after quarter. That, in turn, puts pressure on management teams to think very short term, focusing on the results for each quarter, rather than looking at long-term objectives. To meet a quarter's earnings expectations, a company may be forced to close a sale quickly, settling for a lower price and worse terms, or, more concerning, to pursue less profitable business lines because they provide more immediate revenue opportunities. Thus, management teams might not have the ability to commit to maximizing shareholder value overall, but, rather, they must focus on maximizing *quarterly* shareholder value, and those two things are seldom aligned.

When quarterly reporting requirements were first instituted in 1970, proponents pointed to the need for more transparency to safeguard investors, particularly individuals who may not have had the same access to information as an institutional investor. It was a way to level the playing field. It's hard to imagine anyone could have predicted how those well-intentioned changes might have evolved into what they are today. For companies, what began as a healthy long-term pursuit of organic growth was bastardized by those who pushed the limits with methodologies— some legal and some not—that facilitated growth patterns beyond the normal workings of a company. The GEs, U.S. Filters, and Enrons conditioned the public markets to believe and expect that a company could forever beat and raise expectations, quarter by quarter. And we've been unable to return to a time of proper motivations and responses—it seems that our financial DNA has been altered.

Today, there are fewer and fewer public companies—close to half the number from the peak. More companies are choosing to remain private, forsaking the benefits of going public in order to avoid the costs and pressures of public reporting. This has many implications, particularly in regard to investor access. Private companies are much harder for the average investor to access directly, which restricts those opportunities to private equity firms, the purview of institutions and wealthy individuals. So what we've gained in transparency, we've lost in broader access to investment opportunities. In this way, the democratic public exchange of stock has been diminished by the market's insistence that companies meet and raise their quarterly expectations.

————

A few months after we closed the deal with Vivendi, I strolled through the front gates of the Wet 'n' Wild Water Park in Palm Springs. I lowered my head and let a woman in a floral bikini put a lei around my neck. Typically, when a company celebrates having been acquired, the closing party is a formal dinner with a dozen or so people, senior management, a few lawyers, and the bankers who executed the deal. But that was too dull for Dick, so he rented out the water park for the night, hired the Beach Boys, and gathered about three hundred people, all wearing Hawaiian shirts—U.S. Filter employees, lawyers, bankers, and various associates who had helped the company over the years. He found the women through a rent-a-model agency. Vivendi was footing the bill, so, Dick figured, why not go large? No one would ever accuse him of being frugal or reserved.

Classic Southern California beach-party fare was served—burgers, hot dogs, and booze. One of Dick's gifts for each guest was a T-shirt depicting a fish engaged in coitus with a frog. The cartoon illustration was tricky to pull off anatomically, but the metaphor was clear: U.S. Filter and the Americans had had their way with Vivendi and the French frogs. Emblazoned on the shirt in French was *Merci pour le bon temps!* (which translates as "Thanks for the good time!").

Andy overheard a conversation at the bar between Steve Wirtel, Filter's VP of sales, and Beach Boys frontman Mike Love.

"Man," the musician said, "is it hot here? We had to practice all afternoon. It was hot as shit."

"Wait a minute," Steve said, "why do you guys have to practice? You've been doing this for like forty years."

Mike Love said, "Oh, it's the drugs."

Dick pranced through the crowd with a cocktail in a plastic cup, saying hello to people, grinning and gesturing toward the band. A contingent of revelers did the twist, and Andy recalled "a lot of bad white-people-type dancing on the stage." After enduring a ten-year race against market expectations, scores of acquisitions, train wrecks, and near misses, capped off with a legendary sale to the French, people were cutting loose as if they hadn't tasted alcohol or heard live music since they were in college.

Dick climbed onto the stage to address the crowd. "He was just loving life at that point," Andy said. "I don't exactly remember what he said—we all were a little wasted—but I think he put his arm around Mike Love, like he knew him forever, and said something like, 'My best friend Mike Love and I, we've gone through a lot. And U.S. Filter means so much to me, and I'm so glad that he could come here and play. What a great way to end the epic story of a Southern California company. We're rock stars.' Something like that. I remember thinking at the time that it was a great way to close out this crazy run. Dick was good at that stuff, at the gesture, at making things memorable."

The party continued late into the night. Every so often, someone was unceremoniously hunted down and tossed into one of the pools. "I remember some of the bigger guys grabbing me," Andy said, "and they told me, 'You can either go in easy, or you can go in hard.' I gave up and they just threw me in. I mean, people were completely shitfaced, following around those models like they were the Pied Piper."

I stood off to the side with a beer and watched the scene, taking the opportunity to think back on the wild couple of years working with U.S. Filter. The way they acquired scores of businesses and then ultimately sold to the French just before the bottom fell out, I couldn't help but question what was required to be a good steward of a public company in the modern age of finance. The system seemed too demanding and unforgiving, designed to fail or at least to encourage suboptimal behavior. Success required not only a vision and the ability to execute on that vision but also the sense or luck to exit before one's rocket crashed disastrously back to Earth. It seemed to me that our public markets were evolving in an unhealthy direction.

The pressure on management teams to maximize shareholder value should lead to positive long-term outcomes for stakeholders, but that is rarely the case, since management teams are forced to sell their vision in three-month increments, then sell out when they believe they can no longer execute on that serialized vision.

Further troubling was my new awareness of a financial system that seemed to require the constant stretching of the truth. What, I wondered, were the boundaries? Who set those boundaries and for what purpose? Perhaps it didn't matter, since ultimately the winners would be rewarded for their discernment, while the losers would be penalized for buying a failed story. But could our financial system work any other way?

When I started out, I wanted to believe that the system could be based on absolute truth and transparency. Yet that's not how life works. In how many marriages do the spouses know every single detail about each other? How many home sales, car sales, or any sales happen with 100 percent full disclosure? M&A advisors are paid a lot of money to paint clients and deals in the best possible light. We begin with our picture of what the future will be, but then we formulate arguments and narratives that are much more nuanced, influenced by the desire to meet our objectives. Knowing what to push and stretch—and how far—takes significant skill and experience. To an outsider, these seem like shadowy areas of activity. And sure, it's never an acceptable defense or explanation to say, *Listen, kid, that's the way things work in the real world.* We want pure truth. Of course we do. And yet so much in the world is more complicated than that. Intellectually, I appreciated the utility of a system that produces huge value from harnessing the maximization of self-interest by all participants, but, still, the U.S. Filter deal felt extreme, and it had put me in a position I didn't want to be in again. But was that possible in a profession that would seem to demand it?

In the years following the Filter exit, Dick didn't shake the itch to build companies. He took over as CEO of K2 Sports, a company specializing in ski equipment. He performed the same growth feat he had with U.S. Filter—albeit on a smaller scale—multiplying the size of K2 primarily through aggressive acquisitions, creating a roll-up, then selling.

He likes to tell a story about getting a phone call from Coach Holtz when the U.S. Filter–Vivendi acquisition was finalized. From the beginning, Coach had refused any salary from U.S. Filter, agreeing only to take stock options when Dick pressured him to accept something for all his help. Coach woke up one morning to find that his bank account had jumped by several million dollars. "I get this call," Dick said, "and Coach is whispering into the phone. He says, 'Dick, there's something very wrong.' And I said, 'What's the matter?' He said, 'My broker just called me. All this money is in my account from Filter, and we think it's a screwup. I don't want to get taxed for this shit. You got to get this fixed.' I said, 'Coach, that's your stock-option profits.' There was a pause, and then he said, '*That's* what a stock option is?' He had no idea what a stock option was. He was just astounded. About two years later, I took over K2 and called him and said, 'You want to get on the board of K2?' With no hesitation he said, 'Only if I can have stock options.'"

Andy—who is probably the most mixed about the way things ended, since he was left with the postacquisition mess—still can't help but agree that working at U.S. Filter through the 1990s was a career-defining experience. "Hands down, the best thing that ever happened to me professionally, and there's not even a close second. I'm really proud of some of the companies I've put together and run since then, but just the energy at Filter, the excitement of being young and in a Wild West environment with a boss who was a little crazy but would give you wide latitude to run things. Dick could make you feel absolutely on top of the world, and you never wanted to disappoint him, no matter how jaded you were, even in the later days of U.S. Filter. He was a good leader. It was an MBA's wet dream, the fact that you were young and able to do these things with an unimaginable balance sheet and financial capacity, and you got to test your mettle on every kind of operational issue. The managers and I get together every once in a while and just look at each other and we're like, 'My god, how lucky were we?' What a wonderful time to come out of business school and live every dream you could possibly have. Who acquires that many companies in a short period of time and culminates it with an all-cash deal? Are you shitting me? It was incredible; there was nothing like it."

Damian Georgino, who was U.S. Filter's chief legal officer, is one of the former executives who occasionally gather for a reunion, even now, a couple of decades after the Vivendi deal. "Whatever you think about Dick," he said, "his market timing was impeccable. He had a vision, and nobody was going to get in his way. He was a firm believer. Yeah, there was some weird stuff that went on along the way. But at the end of the day, you created something that still exists in several forms today. Veolia [a Vivendi spinoff] is still a water group. And there's the Siemens business, which was sold to AEA, renamed Evoqua, now a public company. And Culligan, HD Supply, all are the progeny, if you will, of U.S. Filter. All are billion-dollar-plus companies. What I learned at Filter—how to build hypergrowth companies, how to finance them, how to manage them, team building—what we achieved at Filter and the friendships we had, that was all led by Dick. Were there some ugly parts? Absolutely. But we built a company that nobody's been able to replicate, that everybody looks to in the water industry as a standard. We keep on searching for those next adventures. But you won't have an environment like we had back in those days again."

I abandoned my post at the fringes of the party and wandered through the crowd. Andy was standing beside a pool, soaking wet, laughing over some lunacy or another with Dick.

It was late, but the party went on. In the kiddie pool, an accountant was engaged in a passionate splash fight with a rent-a-model. The Beach Boys looked washed out, and they must have exhausted their set list by then, but they continued playing. They were getting into some deep cuts.

Song after song, the people of U.S. Filter kept twisting and dancing, a little slower, a little sloppier, as the beer kegs flowed, seemingly never to run dry. A group of lawyers did the Watusi. An office assistant danced the Mashed Potato on stage, right beside Mike Love. One of my own guys from Salomon was doing the Swim by himself in the bushes. Everyone was determined not to miss a step until Wet 'n' Wild pulled the plug and booted us out. Off to my left, a conga line snaked past a tube slide toward the stage. As they bounced through the crowd and into view, I spotted Dick at the front—surfboard shirt, cocktail in hand, feet kicking this way and that, an utterly blissful smile on his face—leading the conga line into the night.

6

SHOOTING AN ELEPHANT

And suddenly I realized that I should have to shoot the elephant after all. The people expected it of me and I had got to do it; I could feel their two thousand wills pressing me forward, irresistibly.

—GEORGE ORWELL

When Tom Smach landed at JFK and turned on his phone, his voicemail was full. Usually a bad sign. He had just flown in from China and hadn't gotten much sleep on the plane, so he shuffled toward customs and immigration with the rest of the jet-lagged herd, wondering what could have happened to inspire dozens of voice messages during his time in the air. Signs posted along the walls reminded him that using a cell phone was strictly prohibited.

So Tom waited, making guesses at what had caused the flood of calls and texts. As a senior VP of finance at Flextronics, he was scheduled to ring the Nasdaq opening bell with his colleagues the next morning on live TV, a celebratory moment in recognition of their tenth anniversary as a publicly traded company. A handful of senior people from the company were already in New York waiting for him. His phone rattled in his pocket again. He fished it out and stole a quick peek. A text message from his buddy in the finance office: "Where the fuck are you?" Short and sweet. Or was it ominous and urgent? In his exhausted state, Tom couldn't decide. He really wanted to dig into the messages to figure out what was happening, but ever since September 11, people were jumpy in airports—especially in New York. Everyone was on alert, eager for an opportunity to play the hero, so Tom obeyed the posted signs and slipped his phone back into his pocket. The endless banks of fluorescent lights buzzed and blurred above him. He needed sleep.

He figured maybe something had gone awry with the plan to ring the opening bell. Or, he thought, maybe the calls concerned this other issue, a run-of-the-mill corporate lawsuit of which Flextronics had recently been the target, filed by a maker of medical devices in California. The company had claimed that the Flextronics decision to close a factory had resulted in a contract breach and impacted its ability to deliver its products.

Tom stepped onto a long, slow escalator, packed with travelers and rolling bags. Far below, he saw a security guard suspiciously scanning the crowd. His phone went off again in his pocket. This time he could feel that it was a call. He calculated how long it would take to reach the security guard at the bottom and figured he probably had a full minute. *Why not?* he thought and snatched his phone and accepted the call. It was Dave Partinoli, a VP of finance at Flextronics.

"Gotta tell me quick, Dave. I'm heading into customs and not supposed to be on my phone."

"It's the lawsuit," Dave said. "And it's real bad."

Tom couldn't understand how that could be so. The lawsuit had been filed for $3 million in compensatory damages, and since annual revenue for Flextronics was several billion dollars, no one was overly concerned with the outcome. It was something of which Tom and the rest of the senior management team were aware, but they didn't pay it much attention because it was such a small claim. The Flextronics lawyers kept telling them not to worry.

"We lost the three million?" Tom asked Dave.

"Worse. Way worse." Dave reported that not only had the judge ruled in the claimant's favor for the $3 million of compensatory damages, but the jury decided to award the medical-device company an additional billion in punitive damages.

"Wait, what?" Tom said, wondering if this were all a joke. "Did you say *billion?*"

Just then, the security guard below spotted Tom on the phone and shouted for him to hang it up. Several people turned to look at Tom.

Dave confirmed the verdict and started providing details, while the security guard kept telling Tom to hang up the phone, shouting across the crowd of travelers, as if Tom were waving a weapon. "Right now, sir! Right now!" Tom only half heard these instructions. He was completely focused on the lawsuit news, which, combined with his jet lag, made him oblivious to his surroundings.

As he strained to hear Dave, an older man one escalator step below Tom took up the security guard's cause, working himself into a lather surprisingly quickly. His protest intensified from a disgusted shaking of the head, to disapproving comments, to all-out yelling in a matter of ten seconds. He turned and got in Tom's face, as if to execute a citizen's arrest, but Tom was still trying to gather the last few details from Dave, so he put his hand up between their faces to try to quiet the old guy down.

As Tom listened, he mentally shuffled through worst-case scenarios. A bond for the full amount of the award would need to be posted in order for them to have the right to appeal. Yet despite the high revenue of Flextronics, its finances weren't structured in a way that would allow them to post a bond of a billion dollars. If they didn't post that bond by the end of the week, then the claim would come due; and since they couldn't pay the claim, that could force them into bankruptcy. There were hundreds of other details and angles to parse later, once he was with his colleagues, but the one thing he understood right away was that bankruptcy was a real threat.

Tom returned to the present moment enough to realize that on the other side of his upheld hand the old guy was still shouting. He and the airport security guard were going fairly wild by this point, acting like Tom was a terrorist.

And then—*boom*—quite suddenly, the old guy reeled back and

punched Tom in the gut with everything he had. Tom doubled over, but he didn't go down, knowing that falling could create a domino effect on the escalator and topple a substantial number of people. He flipped his phone closed, gripped the rubber handrail, and heaved for breath, descending blindly toward an uncertain future.

———

The next morning, Tom stood with his Flextronics colleagues at Nasdaq. They'd considered canceling their ringing of the opening bell, but doing so would have made a bad situation appear even worse, so there they were, counting down the seconds. "We looked like the biggest jackasses in the world," Tom said, "smiling and waving on TV with the crawl underneath saying, 'Flextronics just lost a billion-dollar jury verdict.' I mean, it was just so awkward." While they were up there feigning enthusiasm and optimism, the stock price of Flextronics plunged.

Just after the Nasdaq bell-ringing, a reporter tapped the Flextronics CEO, Michael Marks, for the customary fluff interview on live TV. "But of course," Tom said, "instead of saying anything about why we're ringing the opening bell or what the occasion was, immediately the reporter attacks Michael on the details of the medical-device claim, suggesting that we harmed patients. She tried to make us look as bad as possible."

The next day, Tom was back at his desk in San Jose, and the horrifying reality of what they were up against set in. They had a matter of days—probably two, tops—to find a billion dollars, or they would face a financial catastrophe that was likely to end in bankruptcy. As the senior VP of finance, Tom was tasked with finding the money. "So I'm calling around to all the banks in the world with whom we had established relationships—all the investment banks, all the commercial banks—and everyone's avoiding my calls like the plague, because no one wants to get involved with this mess. Just for us to post the bond created such a financial hardship that no one knew if we could survive this thing."

Only two days after the celebratory ringing of the opening bell at Nasdaq, and it seemed very likely that Flextronics could be facing its end. Tom stared at the phone on his desk, trying to will it to come alive, needing someone to return his call. But the phone emitted no sound, no light, no promise of salvation. And Tom was nearly out of time.

———

Before Sandy Weill sat atop the financial world as the CEO of Citigroup, the largest financial institution in history, he worked, for a while, as a phone-book salesman in New York. He had grown up poor in Benson-hurst, Brooklyn, the son of Polish immigrants. A lazy student, he was eventually shipped off to military school, then got his act together enough to land a spot at Cornell, after which he seemed headed for a career in the air force. Meanwhile, he picked up odd jobs, bumming around New York until a fortunate encounter one day in 1955, described here in a *San Francisco Chronicle* profile, determined his path: "Sandy stumbled into the world of finance when he passed by a brokerage firm that was bustling with energy. He asked his father about the business and got a lead on a job at Bear Stearns. He started in the back office, earning $150 a month, and spent his lunch break taking in the 'large bullpen' where brokers worked. He was hooked, and soon took the next step and became a broker. In May 1960, he and a neighbor branched off and opened their own firm."

That firm became Shearson Loeb Rhoades, which he and his partners developed into a securities brokerage powerhouse and sold to American Express in 1981 for almost $1 billion. After the acquisition, Sandy served as president of AmEx for a few years, then left to strike out on his own at age fifty-two. He was an exception to F. Scott Fitzgerald's assertion that there are no second acts in American lives. He had already built up and sold an enormously successful company; but instead of resting on his laurels and profits, he decided to do it all over again, buying up finance and insurance companies throughout the 1980s—eventually acquiring the second-tier investment bank Smith Barney, as well as Travelers in 1993 for $4 billion, and portions of Drexel Burnham Lambert and Aetna. He then bought back his old company Shearson Lehman and in 1997 purchased Salomon Brothers, the legendary firm of rogues and misfits and big personalities. It was all folded into a vast empire called Travelers Group. In collecting these companies, Sandy had become my boss.

And his shopping spree wasn't done yet. His dream was to build what he described as a "financial supermarket," a one-stop shop so formidable that it could offer the full range of financial products and services under one umbrella, a symbol that also served as the Travelers logo. Sandy's hope was that his financial supermarket model would not only allow his firm to compete more effectively in the banking world but would eventually lead to industry domination. He wanted to build a platform powerful enough that large customers would be obliged to work with Travelers: If a client wanted the smorgasbord of banking needs—cash management from global services, a line of credit from the commercial bank, coverage from an equity analyst, trading support, debt underwriting, and so on—then Sandy's firm could leverage its size to win the client's lucrative high-margin equity and M&A business. It would be a platform-oriented model rather than talent-oriented, diminishing the importance of the human element, which had traditionally been at the center of investment banking. The feeling we workers had under the new financial supermarket system was of being small spokes in a large complicated wheel.

In April 1998, Sandy made his biggest move, combining Travelers Group with Citibank under the collective name Citigroup. The merger was the largest in history, with a value of $83 billion. He called it the "greatest deal in the history of financial services, the crowning of my career." It would be a merger of equals, with Sandy and Citibank's leader, John Reed, serving as co-CEOs.

In order to have the legal ability to create a financial supermarket in the first place, Sandy needed the abolishment of a seventy-year-old law, Glass-Steagall, which had been a cornerstone of banking regulation since the 1930s. At the height of the Great Depression, Glass-Steagall was devised to distance investment banks from commercial banks. By separating the two, retail banks were prohibited from using depositors' funds for risky investments. The financial services industry operated under that arrangement for seven decades. With President Clinton's support, Sandy successfully lobbied for the end of Glass-Steagall; in 1999, Clinton signed new legislation that repealed the old law, paving the way for Sandy and other Wall Street executives to form financial behemoths.

"Don't waste your time on the little deals," our bosses told us. "You're paid to hunt elephants. You're not paid to hunt squirrels." Now that Sandy had assembled his superbank, he needed to prove that it was a sound concept. One huge new client would quiet the naysayers.

———

Lucent Technologies could be the perfect proof point—one of those highly sought-after business relationships that would normally be the domain of Morgan Stanley or Goldman Sachs, but because it needed Citi for its commercial banking and other global banking services, we also got its M&A business. Lucent could be just the client we were looking for to validate Sandy's vision.

Lucent, a telecommunications equipment company, was created just a few years earlier, in 1996, when AT&T spun off its equipment-manufacturing arm from its core telecom business. The origins of Lucent, however, went back to the 1880s when Alexander Graham Bell, inventor of the first practical telephone, established Bell Labs, which over the decades had earned four Nobel Prizes while fostering the inventions of the transistor, the laser, computer operating systems, programming languages, and many other landmark innovations. AT&T had faced trouble selling its equipment to competitors under its own brand, so the company figured that if it spun off the equipment division under a new name, it could bolster sales.

It proved to be a brilliant move, as Lucent's stock price soared during the late 1990s, growing tenfold under the guidance of lead salesperson (and future US presidential candidate) Carly Fiorina. The company doubled its revenue and added twenty-two thousand jobs during these last few years of the decade. Lucent quickly grew massive, becoming the hottest and most widely held stock on Wall Street, beating analysts' expectations for fourteen consecutive quarters.

Lucent hired Bill Viqueira to create an M&A department right after its spinoff from AT&T. Bill was an even-tempered, no-nonsense, smart Cuban-American who had spent a decade at Merrill Lynch, eventually as a director. It wasn't uncommon for a big company like Lucent to poach talent straight from Wall Street when shaping its corporate infrastructure and planning for a wave of acquisitions. The company encouraged an aggressive M&A culture, driven largely by the trends and expectations of Wall Street. "No matter what we did for a long time," Bill said, "the stock went up. I would argue against an acquisition, and then we would do it. And the next day the stock would go up, and somebody would tell me, 'See, you were worried. The stock went up today. It was a good deal.' 'But what about tomorrow?' I'd ask. 'What about next year? What about the year after that?' Nobody was looking at anything past what happened to the stock tomorrow. If we went through a period of more than a few weeks without buying a company, I'd get an email from [CEO Rich] McGinn: 'What are we doing? Why aren't we buying anything? Can you come upstairs?' It was crazy."

A fresh opportunity sprung up for Bill in 1999 when Lucent's CFO asked him to step into the newly vacated job of treasurer. He was eager to expand his experience beyond M&A, so he accepted the offer. At first, his day-to-day involved all the common things associated with serving as treasurer in a large company—foreign exchange, cash management, receivables. But within the first month on the job, his employees, most of whom had been recruited from the banking industry, were banging down his door, saying, "We have to show you what's going on." Long before Bill's arrival in the treasury office, his staff had been fighting the sales force and the CFO organization, pushing back against what they saw as unscrupulous and risky behavior. No one else in a senior position would pay attention to their concerns, and they hoped that Bill, with his Merrill Lynch pedigree, would see what they saw. "It didn't take me very long to say, 'Yeah, this is a disaster. We're sitting on a time bomb.'"

The time bomb was constructed of what's called vendor financing, the practice of lending money to your customers so they can buy your product. Many companies employed vendor financing effectively and achieved positive results, but Lucent was wielding the tool as carelessly and indiscriminately as a Mardi Gras reveler with a fistful of beads.

"Let's say a deal might have been $50 million," Bill said, "and your customer would say, 'I'll buy $50 million of your equipment, but I need another $50 million for working capital, because I've also got to buy all of these other things.' So the Lucent salespeople, aided and abetted by the CFO organization, would say, 'Sure, we'll do that deal. I'll lend you $100 million, and in return, you buy $50 million of my equipment.' It doesn't take a genius to figure out that that is not a good deal."

One fundamental reason Lucent's vendor financing program was so risky was that many of their customers were unproven and had uncertain futures, so the likelihood that they would be able to pay back their loans was low, yet Lucent still booked those deals as revenue. "There's nothing wrong per se with me lending you $50 million to buy my equipment," Bill said. "What *is* a mistake is not weighing the risk. If I think it's risky, I shouldn't be booking the revenue until I actually see you can pay me. I shouldn't be telling the world that I just made a $50 million sale until I know it's a sale. It got to the point where it became an addiction for the sales force because the only way they could get a deal signed was to offer financing."

Within that first month as treasurer of Lucent, Bill's staff showed him the depth of the problem. And he immediately recognized the potential for disaster. "I went to the controller and asked him how much we had reserved against this stuff. And it was almost nothing. We had $10 billion or so in commitments to lend, a couple billion that already had been lent. All of it, obviously, incredibly risky. All of it in default. In every single one of those deals there was some kind of violation."

Bill weighed his options. He didn't savor the prospect of being the harbinger of doom so soon after stepping into his new job, but he didn't see much of a choice. Two months into his role as treasurer, he was invited to participate in a board meeting, and he figured he'd better use the opportunity to inform the governing bodies that there was major trouble on the balance sheet.

Bill arrived for the meeting, certain that once he delivered his presentation, there would be pandemonium. "I've got sweat going down my shirt on both sides because I'm about to walk in and tell the board that we're sitting on this pile of crap, all of these bad loans, and it was all in default. We needed to get this stuff off the balance sheet. We needed to stop new deals. And I'm sure I'm going to get crucified. I didn't create the problem, but I'm going to get killed for it."

Just before stepping into the meeting, Bill was making final preparations in his office when he was drawn into a conference call with the new head of North American sales and several others from the sales team. "They're all yelling and screaming at me that we need to finance this one customer. And I had already said no five times before. I told them I would not sign off on the deal—it was a $50 or $100 million deal that needed my signature, and I wasn't going to sign it. But they wouldn't quit—and I'm not necessarily proud of this, but it firmly stands out in my mind—I finally said to the head of North American sales, 'Nina, shut up.' At Lucent you did not say things like that. It was a very polite culture—well, to your face. A phrase I learned at Lucent that I'd never heard anywhere else, and that they had mastered, was 'grin-fucking.' To your face, they grinned; behind your back, they fucked you. Anyway, I just got fed up. It was a colossal mistake, but it did shut everybody up. 'The conversation is over,' I told them. 'I've got to go to the board meeting.'"

Bill dabbed at his sweat, gathered his materials, and headed into the meeting. He cued up his doomsday PowerPoint presentation and took the dozen board members and ten other senior executives through the slides, showing them facts and figures and painting the worst-case scenario of what could happen if the problems weren't addressed immediately. Then he braced himself for their response.

"I'm expecting all kinds of fireworks. But there was no reaction. No questions at all. 'Thank you very much, Bill.' That was it. I never got any feedback whatsoever. What I did get feedback on the next day was telling Nina to shut up. I walked in and had to pass the office of the head of PR and IR, a very powerful person at Lucent. 'Bill, come in,' she said. 'Did you tell Nina to shut up last night?' It was eight o'clock in the morning and she had already heard about it. 'Don't do that again.' So that was the big story."

Years later, when thinking back on why the board and executives didn't react to his presentation, Bill felt that either they couldn't understand the risk, or they didn't want to see it. "If they admitted that they saw the risk, that would have entailed pulling the plug on revenue growth. You pull the plug on revenue growth, you pull the plug on the stock price. You pull the plug on the stock price, the entire thing is a house of cards and comes crumbling down. So to acknowledge what I'd found—that what was being booked as revenue was not quality revenue, and it shouldn't have been booked at all—would have been to accelerate what ultimately was bound to happen anyway. And that would have triggered a stock price run in the blink of an eye."

So Bill returned to business as usual, fighting against the sales force and its insatiable hunger for vendor financing. If he couldn't solve the problem, he was at least determined not to contribute to it. A new CFO was hired, and Bill felt momentarily hopeful that she would recognize the looming disaster, but she didn't. "I think she thought I was overly negative," Bill said. "She was hearing from me that it was going to blow up. Everybody else was telling her this was a great growth opportunity. So she replaced me with her own person, and they asked me to go back to running the M&A group. I did it for a little while and then quit in 2001. My feeling, being on the inside, was that these kinds of practices could not possibly end well. I sold my Lucent shares whenever I was able."

———

In the first week of 2000, Lucent announced that it had missed its expected quarterly earnings forecast, and the stock took a quick dive of 28 percent, reducing the company's market cap by $64 billion. Then it came to light that Fiorina and her sales team had been less than forthright in their reporting of revenue and use of vendor financing. *Fortune* magazine later wrote: "In a neat bit of accounting magic, money from the loans began to appear on Lucent's income statement as new revenue while the dicey debt got stashed on its balance sheet as an allegedly solid asset. It was nothing of the sort." Lucent had to admit to massive accounting errors, and the stock dropped further. CEO Rich McGinn was forced to resign. By this point, Fiorina had hit the road. Entirely unpunished for her role in leading Lucent to the verge of collapse, she was rewarded in 1999 with the job of CEO of Hewlett-Packard, the first woman to lead a *Fortune* 20 company. Also from *Fortune*: "In an SEC document filed just after Fiorina's departure, [Lucent] revealed that it had $7 billion in loan commitments to customers—many of them financially unstable start-ups building all manner of new networks—of which Lucent had dispensed $1.6 billion."

"What was going on in the stock market," Bill Viqueira said, "was a big part of what ultimately caused Lucent's downfall. You had this perfect storm—a stock market that was rewarding inherently bad business behavior, overpriced acquisitions, vendor financing, low-quality revenue, and you had a management team that didn't understand fundamentally what it meant to run a public company."

Before its troubles, Lucent was poised to be the poster child and justification for why Citigroup's new financial supermarket model was such a good idea. We had enthusiastically put together a bank loan for them of $2 billion, earning us prestigious M&A assignments. But when the company's performance started to deteriorate in 2000 and 2001, it seemed possible that Lucent might default on the loan. Such an epic failure would not only send destructive waves through the telecom and financial worlds, but it could also undermine the strategic argument for Citi's new financial supermarket model.

———

I typically arrived early to meetings, especially when they were with senior management. On one Monday afternoon in early 2000, a meeting was called with Citi's CEO, Sandy Weill; the vice chairman, Bob Rubin; and other top execs to discuss the bank's consumer internet strategy. We knew it would be a contentious meeting. Sandy hated the interface prototypes he'd seen, so everyone expected him to arrive in a bad mood and dish out sharp criticism to those in attendance, wielding his power to remind us of whom we had the privilege of serving. I brought along Stuart Goldstein, who at the time was a VP in my group.

Stuart and I settled into the conference room early to wait for the others when, to our surprise, Sandy walked in several minutes ahead of schedule. Sandy was an awkward guy. He hated silence and tended to fill it with idle chatter. After asking how we were doing and then not waiting for an answer, he started telling us a story from his weekend.

It was an open secret around the firm that Jamie Dimon—who had been Sandy's protégé and close friend and widely believed to be in line for the top job when Sandy retired—had been fired in 1998 at the behest of Sandy's wife. The rumored dispute was over Dimon's refusal to promote Sandy's daughter, Jessica Bibliowicz, who also worked at the firm and had butted heads with Dimon. He had gone too far in challenging Jessica. She was untouchable, and Dimon had overestimated his safety, considering himself Sandy's de facto son. So Dimon was out. Now, two years later, he had been offered the chief executive position at Bank One, headquartered in Chicago.

Sandy's storytelling took on a boastful tone. "So Jamie called me over the weekend and said, 'Sandy, I just want you to know that I'm thinking about taking this job at Bank One. I have to ask, you're not going to acquire Bank One, are you?'" This was still during the time that Sandy was scooping up companies and other banks to create his giant financial conglomerate. Sandy grinned at Stuart and me and continued: "I told him, 'Oh no, don't worry, Jamie. I have no interest in Bank One.'" He paused before delivering the punch line. "I hung up the phone and thought to myself, *I'll wait until he moves his family, and* then *I'll buy it*." Stuart and I weren't sure if it was a joke or not, but we laughed nervously anyway.

It seemed that Sandy was just warming up. He launched straight into a second story, telling us about another phone call he'd had that weekend with Citi's Jack Grubman, who was by far the most respected telecom analyst in the world—as well as the highest paid, at more than $20 million per year—and he was one of the three most respected equity analysts period, along with Mary Meeker at Morgan Stanley and Henry Blodget at Merrill Lynch. Grubman had built his fame on trashing AT&T, at which, early in his career, he had worked for eight years as a quantitative researcher. During that time, the federal government forced AT&T to split into eight regional phone companies. A 2003 *New Yorker* piece noted: "He made his reputation by arguing that deregulation would allow smaller, nimbler companies to usurp the position of his former employer—an analysis that proved correct. In 1994, he moved to Salomon, where his disdain for AT&T only increased." Grubman either kept a neutral or sell rating on the company, but never a buy, so as AT&T's fortunes diminished into the late 1990s, Grubman was beating the hell out of it all the way down, while building his reputation as a savvy equity analyst.

A central point of tension was that Sandy Weill, who was Grubman's boss, sat on the board of AT&T. Sandy knew that the biggest IPO in history was imminent, when AT&T would spin off its wireless business, and he wanted Citi to win the IPO. But he was in the embarrassing position of trying to get the IPO business while the number-one analyst in the field—his employee—had a sell rating out. You can't hire an investment bank to handle your IPO if they've got a sell rating on you.

"You guys from the investment bank," Sandy told Stuart and me, "you owe me one. I worked hard for you last night."

"Oh yeah?" I said. "How so?" We looked at Sandy expectantly.

"I won you some major business last night. I called up Jack Grubman and twisted his arm, making him change his rating on AT&T so we could win the wireless business."

"Really?" I said pleasantly, though Stuart and I were both thinking, *Holy fuck, is he openly bragging about this?* While an equity analyst's rating was grounded in real analysis, most people understood that it was something that could be influenced—part truth and part marketing. But even so, what Sandy said came across as an extreme flouting of all rules and convention. The markets were doing so well at the time that senior executives like Sandy had apparently convinced themselves that it was okay for equity analysts to be asked to hype stocks for the benefit of the bank, as opposed to providing true and legitimate evaluations. Sandy wasn't even pretending to hide behind plausible deniability. He was bragging.

He went on: "I just told him, 'Jack, you gotta change your rating so we can get this business.'"

The whole conversation—from the casual threat on Jamie Dimon to the strong-arming of Jack Grubman—took all of five minutes. Sandy's tone was casual—we were just killing time while waiting for the rest of the people to arrive—but Stuart and I left the meeting an hour later still stupefied by what we'd heard. The CEO of the most powerful bank on the planet had just told us two stories that confirmed our suspicions that he was a man of questionable character, and he had told us these stories as nonchalantly as if he were describing a golf match or a weekend barbecue.

———

Even before my phone rang, I knew it was coming. Robert Messih, my Salomon colleague, had broken the unspoken code and talked to the *Wall Street Journal*, exposing a shady Wall Street practice that had never previously been discussed in public. We all knew that the firm didn't want employees talking to the press for any reason. Robert was an MD in the tech group out in California, and he didn't report to me, but since I was the New York–based guy in the group with whom all the bosses were familiar, the inevitable phone call arrived from senior management. I rested the receiver against my shoulder and listened to a brief lecture. "We don't talk to the *Journal*, V," my boss said, as if I were the one who had violated firm policy.

"Yeah, I know." Even though I agreed with what Robert had said, the firm's rules were the firm's rules.

The practice Robert had condemned was called spinning IPOs. Here's how it worked: If an investment bank were handling a company's initial public offering, it would set aside premium shares for the personal brokerage accounts of executives of other up-and-coming companies, and then when those shares went public and jolted upward on day one, the lucky executives would enjoy a big payday. This was intended to win their loyalty for when their own IPO came along.

Given that so many people were involved in these processes and needed to sign off, spinning IPOs was never a solitary act; it was done by committee. You would need the buy-in from equity syndicate, senior management, and the investment banking coverage officers. Everybody had to be in on it. Coercing an equity analyst to hype a stock, rather than to provide objective research—as Sandy Weill had done with Jack Grubman on AT&T—was bad enough. But now the investment bank, as an institution, had decided to carry it one step further by using that hyped stock to win future deals.

Spinning IPOs had become a topic of heated debate across the tech and finance worlds. Most banks engaged in the practice quietly during the mid to late 1990s, and the majority of executives who received the spoils were equally discreet, but some people defended the practice vehemently, such as Cristina Morgan, who was an MD at Hambrecht & Quist, a boutique bank focused on technology. "What do you think about taking them out to dinner?" she said in that same *Journal* piece, in an attempt to justify her use of IPO spinning. "We throw lavish parties with caviar. Is that not trying to influence them, their behavior? I suggest that it is. . . . It's not immoral. It's a business practice."

I found Morgan's argument hard to accept. Sure, there were gestures as small as buying a cup of coffee for a prospective client, but stuffing their personal brokerage accounts with a couple of million dollars in stocks was on another level altogether. My colleague Robert's quote in the *Journal* seemed much closer to the mark: "'It's a bribe, no question about it,' contends Robert Messih, a managing director at Salomon Inc., which doesn't have a brokerage arm or engage in spinning. 'You pay them off and expect you're going to get treated in kind when they do the transaction.'"

Since I had refused to endorse the practice over the course of my career at Salomon and later Citi, that made us the only technology group of any material size that wasn't spinning IPOs—which meant we were missing out on a lot of equity business. My bosses regularly pressured me to cave. "Why aren't you distributing IPOs to potential clients like everyone else? That would help us land more deals."

It was unprincipled, I told them. "When the harsh light of reality finally shines on this, there will be no defending the action." The sole reason senior management allowed me to renounce the practice so blatantly and not engage in it was, frankly, because I was bringing in so much M&A business that they couldn't risk losing me. The article appeared in late 1997, as the technology bubble built toward its peak. Over the next couple of years, I became more senior, and the pressure to spin IPOs increased. But as one of the top revenue generators in the investment bank, I had more than a little leverage to continue my resistance.

Robert and I spoke later that week. The bosses had already sent a handful of envoys to reprimand him. "I hope you didn't get in too much trouble for talking to the *Journal*," I said.

"I was just exposing the truth," he said.

———

Selling Lucent's Optical Fiber Solutions Division was the worst deal experience of my life. The pressure and urgency to get it done were enormously high, since Lucent's survival and Citi's new mission—to justify the abolishment of Glass-Steagall and vindicate the creation of a superbank—had come to depend on the success of this one marquee deal. Early in July 2001, we held an emergency meeting in a New York conference room. Michael Carpenter, who ran global banking for Citigroup, kicked it off. "All right, what are we going to do to save Lucent?"

We went around the room, each person presenting challenges and ideas. The conversation kept coming back to the need to move a big asset, to split off some portion of Lucent's business and sell it, giving the company a cash infusion. Everyone knew I'd been working on selling Lucent's fiber division for a while, but those sorts of deals take time. And this one was complicated by three special challenges: The value of fiber was decreasing daily, as the internet industry sank into turmoil; Lucent's reputation was in question; and the markets in general were turbulent. So we were trying to sell an asset that was falling in value for a parent company that was also in decline, in the midst of a difficult market—not good conditions for a sale process.

At the beginning of 2001, when Citi started shopping it around, we expected we could get $8 billion for Lucent's fiber business. Now, only half a year later, its estimated value had dropped to about $2 billion.

"We're working on it," I said. "Believe me, we're working on it."

"Can't you sell it faster?" Carpenter asked, half joking.

"I wish we could." I didn't need to tell Carpenter that M&A doesn't work that way. You can't just put up a FOR SALE sign. The more desperate you look, the lower your chances are of consummating a deal. He knew all of that.

"Is there anything else we can sell immediately?" Carpenter asked. "What about the name 'Lucent'? It's a great name. Or something else. What have we got?"

I shuffled through my spread of papers on Lucent. "There's not as much value here as you would think."

"So what you're telling me," Carpenter said, "is it's a bag of shit."

"Yeah," I said, "but it's a really nice bag."

The tension momentarily broke as we all laughed.

We kept brainstorming, but selling the fiber business seemed to be the only way to save Lucent, and despite the intricacies of the deal, the team figured that we had two to three weeks to get it done before Lucent would default on its debt, which was basically a declaration of bankruptcy. Finding a buyer for the fiber business would demonstrate that Lucent had an influx of cash, which would build public confidence in the company's stability and allow it to shore up its financial position and avoid bankruptcy.

We had first tried to sell the fiber business to individual strategic buyers, but a confluence of issues didn't allow it. After a lot of handholding and persuasion, we finally found a possible solution for Lucent Fiber—an elaborate four-way deal involving Furukawa, CommScope, and Corning. We'd been negotiating the deal for weeks, and by the time it came to a head on July 23, 2001, Lucent was probably forty-eight hours away from defaulting.

That night was my birthday. I called my wife, Jessica, all apologies, explaining that I would likely miss dinner and possibly be at the lawyers' offices late, gathered with all parties present as we worked to get the deal done. "I'm not sure this is gonna end well," I told her. She understood that the future of Lucent—as well as Citigroup, to some extent—depended on closing this deal. It wasn't that Citi would go bankrupt from this one failure, but our stock would certainly take a hit and the rationale for the financial supermarket model would be put into question.

Executing any contract in the eleventh hour is very difficult. The fact that this was a four-way deal added that much more complexity. We weren't negotiating with only one counterparty; we were negotiating with three counterparties, who in turn were negotiating with one another. The lawyers, bankers, and business development teams from each of the firms were there at the table, with people raising this and that issue. Every new point would have ripple effects on the closing terms, which kept compounding: working-capital adjustments, reps and warranties, who would be responsible for this or that happening. Each party had different personalities and levels of sophistication, different deal appetites and risk tolerances. Not to mention, the companies at the table were geographically and culturally diverse—from Japan, North Carolina, and upstate New York.

Every time you asked the Japanese team a question, they said *yes*, even when the answer should absolutely have been *no*. For example, we'd ask, "Is it possible that Furukawa could do the entire deal?" And they'd nod and reply, "Yes." "Great!" we'd say. But there was no way they could do the entire deal. The *Japanese yes*, as I learned it was called, seemed motivated by the need to never publicly disappoint or shame any party with a negative answer. The North Carolinians from CommScope likewise had a problem answering *no* to any question, which was, in its way, a cultural Southern thing. We would ask them, "Do you have your financing in place?" "Absolutely," they'd say. But they didn't have their financing in place. They just wanted to be agreeable and figured they would sort it out in time.

We finally slogged through the deal terms, signed it at dawn, and cracked a bottle of champagne. Disheveled and exhausted, we were sipping bubbly as people started arriving for work. Later that morning the deal was announced, and Lucent had what it needed to regain the trust of the markets and stay alive.

Lucent survived on its own for five more years before it merged with the French telecom company Alcatel and then was absorbed by Nokia.

———

Early in my time at Salomon Brothers, we often had to work through the weekends. The firm had a policy that if you came in on Saturday or Sunday, you'd get $60 each day to cover meals and travel into the office.

My roommate at the time, Jim Crisanti, would take the subway round-trip, and he found a restaurant near the office that served all-you-can-eat baked potatoes for a buck fifty, with unlimited toppings.

Since we shared both an apartment and a tendency toward frugality, I latched on to the Crisanti program. We would ride the subway together, load up our potatoes, and then pocket the extra $110. My French friend Larry Bird occupied the other end of the spectrum. She would hire a black town car to deliver her to work, then order in a nice meal, spending her full $60 each day.

One day Salomon announced: "We're finding that some of you are abusing the stipend." Which meant Jim and me. We weren't using it for what it was intended. So they changed the rule, requiring us to submit expenses for our $120 weekend per diem.

"Okay, fine," Jim and I said. "Now we're on the Larry Bird program." So we took town cars to the office and started eating fancy meals.

"All you did was change our behavior," we argued. "What did you think we were going to do? Continue to take the subway and eat the baked potato? The company is still spending $120 for us to work through the weekend. And now we're less happy."

The only response we received was: "We must follow the rules."

"But you're saving the company no money," we pleaded, "and half the people are pissed, because rather than feeling like they got an extra hundred bucks' pocket money for giving up their Saturdays and Sundays, now they have to figure out how to spend it and deal with submitting receipts."

The bureaucracy of a big company like Citi often led to bad policies. Such a large firm is basically forced to make decisions for a whole organization that don't necessarily apply well to the individual business units. Is it better, one wonders, to have uniformity of authority in decision making at the expense of flexibility? It was a demonstration of the challenges of size, the difficulty of managing a large business with hundreds of disparate units. In the mid-2000s, for example, the firm developed new rules for air travel, insisting that employees reach their destinations on the cheapest fares available, even if that meant multiple connections to get to smaller cities. Saving money was not a bad inclination in an industry notorious for profligacy, but there was no flexibility in the rule, and so my assistant, Angela Murray, was engaged in frequent battles to make sure I could arrive at out-of-town meetings on time. If I had a ten o'clock morning meeting in Omaha to discuss a deal with a potential $6 million fee, Citi still insisted on saving a few hundred bucks by booking me on a flight that arrived in the afternoon, which meant I would miss the meeting unless I traveled the day before. And because those cheaper flights often required an overnight stay, more work hours were wasted as well as any potential savings, since the firm would have to pay for a hotel and meals. I knew for a fact that the policy was revenue-negative.

"It was about following the rules," Angela said. "It wasn't about what was best for anyone. To a certain degree, you did need to have someone who was focused on making sure that money was being spent properly. But when you're dealing with an organization like Citi, you have to understand that in order to make money, you spend money. And sometimes in order to make $6 million, you've got to spend an extra few hundred on a plane fare."

There was another unforeseen consequence, which was that if the bankers were required to churn up full workdays to take cheaper flights with multiple connections to places like Omaha, they simply were not going to book meetings in Omaha. "The firm will make less revenue," I argued to management. "Nobody is gonna waste that many hours to save a few hundred bucks. They just won't do the deal in Omaha."

This was further proof that these new financial supermarkets managed for efficiency and scale rather than empowerment and accountability. One result of this was that employees were made to feel like irrelevant parts of a mighty machine, which of course made us less connected to and therefore less emotionally invested in the wider firm's future well-being.

This division became even more apparent in an improving market, as talented people left Citi to work at firms that prized people over platform. Recognizing this challenge, senior management formed a committee in 2004 focused on culture, with the stated goals of rewarding positive behavior, improving morale, and decreasing the amount of bureaucracy.

To run the committee, they created a new position called culture czar and appointed me. I drew people from across the firm, at all different levels, to join the committee and discuss the company's culture—what was good, what was bad, what needed to be changed. We came up with the corny name Project Passion, with the aim of figuring out "how to return passion to the industry."

Over the course of several meetings, we developed firm-wide surveys, drafted guiding principles, and devised an action plan and mission statement. We identified core issues regarding company culture, pinning questions on the wall and debating them: "What is our identity?" "Do we reward the right people?" "Do we have effective management?" "Can we reduce bureaucracy?" Among our guiding principles were these: "Money is not the answer, even though it is an important part of the answer"; and "The little things matter a lot." Playing off the four *c*'s of diamond quality and the five *c*'s of credit, we came up with our own seven *c*'s, our core values that defined how we wanted to conduct ourselves as individuals and as an organization: *commitment to excellence, client-focused, citizenship, character, cooperation, creativity,* and *celebration.*

The committee brought forth a new set of rules and rewards that would affect promotion and compensation, adopted with a simple goal in mind: to make Citi a better place to work. We knew we couldn't compete with the other big firms on the basis of compensation alone. Sandy Weill was too stingy. People were paid just enough to keep them around, enough that it wouldn't be worth the hassle of switching to another firm for a moderate increase in money. It was evident that if the firm had nothing to offer other than comp, then comp would become the sole factor in determining whether or not someone was happy at Citi.

The culture committee wasn't established as a PR move meant to garner praise from outsiders. It was done in the interest of morale and—as the two typically go hand in hand—profits. If the troops were happier, they'd be more productive, and the firm would thrive. The investment bank adopted our guidelines, and later they were expanded to most of Citigroup.

The changes implemented by the culture committee definitely had a lasting impact, since tying a significant portion of compensation to one's culture score naturally discouraged bad behavior. It became less frequent to hear crude, racist, or sexist jokes, or to see a manager yelling at subordinates or unnecessarily wasting the time of junior people. But while these developments were clearly positive, they also resulted in creating a blander culture, as disruptive individuals were forced to change or move on to another firm or industry. Project Passion snuffed out whatever flickering flames remained of the Salomon Brothers' infamous spirit, as captured so well in Michael Lewis's classic *Liar's Poker*. Disruptors do have an important role within any company or industry that is dependent on evolutionary change to stay relevant to the society it serves. But was it possible to get the good that comes from disruptors without the accompanying negative behavior?

The firm I had once joined could not have been more different from what it later became. Salomon Brothers had been all about the individual; its culture was focused on creating and capitalizing upon star performance. The standard-bearer for Darwinian meritocracy, Salomon shunned bureaucracy and prized personality, chutzpah, and bravado. Citi, on the other hand, was all about the platform; the individual was merely a cog in a global delivery mechanism. Nothing could be done without explicit permission—at least, that was what most of us were told and believed to be true. Citi was a paper tiger that expended significant energy on managing the rule followers in areas that pertained to costs rather than risk. This left the firm with less ability to monitor and manage inappropriate behavior, as evidenced by its significant role in the financial crisis. Salomon Brothers and Citigroup represented the two extremes of culture, but both had one glaring weakness in common: Neither had the leadership to create the standards of personal accountability needed to effectively manage a financial services firm of any material scale or scope. No amount of regulations, compliance officers, or Project Passions could take the place of leaders setting good examples and demanding that others follow their lead.

After Sandy Weill dropped the bombshell on Stuart and me about strong-arming Jack Grubman into changing his rating on AT&T, Citi won the wireless IPO deal, netting nearly $45 million in fees. This victory was looked upon cynically by all, enough so even to attract the attention of the regulators.

New York attorney general Eliot Spitzer went on a tear through Wall Street starting in 2001, first launching an investigation into the activities of Merrill Lynch's equity analyst Henry Blodget, finding through scores of interviews and depositions and nearly 100,000 emails that Blodget had conspired with his firm's investment bankers to attach overly favorable ratings to clients so the firm could keep those clients happy and retain their business. This was done at the expense of regular investors who had trusted the advice of Merrill's analysts, especially Blodget, who had attained rock-star status on the Street. Many people lost enormous amounts of their personal savings, all so Merrill could make more money. (Other firms, of course, were doing the same thing, but Spitzer went after Merrill Lynch first.) Merrill, hit with penalties and fines, agreed to multiple reforms, and Blodget was banned from the securities industry for life.

In November 1999, Grubman had raised the suspicions of authorities—as well as everyone who worked on Wall Street—by changing his rating on AT&T. Since he'd always publicly derided AT&T, the sudden change of position seemed fishy, especially when Citi soon landed the massive wireless IPO deal. Spitzer and his team dug into it, collecting 200,000 documents, including an email from Grubman to Carol Cutler—a telecom analyst with whom Grubman had a flirtatious relationship—that seemed to contain an admission of guilt. Here's what he wrote:

"Everyone thinks I upgraded T [AT&T] to get lead for AWE [AT&T Wireless]. Nope. I used Sandy to get my kids in 92nd St. Y pre-school (which is harder than Harvard) and Sandy needed Armstrong's vote on our board to nuke Reed in showdown. Once coast was clear for both of us (i.e. Sandy clear victor and my kids confirmed) I went back to my normal negative on T. Armstrong never knew that we both (Sandy and I) played him like a fiddle."

A bit of background: The preschool at the 92nd Street Y in Manhattan has long been highly selective, with a mere sixty-five students accepted each year. Press and trial documents later revealed that Sandy leaned on his connections and made a "donation" to the 92nd Street Y of $1 million—using Citi's money—presumably to get Grubman's children accepted at the school. I'm sure Sandy rationalized the use of Citi's money, rather than his own, because this brought the firm one step closer to earning a big fee.

The other side of the bribe mentioned in Grubman's email concerned Michael Armstrong, the chief executive of AT&T, who sat on Citi's board. Sandy's relationship with his co-CEO, John Reed, had deteriorated beyond repair, and Sandy was planning a coup, but he needed the support of Armstrong to get the necessary board votes to make him the sole CEO. Changing the rating on AT&T would win Armstrong's favor and allow Sandy to "nuke Reed."

Initially, it all went down as planned: John Reed resigned, placing Sandy alone atop Citi's throne; Grubman's kids were admitted to the Y; and Citi won the AT&T Wireless business after Grubman improved his rating. But when all the clandestine details finally came to light, Grubman was hit with a fine of $15 million and a lifetime ban from the securities industry, and Sandy was forced to resign from Citi in 2003, ending a long and illustrious career and forever tainting his reputation.

Sandy selected Chuck Prince to replace him as CEO. Chuck had been Citi's general counsel, and the speculation was that Sandy wanted a lawyer and trusted friend in charge, since there was sure to be legal action against the firm and probably a large penalty; having someone at the helm with legal expertise could also ensure that Sandy was kept out of jail. That part worked—Sandy personally escaped unscathed, with the exception of losing his job—but the firm ultimately had to pay a huge fine. And worse yet, Chuck Prince now held the reins of a spectacularly large and complicated bank, and he didn't have the background or knowledge to run a huge, diverse, global operation.

I ran into Sandy years later in 2010 at the Four Seasons restaurant in New York. He brought up his disappointment with Chuck Prince and argued that if he himself had remained in charge, Citi would've avoided the trouble it had gotten into, as he was much more risk-conscious and able to manage that risk. Sandy even implied that the whole financial crisis could have been avoided if he had not been forced to leave Citi. He mentioned having just made similar assertions in a *New York Times* interview. I found the whole exchange sad, a fallen warrior trying to salvage his battered reputation by criticizing others. In the *Times* piece, Sandy claimed that his financial supermarket model had not been the cause of Citi's problems, that rather the failure was managerial, for which he accepted some of the responsibility—but not really: "One of the major mistakes that I made was my recommending Chuck Prince," he told the *Times*, which reported: "Mr. Weill blames Mr. Prince for letting Citi's balance sheet balloon and taking on huge risks."

In Prince's defense, the current worth of financial instruments in the world is loosely estimated to be in the neighborhood of $2.5 quadrillion. That's an unfathomable number. And these instruments are of such varying complexity, with so many different products and types, it's not simply $2.5 quadrillion comprised mainly of government debt; it's $2.5 quadrillion of government debt, municipal debt, corporate debt, equity, derivatives, commercial paper, futures, options, swaps, and a plethora of other financial instruments. How can one person possibly understand the full scope and intricacies of a company that had the largest exposure and reach in the industry?

After Sandy created his financial supermarket, many other firms had followed Citigroup's example and built their own huge conglomerates, such as JPMorgan Chase and Morgan Stanley Dean Witter. Former chairman of the Federal Reserve Paul Volcker called them "bundles of conflicts of interests." Citi was a mishmash of so many disparate firms that, in the end, it didn't have a defined culture—it had size and cost efficiency, but those are not core tenets of a culture. No one at the top levels was concerned enough with holding managers accountable and keeping risk under control. Despite having a compliance department, no one provided meaningful oversight as to how the scores of different departments were being run on an individual basis. Sure, Sandy had his flaws, but he had been a savvy manager and highly focused on risk control. Under Chuck Prince, Citi's business unit leaders were free to run wild.

Several years ago, I became involved with the Aspen Institute, whose mission is to train effective and enlightened leaders. There are a handful of key readings with which every Aspen participant is familiar, and one of those is George Orwell's essay "Shooting an Elephant," which describes a white police officer in Burma, perhaps Orwell himself, being persuaded by the natives to shoot dead an escaped elephant. The narrator doesn't want to shoot the animal, which, by the time the narrator encounters it, is grazing peacefully in a field, but he finally succumbs to the pressure and pulls the trigger.

In an Aspen Institute seminar that had a big impact on me personally, we discussed the story. Our conversation centered on this debate: All your life you are pressured to shoot the elephant when you know you shouldn't. When have you decided to shoot or not to shoot the elephant? Why did you make the choice you made? We went around the room, and people described moments in their lives and careers when they succumbed to pressure and did something they knew was wrong or unethical, as well as when they resisted doing something that was expected of them. No one thought that I, the investment banker, would come forth with a positive example. But I told them about my refusal to spin IPOs. This ignited an impassioned debate about the financial services industry and its loss of character. People on Wall Street are often placed in compromising situations in which it's easy to rationalize IPO spinning, or putting out a positive rating to win business, or issuing excessive vendor financing to boost sales numbers, because everyone else is justifying the action through others' acquiescence.

What would it take for people on Wall Street not to shoot the elephant, not to cave to industry practices and expectations? What's the grounding that would allow them to know where the line is that must not be crossed, to do the right thing? At the end of the day, it requires effective and enlightened leadership to resist bowing to conventional pressures, to shun the seductions of greed, self-aggrandizement, and self-preservation. Firms can't watch every aspect of every employee, and regulation can't control everyone's actions at all times, and so the only way that a company is going to be effectively managed is with a culture that prioritizes the long-term interests of clients, customers, and the integrity of the firm. As the great basketball coach John Wooden said, "The true test of a man's character is what he does when no one is watching."

Citigroup didn't have the sort of culture that would reward people who were focused on doing the right thing. We tried to instill it through Project Passion, but a true commitment would have had to come from the top, and Sandy and others clearly didn't value those things enough. Chuck Prince tried to deal with the 2008 financial crisis by saying things like, "As long as the music is playing, you've got to get up and dance." I neither witnessed nor heard any reason to doubt his integrity, suggesting that integrity alone, without expertise and without a guiding culture, is not sufficient to lead a large financial services firm.

Sandy received a lot of heat for the 2008 meltdown. Back in 2002, *Fortune* magazine had declared Weill to be the most admired CEO in the nation. But by 2009, *Time* included him on its list of "25 People to Blame for the Financial Crisis," stating that "the swollen banks are now one of the country's major economic problems." The factors that led to the crisis are incredibly complex, and culpability should be spread in many directions, but certainly one central factor was the financial supermarket model that Sandy built and that many other firms soon replicated. These megabanks grew complex well beyond the ability of any manager or culture to grasp and effectively govern.

When the dotcom bubble burst, most Wall Street firms either downsized or dismantled their technology banking groups, nervous about the instability in the sector. Citi was similarly spooked, and a lot of heads rolled. Telecom also took a hit, and the banking world in general was fighting to keep its footing in 2000 and 2001. I'd been running the technology group, and now I stepped into a larger role as head of TMT, adding media and telecom to my responsibilities.

I inherited cases of files from my predecessor, and one day while thumbing through them, I came upon an internal memo. The recipient list included all the senior executives who had pressured me to spin IPOs—many of the very top people in the bank—and it showed that they themselves had secretly participated in the practice, spinning IPOs in media and telecom and other sectors over a number of years. It listed allocation amounts, detailing which executives were given shares, how many, and by whom.

That *Wall Street Journal* article from 1997 that had so upset the bosses, in which Robert Messih condemned the practice, had stated that Salomon "doesn't have a brokerage arm or engage in spinning." That, of course, was incorrect, but I didn't know it at the time. The very people committing the acts in question were the ones demanding that Messih be reprimanded for his public comments. A *New Yorker* piece from 2003 reported that Salomon covertly participated in IPO spinning for several years: "Between June, 1996, and August, 2000, for example, Salomon Smith Barney gave WorldCom's Bernie Ebbers stock in twenty-one I.P.O.s, which netted him profits of more than eleven and a half million dollars. Qwest's Philip Anschutz received stock in fifty-seven I.P.O.s and pocketed almost five million dollars."

Eliot Spitzer's assault on Wall Street soon shifted from the shady dealings of equity analysts like Grubman and Blodget to the practice of IPO spinning. Spitzer's team discovered that it was all one big greedy cycle in which the analysts put out undeserved favorable ratings on companies so the investment bankers could land those companies' business, then shares of those hot IPOs would be given as gifts to the executives of up-and-coming companies who would then use that bank to execute their own IPOs. The bank and its bankers made gobs of money, but regular investors who had trusted the bank with their finances got screwed.

By November 2002, Spitzer had completed his investigation and was ready to bring down the hammer on the major financial institutions. The banks were eager to be rid of him, so they all agreed fairly quickly to a host of reforms that would help ensure the integrity of research analysis, as well as fines amounting to $1.4 billion and a ban on spinning IPOs.

———

It became clear to Tom Smach that he and his company, Flextronics, had been banished to a snake-filled island. Storm clouds were gathering overhead, and every desperate bottle he hurled into the sea had bobbed back to his shore, undiscovered, unopened, his rolled-up pleas for help unread.

It was a couple of days after he was punched in the gut on the airport escalator at JFK. Tom had been dialing up his Wall Street contacts for forty-eight hours, but no one would return his calls. In a lawsuit that had been filed for only $3 million by a maker of medical devices, the jury had awarded a billion dollars in punitive damages—and Tom was likely one day from missing the deadline to post a bond in order to appeal the jury award, or Flextronics would probably be sunk.

I'd known Tom for years, back before his former employer, Dii Group, was acquired by Flextronics in 2000, a deal on which I advised. Tom and I had frequently worked together when he was at Dii Group, but when he became part of Flextronics, that relationship was put on hold, since Flex had its own long-term banking relationships in place. Even so, Tom remained a friend, and I always had confidence in his abilities and integrity. Like everyone else, I'd heard about the billion-dollar settlement. And I could pretty easily guess that Flextronics still needed help solving it. Normally I would have called Tom to discuss it, but since I was down in San Jose on other business, I figured I'd drop into his office and surprise him.

Tom's secretary told him I was there to see him, and I had to wait for a few minutes. He probably assumed it was a social call—since Flextronics was not part of my coverage universe. He was in crisis mode and had no time for catching up with old friends, yet finally I was summoned.

Tom was standing at his desk studying papers. "How are you, Chris?" he said, glancing up in my direction.

"Fantastic."

He smiled tensely. He didn't look good.

I got straight to the matter at hand. "Tom, I know you have a problem, and I'm here to solve it for you." He dropped his papers on the desk. "Citi is prepared to backstop Flextronics for 100 percent of the bond. We've got you fully covered."

In response, he fell back into his rolling chair. After a few seconds, he started laughing. I waited until he regained his wits, then we discussed the details.

As good as it felt to help out Tom and Flextronics, I was simply the messenger. On my own, of course, I couldn't have backed Flextronics— no individual or small or even midsized firm could have reasonably helped them, which was why no one would return Tom's calls. I had gone to the senior risk manager at Citi and said, "Flextronics is an important potential client, and we have an opportunity to create a relationship. Here's their challenge. . . ." And he said, "All right, we'll step up for this one."

Backing Flextronics in its moment of crisis arose from the same philosophy to which I subscribed during the worst of the dotcom crash: You build market share when times aren't great, and you help worthy clients with challenges when they get knocked down; and then when times are good again, you've established valuable relationships. So even though I liked Tom and believed in him and the company, our offer was also based on sound strategy and tactics.

"Within a couple of weeks," Tom later said, "not only did we know that the punitive-damage award was illegal, but the plaintiff also knew that. So we started discussions with them and finally settled out the billion for just $23 million."

In building giant financial institutions, there are problems that come with size—weakening of culture, lack of internal controls and oversight, an increase in unnecessary bureaucracy, greater risk and damage if the firm were to fail—but there are also undeniable advantages. Flextronics should not have faced bankruptcy simply because of a misguided and ultimately incorrect jury verdict, but it very nearly did. Citigroup was the only bank that could back Flextronics due to our size and ability to absorb risk. So there can be great value to the financial supermarket. It allowed the firm to provide a critical service to corporate America in the face of the demands created by scale and globalization.

But is providing the service required by large corporate customers worth the challenges that accompany being bigger? Is it worth the breakdown in culture that results from a focus on platform as opposed to a focus on people? When a company grows as large as Citigroup or Lucent, it becomes too easy to justify immoral behaviors by hiding behind accepted industry practices. We saw this with Sandy Weill and Jack Grubman, with Henry Blodget's analyst misdeeds, and all across the investment banking world with IPO spinning. Bill Viqueira encountered the same herd mentality with Lucent's misuse of vendor financing: *Everyone else is doing it, so it must be okay.* Once Citi ballooned to extreme proportions, the firm's top priorities became leveraging its platform and maintaining its size, rather than promoting a positive, ethical, and healthy corporate culture that prioritized individual responsibility and accountability. In the end, that loss of culture was what led to the firm's decline. This occurred throughout Wall Street, with very little differentiating the firms from one another. It used to be that when you named Salomon Brothers, Goldman Sachs, Morgan Stanley, or pretty much any firm, a unique culture would immediately spring to mind. But once these banks were forced to adopt the supermarket model to stay competitive, culture receded and the firms became insipid organizations that esteemed scale and efficiency above all else.

Was it any surprise that Citi—the largest, blandest elephant in the herd, with the mission of hunting other elephants—was at the center of the 2008 financial crisis, even more so than the other major firms, given Citi's size, its global reach, and its lack of centralized risk management? It's not easy to tame or kill these beasts once you've created them. Although many people are concerned that the financial supermarket firms may be too big to fail, they may also be too big to succeed.

7

REACH OUT AND TOUCH SOMEONE

Technology is the knack of so arranging the world that we don't have to
experience it.

—MAX FRISCH, FROM *HOMO FABER*

In the mid-1980s, making withdrawals and deposits via ATM was the
hot new thing in the world of money. Lines of customers would gather
outside the bank at all hours of the day, anxiously waiting their turn. Yet
it wasn't the cutting-edge technology that it seemed to be, as the process
basically involved a customer cramming an envelope through a slot on
one side of the wall, and then a bank employee fishing that envelope out
of a cardboard box on the other side. In fact, it was hardly different from
passing your check and slip to a live, in-the-flesh bank teller—except
that human contact had been lost.

The tellers hated handling the ATM deposits. Everyone except me.
Back at the start of my career, I was only a couple of weeks into the
training program at Bank of America, which required newcomers to
master each job over a one-year period, and my first post was as a teller
in the City of Industry—a thin strip of land just east of Los Angeles,
home to thousands of businesses but only about two hundred residents.
The other trainees found the task of handling ATM deposits boring

and almost offensively menial. But at age twenty-two, in my first job postcollege, there was something I enjoyed about any new experience, no matter how rote.

Each morning before we opened, I would stand beside the head teller as she unlocked the door on the backside of the ATM, and we would wiggle out the deposit box and take it to a table to dump and sort the contents. This gave me the opportunity to sit around the table with the real bank tellers—most of whom were women with families—and talk about their kids and whatever TV shows we'd all watched the night before.

The use of ATMs, for both deposits and withdrawals, required a big leap in trust by customers. I remember the first time I deposited a check of my own into a machine and watched it disappear into the unknown. It felt like I'd fed it into a shredder. I didn't have much faith that it would survive the journey and actually end up as funds in my account. Without a person to hand it to, a real live teller to look in the eye, my very relationship to the world of money started to feel impersonal and detached.

———

Las Vegas in the 1990s attracted the same bizarre clash of cultures and energies as it does today. Tourists in fanny packs or matching neon shirts, showgirls, hustlers, conventioneers, bachelor-party drunkards, magicians, newlyweds, gamblers.

Circa 1996, behold Bozo the Clown holding aloft a scrap of plastic that looks like a credit card. He half turns under the lights and becomes Harvey Weinstein's doppelgänger. This isn't a Vegas illusion; this is CES, the massive annual Consumer Electronics Show, and the man at the helm of this particular booth is plump and short, smiling and pink-faced, clad in an open shirt and gold-chain necklace. The piece of plastic he holds above his comb-over of thinning red hair is the future that most people don't know is coming. Orbiting around him are scantily clad models—"booth babes," as they were commonly known. These women look as though they might have wandered out of the pornography convention and film awards show taking place down the hall—and, in fact, many of them had. They hand out T-shirts and keychains and little bowls of ice cream to passersby, as Bozo the Clown rhapsodizes to the gathering crowd about the wonders of this piece of plastic—the prepaid calling card.

Bob Lorsch, the Bozo/Weinstein hybrid, led SmarTalk, a company that rose to the top of the fast-growing prepaid calling card industry. Lorsch felt right at home at the crossroads of CES and the Adult Video News (AVN) Awards, considered the Oscars of pornography, which took place in the same Las Vegas venue over the same week. He liked to keep company with adult film actors, B-list celebrities, misfits, outcasts, and anyone down on their luck. Those were his people. He was a man built of charisma, compassion, cheeseburgers, ego, and ambition.

Each year, Lorsch tried to make a splash at CES, and he especially enjoyed hiring porn stars to populate his calling card booth, where they would hand out swag and ice cream to the blushing techies and company product reps strolling by. The presence of booth babes at CES has grown increasingly controversial in recent times. But back then, no one nailed that combination of product endorsement and bare female flesh with such unapologetic fervor as did Bob Lorsch.

He was the type of guy most people would despise at first sight. But he was so magnetic and jovial that it was hard not to be charmed by him, even while feeling simultaneously revolted. So when Bob Lorsch held up a calling card and told you to pay attention, it was nearly impossible to look away. He didn't invent the calling card, but he brought it to the masses.

A gifted salesman, he made his unglamorous start selling cigarette filters to liquor stores out of the trunk of his car, then made a small fortune peddling little fuzzy balls with googly eyes called Wuppies, which became a popular promotional tool and ignited a craze in the Netherlands. Later he built a vast empire around the burgeoning industry of prepaid phone cards. There was nothing this man couldn't sell. So much about Lorsch was off-putting—his looks, his volume, his emotional and impulsive nature—but he was brilliant at what he did. At the 1983 COMDEX trade show, Lorsch snuck the Microsoft Windows logo onto twenty thousand Las Vegas pillowcases by bribing hotel housekeepers, bell clerks, and security guards to the tune of $450,000 in folded cash. According to the Chicago *Daily Herald*, this inspired Bill Gates to call Lorsch "a marketing genius and a magician who believed anything was possible and simply wouldn't take no for an answer." Like many business visionaries, Lorsch was an eternal optimist, infecting everyone around him with belief, enthusiasm, and good cheer.

One year at the CES convention, my team from Salomon took over a blackjack table at the Hard Rock Cafe, filling six of the seven seats, leaving one empty on the end. A young woman soon came over wearing a tight, revealing dress. Her arms were heavily tattooed and her eyes made up like a desert sunset. She smiled as she eased onto her stool and arranged her stacks of chips with long painted nails. "Hi, boys," she said. Everyone mumbled a greeting. "Are you here for the conference?"

"Yes," said Bill, one of the more senior bankers. "But probably not the same one as you." He glanced down at his suit and tie. "We're here for the Consumer Electronics Show. I guess that's pretty obvious."

She laughed. "I figured as much. I'm here for AVN, and I'm actually up for an award."

"Oh, really? Congratulations. What is it?"

"Best anal sex scene."

There was a stunned silence, and then the entire table burst into laughter, including the actress.

"It's an honor to be included," she said, "but I've got no chance. The other nominees are so talented."

Everyone started peppering her with questions: *Why do you think you were nominated? What differentiates one scene from another? How does someone become the best?*

Scheduling the CES and AVN conferences in Las Vegas during the same week seemed both cruel and humorous, but the cross section of nerds and porn stars has a long and influential history. Everyone in Silicon Valley knows that pornography, more than anything else, drives innovation, trends, growth, risk, and the ultimate adoption of technology.

In 1992, an old Wharton classmate of mine, Will Fleming, arrived home from work one evening to find a thick envelope in the mail from another Wharton pal, Adam Rubenstein. It contained a draft business plan for a new product—prepaid calling cards, which virtually no one had heard of. Will had a comfortable consulting job in Washington, DC, but after spending the weekend poring over the business plan, he was intrigued enough to quit his job, pack his things, and relocate to Florida to join Adam.

The business plan was built upon the notion that the vast majority of people in the early '90s didn't have an easy way to make long-distance calls away from home, besides getting rolls of quarters to feed into a pay phone. Ubiquitous cell phones were still years in the future. Some portion of the population had a phone credit card, but not many. Will and Adam created a prepaid card that could store phone minutes and slip easily into a wallet. A handful of telecom companies were testing the waters with some version of this idea, but no one had brought the concept to market with much success.

Focusing on convenience stores, supermarket chains, and drugstores—basically, retailers that had pay phones by the parking lot outside the store—Will and Adam quickly learned how difficult it is to change consumer behavior. As they met with the owners of these various stores to explain how calling cards worked, the reactions typically landed somewhere between resistance and ridicule. "They thought we were just making this up," Will said. "They'd say things like, 'This is the craziest idea I've ever heard. Prepaid calling cards aren't a product category. And they never will be.'"

Will and Adam asked the retail executives to describe the hassle of having people come in to request quarters for the phone, which happened frequently enough on busy days that the shift manager would have to send a clerk running to the bank for change, leaving the store short-staffed. Will and Adam pitched their phone cards as a solution to this problem, and it could also be a moneymaker for the store. As an added bonus, the product wouldn't take up any shelf space, and they could brand the cards with the store's name and logo. A few executives were intrigued, but most still thought Will and Adam were either scam artists or half-wits.

Will met with a retail operator in North Carolina who was the owner of a convenience store chain. He rested his feet on his desk and smoked through the meeting. Will got him to admit that people came into his stores all the time asking for quarters, which was a bothersome and un-profitable transaction, and one that actually cost him money. But still he wouldn't give an inch.

"No," he said, dismissing Will's argument with a wave of his cig-arette. "Nobody is going to buy this. It's the stupidest thing I've ever heard. My customers will not pay for something before they use it."

Will pointed at a half-empty twenty-ounce bottle of Coke on the guy's desk. "Well, what's the deal with that prepaid Coke?"

"What?" the store owner said.

"That prepaid Coke on your desk."

"It's not prepaid Coke," the guy said. "That's a regular Coke."

"No," Will said, "it's a prepaid Coke. You paid for it before you used it. Look, it's the same thing with phone time."

A smile crept up from the edge of the guy's lips. By the end of the meeting, he had agreed to carry the product.

That pitch proved effective as Will and Adam darted around the country trying to educate retailers on how they could make money from selling prepaid calling cards. Slowly, their product took hold. Four years later, a larger Ohio-based calling card company, ConQuest, acquired Will and Adam's company, which was shortly thereafter acquired by SmarTalk, sucking Will and Adam into Bob Lorsch's odd universe.

————

From his headquarters in Los Angeles, Bob Lorsch had entered the pre-paid calling card space and built SmarTalk into a success. I was a VP at Salomon at the time and had heard stories about how crazy and fascinat-ing Lorsch was, so I agreed to work with my colleague Mark Davis on a SmarTalk equity offering a year or so after the company's IPO.

We met at their Los Angeles offices at lunchtime. Lorsch burst into the room like a bad caricature of Danny DeVito, and even though I'd been warned that he was an unconventional CEO, I still wasn't prepared for the encounter. We had put together the standard detailed presentation that analyzed the state of the public equity markets, how the SmarTalk stock had been performing, who owned it, et cetera. A young Salomon analyst who had been pulling all-nighters to assemble the books sat in a chair near the door.

Mark and I passed around the presentation books. "So we've prepared a—" I started.

"Just tell me," Lorsch interjected. "Do we have Grubman or not?" Jack Grubman, Salomon's famed equity analyst, had previously endorsed the SmarTalk IPO with a buy rating.

"Yes," Mark said. "We have Jack. We talked to him prior to the meeting and confirmed that he'll continue to cover the company and support the offering."

"Then you're hired," Lorsch said with a smile, pushing his unopened book to the center of the table. "Let's eat."

It seemed reckless to have made his decision on so little information, and I could only imagine how the analyst kid near the door felt, sleep-deprived and probably proud of his hard work, only to see the book tossed aside without so much as a cracking of the spine.

While we ate the catered lunch that was delivered to the conference room, Mark mentioned that I was in the midst of planning my wedding for that summer.

"Don't get married!" Lorsch advised me. "Terrible, terrible idea." He described a few of his own ill-fated unions, dropping in crude one-liners to punctuate the stories: "Why buy when you can rent? . . . If it flies, floats, or fucks, don't buy it! . . ."

Despite his advice to me to stay single, Lorsch had married and divorced and remarried multiple times, finally taking for his bride an aging porn star. His uncontrollable appetites often proved to be an asset in the business world. Similar to the way Dick Heckmann took an unsexy industry like water treatment and transformed U.S. Filter into a powerhouse—through his charisma and vision and drive, along with a lust for acquisitions—Lorsch did the same with SmarTalk. He knew how to tell a good story, and he convinced Wall Street that he was onto something hot. SmarTalk grew into the biggest prepaid calling card company in the nation.

SmarTalk and Bob Lorsch are already forgotten, especially in the age of unlimited mobile phone minutes, and so prepaid calling cards might now seem like an insignificant thing, but nearly all evolutionary developments are made up of a series of incremental changes. As we shifted from a cash to a cashless society, people became increasingly comfortable with monetary value existing in forms besides dollars and coins. We no longer needed to stuff bills into our wallets or carry quarters for the pay phone. The popularity of credit cards helped push this change along, as consumers started thinking about money differently. But since credit cards are not stored money, prepaid calling cards were the first meaningful vehicle to package everyday currency in a different form. Like the convenience store owner in North Carolina, we were beginning to change the way we thought about our relationship with money and commerce.

———

On a recent tour of an internet data center, my host and I discussed a famous legend that has been echoing around the halls of several facilities, even more than two decades after the event. The story was about the day a naked woman was discovered in the server room.

Some people say it happened in the basement of the PAIX in Palo Alto. Others are certain it happened down the freeway at MAE-West in San Jose. Reportedly there are engineers on the East Coast who claim the incident occurred in their own data center. Over the years, the legend spread, magnified, distorted, fraying at the edges. It became a game of telephone, with the facts embellished as the story passed from person to person. One guy heard that the woman was doing a full porn scene in a cage. Another guy heard it was only a topless photo shoot in front of her web servers. Photographic proof must exist somewhere, but no one can find it. The manager on duty got fired over the whole ordeal. Or wait, maybe he didn't get fired. Maybe he was commended for his tactful handling of the situation. It depended on whom you asked.

The naked-woman-in-the-server-room story, which occurred sometime in the mid to late 1990s, has become the stuff of legend, a favorite tale of the small community of people who populate the tangible world of the web. This world can feel so ethereal to the general public that to be able to conjure up the image of a live, beautiful, in-the-flesh woman, right there in a data center, seemed almost to validate and legitimize the corporeal existence of the internet. *She was here, in this place. I swear. I know someone who saw her.*

My host stopped in front of a server cage and pointed with his thumb. "So the story is," he said, eager to provide his own take, "she came in, wanted to get a picture in front of her website, the actual physical assets on her website, nude, and they were photographing her. Supposedly this guy I know who ran the facility called up the boss and said, 'What do we do?' And then from that came the no photography rule. But she disputes it. Who the hell knows?"

Several people connected to the incident—including the woman in question—agreed to interviews. The stories didn't mesh, yet everyone, it seemed, was telling the truth. The facts had veered into a sort of twilight zone in which many versions of the same event could coexist.

But what was the real story of that infamous photo shoot, and what details were enhanced as this bit of tech world lore was passed around? The story had become so bloated and misshapen over the years, was it still possible to know?

After some digging, it became clear, as is often the case, that the truth is much more interesting than the legend.

———

To most of us, the internet doesn't feel like an actual place. That's part of the magic of it. But it is in fact constructed of a constellation of real physical locations—giant, usually unmarked warehouses, hiding in plain sight in our communities, linked to one another by millions of glass fibers. All companies on the planet that have an internet presence are

physically hosted in one or more of these data centers—as are the internet service providers and telecom companies—where they store their
digital information, operate servers, and run thousands of cross-connect
lines between one another's equipment. These days, we call this network
the cloud. Our photos and playlists are found there. Our files are backed
up there. Our transactions are executed in the cloud.

Most people never physically set foot in a data center—why would
they?—but anyone with a computer or smartphone probably does dozens
or hundreds of things each day that are only possible because of these data
centers. Every time we send a text, check email, buy something online,
map a route, play a game on a phone, post a photo to social media, check
the news, order food delivery or a car service, all of these operations occur
within the fortresslike walls of data centers—arriving at the speed of light
via fiber-optic glass, pinging around the facility through various cables and
cross-connects, then exiting at the speed of light back to the device.

Data centers aren't just selling storage; they're selling security. Guards
are on duty at all times. Getting anywhere in the building requires strict
clearance or a senior level chaperone. The building structure is Kevlar reinforced, with bullet-resistant glass. Some are built on giant rubber shock
absorbers to protect against earthquakes. There are thousands of monitored cameras, mantraps, and several layers of hand-geometry-reader access, with level upon level of identity authentication. The reason for the
extremely high security is that today's data centers are, in many ways,
the new banks, as money has become data, and data has become a sort of
currency.

The data centers are organized in long corridors that are bordered by
metal cages. Inside the cages sit squadrons of humming servers stacked
in cabinets. The lighting is low, blue-lit, as if you'd wandered into the
least popular nightclub on the planet. The room screams with the white
noise of air-conditioning, monstrous systems installed to temper the heat
radiating from the thousands of servers that run 24/7, 365. (The electric
bill for many facilities exceeds $1 million per month.)

The woman who allegedly infiltrated the facility and disrobed—so
she could show her audience how the internet worked and where her

website physically existed—was one of that data center's most important and powerful customers: Danni Ashe, founder and star of Danni's Hard Drive. One of the first-ever pornography websites, Danni's Hard Drive was a softcore destination of nudes and pinups that was originally conceived with a simple goal, a way for Danni to broaden her audience and sell more merchandise. She had toured the strip club circuit as a featured dancer for some years, but after a few traumatic experiences with sleazy club owners, she exited the scene and turned her attention to building up a fan club—mailing autographed photos and magazines and other collectibles around the country, which, in the 1980s and '90s, could provide a decent income for an adult-magazine model. Most evenings when her husband returned home from his job as a senior executive of the Landmark movie theater chain, Danni would be sitting at the table faithfully filling orders. Sign, stuff, lick, seal, stamp, repeat.

She and her husband were early adopters of personal computers, at a time when having a computer in your home was still highly uncommon. Danni heard rumors that photos of her were already being shared widely in Usenet newsgroups—a primitive network of topical chatrooms that predated the internet we know today—so she started to frequent those discussion pages, engaging her fans in conversation and posting her own photos. She soon became the Marilyn Monroe of the nerd community.

One evening in early 1995, her husband showed Danni his company's new website. "It was very, very simple, bare bones," she recalled, "as everything was on the web at the time, but the whole concept of hypertext was designed to work like the human brain, creating a massive web of associations. . . . When I saw that, I was really intrigued. I had that instant light-bulb moment." With plenty of encouragement from others in the Usenet newsgroups, she warmed to the idea of creating her own website. But she had no idea how to go about doing that. There wasn't an industry for web design and development as there is today. She first hired the web developer who'd built Landmark's site, but he couldn't figure out how to create the hypertext structure that Danni envisioned.

A high school dropout from South Carolina, Danni was deceivingly smart. In a 2001 *Frontline* interview, she described herself to PBS as "a geek with big breasts." She picked up a couple of manuals before she and her husband vacationed in the Bahamas, and she essentially taught herself the basics of HTML while lounging on the beach. Returning home, she built the website in two weeks. "I was talking to this colocation facility in Anaheim about a hosting agreement," she said in our interview. "They were going to put me on one of their shared servers, and I said, 'You know, I really think I need my own server. I have this feeling that the site's going to get a lot of traffic,' and they were like, 'No, no, you'll be fine.'" Danni finished the site and emailed a link to five people she had connected with on Usenet, then she boarded a plane for New York, accompanying her husband on a business trip. "The next day I got these frantic phone calls from my ISP [internet service provider] saying, 'Oh my god, oh my god, you've crashed the servers.' So somebody had let the word out. They pretty quickly gave me my own server." Danni's Hard Drive had more than a million hits in its first week. It became the internet's most visited site over the next two years.

There was, however, one big problem. In those early days, the backbone of the internet wasn't robust enough to handle such volumes of traffic. The data centers were largely a mess, poorly organized and overwhelmed by traffic and server demands. While Danni's Hard Drive and other newly popular sites drove the demand, the appetite for their content far outpaced the development of infrastructure, leading to bottlenecks and severed connections. And those limitations only became more troubling as the '90s chugged along and thousands of startup founders began to descend on the Bay Area to hunt their fortunes. The bigger the internet grew, the more it was crushed under the weight of its own activity. Some leading experts predicted that the internet wouldn't survive.

It needed a savior.

———

A couple of years after Danni Ashe crashed the web servers in 1995, a handful of companies were trying to figure out what could be done to address the internet's increasingly dire structural issues. One of those companies was the behemoth Digital Equipment Corporation (DEC), a

Massachusetts-based computer firm founded in 1957 that rivaled IBM in size. DEC had sent a team of researchers and engineers to set up shop in the basement of a defunct telephone switchboard building in Palo Alto, which became known as the Palo Alto Internet Exchange (the PAIX). Their task was to identify the infrastructure problems plaguing the internet and then create a new kind of data center that might solve those problems. Other internet exchange points were run by companies that also sold telecommunications services, which meant that they were compromised by conflicts of interest, but DEC wasn't in the telecom business, so its team members at the PAIX figured that if they could create a truly neutral space where the various elements that form the internet could connect with one another, free from conflicts of interest, that could be the infrastructure development that was so badly needed.

The two guys leading the effort, Jay Adelson and Al Avery, labored over this task with full knowledge that it might not be possible. In time, however, they had a breakthrough. Confident that they'd come up with a successful model for a neutral exchange point, they brought it to their superiors—a concept that very well might save the internet—and yet the bosses at DEC didn't recognize the urgent need to expand the model to multiple facilities around the world. Adelson and Avery knew that the internet was at a pivotal moment, desperate for a large-scale solution, so they quit their jobs and decided to go it alone. They set for themselves an unimaginably lofty goal—to revolutionize the way the internet worked, worldwide. They called their new company Equinix, a loose mashup of *equality*, *neutrality*, and *internet exchange*, and they pretty quickly raised their money. "We knew that a company like Equinix would need to exist," Adelson said. "Somebody would have to be the steward of all this infrastructure."

It seemed that their timing couldn't have been better, as the dotcom craze built toward a crescendo. Similar to homesteaders during westward expansion, a land grab took hold, with newly sprung Silicon Valley companies racing to plant their flags in the virgin soil of the internet. Salomon's senior management started calling me around this time. "What's happening with those big IPOs out there on the West

Coast?" they asked. "Why aren't we getting that action?" Taking companies public wasn't my area of focus; I specialized in M&A and was still based in New York, not Silicon Valley. But since I worked in the tech sector, my Salomon bosses came to me to find out how real the dotcom craze was and why we weren't landing any of the major public offerings, which seemed to be occurring almost hourly.

During the best of times, Silicon Valley brimmed with opportunity. It seemed that every kid with a laptop and a hoodie could slap the dotcom suffix on the end of almost anything—stamps.com, shoes.com, drugstore.com, webvan.com, eToys.com, garden.com—and become a millionaire overnight. Venture capitalists poured money into these companies, and their valuations soared.

But there's no piece of music in which the crescendo doesn't eventually crash. Most people can't recognize when they're in a bubble—or they don't want to recognize it. Markets and industries are cyclical by nature. During periods of significant innovation, bubbles form because expectations grow faster than reality, and hope gets too far out in front of a future that doesn't currently exist. The problem was that the structures, timing, and valuations of these startups were all dependent upon assumed growth and the execution of ambitious business plans, and those assumptions and executions often weren't reasonable or achievable.

One example of many was the perfect catastrophe of pets.com, which sold retail pet supplies. The company launched in early 1999 and found quick success, mainly through ultra-aggressive advertising campaigns and by offering its products for a third of the price at which it had purchased them, with free shipping. The management team running pets.com gambled that if they could convince enough people to begin buying pet goods online, then they could capture adequate market share—even while losing money on every sale—to establish themselves as a viable company. But as their sales increased, so did their losses. Yet they pressed on, spending lavishly to erect a "falloon" of their sock-puppet mascot (a thirty-six-foot-high balloon attached to a float) and entering it in the Macy's Thanksgiving Day Parade, then purchasing a Super Bowl ad for $1.2 million, even as the company hemorrhaged money. Seventeen days after the Super Bowl, they had a successful IPO on the Nasdaq at $11 per share. Less than nine months later, the stock bottomed out at nineteen cents, and they liquidated all assets and went out of business. The entire meteoric run of pets.com—from launch to falloon to Super Bowl to IPO to handing in its keys—spanned barely more than two years.

There was a gold rush atmosphere in the fledgling days of the internet boom, and indeed it evoked memories of the first California gold rush, which was its own sort of bubble. Exactly a century and a half earlier, gold was discovered in the foothills of the Sierra Nevada by a former carpenter from New Jersey. Hordes of fortune seekers then invaded the state from every corner of the globe, striding into the hills with picks and shovels and pans—and nearly all of them ended up penniless. Yet there were some pioneers whose wealth and success endured, and typically they were the people not especially interested in pulling gold out of the ground. A famous maxim was coined: *If you want to get rich during a gold rush, sell shovels.*

Those who provided the miners with their tools, services, and transportation raked in the cash. A Bavarian-born businessman named Levi Strauss launched an enterprise selling dry goods, camping gear, and of course blue jeans, which he produced in his San Francisco shop. Henry Wells and William Fargo set up a shipping and financing service. John Studebaker made wheelbarrows for the miners, long before he became famous for automobiles. Sam Brannan, who first shouted news of the discovery in the streets of San Francisco, didn't spread the word until after he'd bought up every available shovel, pick, and pan, multiplying the prices. It was these pioneers, the providers of tools, clothes, housing, roads, entertainment, food, financial services, transportation—these creators of infrastructure—who allowed the budding gold rush communities and economy to function and thrive. Those are the names we remember today.

Equinix became the shovel salesman of the internet. As dotcom startups flooded California to seek their capricious fortunes, Equinix was busy creating the infrastructure to make it all work. But what had first seemed like fortuitous timing quickly reversed course. Equinix was reliant on the success of those startup clients, and by 2000 the dotcom bubble had burst. Those crumbling companies, whose guiding vision had been hope, no longer needed the infrastructure assets they had acquired in pursuit of that hope. Equinix was stuck with a lot of unsettled accounts and increasingly deserted data centers. And now it faced the insistent challenge of having to pay off its substantial debt, which it had accumulated in order to build the infrastructure that would support all those companies that had just gone up in smoke.

———

In the sanguine early days, before the bubble popped, Danni's Hard Drive quickly grew beyond its original vision of running her fan club. "I went on this thing called the Boob Cruise," Danni said in our interview, "which used to be put on by *Score* magazine. They booked several models for this cruise, and then fans could pay to be on the boat and watch photo shoots and have dinner with the models. So while I was on this—I think it was my second Boob Cruise—I had dry-loaded my website onto my laptop so that people could look at it."

One of the publishers of *Score* also ran a large mail-order video operation, and when he saw Danni's site on the Boob Cruise, he recognized the internet's potential as a new kind of marketplace. He asked her to put his entire video catalog on her website, hundreds of titles. Danni, of course, was one step ahead of him. "My whole concept was to use hypertext to get people to link into products—you start reading about a certain model and then, oh look, she has this signed magazine over here, oh look, she has this videotape over there. So we started negotiating. I'm like, 'I can only sell your products if I also have content, if I have photographs and bios and pictures of all these models, because that's the way it all works.' To get all of that, we had to go to the magazine and make a deal to get their entire library of content, so then I would have material to sell the videos."

In that process, the idea was floated to create a subscription pay area, since so much valuable content would be uploaded to Danni's site. A paywall was another new concept for the internet. "That was launched in February of '96, and again it was like *wham*, overnight success, unbelievable. It just completely overwhelmed me. I was working sixteen hours a day, getting order forms with credit card numbers and then manually punching them into a piece of software that would authorize the credit card. This was way before anybody had real-time credit card processing."

Around 1997, Danni started taking meetings with companies that were creating payment-processing software, hoping she could find help in handling the avalanche of sales and memberships. "They'd come in, and I'd say, 'Well, okay, how secure is my customers' data? What happens if this happens? What happens if that happens?' And I didn't feel comfortable with any of the answers that I was getting. That's when I started hiring software engineers and building my own credit card processing engine."

The legend of Danni Ashe isn't about a nude photo shoot in a data center. That was a distraction. The real legend is about a smart, enterprising woman whose name should be remembered for her brilliant tech innovations. Danni's Hard Drive provided a blueprint for how to construct and operate a successful e-commerce website—not only pornography, but all of e-commerce—as Danni developed several brilliant, cutting-edge solutions to handle transactions more efficiently and securely. "The innovation was always out of sheer necessity," she said. "It was out of an urgent need to solve a problem. It wasn't so much like, 'Oh, I'm going to become somebody who builds technology.' It was more like, 'I have an urgent need to make *this* happen.'" Urgent problem solving is so often the catalyst for successful companies. Danni told PBS: "Over the years, we've had to develop a lot of technology to support the business of Danni's Hard Drive—streaming video technology, hosting technologies, credit card scrubbing technologies, processing, customer service. And all of these things are now working so well that they have value to other companies, and we're beginning to market those technologies to other companies. And that's actually the largest area of growth in our business right now."

From some combination of sexism and a bias against the porn industry, Danni Ashe has rarely gotten the recognition she deserves for her technological and entrepreneurial prowess. The science and tech journalist Patchen Barss wrote: "She and other pornographers pioneered the e-commerce and security solutions that paved the way for PayPal, eBay, Amazon, and the commercialization of the internet."

It's telling to imagine those first moments when someone pulled a card from his wallet and had the nerve to enter the numbers onto a form and send it off into the ether, hoping that the person on the other end had the diligence and integrity of Danni Ashe. What motivated the consumer's leap of faith? The promise of seeing naked flesh. It seems ironic that raw human drive—in the form of pornography—was largely responsible for forcing the tech innovations that ultimately led to the reduced need for personal interaction in our daily lives. We craved human contact so badly that we devised ways to destroy it.

Buying something online with a credit card is so commonplace today that it's difficult to remember the recent past when it was a completely foreign concept. The advent of that digital transaction was another important step in our physical disconnection with money and in the diminishment of human contact in the financial world. Commerce no longer required one person handing cash or a card to another in exchange for goods and services. The removal of transaction friction—as it is called in business parlance—facilitated massive efficiency and productivity gains for so many companies. Yet while a lack of friction has been positive in many ways, it has also compromised our proximity, awareness, and sensitivity to others. For many of us, commerce was one of the few opportunities in our modern world to interact with individuals different from ourselves. That's a loss that has reverberated throughout society, politics, and the financial industry.

After the dotcom crash of 1999–2000, most Wall Street firms ran screaming from the technology industry. They had made their money when times were good, but now the risks had proven too great, the potential losses too steep. The name *dotcom* became a curse word; Wall Street wanted nothing to do with it. The managing director leading our own tech group, based in California, quit. So I met with the head of banking and nominated myself for the job. "Are you sure you want to do that?" he asked. Most people considered it a terrible career move, since the industry was in such turmoil. But my wife, Jessica, and I had long been enticed by the notion of returning to California—where I'd spent my high school, college, and early working years and where Jessica had also lived for a time, plus her father was a professor of political science at Claremont McKenna College. So while fleets of U-Hauls were rolling east, away from the smoldering embers of the tech industry, our truck rolled west.

A crisis is a terrible thing to waste, as many people have noted. It's when relationships are cemented; it's when franchises are established. In this case, with tech IPO and M&A activity having slowed significantly, there was a great opportunity to develop relationships with the companies that were still standing in the scorched landscape of Silicon Valley. We were setting ourselves up for when the market would recover.

I had a loyal group in New York, and I gathered my top people and suggested that we make a go of it, that we head west together and try to build something. They all consented, willing to give up their stable positions in New York to take a risk in California.

When I arrived to assume control of the office, there was an air of PTSD among the staff. They had been there for the high times, then seen it all crumble, and now everyone was worried about being laid off. I wanted to establish a positive environment right out of the gate. I wanted them to know that I would reward good work and cooperation, that I intended to promote a healthy culture.

On my first day, the office manager came up to me with a sheet of paper. She seemed friendly but very serious.

"Mr. Varelas, you need to send this memo to the entire office. I've drafted it for you."

I figured it was some sort of welcome note. "What is it?"

She held it out to me. "Don't feed the ducks."

"Did you say, 'Don't feed the ducks'?"

"That's correct. The ducks in the pond out front. If you feed them the wrong food, it makes them poo in a way that clouds the color of the water." She said this last part in a hushed tone, as if we were sharing an important secret.

I skimmed the memo and handed it back to her.

"Leigh, right?" I asked. She nodded. "Leigh, I appreciate this, but I'm not gonna have my first official memo to the office be *Don't feed the ducks*. My third or fourth memo maybe, but not my first. We're gonna have to put this one on hold for a while."

She looked crestfallen. She seemed very earnest.

"Why don't you send it, Leigh? You're the office manager."

"I guess I could," she said.

I smiled encouragingly. "I fully support the message if it comes from you."

My wife, Jessica, had been darting back and forth to New York, where she was finishing her work as a lawyer for Goldman Sachs. By the end of the summer of 2001, we moved the last of our things to California and settled into a rental house in nearby Hillsborough.

Citi's big tech conference was in Manhattan during the first week of September 2001. I remember walking around depressed because New York felt like one of those places that, once you left, you never moved back, and I loved New York. The streets that week were filled with happy people enjoying spectacular weather after the oppressive August heat.

Days later, I was asleep in our new house in California when the planes crashed into the World Trade Center. My sister called at six that morning to make sure I wasn't flying that day. Her husband, Eric, was in Manhattan, on the fortieth floor of Citi's building at 388 Greenwich. The second plane flew right over his head.

After I awoke and heard the news, I sent out a voice message to the office, knowing everyone would check before reporting to work. I told the staff to take the day off, watch CNN, make sure their loved ones were okay, do whatever they had to do. "But," I told them, "you've got to come into work tomorrow because we're going to have to help every-body in New York. They don't have an office; they don't have anything. So we're going to have to be a sort of emergency center for our friends there."

———

During the year or so after 9/11 and the dotcom crash, the technology industry continued to flounder. While Salomon had allowed me to take over the tech group and develop new relationships with potential future clients, the firm had grown just as wary of the dotcom world as everyone else on the Street, and there was simply less action in the sector, meaning fewer and smaller fees, so we couldn't maintain the staff size we had built up during the boom times. Each quarter, we would wait to hear whether we needed to trim our staff, hoping we would get lucky and be passed over until the next quarter, which rarely happened.

One particular quarter, I knew I had to lay off a few people, and I had a hard time figuring out who would come under the axe and how to deal with it. I walked to my wall of second-story windows and looked out at the manufactured duck pond that graced our industrial complex in Palo Alto. A haggard old duck limped along the shoreline, oblivious to a hawk passing over. She was conspicuously, maybe even defiantly, alone. In spring and summer, I would watch these mother ducks lead half a dozen or so of their young around the pond, and occasionally hawks would swoop down and pick off the ducklings. By the end of the season, each mother had only one or two offspring left, which was all she could defend. The rest were victims of the almighty food chain. It was sad to see, but those were the cruel and necessary laws of nature, even on a manufactured pond in an industrial park at the center of the tech world. It was a blustery autumn day. The lone duck slipped into the water and swam against the wind for the far shore.

I concluded that I had no choice but to lay off an associate named Andy Rigoli. His career had begun at the CIA, as a junior trade and finance analyst in the Directorate of Intelligence in Langley. His duties there involved reading and writing about the New York financial world.

After a few years of that, he felt too removed from the excitement—tucked away at a desk reading *about* the financial world, rather than participating in it—so he quit the agency and enrolled in business school at his undergraduate alma mater, UCLA. Andy received a lot of interest from bank recruiters who were intrigued by his CIA background, and he landed at Salomon, working in New York and then offering to shift to the West Coast headquarters of the technology investment banking group, since, at the time, it was the most exciting sector on the Street. When Andy joined us in California, his main task was to develop models for what it might look like if various Silicon Valley companies were to merge. He was good at it and very well liked at the office, but after he'd been with the firm for three years, most of the tech companies he'd been covering had disappeared when the bottom fell out of the industry.

After Salomon laid him off, he spent a few weeks floating in the pool of his Mountain View apartment building, feeling adrift and watching the clouds pass. He had taken a risk leaving the CIA, hoping it would pay off with a thrilling and lucrative Wall Street career, but now here he was, unemployed, 350 miles from his girlfriend, not knowing if he should stick it out in the capital of the tech world or hightail it back to LA to begin anew.

I hated letting my people go and worked hard to make sure every one of them landed in another good job somewhere. I felt a personal stake in their well-being. At Salomon, we were digging through our contacts of clients, friends, and other firms, trying to find a job for Andy, something that would suit his talents of analyzing and building financial models. We had done a lot of work with Equinix, and I was particularly close with the new CEO, Peter Van Camp. PVC, as everyone called him, had been a senior executive at CompuServe back in 1997 when I helped negotiate a three-way deal to sell the company to WorldCom and AOL. PVC was deeply liked and respected by all who encountered him. My associate Stuart gave Equinix a call to see if they had a place for a guy like Andy. Soon after, Andy was reporting for his first day at a company that he had never heard of a few weeks prior.

PVC's integrity and professionalism were unquestioned. Everyone wanted to be on his team. When he announced his intention to leave WorldCom, Bernie Ebbers—the infamous CEO who would later be convicted of fraud and conspiracy and serve jail time—recognized PVC's value and offered him a retention bonus with indications that it would contain a seven-figure number, which was an amount that PVC had never before contemplated receiving. Ebbers didn't want to lose PVC, but PVC knew that things weren't quite right with the company. "I could see we'd amassed a strong set of assets, but we lacked the leadership or vision to align them into a market leader. I just knew it would collapse under its own weight. No amount of money would change that." PVC exited WorldCom, leaving the check on his desk—still sealed in its envelope. He didn't want to be tempted by what it contained.

Unbeknownst to us, we were sending Andy from the frying pan into the fire. Equinix had suffered mightily after the dotcom crash. It was a real company that had been built on a model of providing a necessary service to a bunch of companies that turned out to be ephemeral startups. When they evaporated, Equinix was in serious trouble. Its IPO happened in August 2000, in which it raised $240 million, with its stock debuting at $12 per share, then briefly running up to $16; and a mere two years later, everything had fallen apart. Equinix's stock plunged to seventeen cents per share. Its remaining cash reserves could cover only a single month of payroll. It wasn't that Equinix was teetering on the brink of disaster; disaster had already arrived. The main debt holders insisted that the company declare bankruptcy, but PVC and his team instead devised a complicated and ambitious restructuring plan and capital raise that might save the company. To say it was a long shot is an understatement. The plan almost seemed like a gag. No one had confidence it could succeed. And that was the moment when Andy Rigoli walked in, smiling, unaware of the problems, eager to start his new job.

He was asked to join a meeting on his second day at Equinix. When he arrived at the conference room, most of the senior-level people were present. The mood felt decidedly grim.

"Right here, Andy." He was directed to a seat beside the notoriously volatile president and chief operating officer, Phil Koen. Andy sat down at the laptop waiting for him, on which was displayed a spreadsheet with Equinix's financial models. The screen image was projected onto the wall, so everyone in the room could follow along.

After a brief preamble, Koen turned to the projected image. "Okay," he said. "Let's turn off Bangkok and Seoul."

Andy looked at him for a couple of seconds, to be sure he understood what his boss wanted him to do, and then with a few keystrokes, Andy wiped out those Equinix operations. That would result in the termination of about forty people.

Koen squinted at the bottom-line numbers on the wall. "Now turn off half of Singapore."

Andy did. The meeting continued in this fashion, scanning profit and loss summaries, then zeroing out Equinix employees and whole teams around the globe.

After a lunch break, they reconvened. Koen continued as remorseless and unemotional as a medieval executioner. He didn't take kindly to dissent. When a few people in the room gathered the courage to protest some of the deeper cuts, Koen said, "This is like battlefield triage here. We have to cut off the arm to save the patient."

Even though it was only Andy's second day on the job, and he'd never laid eyes on any of their staff in Asia, he felt awful carrying out these orders. It was almost like being caught up in a mafia initiation where you were handed a gun and told to shoot someone. But no matter what dark metaphor he reached for to understand the situation—medieval executioner, battlefield triage, mafia assassination—he did as he was told, and the financials adjusted accordingly, gradually steering the company back toward the possibility of survival.

By the end of the eight-hour session, seventy or eighty people would soon find out they'd lost their jobs. But there also seemed to be a clear path forward for saving the company. "Phil may have been rough," Andy said, "but there was a logic to his decisions that I could respect." Andy arrived back at his apartment that evening feeling some combination of nausea and exhilaration, but the experience helped him understand why he had just been laid off from Salomon, and he was guardedly excited about Equinix's future. He dialed up his girlfriend in LA. "I think this company's either going to go bankrupt in six months," he told her, "and we'll be handing in the keys to the landlord and turning off the lights, or the stock is going to take off."

———

Despite Phil Koen's forcible downsizing and the bloodbath that Andy witnessed during that first week, the culture at Equinix remained positive and healthy, even in the lean times that were to come. Much of this was due to the founders, Jay Adelson and Al Avery, who, at a certain point, hired a new management team to replace themselves, so the company could move forward and grow and evolve. Most startup founders don't have the maturity and selflessness to do this, but Adelson and Avery cared too much about Equinix and its larger vision to let their egos stand in the way.

PVC took over as CEO at an inauspicious moment. The company's IPO was a few months away, but the internet bubble was already bursting. "I think there were five online pet stores at the time," PVC said. "You know, that just isn't going to work. We were walking into road shows and meetings, and investors would open the meetings by asking, 'Why are you even here? Haven't you been reading the press?'" Even the big dotcom survivors were badly hobbled by the crash, so of course that affected their relationship with Equinix. "Mainstream names like IBM, they had wanted 5 to 10 percent of every data center we built. That was in our contract with them, because they thought they were going to build so many websites. In that first year, everybody was buying—they all wanted to have a presence near the networks at Equinix, which was a great selling tool. But by the end of that year, as the bubble burst, everybody was coming back to renegotiate their contracts, so we started facing that."

Equinix had borrowed $150 million to cover the considerable expense of building new data centers, but as its customers began to fail and disappear, Equinix slowed construction but still needed to address the threat of not being able to make payments on its debt. The banks were very close to taking the keys to the company.

In order to retain any shred of investor confidence and hope to avoid bankruptcy, Equinix needed the endorsement of a major investment bank to help raise the capital necessary for survival. No one would go near them, but from my previous experience working with PVC at CompuServe, and from our recent exposure to the rest of the Equinix management team, I had full confidence in their integrity and abilities. Our endorsement still didn't mean they would survive, since the cards were stacked heavily against them, but I was in a position to take a chance on someone; and who better to support, I figured, than these good people? What was the point of having built up goodwill and authority within my firm unless I could actually use it in situations like this? I didn't even want to see the financial analysis, because the numbers might dissuade me from helping Equinix for what I felt were more important reasons. Integrity and relationships are the only things that will get you through a bubble. So with my recommendation and approval, Salomon backed Equinix as it hit the road to raise the funds that might save the company.

"The survival plan was launched in mid-2002," Andy Rigoli said, "a few months before I joined the firm. Had I known all these details, I would have certainly packed everything I owned into my Lexus and driven down the coast to be with my girlfriend in LA." The feat that Equinix needed to pull off was hard to understand, let alone accomplish. To a normal person, it was as if Andy were speaking in tongues when he described it: "We had to complete a 32-for-1 reverse stock split to take the stock price back above the mandatory minimum $1 threshold to avoid getting delisted, simultaneously renegotiate the company's debt with the bondholders, raise new capital through convertible debt, sever and divest several underperforming assets, renegotiate unfavorable leases locked in during the real estate peak, lay off more staff, and sell the hell out of our remaining assets to get back to EBITDA and cash-flow positive." If they could do all that, then the next step would be to merge the now-cleaned-up company with two Asian companies in exchange for Equinix shares.

"It wasn't a 10 in complexity," PVC said, "it was a 25. But I think back to the human element again—it's about relationships, affinity for the team, the promise of the business model, all these were enough inspiration for everybody to say, 'This thing needs to go on, and we're all in.' On December 31, 2002, the deal closed, and our bookings from the end of 2002 to the first quarter of 2003 quadrupled. All our competitors failed. We were the survivor at that point, and so by being the survivor, all the business came to us, and we started ramping again."

Yet even having survived that near-death experience, Equinix still had to make it through another bubble not long after, somehow riding out the financial meltdown of 2008. In the few years leading up to that event, Equinix had built a robust presence in the financial services industry, providing the infrastructure for one of the biggest financial evolutions of our time—money moving to the cloud.

John Knuff first encountered Equinix as a customer while he was working for an electronic-trading-solutions firm called NYFIX, and he was so excited by what he saw that he asked Jay Adelson for a meeting to discuss how Equinix could be scaled in a way that would benefit global markets. "If Equinix could become that hub," he told them, "or that dense interconnecting point in cities like New York, London, Tokyo, Frankfurt, it would change the way people do electronic trading worldwide."

Knuff joined the company in 2007 and began crafting Equinix's presence in the financial world. The firm built a large new data center just outside of New York City. "Little did we know," John said, "that the four horsemen of the apocalypse were going to ride right through the financial markets a short time later. All the banks started to collapse. I don't think that that site would have been built if we could have looked into a crystal ball and seen what was coming. But the fact that it was built and that we were making investments is really what won us a lot of business and made us the home to the financial markets. Equinix was willing to invest when other people were reeling from the impact of the financial apocalypse."

One way that Equinix distinguished itself in the financial sector and set itself up for long-term success was by rejecting the popular yet controversial trend of high-frequency trading (HFT), which is the rapid buying and selling of large volumes of stock at very high speeds, using algorithms. With HFT, stocks are never held for long—their purpose is for rapid arbitrage. At its peak, HFT accounted for well over half of US equity trading volume. Equinix shunned this opportunity and instead focused on supporting low-latency trading—an approach that also minimizes the time between the decision and the execution of a transaction down to microseconds. But even though both practices prioritize speed, arbitrage isn't the intent of low-latency trading. "For example," John Knuff explained, "Berkshire Hathaway might be trying to own most of a railroad over a few years, and they may try to get into the market at specific times to buy stock, and they want to do that very quickly. So they care about low latency, but they have no intent to turn over that position quickly. Equinix became known as the hub for intelligent trading, the place where you could aggregate all of the information and market data and then route orders to your trading infrastructures at the exchanges. Our tagline was: 'Trade smarter, because speed won't make a bad trade better.' So when high-frequency trading was at its peak in 2007, '08, and '09, we missed all of that growth. But that was also luck beyond measure because then when it started to die off in 2010, we also missed the extinction event of a lot of the HFT folks."

At its low point, Equinix stock was worth seventeen cents a share. By July 2019, it would be almost three thousand times higher, soaring past the $500 mark, which made it one of the best-performing stocks since the dotcom crash. Equinix is now the world's largest operator of colocation data centers, with more than six thousand employees across the globe, from Dallas to Dubai, from Helsinki to Hong Kong. The company's neutral exchange model revolutionized the industry and provided the necessary backbone for the internet to grow and the cloud to be established. And yet, if you were to survey a hundred random people, probably no one would know what Equinix is or what it does, even though most of us touch the company dozens of times each day on computers and phones. It may be the most important company that you've never heard of.

———

One day, not long after I relocated to California, I was driving to a meeting in Palo Alto when I spotted an amusing bumper sticker on the beat-up Porsche in front of me: PLEASE, GOD, ONE MORE BUBBLE BEFORE I DIE. The fallout from the dotcom crash was still fairly fresh. Was this someone who had missed out on the boom times, I wondered, or someone who had profited and then lost it all?

Either way, the sticker highlighted a fascinating mindset that still pervades Silicon Valley: Are we out there just wishing that another bubble would come along, to boost our spirits and our bank accounts for as long as the party lasts? It's a dangerous wish. Where would that leave us when the next bubble breaks? Many generations have seen true progress and growth, but not without moments when reality falls out of alignment with inflated bubble metrics. Hope, by its very definition, gets too far out in front of reality, and many of those hope-fueled companies don't survive. The general formula in Silicon Valley is that there will be nine failures for every success—that high rate of failure is a necessary consequence of the freedom to take the risk to innovate. Even so, those failures leave damage and casualties in their wake. Part of the brilliance of startup culture is its dexterity and speed and conviction. Those same characteristics, however, can also manifest as vulnerability, as they frequently lead to shortsightedness, impatience, and volatility.

Jay Adelson and Al Avery, the visionaries behind revolutionizing the data center, constructed Equinix as a company that would provide the backbone of the internet for years to come. They exited before they could share in its great success. Al died while Equinix was still struggling to survive, and Jay has gone on to do many other impressive things; but, outside of Equinix, they've never gotten the recognition they deserve for saving the internet at a crucial moment and revolutionizing the way it operates.

Danni Ashe, the mother of e-commerce, quit her industry while still in her thirties, dismayed at the direction online pornography was headed and unwilling to be associated with the darker corners of that realm. She sold her company, which was eventually acquired by Penthouse, and moved to a horse ranch in the Northwest.

Bob Lorsch, that tragic, larger-than-life evangelist of the prepaid calling card, stepped away from SmarTalk and started a medical-records storage company, while serving on several boards. He stayed married to his former porn star wife until death did them part. Lorsch's tireless optimism was finally overcome by a long, painful battle with illness. In May 2017, lying in bed at home, Bob Lorsch shot himself in the head.

These people, forgotten or not, each represented essential steps in the evolution of modern money. Lorsch's calling cards made us comfortable with the fact that money could exist in other forms. Danni is responsible for e-commerce as we know it today. Equinix created the backbone that made it possible for money to move to the cloud.

Money keeps shifting into new forms to meet evolving needs. The concept of phone minutes as currency has recently taken hold in some African nations, where the public has so lost faith in their government and its fiat currency that it has become common for people to pay one another or make financial transactions by transferring phone minutes, or "airtime," between mobile devices. *The Economist* covered the phenomenon in a 2013 piece: "Unlike mobile money, airtime's value does not rely directly on a government's stability or ability to hold down inflation by, say, showing restraint printing money." Money doesn't have to be money anymore. And a lot of that evolution has been fueled by a loss of trust in government and our financial institutions.

Consider the rise of cryptocurrencies. People have become so comfortable with alternate forms of currency, while simultaneously disillusioned with our traditional financial structures, that they're willing to put their money into something that an anonymous entity created and is nearly impossible to use for anything legal other than speculation and trading. Stories are common of people having mortgaged their houses to buy Bitcoin. They may not trust the bank, but they'll trust sinking their savings into a currency with little history and unproven legitimacy. That's how cynical we have become, how disconnected we now are from conventional forms of money.

A recent trend in Silicon Valley—which capitalizes on the popularity of cryptocurrency—is to issue an initial coin offering (ICO) when raising funding. With an ICO, companies essentially form their own currency and sell it to investors, who in turn can only use the coin to purchase the products or services of the issuing startup. The startup world is already fraught with risk and inflated promises, and ICOs magnify those problems by injecting the crypto landscape with flimsy new currencies, further corrupting the trust and integrity of that market.

A lot of people believe that what will survive the crypto bubble will be the infrastructure, rather than many of the currencies themselves. Blockchain is a digital ledger originally created to record Bitcoin transactions, but it has since found a multitude of other valuable uses. Blockchain, as the infrastructure that allows the majority of cryptocurrencies to operate, is the shovel salesman, just like Equinix was for the internet, while the cryptocurrencies are the gold seekers or the startups. One use of Blockchain that will have a dramatic impact on wealth management and the way we look at value will be the ability to divide an asset into as many parts as desired and sell those to third parties. Any asset, in theory—including your house or even your future earnings potential—would be eligible to be parsed and sold, creating a world in which partial ownership across existing and potential new asset classes would likely be the norm. How will that change our view of and relationship to value when we no longer own an entire asset but only a piece? Will we be as invested in the viability and success of the whole?

As much as any other evolution in the world of money, one of the most influential has been the gradual diminishment of human contact. It started with the false magic trick of ATM deposits, then the very idea of money shapeshifted into calling cards and other new forms of currency, and finally the advent of the internet pushed us into an entirely new realm; in a few short years it became possible to execute everyday tasks and transactions—like hailing a ride, buying groceries or clothes or books, ordering food delivery, chipping in for your share of a restaurant meal—with the mere touch of a screen. So many popular apps and tech forces—Amazon, Uber, Venmo, Airbnb—simply provide the means to disintermediate humans from commerce. It's not uncommon in several cities to see a knee-high robot, basically a fancy cooler on wheels, navigating through pedestrians en route to deliver lunch to some hungry office worker, who not only doesn't need to offer a gratuity, but can skip the small talk and pleasantries too. There is something wonderful about the swiftness and convenience of these technological developments, but there is also something perilous, as we become increasingly disconnected from money and commerce. As several companies work to perfect the driverless car, it'll soon be possible to get from home to the office and back with essentially no human contact. We can protect ourselves from anything and anybody that might disrupt, challenge, or unsettle us.

But what will protect us when the next big bubble bursts? In the case of Equinix, it was their integrity and the trust they had built with their employees, partners, and customers. But in a world with less and less human interaction, and therefore fewer opportunities to develop trust, how does one build the relationships that will be there for us in times of need?

It used to be that when we needed bread, we went to see the baker. And in doing so, we would talk to our neighbors. *Has your mother recovered from her hip surgery? How's your garden? Did you take care of that roof leak?* Commerce grounded us in the physical world, forcing us to be present in our cities and towns and communities. We would pull out our wallets and count dollar bills onto the counter in exchange for our goods, back when money used to be real, tangible currency, built of paper and metal. We stored it in purses and pockets and bras, safes and mattresses and backyard holes. The quality of our bank was measured by the impenetrability of its vault and the alertness of its armed guard. Then one day the cloud appeared overhead. We stayed indoors and took up our devices, checked our balances, played our games, ordered dinner, scrolled our feeds. Our relationships, transactions, and net worth could now be found and managed on a screen. Main Street became somewhere we no longer needed to go. Our money began to evaporate into the cloud like dew on a bright morning, lifting up, up, and away, becoming digital raindrops in a sky of ones and zeroes.

8

DIAMOND DOGS

To be without some of the things you want is an indispensable part of happiness.
—BERTRAND RUSSELL, FROM *THE CONQUEST OF HAPPINESS*

I sat facing my boss's desk, waiting for him to speak the number and tell me my worth. He shuffled through a stack of pages, fished one out, and told me my year-end bonus amount with a total lack of expression or emotion. He could have been reciting the evening train schedule, but to my ears, it was Beethoven's Ninth. I was thrilled. As a freshly minted Salomon Brothers investment banking associate, this was my first important bonus meeting. The number was greater than zero, which meant that I wasn't getting canned, and it was in the ballpark of what they told me to expect when I joined the firm. In fact, it was triple the best money I'd ever made.

I rose from my seat to shake my boss's hand, gushing my appreciation for the generous compensation and the opportunity to work at such a great firm. He looked at me askance, as if he were trying to detect sarcasm in my tone. But my enthusiasm was unfeigned. He handed me the sheet of paper and said, "All right then, Varelas." Apparently we were done. So that was a bonus meeting. No recap of the past year's successes and challenges. No warm encouragement for what lay ahead. Just a routine delivery of a dollar amount, a limp handshake, and out the door.

Back at my cubicle, I sat down, laid the paper on the desk, and leaned in to study it carefully. Finally I slipped it into the center drawer of my desk and returned my attention to the presentation on which I'd been working—even though I suspected it might never be put in front of a client nor generate a dollar of revenue for the firm—and I attacked the work, reinvigorated by my bonus, which I felt sure was proof of my value to the firm.

That buoyant feeling lasted a few hours.

At the end of the day, congregated in a cubicle encampment with the thirteen associates in my class, I held a small scrap of paper, watching Kelly circle with a hat. "Drop it in, Varelas." She shook the hat in front of me, inside of which other scraps of paper tumbled like deflated lottery balls. I noticed the hat's Yankees logo. An ominous sign for a Red Sox fan. I felt as though I'd already lost, and the game hadn't even begun.

Kelly and Billy were the ringleaders. On the scraps were scrawled the bonus numbers we'd each received that day. Management had told us never to share the amounts of our year-end bonuses, but they had also instructed us that information is power. And of course, as Salomon Brothers employees, we were almost expected to push boundaries and test rules. So there we were, the entire first-year investment banking associate class, having anonymously scrawled our bonus numbers on scraps of paper, dropping them into a hat to be read aloud, so we would have an idea of where each of us stood within the full group.

Kelly orbited the cubicles with her sinister Yankees cap, while some of the cockiest or loudest in the group provided commentary as they tossed in their scraps.

"Undoubtedly the high."

"Bingo! Sorry, suckers."

"I just hope I don't get too bummed out when I learn that some of you worthless slugs got paid within the same zip code as me."

I relinquished my scrap without a word. I knew I wouldn't be the high, but I was hopeful that I wouldn't be the low.

My stomach tightened as Kelly handed the hat to Billy, and he stirred the papers and began pulling them out one after another. From the first number he read, I learned that I wasn't top bucket. But with the third and fourth numbers, at least my misery had company. No one owned up to their amounts, as we'd all agreed upon ahead of time, but still, rumors and reactions were lobbed across the room.

"I heard they're planning to let go of 20 percent of the class next week."

"I heard it could be half."

"Wouldn't want to be bottom bucket going into that firing squad."

"Nah, they aren't going to fire any junior associates. Sends a bad recruiting message."

I didn't know what to believe, but that last line of logic was mildly comforting. They wouldn't fire us right after doling out bonuses, right?

As Billy spoke the numbers, I did some quick mental math, in case the 20 or 50 percent rumors were true, calculating my odds of keeping my job. A 20 percent layoff I could *probably* survive. If it were half, I could easily be among the departed. The fourteen of us represented the smallest investment banking class in years, which reflected the struggling markets.

Once all the numbers had been read, I felt some sense of relief to find that many of us had been paid nearly the same amount, with a few standouts who'd been paid roughly 15 percent more. We could pretty easily guess who had landed in the top bucket. I began to assess my classmates—and myself—in light of this new information. Those of us who had been paid the least must have failed to differentiate ourselves in any significant way.

The pleasant fog of optimism and abundance I'd enjoyed that morning had now burned off, replaced by disappointment and a sprinkling of panic. I hadn't recalled experiencing these emotions, at least not to this degree.

I'd have to work harder and better and smarter. And not just on the projects assigned to me—I needed to land more impressive projects, to work with more influential people. It was the only way to guarantee survival.

Just months earlier, I'd been happy with my pay and place in the world.

Hell, I'd been happy just a few *minutes* earlier. I supposed I had wanted to know where I stood among my fellow associates, but the knowledge plucked out of Kelly's hat had made it difficult to feel positive, despite being paid more money than I'd ever dreamed of making. Such was my first hard lesson in the double-edged sword of compensation transparency: What I gained in motivation, I lost in contentment.

———

Over the next few years, I learned to survive without sleep. Dinner happened when most of the city was tucked into bed, usually cheap pizza or Chinese. In busy stretches, we ordered delivery six or seven nights per week. Typically our exhaustion would lead to philosophical discussions about happiness, purpose, and future plans.

I was working on a project with Kevin Tice, who had been at Salomon one year longer than I had, and we dined on Chinese in an empty conference room.

"What's your number?" he said, across towers of steaming takeout containers from Au Mandarin, one of our favorite spots.

"My phone number?" I asked, between chews.

"No, man, your *number*. How much would you need? To be done?"

"Done with what?" I glanced protectively at the egg rolls.

"Done with the business. Done with this thing." He waved his chopsticks, encompassing the room.

I looked cluelessly at him. "You mean when do I want to retire? I'm not even thirty."

"Not retire, just do something else. What's the number you need so you can just walk away and live the life you want? Do something you've always dreamed of doing."

"I've never really thought about it," I said.

"Come on!" Kevin shouted. "Everyone's thought about it. Everyone has a number."

I looked through the conference room's glass wall to where dozens of people, also working late, barked into phones, jawed at each other across desks, rushed around with papers and dealbooks. This place was exciting and frenetic, even at ten at night. It was alive. Were all these people just biding their time until they could jump ship and do something else? I began to wonder whether the infectious energy of the investment banking department was in fact born from a wish to escape. "I love this job," I said. "I don't want to be anywhere else right now."

"Bullshit."

"Are you really that miserable here?" I asked.

"Not at all. I love my job too. It's not like I'm counting the freakin' days, saying, 'God, when am I going to get that check so I can bolt?' But everybody has a number and something they'd rather eventually do."

I didn't know what to say. I shrugged and scooped some rice onto my paper plate. "What's the other thing you'd rather be doing?" I asked.

"Don't you want to know my number?"

"Sure." I couldn't help but be curious, even though it seemed like awfully personal information to be sharing so casually.

"Four million." Kevin paused for effect, holding a bite of chow fun poised in the air between us. "That's the amount of money I know I can live on comfortably for the rest of my life, take care of my family, and leave them something." He devoured the chow fun, wiped his face, and wadded up his napkin.

"Okay," I said. "You should be able to get that."

"And *then*," he said, lowering his voice conspiratorially, "I'm gonna coach basketball and be a Colorado ski bum."

Kevin leaned back in his chair and launched the balled-up napkin toward the corner of the room, banking it off the wall and missing the trashcan by a few feet.

A bit later, I plopped down in my cubicle and surveyed its things—a mess of papers, presentations, annual reports, a folded *Wall Street Journal*, a half-drunk bottle of water. Unlike the other guys, I didn't decorate my area with photos or mementos of any sort, yet this place still felt like home, especially since the job often required eighty to a hundred hours per week. It was more home to me than my shared New York apartment, where my grand total of furnishings consisted of a bed and a secondhand black-and-white TV.

Midnight arrived, but I felt no fatigue. I'd been contentedly analyzing the potential sale of a company that built most of the world's airplane jetways, when I paused to look around the office. The place had mostly emptied out, but still there were at least half a dozen twenty-two-year-old analysts creating financial models and preparing presentation materials. A cleaning woman was vacuuming, listening to a Walkman. From my desk I could see north, toward Midtown. The lights of the city sparkled around the dark expanse of Central Park. Yes, the money was incredible, but I truly felt at that moment that I would have paid Salomon Brothers for the privilege of sitting at that desk. Even at such a young age, I worked directly with the leaders of *Fortune* 500 companies. Every day was intellectually stimulating.

But was I supposed to have a number? I hoped not. I sensed even then that to have a number might introduce dissatisfaction with the life I was building, and I was only a few years into a career that I found enjoyable and challenging. I didn't want to poison it. To have a number might shift my focus toward compensation rather than the work, rather than the deals and clients and colleagues. But was I being naïve? Was it only a matter of time before I became disenchanted enough to start looking at my job as simply a number to attain?

———

Bonus day, a dozen years later. Salomon Brothers had been acquired by Travelers Group, which in turn had merged with Citibank. I was now head of TMT—technology, media, and telecom—the largest group in the firm's investment bank, and so it fell to me to divvy up and hand out hundreds of millions of dollars to the scores of people working in my department. Based in Silicon Valley by this point, I would follow the sun around the globe, starting predawn by calling each member of my team in Europe and New York to tell them their year-end bonuses, then I'd meet in person with my West Coast team, and finally I'd get back on the phone until midnight to cover the Asian territories. I would give each of them more money than most people see in a lifetime.

I hated bonus day.

The only guarantee on bonus day was that almost no one would be happy. The duty of most investment bankers was to be disappointed with whatever enormous compensation he or she was due to receive. The amount was almost irrelevant, as their displeasure was predetermined.

While a bonus meeting marked the end of the year, it also signified the first negotiation for the upcoming year. Most people seemed to believe that if they were simply thankful and appreciative when told their bonus amount, that would make it less likely that you would fight hard for them next year. Yet if they argued that you had shortchanged them, then that might inspire you to push harder the next year to make up for the shortfall. They were like college basketball coaches complaining about a missed call, knowing it was too late but hoping their disgruntlement might pay off later. I'd like to believe, being the referee shouldering the abuse, that the strategy didn't work on me, but sometimes I wondered if it may have had some impact. Whatever their reactions, I still had to try to make the fairest and most measured decisions.

Looking over my list of meetings for the day, I tried to guess who was going to be awful to deal with and who would be relatively pleasant. It was never a fun day. But it was the most important day of the year as a manager, because this was the single occasion on which my people were told their value to the firm and the team, and they knew that the assessment would be backed by hard data. Some managers, like my first boss, simply delivered the number and pointed to the exit, but others used bonus day as an opportunity to check in with and refocus the members of the team. The way I conveyed this message to them could drive their motivation for the coming year; or, conversely, one wrong word or misplaced sentence could blow up in my face, occupying their thoughts and harming productivity, performance, and morale. Sensitivities ran high on bonus day.

There were three levels of analysis that determined how someone would react to his or her compensation. The first level was the most grounded in real-world sentiments—pretty much everybody on Wall Street would acknowledge that his or her bonus was a huge amount of money. Their moms would be proud. But the next level of analysis

entered a sort of alternate reality, as someone would look at his or her bonus and want to know how it stacked up firm-wide, relative to everyone
else at the same level. The absolute number didn't matter anymore. The
concern was whether he or she got paid more than Joe down the hall. *I'm
better than Joe*, the person would think, *so I damn well better have gotten
paid more.* The third level of analysis stretched out against the industry,
asking: *What did my firm pay for my job, my class, my level, compared to
the same people at Morgan Stanley or Goldman Sachs?* At this point, the
bonus amounts had become unmoored from the common experiences
of the general public, although they were still within Wall Street's expectations and standards. Over time, these folks would normalize their
situation and stop thinking about their world of megabonuses as the alternate reality, and they'd begin thinking of their mothers' world—of
Main Street—as the strange place.

While bonus day would usually bring a steady downpour of bitterness, occasionally there were a few breaks in the storm clouds. In those
rare cases, the recipient of what to most people would be a king's ran-
som was actually grateful and appreciative. After a few predawn hours of
combative phone calls, one of my first in-person meetings of the day was
with Tim, a second-year associate. I could see the tension on his face as
we finished up the minute of small talk.

"And that," he laughed nervously, "is why you don't eat Indian food
in Spain! So anyway"—hard swallow—"how are we doing?" He'd already
seen his review, so now he simply wanted the number.

"Well, Tim, based on your review, you had a good year."

"Thank you. I really enjoyed it, and I'm excited about next year."

I skimmed down the page. "Your previous bonus was $300,000. This
year we've raised you up to $320,000, which is nearly a 7 percent in-
crease." I tried to make that sound impressive, even though it was an offensively minor raise for a second-year associate, and it put him at a lower
mark than other people at his level. But Tim just smiled.

"Oh, wow," he said. "Thank you very much."

"Okay then." I was relieved, although I didn't show it. I couldn't admit
to Tim that he was what we called "the plug" this year—someone who,

in order to make the numbers work, ended up with the scraps of the pool after everyone else's bonuses had been determined.

"My parents aren't gonna believe this," he said as he got up and moved to the door, pausing with his fingers touching the handle. "My dad always says, 'We know you, and there's nothing you can do that is possibly worth that much money. Something must be wrong.'" Tim laughed. "Anyway, I hope your bonus is good too. Happy New Year." And he left the room. What a guy. I made a mental note to fight harder for him next year.

I scanned my list of remaining bonus meetings and calls for the day. Less than sixteen hours to go. Maybe this wouldn't be so bad after all, I thought.

But of course it would. People's reactions usually landed in one of five categories. Tim was a rare Category 1, the gentlest of hurricanes— there was tension, but you knew you were going to survive it, as he was genuinely gratified to learn that more than $300,000 would be handed over to him in a matter of days. His contentment was probably due to his bonus-day inexperience as a second-year associate. Most likely he would change over time and with knowledge, escalating to one of the less agreeable, more vicious categories.

I met with Alexandra later that morning. Her reaction was a classic Category 2. She was a VP who had made $600,000 the previous year, and now I had her at $775,000. "Thank you," she said evenly. "I want to feel good about this number. So please tell me that you did everything you could, and if you did, then I'm satisfied." The Category 2s would typically remain civil. They didn't feel the need to challenge my process or conclusions directly, but they wanted my assurance that I'd fought for them.

Category 3 was the most common, comprising more than half the people with whom I'd meet. The main characteristic of Category 3 was incessant questioning, usually with a facial expression that suggested that they'd just caught a whiff of bad gas or a dead rodent. The purpose of their inquisition was to make me feel uncomfortable, but they preferred to avoid all-out confrontation. Jack was a textbook Category 3, a director whom I'd bumped up to a million from last year's $800,000—"a 25 percent raise," I pointed out. He wasn't appreciative, yet he wasn't violently upset; he just wanted me to feel shitty about giving him a bunch of money. "A million?" he said. "God, are you reading the sheet right? I had a great year, and a freakin' million? That's horrible. I thought the firm really valued me. I don't know if I can go home tonight and face my wife."

I had planned to congratulate Jack with *How does it feel to be paid a million dollars?*—a line I'd used before with some success—but that clearly wouldn't have been well received. After his initial wave of revulsion, the questions started to rain down: "Was I top of my class? How did you come up with this number? Was it hard to get it? Did you fight? How many people were top bucket?"

With Category 3s, you knew they were putting on an act, but it was method acting—they really did believe their sob story; they could actually feel their feigned disgust. They might not blame you directly, but they would blame the firm. They would blame the invisible committee in the conference room who had screwed and undervalued them yet again by having the gall to offer up a measly million dollars as a year-end bonus.

Category 4, of course, came with even more venom. Rick was a young managing director, an alpha Ivy League kid who smacked of privilege and entitlement. "Listen, Rick," I started. "You're not gonna like this number."

"Oh, Jesus Christ," he said. "What."

"Let me first say that, although you had a good year on paper, the reason your bonus is flat is because of the new policy we've put in place that—"

"Wait," he cut in. "Did you say fucking *flat*? You better have said *fat*, not fucking *flat*."

I tried again. "The main factor here, Rick, is our new policy that states that 25 percent of bonuses are tied to culture, to how you operate within the firm's community. People get rewarded or penalized for their contributions outside of just pure revenue. Everyone gets a 360-degree review by his co-workers, and we don't feel that you've made the cultural contributions that you're capable of." He knew as well as I did that this was simply code for *You're a complete asshole.*

"So let me get this straight"—he put fingers to his temples, as if trying to summon special powers—"'cause I'm having a hard time here understanding what the *fuck* we're talking about."

"Okay." I would give him as much line to run with as he wanted. That was the only way to handle these upper-category guys.

"So you're saying that a bunch of tools evaluated how tender of a guy I am, and because of that—despite that I brought in fifty-five fuckin' million in fees this year—my bonus stays flat at two million?"

"I'm afraid so," I said calmly. "And I happen to have been one of those tools who evaluated you. You did great work, Rick, but I think you can be a more effective culture carrier."

"*'Culture carrier'?*" His contempt could have powered a skyscraper. "This isn't fuckin' summer camp. It's an investment bank."

Most Category 4s were similar to Rick. Their blood would simmer, and they might threaten to go find another job. Or, conveniently, they would tell you that they had just received a strong offer from a competing firm, perhaps that very morning, and goddamn if they weren't tempted to walk straight out the door.

When it got to the Category 5 guys, you were dealing with all-out shitstorms. It would have been wise to have boarded up the windows and evacuated, but now it was too late. Shouting, swearing, fury. They'd throw a desk if there were one to throw. You had attacked their honor and smeared their reputation. You had pissed on the graves of their ancestors. You had slept with their spouses and spanked their children. "But, Chip," you'd try, "it's $4.5 million . . ." And the hurricane would rage anew. There was always a handful of Category 5s, and nothing made you want to help them in the future.

Chip was a managing director and headed up one of the technology subsectors. I'd bumped him up to that $4.5 million from $3 million—a *50 percent* increase—and I'd fought hard to get it. I honestly thought he'd be thrilled. But it was tough to predict who was going to be sweet and appreciative, like Tim, and who was going to go off the deep end, cursing and spitting insults, like Chip.

In general, the categories of reaction correlated with bonus levels—Category 1s and 2s, who were often fresher on the job and paid on the lower end of the scale, were still gracious and happy. The highest-paid people, on the other hand, who had typically been around longer, tended to react with a combination of discontentment and self-righteousness, since their jobs had become more plainly about the money. Therefore they got upset when the money didn't surpass their expectations.

The phone meetings rarely went better, but at least I didn't have to see their faces as they expressed their eternal displeasure. Finally midnight rolled around, and I dropped the phone in its cradle and grabbed my jacket. "Ungrateful bastards." I flicked the light switch and made for the exit.

———

Let's state the obvious: This level of compensation, and the behavior that often accompanies it, is crazy. Securities firms paid an estimated $31.4 billion in bonuses in New York in 2017, according to the state controller, out of the highest profits earned since the financial crisis. The general public's visceral reaction against Wall Street and the banks is often centered on the belief that people in finance are excessively paid. Most Wall Street people would agree with that, even if, over time, they may lose touch with that reality. Okay, so it's crazy. But why are things the way they are? Why is compensation so extreme?

The 1986 *Fortune* magazine cover that featured a young investment banker cockily holding a cigar and gazing into the camera with an expression of callous confidence had in big red caps: WALL STREET'S OVERPAID YOUNG STARS, and a caption that read: "At 31, Kansas-born David Wittig makes some $500,000 a year at Kidder Peabody." (Wittig was the same guy who would later run Salomon's M&A department, the managing director who played golf with my sister and interviewed Michael Soenen for a job, tormenting him about Teterboro tail numbers and Dumpster-diving for *Wall Street Journal* throwaways.) The *Fortune* magazine cover made waves throughout and beyond the industry. It was the first widely discussed example of Wall Street compensation, and, in many ways, it was the moment that triggered a seminal change in the financial services industry toward compensation transparency. While people on Wall Street were stunned that the numbers had been so cavalierly hung in public, Main Street was equal parts shocked, disgusted, and intrigued by how much Wittig was being paid.

"That's why I went to Wall Street," Kevin Tice recalled. "It was David Wittig on the cover of *Fortune* in 1986, smoking a cigar, $500,000 a year—and I remember sitting there like, *What?* I was making $24,000 a year at the Central Bank of Denver. That was a symbol, Wittig on the cover. All of Wall Street was aghast, because the ethos before then was that you didn't brag about how much money you made. Wittig put it out there, how much you could make on Wall Street."

Greater transparency usually has a positive ring, but in the case of Wall Street comp, Wittig's *Fortune* cover and the discussion it ignited changed Wall Street's culture and Main Street's perception of the financial world in innumerable ways—and mostly not for the better. Compensation became even more of the driving focus of many who pursued careers in the financial services industry; bonus amounts became the barometer of one's sense of value and contentment.

As transparency around compensation numbers increased on Wall Street, the complexity and opacity of the financial industry was also increasing. It became harder for the man on the street to understand what the hell those people did for such huge paychecks. And that surge in compensation, combined with an obscurity of purpose, created a general distrust of Wall Street. When things did go awry, the negative stories highlighted only the worst aspects and most unscrupulous people, making bankers an easy target for Main Street's ire. So much of the financial services industry happens out of the public eye—not for the distinct purpose of being dodgy, but because that's the nature of the work. In a lot of what's done in mergers and acquisitions, for example, the advantage comes from a perspective on information that is unique and proprietary. By definition, one can't provide a play-by-play of what's being done to shape a deal. That means that the only things reported are final outcomes and bad behaviors. Everything else—nuanced processes and negotiations—is done out of view.

So what specifically are these Wall Streeters doing? What's the unique talent required to earn the big bucks? In the case of mergers and acquisitions, a special set of skills and knowledge is needed—in areas ranging from your client's industry and strategic landscape, understanding the forces driving the two entities together, advanced financial analytics, merger accounting, deal tactics, governance, to price and terms negotiations. All the while you have to manage and massage the psychology, agendas, and egos of your own clients, as well as those on the other side of the negotiation table. The question of who will sit in the corner office after the deal is consummated is often a leading consideration, even more so than the synergies and value created by the merger or acquisition. I loved the job because it demanded just as much, if not more, of my qualitative skills, such as the ability to build trust, as it did of my quantitative and analytical skills.

M&A is a tough game with big winners and losers, involving a lot of stress, complexity, and risk—not dissimilar to what any athlete deals with at the highest levels. It's more apparent, however, what pro athletes do for their money. We can turn on the television and watch them swing the bat or shoot the three or go for the green on a long par five. Yet Wall Street is not a spectator industry, the way that pro sports and Hollywood are, so high compensation is tougher to understand and justify.

But even if we struggle to justify Wall Street's crazy levels of compensation, can we attempt to understand how we got here? What exactly do the tech groups at Goldman and Citi do to generate $1 billion in revenue? They're underwriting the largest equity offerings or negotiating the biggest deals in the technology world, such as Oracle's hostile takeover of PeopleSoft in 2004. Those companies wanted to hire the best firms with the best talent to represent their interests, and if you're doing a complex $10 billion deal that involves multiple defense strategies, as well as navigating complex governance issues, you're willing to pay a

$47 million fee—less than half of 1 percent of the deal amount—to get the premier talent working for you.

The same is true in every industry. There are a few people who are simply the best at what they do, and if you're one of the best in a market that generates massive revenue, you basically earn a percentage of that revenue. If you're one of the top film actors in the world, your performances can command huge paychecks. If you're one of the elite quarterbacks in the world, bank. And if you're one of the most talented entrepreneurs or deal makers or traders, you're likely to be very well paid—and despite how it may seem, talent *is* required to reach the highest levels in finance.

But even if you accept the argument that Wall Streeters are people with unique skill sets, do the compensation amounts need to be so astronomically high? Wouldn't people do the same job for less? Most likely, but once the market determines the value of the talent and experience necessary to succeed in the job—a value that is always being recalculated, again and again—it becomes difficult or impossible to rewind the tape to more modest times. After the early 1990s Treasury scandal at Salomon Brothers, in which Paul Mozer tampered with bond auctions and almost brought down the firm, Warren Buffett agreed to serve as temporary chairman to help save Salomon and correct what he saw as flaws in its system. One of his main objectives was to lower bonuses. He felt—and of course he's not alone—that Salomon's bankers were paid too much, and that the overpayment had led to a culture of high risk and corruption. So he announced plans to slash bonuses throughout the firm.

The threat of mutiny quickly spread. This happened during my second year working there. While I was still amazed that I was being paid anything at all, I remember Caesar Sweitzer, a more senior colleague, saying that if they offered him the rumored bonus amount for MDs of "only" $500,000, he would march up to his boss and say, *Fuck you, I'll walk out the door.* A lot of people at the firm felt the same way, and more than a few were as outspoken as Caesar. He wasn't ultimately affected by the bonus cuts, but many others were, and they packed up and headed for greener shores, since competing firms were willing and eager to hire them at market rates. As the exodus continued, Buffett realized he had no choice but to reverse the directive, bringing Salomon's bonuses back into balance with the rest of Wall Street. In order to retain premier talent, he learned, you have to pay for it.

———

Kevin and I made managing director the same year, 1998. The market had been going wild with big deals, which meant big fees, and it was no secret that the best guys were getting paid handsomely across the industry. There was a lot of poaching going on between firms, and Kevin soon became a target.

In April 2000, he got an offer from Frank Quattrone to join the tech group at Credit Suisse First Boston. Or, rather, he got two offers from Quattrone, and he wasn't sure which one to take. Either deal was a tremendous step up, so there was no question Kevin was going to accept one of them. He came to me with his dilemma.

"It's a tough call. For a two-year contract, Quattrone says I can either take a guaranteed $8 million a year, or I can take $4 million a year with points—no tears."

"He actually said 'no tears'?" That was tough-guy Wall Street parlance for *Accept your decision and don't whine about it if it turns out to be the wrong one.*

"Yup."

The points deal was intriguing, as it meant that Kevin's comp would be directly tied to the success of the group. It was a riskier choice, as the markets could change on a dime, but it could also end up being a higher number than $8 million per year. It was a matter of how much certainty Kevin wanted in his earnings. The eight-by-two deal would ensure a payout of $16 million, regardless of what happened with markets or with Credit Suisse.

"Kevin," I said, "I don't know if you remember this, but way back when we were associates, you asked me what my number was. And you said yours was $4 million—if you made that, you wanted out. Credit Suisse is offering you four times that amount over two years. Why would you not lock in the eight million by two?"

He thought for a moment. "Yeah," he said, with some reluctance, "good point," and he took the eight by two.

Now that he would far exceed his number over the next couple of years, I wondered if that meant he would cash out and finally coach basketball. It wasn't an appropriate question to ask right then, since he was embarking on an exciting challenge at a new firm, but I couldn't help but be curious as to what would happen after he surpassed his goal.

―――――

When Citi allowed my colleagues and me to form Project Passion to improve the firm's culture, the new guidelines put in place included fifty-five changes, the most impactful of which was the bonus rule—if a guy killed it on paper but was an insufferable prick, his bonus could be docked up to 25 percent. He would receive a 360-degree review, rated by those who worked beside him, above him, and below him. (My favorite comment from one of our culture reviews was: "My manager beats me with both the carrot and the stick.")

Once we established that 25 percent of each person's bonus would be determined by how he or she was rated from a culture perspective, many of the senior managing directors thought they would be exempt. They'd gotten the same review as everyone else, and even though most of these guys were my peers, I had no problem holding their feet to the coals.

In one meeting, we were discussing the comp for a managing director who'd had a good year but had been very poorly rated on culture from all angles. The committee wanted to pay him max money.

"We can't pay him that," I said. "His culture marks were a disaster."

The people in the room looked at me like I'd pissed in the punch bowl.

"You've got to be joking," someone said. "We're not taking that culture shit seriously at this level, are we?" These were the same executives who had signed off on the new rules and appointed me culture czar.

All heads swiveled for the reaction of the two bosses at the end of the table, and they composed themselves quickly. "Of course we're taking it seriously," one said, while the other nodded. "We have to model the behavior we want from the rest of the firm."

But we all knew the truth of it—that adjustments would most likely be made later, in private, to bring the MD's comp back up. Sure, the bosses had to display their support in the meeting, yet it was obvious that culture would rarely have an impact when it came to the compensation for those who made the rules.

But I stayed faithful to the new directive in regard to my own people, which was how Rick, the Category 4 MD who had reacted to his comp with such disdain, had ended up stagnant at $2 million, even after an impressive performance on paper. He was terrible to work with—everybody agreed—so when we debated his bonus in the managing director comp committee, we concluded that he needed to be docked the full 25 percent for being an asshole, and I made sure we stuck with the decision. Ultimately Rick was moved to a different group that didn't adhere to the new culture rules as strictly. I'd like to believe that even though we were losing a high-revenue generator, the group performed better after Rick's departure because it assured my team that there was somebody in charge who cared about fostering a positive work environment.

It was effective, I believed, to tie an individual's cultural contributions to his or her compensation, as it would keep the firm's focus in balance and avoid the myopic obsession with comp and revenue generation. But most firms—and even much of Citi—declined to make a real commitment to culture, at their own peril.

———

The year before I moved to California—when I was still a young MD in New York—I got back to the office from a meeting one afternoon to find a couple of dozen investment bankers gathered around a desk, yelling and waving money in the air, as if cheering on a dogfight. "Get him! Yeah, that's right! You got it!" I stepped closer and peered into the circle. There was our leader, Gregg, the head of M&A, arm-wrestling with a young analyst. A rivulet of sweat rolled down Gregg's bald dome. The bankers were making bets, and many of them had their money on the boss, although the crowd was clearly pulling for the kid.

Gregg was big and muscular, an arm-wrestling aficionado, a champion of testosterone who would walk around the department with a baseball bat, flipping it in the air and practicing his swing. His greatest desire, more than anything, it seemed, was to be well liked. The arm wrestling was all part of the machismo—Gregg would clear a desk and challenge anyone with the guts to battle their supervisor. It might be expected that a guy like him would rarely lose, but that wasn't the case. On this day, the young analyst had Gregg against the ropes.

I'd seen the whole pageant many times before and had a deadline looming, so I backed away and walked to my desk. Just as I sat down, the group of spectators erupted. The kid had won. Money changed hands as people dispersed, with those who had bet on the winner bragging loudly about how they planned to spend the cash—steaks at Peter Luger, a weekend away with the girlfriend, a piece of jewelry for the wife. I caught a glimpse of Gregg storming off, rolling down his sleeve. He hated losing.

Gregg scheduled a meeting with me the following week to discuss, as he put it, my important role in the firm and the historic gains in the tech market. It was May of 2000. Like Kevin Tice the previous month, many people had been poached by other banks, so the biggest firms wanted to lock down their good people and make them feel confident that they were being paid well. The atmosphere around the tech market sizzled with excitement and frantic profit grabbing, seasoned with a pinch of paranoia that the good times might suddenly end. Even though the tech market had plunged by that spring, no one wanted to entertain the possibility that the party was over—people preferred to believe it was simply a market correction. I figured that Gregg and his bosses were concerned I might be tempted to leave, especially since Kevin had so recently been drawn away by a big payout. At that point, I was the only MD they had doing tech deals. My departure would injure the firm's tech effort, and the market was too hot to risk losing another key figure.

Gregg knocked as he entered my office, not waiting for an invitation. "V!" he boomed. His default management style was of the just-one-of-the-boys variety, as if he were president of a frat house to which the rest of us belonged. Making himself comfortable in one of my chairs, he got right to the point. "Listen, you've had a hell of a year already, and we want you to know that you're appreciated, so we've circled you."

"You've circled me?" I knew what the term meant—that he wanted to give me guidance on what my year-end bonus would be to discourage me from considering offers from other firms—but I was still taken by surprise. It was only May, a full seven months before bonuses were usually determined. Sure, I'd had a great year so far—truthfully, it was hard not to do well during the dotcom boom—and while I could have guessed that my bonus would end up higher than the previous year's, I hadn't given it any thought.

"That's right," Gregg said, rapping his knuckles on the desk to punctuate his words. "We've circled you for $4.3 million."

All I could think was *Holy shit.* That was more than triple my previous bonus. But my M&A training had taught me never to reveal my reaction to anything offered across an expanse of laminated wood, so my expression remained unchanged. Gregg's grin faded as he looked at my unsmiling face, and after a few seconds, I leaned forward and spoke. "It would have been better for you to have given me no number, leaving the small possibility that you would pay me fairly, than to have offered me this and removed any hope that you were going to do the right thing."

I sat back and thought, *What the fuck did I just say?* And Gregg's face mirrored that same sentiment. All his swagger had evaporated. He stood up to leave, mumbling that he would be back in touch soon. I stared him out the door, wondering briefly into what category my reaction had put me.

I took a walk at lunch to release the pent-up adrenaline. Citi's investment banking operations were in Tribeca, near downtown Manhattan, and one of my favorite routes was south to Trinity Church and then down the seven cobblestoned blocks of Wall Street to the East River. When I first moved to New York and would close a big deal, I'd stroll along Wall Street as a kind of small private celebration. It made me feel for a few minutes that I was part of a larger history, that I had *arrived*, in some sense. It surprised me how short the street actually was—for what was arguably the most famous and influential location in the world, you could walk from top to bottom in five minutes at a quick clip. But I liked to take my time, marveling at the quaint feel of the place, the old marble fortresses, the New York Stock Exchange, the few financial institutions that still kept offices there, while most had scattered to other areas of Manhattan.

I pondered the source of my reaction to Gregg's offer. I would have been fully content with the four-point-three, but I knew, almost reflexively, that I could not reveal that contentment. I insisted with regularity that I wasn't fixated on compensation, and it still wasn't the source of motivation in my career. But I won't pretend that I didn't care at all about getting a raise each year. It's human nature—whether we're schoolteachers or bankers or long-distance runners—to set goals for ourselves, then strive to meet them, then set new goals. So I was satisfied when my bonus went up each year because that was the way Wall Street signaled that I was doing my job well. And why should the firm, I figured, get the benefit of me not caring? Not to mention, if you didn't demonstrate that you were a good negotiator for yourself, they wouldn't respect you as a negotiator for clients. I believed those arguments, and yet I still couldn't help but question my motivations for wanting more.

Of course I wasn't the only person on Wall Street who tried to view comp with a healthy perspective. My buddy Stuart Goldstein took his wife, Anessa, to McDonald's each year on the day he received his bonus to remind him of his humble beginnings. Stuart had grown up in Philadelphia, the son of a cardboard box salesman. He didn't want to forget where he was from, no matter what advantages and comforts might come his way.

Most people, however, became less content the longer they worked on Wall Street—and they had to learn their unhappiness. They were always trying to get perspective and context on their compensation, looking to others to help them determine whether or not it was adequate. I remember first hearing these numbers and saying, "How could you be anything but happy?" And then people started telling me why I shouldn't be happy: "Well, Pete got paid more than you. Doesn't that piss you off?" And I'd say, "Not really." And they'd say, "What do you mean? You should feel burned. You're smarter than him. You're better than him. You worked harder than him. Why is he getting more than you?" Transparency, in this case, was the mother of discontent. I tried to avoid those pitfalls, and I felt sorry for the people for whom the job was primarily about money. They often didn't enjoy the work, but they liked telling people what they did, and they liked the spoils.

At the end of the year, they all seemed to buy themselves a holiday gift—a car, a new wardrobe, a beach house, some sort of personal reward for their big bonus. It was as if they needed material things to make the bonus feel real, to prove to themselves that their sacrifice of another year was worth it. They needed to overcorrect for the loss of control in their lives by manufacturing the feeling of happiness, by doing something like buying a yacht in January.

I reached the river on my lunchtime walk, where some of those very same yachts bobbed in the chop, and ferries departed the pier for Brooklyn and points south. To my right, the Manhattan heliport buzzed with activity. On the horizon, two incoming helicopters drifted into view, probably delivering executives or politicians. Thousands of taxis careened and screamed around the corners in every direction. The constant comings and goings of New York—everyone and everything lurching forward, backward, up, down, sideways.

Gregg came back to my office a week later, empty of bluster. "All right," he said, "we've thought about it. You're right. You're super valuable to the firm. We have you circled for six-point-seven." His lack of enthusiasm, as he delivered the revised offer, proved that he was simply the messenger. I knew he didn't want to see me paid this much, but the bosses must have decided it wasn't prudent to risk losing another senior tech banker, so they'd raised the number from four-point-three to a staggering six-point-seven.

"Okay," I said. "I'll take it. It's not quite market, but I understand that to get market at this firm, you have to threaten to leave. There's some value in not changing firms, so I'm willing to take a market discount in order to stay." Gregg looked relieved and a little bitter as we shook hands. My bonus had been $1.4 million that previous January—not even five months before—and now I was circled for six-point-seven. I didn't thank him or smile once. I had become the ungrateful bastard.

Everyone who worked long enough on Wall Street was at some point a Category 1, 2, 3, 4, and 5. I myself had run the full spectrum at different moments in my career. I'd like to believe that I was more civil and cordial than most, but I have to acknowledge that I had bought into the process of feigning disgust at a big bonus in order to maximize my pay and my supervisors' respect—or was it their fear I was after?

Transparency, in this case, had made everyone dissatisfied with what most people, and even those receiving the big paychecks, would easily agree is outstanding compensation. Having detailed knowledge of what others earned drove us to push for more, creating a compensation arms race that resulted in mentally and psychologically aligning us more with the compensation and less with the work. It wasn't enough to be paid the most in any one year; you wanted to be paid the most every year. It was your way of knowing you were on top, considered the best by those in charge. Simultaneously, people outside the industry had become more aware of compensation levels within finance, but there still was relatively little transparency as to what had been done to earn those paychecks, so outsiders grew skeptical if not downright appalled by the high amounts.

It turns out that there was good reason to be skeptical. Thanks in large part to increased transparency, the financial services world is now unhealthily tied to an annual compensation cycle. The desire to be paid the most each and every year has created perverse incentives directly impacting almost every facet of the banking and investment world. As the focus on and opportunity for outsized compensation in the financial industry has shifted from investment banking to the investing world, the short-term compensation arms race has moved to the realms of private equity, hedge funds, and managers of public market securities. Given investment managers' desire to boost their annual—and, in some cases, quarterly—compensation, they're motivated to pursue strategies that maximize returns on an annual basis, rather than allowing for longer hold periods. As such, these annual compensation structures often lead to shorter-than-ideal investment horizons and lower relative returns, all at the expense of investors—and, arguably, at the expense of the long-term compensation of the investment managers themselves. This was not always the way things were done. Of course it happened, but much less when the investment strategy wasn't so laser-focused on an annual bonus cycle.

———

In the dead of night, exhausted, wracked with self-doubt, you would sit at your desk and do a full accounting of yourself. Why were you working on Wall Street? Was it to impress others? To satisfy a societal definition of success? Or was it simply for the money? You'd rock back in your chair and stare at your cubicle wall and crack a warm soda if you had one. While waiting for documents to come back from word processing, you'd torture these thoughts.

Wall Street didn't simply exert a tax on your personal life—it obliterated your ability to maintain healthy relationships outside of the office. There just wasn't time. Even basic hygiene and errands seemed impossible, unless you could cram them into a scant, rushed hour, leaving the other twenty-three hours of each day for work and maybe a touch of rest. You canceled plans again. You skipped another holiday with your family. You returned a friend's call seven months late. Days like this would stretch into weeks or even months. Every now and then you might get a few days' furlough, but that respite would arrive without warning, so there would be no way to plan anything special. You'd keep it simple—walking in Central Park and reading the Sunday *Times* seemed like the ultimate luxury. Catching a movie. Drinking a cappuccino. *So this is normal life*, you remembered. *These are basic pleasures.* And then you'd be sucked back into the vortex just as quickly, and you might not know those pleasures for many more months.

It was in those sleepless nights at the office that you asked yourself why you were doing it. You didn't care, in those moments, about the money. The sacrifice seemed too great. And despite your self-pity, you knew nobody felt sorry for you—if they even believed that your crazy schedule was real. This was a choice you had made.

But you wondered, in the dead of night, if you really did have a choice. It wasn't only the years of schooling and the accumulation of debts that first kept you shackled to the job. It wasn't only the fact that thousands of others would gladly step into your place. It wasn't only that you'd have to explain to everyone why you were giving up, especially after you'd projected it as such a big accomplishment. Was it because Wall Street was the greatest game in town, and how could you walk away from that? You'd be admitting that you didn't have the smarts or the stamina to play in the majors. You'd be settling for a lesser challenge and a duller life. You also knew there was no return—that once you quit the game, you couldn't get back in. So you kept going, trying to convince yourself that it was all an investment in your future, that one day you'd have a more balanced life, including love and possibly a family, and that the money would later allow you to do whatever you wanted. You could become a bad landscape painter, write a book, coach basketball, anything. But even if you one day achieved those things, would you be able to enjoy them, or would that part of you have died?

My god, you'd think, *have I become a cliché? Am I just regurgitating an internal monologue from some book or movie lodged in my subconscious?*

But the anxiety was real. You worried that the job might be changing you in ways that couldn't be reversed with any amount of time off and financial security. *Have I become a slave to the money*, you'd wonder, *without the will or fortitude to prioritize anything above work and compensation?* Whenever you convinced yourself that it was okay to sacrifice another year, you were losing a little more of your integrity and your ultimate ability to achieve true happiness. Maybe you should exit the game after all. You could always fine-tune the assumptions that went into your number-calculating algorithm. *I don't need that big a house*, you'd think. *It doesn't need to be on the beach. Vacations can be more rustic. I can learn to make gourmet meals myself rather than dining out.*

It was two in the morning, then four, then the eastern sky grayed with dawn outside the office windows. Get up and splash some water on your face. No time for breakfast.

Yet perhaps today would be the day. Today you'd retake control of your life. Today you'd walk into your manager's office and throw in the handkerchief. *Bob*, you'd say, *I loved working here, but I need to have a life*. It would be so easy! Today would be the day you'd speak those two, elusive, magical words: *I quit*.

But you knew you never would.

———

After Kevin Tice had been in his new job at Credit Suisse for eight months, he called me one weekend day. I was lucky enough to be home watching a late-season Patriots game and eating a sandwich when the phone rang.

"I fucked up," he said.

My immediate thought was that he'd gotten caught in a scandal or affair, even though that would be very out of character. I muted the ballgame. "What did you do? What happened?"

"Should've rolled the dice."

"Where are you? Vegas?" I sat forward.

"No, man. I'm talking about the eight by two. I should have taken the points."

"Oh." I slumped back on the couch and picked up my sandwich. "You mean your comp offer?" I took a bite. Drew Bledsoe converted a long third down to Terry Glenn—wait, he bobbled the catch. Incomplete. Our new coach, Bill Belichick, paced the sideline in a hoodie and a scowl.

"Yeah," Kevin said, "the goddamn comp offer. Remember I could've taken $4 million a year with points, but instead I took the sure thing?"

"Right."

"I should've known—scared money never wins." That was a favorite phrase of Kevin's, his motto in life, business, and casinos. "If I had taken the four with upside, I would've cleared $12 million this year. I don't know what to do."

"What *can* you do?" I asked through a mouthful of sandwich.

"I think I should call up Quattrone and say, 'Hey, I know I took the eight, but I left money on the table. Can you throw me a bone?' He's a reasonable guy. He's gotta see that eight wasn't fair for what my team and I accomplished."

"Kevin," I said, "you made your choice. Just be happy with it. Don't worry about the fact that you turned down the points." I didn't even mention the *no tears* part of the agreement. "Besides, $8 million dogs don't get thrown bones."

As much as anyone on Wall Street, Kevin Tice had fallen victim to the mentality of chasing the number, then reaching it, only to find that it had gotten larger and farther away, then chasing it again. "I remember I started at $2 million," he recalled much later. "I was a couple of years out of business school and thought that if I made $2 million, that would have been it. And then the heroin starts to kick in—the heroin is the compensation—so then you're like, *Well, I always thought I'd have a $500,000 house, but now I could have a $2 million house, so my number's now $8 million*, and it continues to escalate. It almost becomes this elusive dream that you're chasing. We would joke that it was always, 'Two more bonus cycles and then I'm done.' And then you do two years and you're like, 'Two more years and *then* I'm done,' and your number would grow bigger, and you'd continue chasing it."

But eventually Kevin escaped the cycle. After twenty years on Wall Street, he stepped away, moved back to his home state of Colorado, and took up the life of a ski bum and basketball coach in the Amateur Athletic Union league—exactly what he told me he wanted to do all those years earlier.

Despite Kevin's fondness for the work, he was ready for a change. "I walked away from a millions-of-dollars-a-year job because I wanted to do something else. It wasn't so much running out of gas; it was more what anybody deals with in any profession—whether you're a dentist for twenty-five years and you're like, 'I'm sick of cleaning teeth and doing cavities,' you know? I got to a point where I wanted to experience something new. I wanted different challenges, different horizons. I wanted to meet different people, a different experience set. I get emails all the time from my buddies who are still slogging it out, and they say, 'You're the luckiest guy alive,' and, 'I wish I had the guts to do what you did,' and blah, blah, blah. You know, to each his own."

Kevin had the courage to get out while still on top, which is something I've seen very few people do in the finance industry. Most aren't willing or able to exit of their own accord. Their end ultimately comes when the rest of the world has already figured out that their heart is no longer in it, and they're asked to leave the playing field. Kevin's situation was unique, perhaps because of his relatively humble roots, or perhaps from his coming to terms with the fact that a number is just a number, and if you're lucky enough to reach yours, then it's time to find a new goal—one that is personal and can't be measured by your accountant.

———

The compensation transparency that began on Wall Street eventually spread to the corporate sector. Annual compensation levels for the executives of the largest public companies are now posted like box scores to be studied, parsed, and argued over by colleagues, competitors, and the general public. Human nature being what it is, these CEOs—in fact all members of the executive suite—use the numbers to argue for their own increases in compensation, and board members often have no choice but to yield to their demands. "Look, Bob at Company X got paid $5 million more than me, and you can't deny that, as CEO of Company Y, I've done a far better job than him." As a result, the increased disclosure of CEO compensation has driven up executive pay while igniting the public's ire over the disparity between people at the top, middle, and bottom.

Having advised and served on many boards, I see firsthand that the value of leadership is indisputable. Warren Buffett has said he would rather own a company with an outstanding management team that sells an average product than own a company with an average management team that sells an outstanding product. Attracting and maintaining leadership talent is the most important responsibility of any board—public, private, or philanthropic. As such, when it comes time to decide on the compensation of the CEO and the executive team, the task receives significant time and attention. To prudently determine appropriate compensation levels, the board must obtain compensation information from comparable firms, usually with the help of an outside consulting service.

Each conversation goes something like this:

"James had a great year," says Board Member One.

"Not so the stock price," says Board Member Two. "We shouldn't be compensating a CEO so handsomely when the stock is down 7 percent."

"But that's not his fault, and you have to admit that he has set this company up for positive future results with all the strategic initiatives he's put in place," says Board Member One.

"Well, he should get paid once we see those initiatives translate into a higher stock price," says Board Member Two.

"If it were only that simple," says Board Member Three. "We know Competitor X has been courting him for the past year. We can't take the chance of them stealing him."

No board wants to risk losing a good CEO and have to deal with finding a replacement. So they check the consultant charts and agree to offer a compensation level above the median but not at the top, often within spitting distance of the 75th percentile so they can argue they are generously placing James in the top quartile.

The public then sees that James was paid an exorbitant sum, even though he hadn't delivered on the understood objective of every CEO—maximizing shareholder value. And so it may look like an inside job, a hypocrisy that at worst is a sign of the board being in the CEO's back pocket and at best seems to assert that every CEO in America is above average.

———

People go into their professions for a host of reasons. In the best cases, teachers or doctors or pastors decide to pursue their jobs because of passion, interest, belief, and the desire to be of service to others. Their job is a sort of calling. Someone else might be born into his or her profession—you grow up in a factory town, and working on the assembly line is the opportunity you inherit. For teachers or factory workers, compensation never goes up enough to afford them the luxury of having an exit option. They don't ask, *What's my number?* If they have a number, it's probably four digits—the year that they'll qualify for their pension or the year they'll pay off their mortgage.

One recent development in the financial services industry is that people no longer feel good about working there. Many who now go into finance see it as a stepping stone on the path to something else, much as I did when I took my first full-time job in commercial banking. Today, the youth of America flock to Silicon Valley the way they used to flock to Wall Street—because they can make a lot of money in the tech world, but they can also convince themselves that it's a noble pursuit. Or they target private equity, where the opportunities to make big money still exist.

These days, to lure talented people to Wall Street, investment banks have to pay more than they otherwise would because they're not only competing with the fortunes to be made in tech but also with Silicon Valley's mantra that each new gadget or app or startup will "make the world a better place"—regardless of whether there's any truth to that assertion.

And so with the center of power and excitement having shifted, Wall Street no longer attracts the best and brightest. If young talent does come to work on the Street, many of them treat it as a sort of boot camp where they can gain experience and skills before heading for the Valley. When I got my start at Salomon Brothers in 1989, there was little question as to the societal value of Wall Street. Now there is. Even if it would be fair to say that most people who work in the financial services industry today indeed still contribute positively to a functioning society, the increase in complexity over the past thirty years has so obscured that connection that it has become all but undetectable to Main Street.

Not many decades ago, only a handful of people reached such rarified stratospheres of wealth—the Rockefellers, the Carnegies, the Vanderbilts, the Fords—people whose names everyone knew. Today the situation is quite different. In 2016, there were more than five hundred billionaires in the US and nearly two thousand in the world; the United States was home to eleven million millionaires, many of whom made their wealth in the financial services industry. We have fairly recently entered an age in which droves of highly paid people regularly hit and exceed their numbers, and they grapple with what that means and how it affects their psychology and contentment. Everyone knows the cliché that having lots of money doesn't make you happy—and in many cases it can make you unhappy. Perhaps it's true—or could it be that having a *number* makes you unhappy?

People on Wall Street, and now many others with high-paying positions elsewhere in the financial services industry, fall somewhere on the map of two crossing arcs. You pursue the job because it's exciting. The opportunity to make a lot of money is there. Then you start to make that money, and the job loses its luster. Like the decay curve on a big deal, a high-stakes game of poker, a bungee jump—as you get more comfortable with it, the excitement deteriorates. And so at some point in a finance job there's an X—that sweet spot in which you're still engaged and enthusiastic, and the money is good—but then when you move to the extremes, the thrill is gone. The job turns into a slog. Dealing with clients, boards, or investors is less and less enjoyable. They almost become annoying, as if they are simply hindrances to attaining a good bonus.

At that point, you feel like a sort of prostitute, in those rare moments when you allow yourself to feel anything at all. You're selling yourself because you can no longer hide behind need, you can no longer hide behind paying the bills and taking care of your children, and you can no longer hide behind loving the job. You don't know how deeply the money has complicated your ability to enjoy the work, but by now it's too late. It has become a treasure hunt—more, bigger, better. You pretend that isn't the case, but it becomes tougher to fake it. Some sacred, fragile, essential part of yourself—call it authenticity, or soul, or passion—has been bought and sold on the trading floor of happiness. You've wheeled and dealed your contentment, your friendships, maybe even your family.

Compensation levels in the financial world have created internal struggles that have never existed to this scale in human history. The realization that there's a tradeoff between personal freedom and long-term financial comfort is nothing new. But the significant wealth amassed by people working primarily in finance and technology has brought more fundamental, almost existential, questions to the forefront: *How am I spending my life? Why do I work? Is there something else I should be doing?*

Money once provided the simple necessities of survival—food, shelter, and clothing—along with some pleasure. The leaves were full on the trees; the grass seemed to be green everywhere. It was our spring and summer. Then the leaves turned and fell earthward, and we could start to see the fields across the valley, and they looked better than our own—larger, more fertile—so naturally we coveted them. There was a new chill in the air, and we prepared to hunker down, filling our cellars, stockpiling firewood and supplies, closing our doors and windows. And finally the trees stood bare against a silver sky, and we could see for miles—hills and glens, farms and houses—and we wanted it all. Our own plot of land suddenly felt small and inadequate. At dark, we encountered our reflection in the window, and we didn't like what we saw. The winter of our discontent had arrived.

9

THE OTHER LINE

There is no subtler, no surer means of overturning the existing basis of society than to debauch the currency.
—JOHN MAYNARD KEYNES, FROM *THE ECONOMIC CONSEQUENCES OF THE PEACE*

We strolled out of the Cosmopolitan after a late dinner at Momofuku. The taxi line was typically long for a busy night in Las Vegas. The prospect of waiting for half an hour or more dampened our enthusiasm for the night ahead.

My friend Ivan, who was no newbie to the workings of Sin City, stepped toward the head valet, drawing some bills from his wallet and folding them over.

"Excuse me, sir."

The valet glanced at the money in Ivan's hand and smiled attentively. "Yes, sir?"

Ivan extended the cash and asked, "Where is the *other* line?"

In one practiced motion, the valet slipped the folded bills into his pocket, signaled to a nearby black car, and said, "Just a moment, sir." The driver pulled up, doors were opened, and the four of us piled in with no discussion of fare, happy to have avoided the wait.

Born in 1963, I grew up in a time when the concept of "the other line" was unknown. In my neighborhood in Springfield, Massachusetts, some families had more money than others, but we all rode our bikes around on the same streets, watched the same TV shows, got the same news, and when we craved things we didn't have, it was usually something simple and reasonable like a better bike or a new baseball glove or the hot Atari game of the moment. Our parents might have wanted the latest car, a more reliable oven, maybe a bigger house. But those were common desires. We didn't know anyone in the upper echelons of wealth or anyone who had flown on a private jet—hell, I didn't even know private jets existed. There were no smartphones, no internet, and only a few channels on the television. In our little world, it was a classic case of keeping up with the Joneses, and they didn't typically have much more than the next neighbor, so our aspirations were more modest. Widespread discontent wasn't the societal norm that it would later become. People strove for better lives, but not in a way that consumed their present happiness.

In my family, we were frequently reminded of our humble origins in Sparta, Greece. My father was raised in a Boston neighborhood that was so thoroughly Greek that he didn't know English when he started school, and my mother was an immigrant who had come to Quebec, Canada, in her twenties, then later to the States. She learned English by watching *The Flintstones* and *Leave It to Beaver*, mastering the language so completely that she ended up teaching English, as well as physical education, in Montreal schools.

We were firmly middle class, yet our household was run with that Depression-era commitment to thrift and frugality that comes from growing up with a lack of modern comforts—never throwing anything away, patching holes in our shoes with scraps of cardboard. My father would describe how they used to hunt pigeons with slingshots to put food on the table. My mother would pick dandelion greens from the neighbors' yards for our meals, which ensured that my friends always avoided our house at dinnertime. She had been raised in Sparta with no electricity or running water. I once asked her why we didn't go camping like other families. "I grew up camping," she said. "We are never doing that." While I myself never dined on pigeon, and it took years before I developed a taste for dandelion greens, the Spartan way of life was instilled deep in me and has remained.

I remember the day when I became aware of the other line, of the class system lurking beneath the surface of our suburban American lives. At my high school in Anaheim, California, I noticed that the parking lot was bigger than the school. And the student armada didn't consist of standard-issue teenager cars—these were Mercedes, BMWs, Trans Ams, Camaros. I seemed to be the only kid who didn't own a car. When I did finally get one in college, it was a used Caprice Classic that had been repaired after an accident by a mechanics' school for free, so each panel of the car was a different color—red, white, or blue, depending on which group in the class was responsible for that section. It looked like a patriotic quilt stitched together by a lunatic. I drove that ridiculous automobile almost as a point of pride.

Not long after I graduated high school, the television program *Lifestyles of the Rich and Famous* debuted in 1984 and quickly found a large viewership. Each episode offered a detailed profile of the unimaginably luxurious life of a celebrity or business magnate, with tours of their mansions and yachts, airplane hangars and thoroughbred stables, summer homes and beach chalets. Robin Leach, the English host, would sign off each episode with his catchphrase, "Champagne wishes and caviar dreams." For many Americans, the program was our introduction to the other line. We didn't know people lived like that. We didn't know such extravagance was possible.

Perhaps the seeds of discontent were there all along, but then the field in which they were sown expanded from the neighborhood to the globe.

———

A generation later in the suburbs of Cleveland, Ohio, a ten-year-old named Logan Paul was learning to use his new camcorder, shooting stunts and pranks with his little brother, Jake, editing the videos with what crude skills they had, then uploading them to YouTube. The brothers steadily built a following. Later, the now-defunct app Vine, which allowed users to post six-second films, became the home for their budding breed of online celebrity.

A football and wrestling star in high school, Logan was "internet famous" by the time he matriculated at Ohio University. He bagged his plans for a career as an industrial systems engineer, dropped out of school after one year, and relocated to LA in hopes of parlaying his internet fame into Hollywood stardom.

Logan comes from a normal middle-class family. There's nothing remarkable about him, except perhaps slightly heightened levels of charisma and good looks and an excess of narcissism. He's tall, blond, Midwestern, a basic American boy who would be popular in high school and maybe a contender for prom king. But the one thing that was remarkable about Logan Paul was his timing. If he'd been born before widespread internet, before apps and video sharing, before camcorders and smartphones, probably no one beyond suburban Cleveland would have ever heard of him. Yet when he arrived in LA, he found that other internet celebrities were also making a go of it, and enough of an audience had gathered around Vine that a few forward-thinking brands were willing to pay these kids to plug products in their homemade videos. Suddenly, the bourgeoning amateur industry was monetized, and it quickly became less amateur, as the internet stars began hiring camera operators and crews, while still being careful to affect a do-it-yourself vibe.

Logan and his fellow internet stars—who are often called *influencers*, for their massive audiences and their ability to sway tastes and trends—were surprisingly savvy about developing themselves into effective brands, and in doing so, they disrupted the advertising world. Rather than hiring an ad firm and landing a big celebrity to come into a studio to shoot a traditional commercial, companies could pay the influencers to promote their products in "homemade" online videos, reaching an enormous following of young people.

"What's most unique about the influencers," my friend Michael

Tedesco explained, "is that they have no talent." He described the genesis of these new media and marketing platforms and the online celebrities who are perched atop that world. "Really, they're content creators. They use video platforms like YouTube and Instagram to create funny sketches or for beauty and health tips. I guess it's unfair to say these people have no talent. They don't have talent in the traditional media that we grew up with—music and broadcast TV and movies—but they have talent in the new media, which is an Instagram feed."

As their fame and wealth and access grew, many of the internet stars were no longer just peddling products for easy money; they began peddling an entire lifestyle. Because of technology and social media, millions of kids gobble up the posts of these nouveau célébrités, craving the products, the popularity, the glamour. Gone are the days of riding bikes in lazy circles around the neighborhood. Now kids are tapped into a much bigger and more complex orbit, and they are relentlessly aware of the existence of the other line.

May 1990, springtime on the campus of the University of Pennsylvania. I was already nostalgic for the Wharton life, and graduation wasn't until the following week.

Despite the savings I'd amassed from working before entering the program, along with the scholarships, part-time gigs, and what I earned as a summer associate at Salomon Brothers, I was set to graduate with $43,000 in student debt. Fortunately, I'd secured a job with a starting salary almost double that amount, and I lived frugally, or else it would have been a frightening situation.

As instructed, I visited the financial aid office to discuss the terms of my debt repayment. Everyone there had always been welcoming during my few appointments, and that day was no different, as I was met with the warm smile of the young woman behind the desk, Jenny. Before getting to the bill-settling part of the conversation, Jenny and I made small talk and discussed summer plans.

"Yeah," I said, "this may be my last opportunity for an extended trip for quite a while."

"You're telling me," Jenny said. "I'll be right here in this office all summer long, with the exception of a week on the Jersey Shore visiting family. So go ahead and make me envious—where are you planning to travel?"

"I'm going with some other MBAs to do volunteer work on a remote Caribbean island called Dominica, then I was hoping to visit a friend in Paris, but I'm not sure it'll happen, given my limited funds. I'm pretty much graduating with the tank on empty, which I guess is how the system is designed."

"My god, the Caribbean *and* Paris?"

"Well, the Caribbean part won't be fancy. We're staying in thatch huts and helping to build a school. Apparently Dominica is one of the poorest places on Earth."

"That sounds like quite a summer. Make sure you save some time for those Caribbean beaches."

"Yeah. I'm sure we'll have a day off here and there."

Jenny squared a stack of papers on her desk. "Have you thought about further borrowings in order to help fund your summer plans?"

"Is that allowed?" Having been a loan officer in the LA jewelry district a couple of years prior, I knew that I was far from an ideal candidate to borrow further funds to be used for a long vacation.

"Absolutely," she said. "We're comfortable loaning up to $50,000 to every one of our business school students. Let's see"—she checked my file—"you're at $43,000, so that leaves you with $7,000 of borrowing capacity."

"Just so I fully understand," I said, "I can borrow $7,000 and use that money to pay for a summer trip?"

"Yup. Whatever you like. But I recommend you put a few dollars aside to cover your moving costs and setting up your new living arrangements after the summer."

Smart advice, I thought, even though Jenny had no idea how small an amount that would need to be, given how little I had to move. How much did a duffel bag cost?

"Well, I'm in for $43,000," I said, "so I might as well go all the way to $50,000." I figured that if my job went as planned, then repaying $50,000 wouldn't be much more difficult than repaying $43,000. Sure, if it all blew up and I was forced to take a less lucrative position, then I would rue repaying every cent of that additional $7,000. But all things considered, it seemed a risk worth taking.

Financial aid for business school students, I later came to understand, operated much differently than for undergrads. Because of our earning potential, loans to MBA students were actually a profitable venture for the school, as we were a good bet to pay them back. The school was eager to give us the money.

Jenny helped me fill out the paperwork, and I traveled the full eight weeks from graduation to the start of training at Salomon Brothers. In Dominica, I helped build a school and meeting house by day, while fighting off the huge, feisty banana rats that populated our hut each night. Afterward I backpacked from Paris to the islands of Greece, and all that time I seldom thought of my additional debt other than to be thankful for the life experience it had afforded me. Although it seemed shocking at the time that Wharton would be willing to finance my vacation, I later understood that since the MBA degree gave me an opportunity to work on Wall Street, that would likely lead to enough financial success to change my line. So even though I couldn't fully appreciate it at the time, while I was still saddled with debt, I had pretty much arrived at the cusp of the other line.

———

When my first summer arrived at Salomon Brothers, I kept overhearing colleagues asking one another an incomprehensible question: "Where's your hamptonshaus?" I had no idea what that word meant; it sounded vaguely German. Then inevitably someone asked me the question— John, a second-year associate I'd known back at Wharton.

"Sorry, John. What was that?" I hoped I might figure out a translation through repetition.

"Your hamptonshaus," he said. "Where is it?"

I shrugged.

"You do have a hamptonshaus, right?" he asked.

"I don't think so," I admitted.

He squinted at me. "Well, you do or you don't."

I couldn't avoid it. "What *is* a hamptonshaus?" I asked.

"A hamptonshaus? It's a goddamn house in the Hamptons."

"Of course! A Hamptons house." He still seemed to be waiting for an answer regarding whether or not I had one. "What are the Hamptons?" I asked, surrendering all hope of saving face.

"Are you fucking kidding me? The Hamptons, out on Long Island."

"Oh, right, right. Where *Gatsby* is set." Having spent my high school years as a Californian, I wasn't exactly up to speed on the vacation destinations of the New York elite. After a few more humiliating questions, I learned that there was an expectation on Wall Street that everyone would rent places in the Hamptons each summer, often spending as much as $50,000 for the season. Bragging rights and status would be determined by the size of the pool, the decadence of the gardens, access to the beach, and the profligacy of the weekend parties. Later in their careers, when they were making a lot more money, it was normal to part with six-figure sums to procure and enjoy their very own Hamptons houses.

I recalled another confusing moment with John when we were back at Wharton. I was at a table with him and five other guys at the campus pub when I realized that all six of them knew each other from a few elite boarding schools, such as Deerfield Academy or Andover, and that they'd all gone to Dartmouth or Yale or Princeton. What were the chances, I thought, that they had all gone to the same few schools? I couldn't imagine that a single other person at Wharton had gone to my public high school in Orange County, and there were certainly no other Occidental College alumni, either. Then the obvious became clear: It wasn't strange at all. These guys had been admitted to an exclusive club at birth. Entire fleets of them had sailed together from Deerfield to Dartmouth to Wharton to Wall Street, and then to the Hamptons each summer. It was their common path of travel.

I didn't have a Hamptons house, and I didn't see the point of getting one. I was clearly the Nick Carraway of the group; a modest cottage at the edge of the lawn would have suited me just fine. A realization struck me that first season, as I mastered the art of landing invitations to everyone else's estates. I called it "the Hamptons effect." So many people were struggling to get into the other line that it actually made a contrarian play advantageous. As the weekend guest, I would insist on paying for everything—drinks, dinners, tolls, gas money—and that made me a coveted guest, allowing me to go wherever I wanted, whenever I wanted, and it cost me a fraction of what the others were spending to lease their summer places. As a result, I had full flexibility and none of the logistical or financial headaches associated with having my own Hamptons house.

———

I've never tired of returning to my old stomping grounds at Disneyland every couple of years or so. On a recent visit, the weather was scorching, and the lines were murderously long. Signs posted above the entrance to each ride estimated the misery: APPROXIMATE STANDBY WAIT TIME 150 MINUTES. No one seemed overtly upset by this. Having paid hundreds of dollars to access the park, the guests had no problem standing for hours under the baking sun to board a ride that would last a few short minutes. Rumor had it that the new Guardians of the Galaxy attraction over in the adjacent California Adventure Park had wait times of five full hours.

Our group of ten had no intention of joining them. We stayed close behind our hostess, Michelle, who wore a plaid riding outfit—cap, breeches, boots, and all—as she led us around the waiting masses to the Pirates of the Caribbean exit, where we entered right away and took our seats in the boat. I felt a pang of guilt for skipping the line, but that quickly subsided as we drifted into the bayou among the fireflies, passing the old man sitting on the front porch of his cabin.

For three hundred dollars per hour, we had hired Michelle as our

VIP hostess, which allowed us to skip all lines. Over the course of six hours, our group would go on every ride, have front-row seats for the parade, and enjoy a leisurely lunch at the Blue Bayou.

Most of the newer rides had hidden VIP entrances, so the people in line wouldn't feel more bitter about their wait—seeing us coast by, of course, wouldn't positively impact the guest experience—and for some rides we could enter through the exit; but since the park was not constructed with a VIP option in mind, the majority of the rides required us to cut directly in front of those who had been standing for hours. Michelle would raise an arm in front of the waiting guests and say, "Just one moment," and our group would step into the next boat or car or spaceship or whatever.

We headed straight onto the Buzz Lightyear ride. The space cruisers were outfitted with laser guns for battling evil robots, and you racked up points for each kill. We made it a contest among our little group. As we came off the ride, each of us reported our results. I tallied a measly 55,000; my nephew got 60,000; my daughter 80,000; and my sister-in-law took the title with 110,000 points. I asked Michelle her score. "Two million," she said with a smile. "An off day. That's not even close to the top scores for me or the other VIP hostesses." Evidently she had a lot of laser gun experience and was a seasoned pro. Quite a few people must have been taking advantage of Disney's other line.

As Michelle escorted us to lunch, we passed my old Café Orleans, which I pointed out to my daughter for the twentieth time. "That's where I worked in the early '80s, when I was barely older than you."

"I know, Dad." She'd heard all the stories.

Later, while dining at the Blue Bayou, feeling uneasy about cutting in front of waiting guests, I considered some of the reactions we'd gotten, which ranged from awe to envy to resentment, often accompanied by commentary: *Wow, they don't have to wait. How cool would that be?* or: *Why do they get to skip the line? What makes them special?* or: *That's not fair. They should wait in line like the rest of us.* One consequence of the other line is that it can make people in the traditional line feel angry or disadvantaged, as if the system is rigged against them. Most of the people standing in those long lines at Disneyland had carefully saved the money to be able to afford their visit. (A family of four might spend thousands of dollars for a long weekend in the Magic Kingdom.) Their visit was a special occasion, sometimes a once-in-a-lifetime occasion. So to see privileged people skip the line must have demeaned and debased the guest experience.

I wondered how I would have felt about Disney's other line back when I worked there, before the notion of VIP treatment existed at the park. I couldn't decide. Part of me thought I would have been perfectly fine with it, appreciating the pay-for-value proposition that now seemed to infiltrate every part of Disneyland. But I mostly felt that my eighteen-year-old self would have been shocked. Equality seemed a core tenet of the happiest place on Earth. *Would Walt have approved?* I wondered. *Is the VIP experience consistent with the values that Disneyland was created to exemplify and promote? Would I even come to Disneyland if I had to wait in line? What is my daughter learning each time we skip a line?*

A 2013 report by the *New York Post* found that wealthy Manhattanites were hiring people with disabilities as "black-market guides" for visiting Disney, paying them $130 per hour to pose as family members so the groups could skip to the front of lines. One woman who used the service was quoted as saying: "This is how the 1 percent does Disney." In response, Disney was forced to change its policies regarding disabled guests, revoking their instant access to rides. It's repulsive that there was a market for such a thing, but then again, there's now a market for everything.

In our new culture of special access, bribery, and other lines, what has been lost? And why should we care? Is it more efficient to create a price list for every advantage, social need, desire, and activity? Or are we propagating a new class system that will only grow more extreme and divided in time?

The Disney VIP hostess is just one manifestation of a growing societal trend. As increasing numbers of people become wealthy, they look to spend that wealth, accumulating all the material things one could want. But what to do with their excess wealth? More and more often, they spend it on better access—the other line.

The other line can be better healthcare: For a monthly fee, you can employ an on-call concierge doctor who will use his or her contacts to get you the best treatment for whatever medical issue may arise. Large gifts to hospitals or medical foundations also secure priority access. And of course there are other lines in the political world, the entertainment world, the nightclub world, and so on. Special access is not a new concept. But never before has it been so pervasive, accepted, and sought after by such a large group of people.

A central objective of those in the other line—whether they're conscious of this or not—is to reinforce and extend their privilege across generations, so that their children can maintain the advantages that they enjoy. Once the wealthy have attained all the desired access and material things, then they start to look at lengthening their legacy and making sure their progeny will enjoy the same lifestyle and benefits. One increasingly popular way to do so is through the development offices of education and philanthropic establishments, which sell access as a fund-raising tool. The price for "special consideration" at Stanford is said to be $25 million. "While a donation does not guarantee your son or daughter admission," goes the typical line, "it does ensure that the admissions office will pay close attention to his or her application." Students who are admitted with the help of a large gift now have a name: *development admits*. While upsetting, these are perfectly legal ways to grease the skids.

Other methods, which are not lawful and aboveboard, are perhaps no less uncommon. In March 2019, the Justice Department arrested several celebrities and business moguls in connection with a vast college admissions scandal. A man named William "Rick" Singer, who claimed to run a college preparatory service, accepted roughly $25 million to fix standardized test scores and pay off coaches in order to land enrollment for undeserving students. Some parents were accused of having shelled out as much as $6.5 million to buy their child's access to the "side door," as Singer put it. Sitcom actress Lori Loughlin allegedly paid $500,000 to get her two petite daughters admitted to USC under the guise of their joining the crew team. One of the daughters, Olivia Jade—a social media influencer who decidedly does not row crew—approached college as a marketing platform, striking deals with Amazon Prime and launching a makeup line with Sephora. Before her freshman year began, she posted a YouTube video for her couple of million followers: "I don't know how much of school I'm gonna attend, but I'm gonna go in and talk to my deans and everyone and hope that I can try and balance it all. But I do want the experience of, like, game days, partying. . . . I don't really care about school, as you guys all know." Since the scandal, Sephora has severed ties with Olivia Jade, and the public backlash has been spirited.

In order to make college available to more people, federal student loans were created in the 1950s. While that program started with good intentions—to assist those without the means to attend college—it later contributed to a financial and social ill. Rather than reward and encourage vocational careers, we have instead come to define success in relation to acceptance by a well-known college, with a greater emphasis placed on the institution's brand name than on the actual education it provides. The student loan market has facilitated schools' raising the cost of education astronomically, which in turn has made it even less viable for those unable to access loans and scholarships.

Our national education bubble has swelled to $1.6 trillion in debt outstanding—that's larger than both credit card and auto loan debts, a consumer debt market smaller only than mortgage debt. Two million people in our country owe more than $100,000 in student loans. After being told their whole lives about the importance of a college education, then working hard to get into the best school they could, they graduated into a Kafkaesque existence, shackled to debts they have limited ability to repay while working jobs that leave them living at subsistence levels. Meanwhile, the children of the rich and famous are matriculating at even better schools, unburdened by financial considerations as they set up their cameras to plug new products and vlog about their glamorous lives.

———

I headed to Coachella with my friend and former Salomon colleague Michael Tedesco, whom everyone called T. We were going down for the music festival as the guests of a company in which we had invested. A kid with a flowing mane of blond hair shot across the tarmac on a skateboard, wearing loud floral-patterned shorts and a matching tank top. He skidded to a stop in front of the private jet that would take us to Palm Springs, uncapped his Fiji water and took a pull, and said, "Fuck yeah! We're flyin' PJ!" After a series of hand slaps and fist bumps for me and the others standing outside the plane, Logan Paul passed his phone to one of the other internet stars. He struck a few poses in front of the plane—invoking childish excitement, then innocent surprise, then comic triumph—not yet sure what vibe he was going for. The guy with the phone checked the photos before handing the device back to Logan.

"Wait, dude," Logan said. "Get another one with this EMERGENCY sign in it."

They set back up as we all watched. Logan climbed onto the plane's stairs—one foot on the bottom step and the other waist-high, legs spread wide—and he raised his chin and flexed his biceps. He appeared, perhaps intentionally, as some cross between a Greek god and a circus clown. Once they wrapped the shoot, we boarded and took our seats. Logan made adjustments to his favorite photo and, while we were taxiing, posted it to Instagram. He spoke the caption aloud as he typed it: "My outfit is the emergency." They all laughed, these internet celebrities.

The flight from LA to Coachella, the site of the giant music festival in the desert outside Palm Springs, only took half an hour. T and I were investors in The Influential Network, a company that paired social media stars with brands looking for fresh ways to advertise, and we were accompanying a few of the top online celebs on a private jet to Coachella, where The Influential Network was throwing a several-day party in a mansion called the TIN House.

By the time of this writing—and this stat often changes by the hour— Logan Paul had more than 59 million followers across several social media handles, with views of his videos estimated at north of 5 billion, rewriting the very definition of celebrity. Gone were the days of making backyard videos with his little brother in the Cleveland suburbs. *Forbes* reported that Paul earned $14.5 million in advertising revenue from June 2017 to

June 2018, some from peddling products and some from brands running ads on his YouTube page. No wonder, in his vlog posts, his enthusiasm often bordered on hysteria. Even Logan's pet parrot, Maverick, had 1.3 million Instagram followers. His fluffy Pomeranian dog, Kong Da Savage Pom, built up 3 million followers before he was killed, in April 2019, by a coyote.

Brands have continued to find success with this sort of advertising, reaching their target audience in a more organic and direct way. When *60 Minutes* spent an afternoon with Logan for a profile piece, he was improvising an advertisement for Dunkin' Donuts in New York's Central Park—executed with no corporate oversight or interference—then he posted it to Instagram, collecting nearly $200,000 for the day's work. Dunkin' Donuts claimed that the post, which swiftly reached 7 million views, was at least as effective as a primetime television ad. In 2017, *Forbes* reported that Logan typically earned $150,000 for a sponsored Facebook post and $80,000 for a single Instagram photo.

"They're the cultural icons for younger people and Millennials," T said. "That's why it's so powerful to advertisers—it's a demographic that you really can't reach through traditional media. They're cynical about ads on TV and large campaigns. But when it's social media and somebody's telling you what they like, there's a higher level of trust that they're telling you the truth." A 2014 survey conducted by the McCarthy Group found that 84 percent of Millennials distrust traditional advertising. Their skepticism has only grown deeper and broader. In 2017, MediaPost reported on the results of a poll conducted by Harvard's Institute of Politics: "88% of Millennials said they 'only sometimes' or 'never' trust the press, and 86% of Millennials said they distrust Wall Street. Millennials were equally dubious of government, with 74% saying they 'sometimes' or 'never' trust that the federal government will do the right thing." With such a loss of faith in our societal institutions, it's unsurprising that these homegrown online personalities have reached unprecedented levels of stardom.

When you look at the influencers' feeds, the majority of the posts are unsponsored—unless you consider their tireless promotion of a lavish, jokester lifestyle to be a sort of sponsorship. When they are selling a particular product, the most subtle and deceiving native advertising tactics are often employed. An Instagram photo from July 2017 depicts Logan splayed across the hood of a Mercedes-AMG G65, a luxury SUV that retails for a quarter of a million dollars. He's wearing short-shorts, a fur coat, mirrored sunglasses, and slippers. Sitting next to him, also in a fur coat, is Logan's frequent sidekick, a dwarf known online as Dwarf Mamba. The caption reads: "fur soft but we hard af" (*af* is internet slang for "as fuck"). The post quickly racked up more than 1.3 million likes and 21,000 comments. Most of Logan's fans probably wouldn't have thought of the photo as an advertisement—which is precisely the point. Perhaps Mercedes paid him for the post, or perhaps he traded the product placement for a free automobile, or perhaps he simply used the association with the luxury car brand to boost his own personal brand, but no matter which, the Mercedes logo is prominent in the image.

Some posts don't attempt to hide their transactional nature. A photo might show an influencer, for example, buried under a mountain of JBL headphones that he's giving away to people who like and share the image. Or a post might show an influencer applying her favorite hair-removal cream on the edge of a bathtub, showing a lot of leg and plugging the product in the caption. Other posts try to use clever misdirection, such as an April 2015 Instagram photo by Logan's little brother, Jake, who had become a social media star in his own right. The image, set in what looks to be the kitchen of the TIN House at Coachella, shows a shirtless guy standing at the stove and shooting a massive flame from an aerosol can, while Jake sits at the counter riveted by his laptop. Beside the computer is a bottle of Coke. The caption: "Can't even pay attention to Richie right now, I'm busy playing @CocaCola's Tongue Hero game. Check it out (link in bio) #TasteBudTalent #DontTryThisAtHome." Despite the overt plug for the largest soda company on the planet, the post still gathered 90,000 likes and climbing.

Many influencers have other talents for which they hope to become known. Logan wants to make it as a legitimate actor. Jerry Purpdrank, who was also on the plane, is an aspiring rapper. In spite of my skepticism,

I couldn't help but be charmed by them. And I guess that's their true talent, after all. They're relatable, good looking, and charismatic. Their success has a homemade quality, which seduces millions of young fans into believing they too can attain fame, wealth, and a glamorous lifestyle. *Logan is a suburban kid from Ohio*, they think, *not much different from me, and look at him now*. The job of these influencers involves flying to music festivals on private jets, vacationing in exotic locales, lying across the hoods of expensive automobiles, striking suggestive or falsely modest poses—and then making sure someone is nearby with a good camera to capture it all. They live entirely in the other line, allow corporations to finance it, and make everyone covet it.

We touched down at the private airport in Thermal, and Logan tapped into his app to see how his post was doing. "Check it," he said, holding the phone toward me, "50,000 likes in half an hour."

At Coachella, The Influential Network's rented mansion was in an exclusive neighborhood with high security where many celebrities leased estates during the festival. The TIN House was meant to be a microcosm of the world that The Influential Network existed to promote—the world of luxurious leisure, of self-indulgent slackers. Attractive people strolled by with tropical cocktails from the open bar. Young women sunned themselves in scant bikinis. Each of the interior rooms was occupied by one brand or another, so the influencers could make money peddling products while they enjoyed themselves. It was an advertising agency masquerading as a nonstop house party—absurd and brilliant.

T and I expected to feel completely out of place—and we did, but everyone was surprisingly nice to us. I knew that some of the big influencers were there, but I couldn't figure out how the rest of the crowd ended up at the TIN House. Who were these women having a splash fight in the pool? Why was that guy doing push-ups beside the Jacuzzi? Did Justin Bieber just walk by?

The news burning through the party was that Bieber was renting the house next door, and he was throwing a rager later in the day that everyone wanted to attend. I kept thinking I saw him at the TIN House party—walking past in a white T-shirt and green bandanna, then a few minutes later wearing a Hawaiian shirt, talking to a group of women on the lawn, then cannonballing off the diving board in his underwear. When I saw two Biebers side by side, yelling from the balcony, I tracked down T to ask what was going on.

"T, I've spotted Justin Bieber half a dozen times, in different places, in different clothes, and now I think I'm seeing things." I gestured at the balcony with my drink. "Did somebody dose my tequila, or are there really two Biebers up there?"

T explained that one of the guys at the party gained his fame as an actual Justin Bieber impersonator. That was his shtick. The others, including the twins on the balcony, had simply made themselves so completely in the image of Bieber that they were unofficial doppelgängers. Most of the people at the party, T explained, were "aspiring influencers," busy building their followings and developing their marketing relationships. The biggest online celebrities had outgrown The Influential Network and assembled their own armies of publicists, agents, stylists, and managers, dealing directly with brands.

Just then one of the top stars, Rudy Mancuso, entered the party, creating a stir. I eavesdropped as a couple of guys behind us quietly cataloged and admired his outfit—a baggy purple-and-black striped T-shirt, tight black jeans, rounded aviator sunglasses, hair in a bun on top of his head—things I never would have noticed or cared about in my normal day-to-day.

"Look at those boots," one guy muttered.

"Dope," said the other. "I think they're Berlutis."

Even T was a big fan of Rudy. He had described to me how Rudy was one of the original Vine stars, funny and magnetic, as they all were, but also an accomplished musician. His Instagram feed is filled with piano and guitar performances, goofy comic video skits with the likes of Mike Tyson, Mariah Carey, and Steph Curry, photos with international superstars like Neymar, and jokey interviews with Floyd Mayweather and, of course, Bieber. "Rudy's super savvy," T said. "He's a Brazilian from New York, and he's definitely one of the most talented, because he's actually a really good musician." Rudy was once approached by Tom Hanks at a party. "I need to get a selfie with you," the legendary movie star said, "or my son will never believe this."

After making his proper entrance at the TIN House, Rudy came by to say hello to T.

"Sorry not to see you on the plane," T said.

"Man," Rudy said, "I had to roll out here in a new Mustang convertible. You should see this thing. Ford gave it to me the other day."

Rudy hadn't even done a plug for Ford in exchange for the car. It was basically given to him on spec, with the hope that he might post something about it later, which would bolster the cool factor of the brand and hopefully help sell some Mustangs. This was a common occurrence in the lives of the influencers. A couple of years later, another influencer with whom T was familiar claimed to have been given a BMW i8. "It's a $140,000 electric car," T said. "That shows you the evolution of this world. I don't think Rudy would even accept a Mustang these days." For some of us regular people, we might move from Caprice Classic to minivan to Mustang, and *maybe* on to something like a BMW or Tesla or Bentley, and that evolution would probably span thirty years. For these social media stars, the full evolution might happen over a matter of months, although of course they'd skip the Caprice and the minivan.

I stuck around the party for a few hours, and in spite of my reservations about this brave new world, I had fun. It was hard not to. Having a good time was what the marketable lifestyle was all about.

Here was the youth of our nation—the most followed and liked and tagged and admired—hawking the other line as a way of life. And millions of kids were buying into it, hook, line, and sinker. Pop culture and advertising have always been filled with misguided messages about body image and materialism, but this was on a whole other level. The very existence of these influencers screamed out the new ambition: You can drive a luxury car, wear a fur coat, fly to Rio on a private jet, maintain a perfect body, acquire the best clothes and accessories and devices, surround yourself with beautiful people, at beautiful places, in beautiful weather—and photograph it all for others to see. It was a radical redefinition of success, and at its core was a frenzied craving for the other line.

Jake Paul, Logan's little brother, was also at the party. He had coasted to fame on his brother's coattails, eventually capturing his own sizeable social media following and forging his own identity. He had even transcended the internet audience by landing a role on a Disney Channel show called *Bizaardvark*, but despite his connection with Mickey Mouse, Jake Paul clearly had a wild streak.

The rest of his crew had left the TIN House and gone next door to Bieber's party, but since Jake wasn't twenty-one, he'd been turned away at the door. It must have been torture for him to know what celebrities and other VIPs were there. He marched into the backyard with a look of desperate determination and scanned the wall that separated the two properties. Nothing and no one were going to deny Jake Paul access to Bieber's party. He belonged there. He deserved it.

If you can't get to the other line through the front door, you can always scale the wall. Jake finally got some purchase, scrambled to the top, and disappeared over it. I could only imagine him, this teenager famous for being famous, wandering through the manicured gardens of flesh, money, products, and cameras, feeling completely within his element. He had arrived, and soon his followers would know all about it.

In a scene from the 1996 film *Jerry Maguire*, a working-class mom named Dorothy Boyd (played by Renée Zellweger) is sitting on an airplane, worried about her sick son beside her, as he promptly fills a barf bag. Meanwhile, up in first class, Jerry Maguire (Tom Cruise) is flirting with a blond woman while a spread of fresh fruit and cheese is delivered to him. He and Dorothy work for the same talent agency, but on different ends of the corporate hierarchy. He's the famous agent enjoying first class, and she's a secretary crammed in coach beside a vomiting child. From her seat, she can just hear the story Jerry is telling the blonde, describing his elaborate Hawaiian proposal to his fiancée. Dorothy leans into the aisle, listening, transfixed, as she snacks on her bag of peanuts and watches the blonde hold her champagne flute aloft for a refill. Suddenly the flight attendant whips the curtains closed. Dorothy sinks back into her seat.

"What's wrong, Mom?" her son asks.

"First class is what's wrong, honey," she says in a tired voice. "It used to be a better meal. Now it's a better life."

In few places is the other line more apparent than in air travel, with vast differences in comfort and luxury between economy, business, and first class. VIPs can skip the wait at check-in, security, and boarding. While air travel's other line has been the aspiration of many of us, it is simply one more example of how we've been segmented, spliced, and diced into groups, which by definition has made us less proximate to people different from ourselves. In pursuit of the other line, we have constructed personal bubbles to protect us from unwelcome information and unwanted interactions. We control our own narrative by limiting the information we receive that might challenge our beliefs, yet at the same time, we seek information about how people in the other line are living, so we can know what we're missing. That way we can ensure our discontent. By controlling our proximity to the unfamiliar, we have become less connected, more insular, locked into the narratives we want to believe and propagate.

I think about this every time I board an airplane and see people quickly reach for their headphones so they don't have to speak to the person next to them. Many first-class cabins these days solve the problem for us, as they've been redesigned to simulate individual isolation booths. There was a time when I looked forward to meeting the random stranger on the way to an exotic backpacking trip. I might spend the entire flight talking to that person, often making plans to meet up while traveling. We're all under such a constant barrage of information and stimulation that airplanes have become a place to disconnect. It's ironic, or maybe sad, that the moment when we're together with a bunch of strangers is the time when we go out of our way to disengage with them.

─────

After reaching unprecedented heights of online celebrity, some cracks have appeared in Logan Paul's armor. In January 2018, he was sharply criticized in global news for bringing his posse and camera crew to romp through Japan's famed "Suicide Forest," a remote location at the foot of Mount Fuji, where many people have gone to end their lives. There they stumbled upon a man hung from a tree. In the fifteen-minute vlog post of the incident, Logan shows graphic footage of the deceased to his millions of young fans. At one point, he says with mock toughness, "What, you never stand next to a dead guy?"—then he sniffs comically and bursts into laughter. He brags in his intro to the video that "this definitely marks a moment in YouTube history" and that viewers should "buckle the fuck up, because you're never gonna see a video like this again."

Suicide prevention groups, the media, and the general public attacked Logan for his insensitivity. Author Caitlin Doughty posted one of countless disapproving tweets: "It is the purview of the privileged young to believe everything is for them, to be commented on by them. The young person who died was not for Paul—not their body, not their image, not their story. . . . You're not Neil Armstrong bro, it's simply a thing no one else has been tacky enough to do. . . ."

Logan was part of YouTube Preferred, a program that places ads before the site's most watched videos, allowing these stars to collect big payouts. After this scandal, YouTube temporarily demonetized Logan's channel. He issued a handful of public apologies, with differing levels of sincerity, but the stunt badly hurt his personal brand and cost him multitudes of followers and fans. Other vlog posts from Logan's visit to Japan displayed a startling level of racism and cultural disrespect. After a monthlong hiatus from his various platforms, apparently for a period of self-reflection, Logan returned to YouTube with a video in which he Tasered a dead rat, which brought further YouTube restrictions and widespread disgust. In April 2018, he announced the end of his daily vlog. As Logan's falling star has demonstrated, the influencer world is an ephemeral one. Admirers and riches can depart as quickly as they arrive.

His little brother, Jake, has seen his own share of bad press, as he remade his image from Disney Channel star into the antihero of the internet. In June 2017, a local Los Angeles news station reported that Jake was so reviled by his West Hollywood neighbors that they were considering a class-action public-nuisance lawsuit—an achievement for which Jake expressed pride and amusement. He and his gang pass their time by doing things like filling his empty swimming pool with furniture and setting it on fire, or performing motorcycle stunts in the streets of the family-oriented neighborhood, or publicizing his address and encouraging hordes of fans to flock to his house. Neighbors described the scene as a "living hell," a "war zone," and a "circus"—to which Jake chuckled and said, "I mean, but people like going to circuses, right?" The *New York Times* picked up the story, titling it "Jake Paul, a Reality Villain for the YouTube Generation." Soon after, the Disney Channel parted ways with Jake.

The Paul brothers and their fellow influencers seem to have descended straight from the godfather of stunts, pranks, and gross-out videos, Johnny Knoxville, who launched the *Jackass* series on MTV in 2000, when Logan was five years old. The subsequent *Jackass* films would have been a cultural force during Logan's formative years. The main transformation from *Jackass* to today is that the new generation has cut out the middleman and figured out how to monetize their videos, create personal brands, and market themselves as commodities. When I was younger, we would have called that selling out. Not anymore. If you're savvy enough to make a dollar, by whatever means, then that's cause for adoration.

At the risk of sounding ridiculous, compared to today's amateurs-turned-stars, Knoxville is an old-school traditionalist. He paid his dues, first pitching stories and video ideas to *Big Brother* magazine, then developing the concept for television, eventually selecting MTV after a bidding war that included Comedy Central and *Saturday Night Live*. Success used to be achieved through hard work, perseverance, talent, and, sure, some measure of luck. The goal for many young people these days is to skip the line, hack the system, and gain maximum success while paying minimum dues. And that creates a sense of entitlement to the other line, along with resentment when you don't reach the other line with ease. Logan went straight from the Cleveland suburbs to stardom. The millions of kids who venerate him—that's what they all want too.

The size of their following becomes a sort of currency, and they sell that currency to fans and other aspiring influencers. What people are buying is the hope that they can collect the same spoils and maybe even become an influencer, so that they too can sell their currency to others who would want to become them.

Even many who aren't influencers are obsessed with crafting their public image. There's a Moscow-based company called Private Jet Studio that offers hourly rates for a Gulfstream G650, which never leaves the tarmac. One can pay extra for a professional photographer, makeup, and hair stylist. At the end of their staged photo shoot, they leave with Instagram-ready images to conjure the illusion that they're flying private and living the high life. The National Institutes of Health conducted a global study of the mortal dangers of selfies: "From October 2011 to November 2017, there have been 259 deaths while clicking selfies in 137 incidents. The mean age was 22.94 years."

Aspiring social media stars in Russia often go to fatal lengths in pursuit of internet fame and its associated riches. These kids are notorious for performing incredibly dangerous acts—climbing skyscrapers and bridges, hanging from construction beams hundreds of feet in the air, jumping from tall buildings into snowbanks. Many die in the hunt for status and wealth.

In the summer of 2017, the quest for YouTube fame ended the life of a twenty-two-year-old Minnesotan named Pedro Ruiz III. He and his nineteen-year-old girlfriend, Monalisa Perez, had been posting harmless pranks and stunts in an attempt to build a following worthy of influencer status. One day he held a book against his chest and encouraged her to shoot a bullet at it, confident that it wouldn't pass through, but of course it did, killing Ruiz. From the *New York Times* report: "It was a preventable death, the sheriff said, apparently fostered by a culture in which money and some degree of stardom can be obtained by those who attract a loyal internet following with their antics. In the couple's last video, posted on Monday, Ms. Perez and her boyfriend considered what it would be like to be one of those stars—'when we have 300,000 subscribers.'" At the time of the shooting, Perez was visibly pregnant with the couple's second child. In December 2017, she pled guilty to second-degree manslaughter and, through a plea deal, was sentenced to six months in jail and ten years of supervised probation. "I just don't understand the younger generation on trying to get their fifteen minutes of fame," Sheriff Jeremy Thornton said.

"The original promise of the internet," Tedesco said, "was that we would remove the gatekeepers and arbiters of taste, which would democratize it. But we're finding that having a gatekeeper, to some extent, having to build your road, having some societal rules, as unfair as they often were, this served an important function. There are pitfalls of being able to hack the line and jump to the top and skip the twenty years of honing your craft and paying your dues."

These homegrown celebrities can wield enormous power, for both good and evil. The biggest YouTube star of all is a Swede named Felix Kjellberg, who posts under the handle PewDiePie. He first gained fame through posting YouTube clips of himself playing video games. In January 2017, after he became the first person to surpass 50 million subscribers, he posted a video in which he paid two young Indian boys to dance around with a sign that read DEATH TO ALL JEWS. YouTube reprimanded PewDiePie by removing him from its Preferred advertiser program, and Disney cut ties with Kjellberg after the *Wall Street Journal* highlighted nine anti-Semitic videos that had been viewed by millions of followers, many of them children. Kjellberg claimed the videos were not meant to express sympathy with hateful views. "I'm not trying to push the envelope," he said. "I'm just trying to stay true to my sense of humor." The Daily Stormer website, home base for white supremacists and other hate groups, added the tagline to its homepage: "the world's #1 PewDiePie fan site." Kjellberg, who now has more than 90 million YouTube subscribers, pocketed $15.5 million for his posts in 2018, according to *Forbes*.

In March 2019, a white supremacist in New Zealand shot and killed fifty-one Muslims worshipping in two separate mosques, injuring another forty-nine. True to the era of homegrown online celebrity, the killer livestreamed the attack on Facebook. As he strode into the first mosque with his arsenal of weapons, viewers heard him say: "Subscribe to PewDiePie."

Most social media stars don't inspire mass murder, and many are not reckless, thoughtless, or racist, but these influencers, who are shaping the tastes and identities of our youth, rarely use their considerable reach for positive ends. Whether they're fostering in their fans an obsession with products and body image, or selling the other line as a way of life, or acting on darker, destructive impulses, the market economy has taken over the social order, and it has become a fierce, fast, scary new world.

———

Maybe we'll be spared from worrying about whether PewDiePie is a Nazi or whether Jake Paul will further irritate his neighbors, and the world will soon come to an end. That's what a growing number of wealthy people are preparing for.

The collapse of civilization has always been a favorite topic of humankind. Each generation seems to have its own stark vision for Armageddon. Technology is partly the cause for our modern paranoia, as is globalization. In recent decades, our world has expanded beyond the neighborhood, beyond the local community, so now we can witness atrocities around the planet in real time, streaming them live, following them on social media, watching them on cable news, twenty-four hours per day.

As such, a new breed of survivalist has sprung up. When I was a kid, a survivalist was viewed by the general public as someone just a few camo vests and crossbows short of a padded room in the mental institution, but not so today. It has become startlingly common for the wealthy classes to make preparations for the end of the world. The interesting thing about preppers—as they're often called—is that the movement transcends all the labels that we typically associate with survivalism. Today's preppers don't come from one political persuasion or another. They don't come from one background or age group. They are found in both Silicon Valley and Wall Street, are both liberal and conservative, young and old. The single unifying thread seems to be that preppers have lots of money, resources, and unlimited access to the other line.

They typically don't agree on what will be the cause of the fall of humanity. Some expect it to be climate change or a natural disaster. Some are worried about political, racial, and social tensions leading to broader unrest, riot, and civil war. Some are watching the skies for a nuclear missile. But they all seem to feel that the system—the financial system, in particular—has become too complicated and unstable, and if one of these disasters were to occur, the center could not hold; the financial structures on which our society rests would become untenable. So these people, anxious that the world could blow up any day now, one way or another, are willing to go to great lengths to be ready.

Evan Osnos covered the prepper phenomenon for the *New Yorker* in January 2017, interviewing people from both the Manhattan financial world and the Bay Area technology industry. He spoke with the head of an investment firm who has an underground bunker and keeps a helicopter gassed up. "A lot of my friends do the guns and the motorcycles and the gold coins," he said. "That's not too rare anymore." A Silicon Valley venture capitalist told Osnos, "I kind of have this terror scenario: 'Oh, my god, if there is a civil war or a giant earthquake that cleaves off part of California, we want to be ready.'" He keeps suitcases packed and has invested widely in real estate, so his family would have multiple escape options if the end drew near.

A common trend in the prepper community is to purchase land and an airstrip in New Zealand and then buy your way into citizenship. As Osnos reported: "In the first seven days after Donald Trump's election, 13,401 Americans registered with New Zealand's immigration authorities, the first official step toward seeking residency—more than seventeen times the usual rate. . . . Much as Switzerland once drew Americans with the promise of secrecy, and Uruguay tempted them with private banks, New Zealand offers security and distance. In the past six years, nearly a thousand foreigners have acquired residency there under programs that mandate certain types of investment of at least a million dollars."

The rise of doomsday preppers is just one extreme symptom of a larger cultural illness. We used to interact with people who didn't share our belief system. That's no longer the case. We used to live in the same neighborhoods, watch the same sitcoms and nightly news, share a flight, a sports experience, we used to chat with one another in the grocery store. But we no longer intersect with that which might disrupt our narrative, allowing it to harden, bunkering it from opposing viewpoints. The very definition of *community* has changed. It's no longer based on the people to whom you are physically near; it is increasingly defined as a network of people to whom you have an electronic connection and with whom you share similar views and tastes and experiences. The randomness of forming a community with those around you is vanishing and, with it, diversity. Many people's circles of friends are now determined in some measure by algorithms on social media.

The insulation we've constructed for ourselves is what led to the political landscape that emerged in 2016, a starkly divided nation in which there is not only a dearth of appreciation for the views and plights of others but also judgment and condescension toward their beliefs and priorities. The individual bubbles that we live within play an integral role in the formation of large financial bubbles too, as we choose to ignore the rise of government debt, unfunded pension obligations, and student debt—just as we failed to see the mortgage bubble that blew up into the 2008 financial crisis.

It's rare to find someone in the upper stratospheres of wealth who vocally opposes the survivalist trend. Max Levchin, a PayPal founder, also talked with Osnos for the *New Yorker* piece: "It's one of the few things about Silicon Valley that I actively dislike—the sense that we are superior giants who move the needle and, even if it's our own failure, must be spared. . . . I typically ask people, 'So you're worried about the pitchforks. How much money have you donated to your local homeless shelter?' This connects the most, in my mind, to the realities of the income gap. All the other forms of fear that people bring up are artificial."

What are the preppers really afraid of? They're not afraid of the zombie apocalypse. They're not directly afraid of an earthquake. Their fear is this: They know the system is being debased and becoming more fragile. They don't know what's going to precipitate the end of the world as they know it, but they're worried it's going to happen; and when it does, they want to make sure that their advantages are protected.

It's pretty scary that the people with the most knowledge—those from Wall Street who built our financial world and those from Silicon Valley who built our technology—are the ones who are most worried that the whole system could melt down. This has inspired the rise of things like Bitcoin and other cryptocurrencies. When people lose faith in their civil society, government, and financial institutions, they begin to invest in alternatives—store up gold, build a compound, buy crypto, assemble a personal arsenal.

But what if their strategies are misguided? I have many friends who are preppers. They don't broadcast it, of course, and they usually tolerate my arguments about their motivation and whether their survival approach would be effective. The problem I see with preppers is that their assumptions may be off. What if, rather than isolation, joining together with a community is how one survives? If civilization fails, it's likely that we won't be living in a world in which the old constructs persist. Why would a doctor come out to your bunker, for example, if money loses its value? The preppers might be devising sound strategies to survive a month of chaos, or maybe a year or more, but those are temporary solutions. Yet, like modern-day pharaohs, they're committed to the belief that if they get buried with all their assets and resources, those advantages might transfer to the next world.

———

We recently moved to a different part of the South Bay so we could be closer to my daughter's school and my work. We'd grown sick of the daily gridlock of Silicon Valley traffic. So it was a convenient move, but also a bit culturally jarring, even though it was only about twenty miles from our previous house.

Where I'd grown up, in Springfield and Orange County, I was used to living in a neighborhood where, sure, you were trying to keep up with the Joneses next door, but you would also gather with them for backyard barbecues on the weekends. On any given night, it seemed as though half the neighborhood would drop by our house; they'd just make a social call with no warning or invitation. Neighborhood was synonymous with community.

Fifteen years before we bought our new house, we had visited the area with our real estate agent. At one point she said with a wink, "Don't worry, none of your neighbors will ever come by to borrow a cup of sugar." The confidence and ease with which she delivered the line made it apparent that it had worked well for her in the past, even though I found it both depressing and alarming. And I never forgot it. We decided to live elsewhere. But when we ended up buying a house in that neighborhood a decade and a half later, I wondered if the atmosphere of privacy and seclusion she described would still be accurate. We tested it out. After moving in, we sent letters and emails to our immediate neighbors to introduce ourselves and invite them over. We didn't get a single reply. Even a year later, we've still never met them. If the world does approach its end, I don't expect my new neighbors will be banding together.

Access to the other line is first and foremost determined by the birth lottery. Race, nation, and gender are all factors, as well as the socioeconomic status and psychological functionality and resilience of your family. I'd been lucky on those accounts. But if not for the Wharton MBA, I likely wouldn't have had the opportunities and resources that offer entry to the other lines that now permeate all facets of modern life.

These considerations are not only for the wealthy. Today, many more people face the challenge of figuring out how to set limits in a society that makes it easy, acceptable, and often celebrated to yearn for special privilege. Anyone with some level of success grapples with these questions: *What are the perils of chasing the other line? How much privilege should we take advantage of? What is the impact of the other line on our happiness?*

What sort of lives do we want for our children? How much do we utilize the other line on their behalf? How much do we expose them to the negative effects of the other line? By exerting our influence, power, and money, are we hampering their development and understanding of how a healthy society should function?

On the other hand, incentives do matter. The fruit of our labors must be something worth working hard for. Expecting people to contribute to society and create value for reasons other than personal motivation has been proven untenable time and again. To imagine a world without the other line is unrealistic.

But where is the balance? Social currency used to be based on a combination of personality, integrity, intelligence, appearance, family history, demographics, and connections. And that currency could be wielded only in the limited circle in which one resided—a place of work, a community, and perhaps an extended social circle. Merit played a predominant role in determining our ultimate success. To achieve the American Dream, we believed, one must work hard. Merit has since been debauched, leaving access as the most powerful currency of modern times.

The world seemed a better and happier place when our experiences were punctuated by special, memorable moments, rather than the other line being an end in itself. We used to want a rewarding job, a nice house and car, and the ability to support a family, send the kids to college, and retire comfortably. But now we yearn for the most exclusive, private, elite luxuries. What has the American Dream become?

10

EVERYTHING RHYMES WITH ORANGE

"How did you go bankrupt?" Bill asked.

"Two ways," Mike said. "Gradually and then suddenly."

—ERNEST HEMINGWAY, *THE SUN ALSO RISES*

A boy named Michael was born in Stockton, California, in 1990. Stockton would later be labeled the most miserable city in America. Hunger and need, in this place, were accepted as facts of life. Hundreds of children lived in tents and cardboard boxes in the arroyos. Everyone dreamed of getting out, but they didn't know how such an exit might be possible, so many of them gradually stopped dreaming. The shackles of poverty, and a certain measure of pride, kept them bound to their city.

Michael's mother, Racole, was a high school senior when he was born, while his father—also a teenager—was incarcerated in a juvenile facility. After graduating, Racole worked at McDonald's to keep her family fed and dressed, later finding a job in the healthcare field, and she enforced strict rules to keep Michael and his younger brother indoors and glued to the books, while many of their friends often encountered trouble in the streets. Michael was allowed to go to church and to play basketball within view of the house, but that was the extent of his domain. The South Stockton projects spread out around them, rampant with violence and drugs, a soundtrack of gunfire and sirens. Crack dealers and gang members ruled.

Racole wanted her bright, curious son to experience a world beyond the destitution of their neighborhood. She got him into a private elementary school in the northern part of town. On his first day, she told him, "You'll be going to school with the kids of doctors and lawyers, but you're just as good and smart as they are." He believed her, but that still didn't temper his astonishment when he was invited by classmates for sleepovers and found that they lived in gated communities and their houses rose to a second story and had giant backyard swimming pools. He'd never seen any of these things before. It was the first time he was aware of his poverty. Most of the kids he'd grown up around never strayed from the neighborhood.

I spent my teenage years in Orange County, where that sort of wealth and luxury was plentiful. While people still thought about money, they weren't occupied with the basic concerns of survival and sustenance. I was a transplant from the East Coast, and I still recall feeling amazed by the estates of some of my high school friends—tennis courts, pools, Jacuzzis, gardeners, maids, and wine cellars. My own house was a ranch-style tract home—nice, but not that nice. I was somewhat of an anomaly in that affluent world. I worked several part-time jobs to pay for college and drove a beat-up Chevy, but still there were many advantages stacked in my favor. I lived in a safe and bountiful place, and that made everything easier.

Michael's hometown, by contrast, was hardscrabble and unlucky. The longest stretch that his father was out of jail was a few months, and finally he landed in state prison on a life sentence under the three-strikes law. When Michael was twelve, he paid his only visit to his father in jail. "I didn't like the way the guards treated everyone, all of the searching, the sadness of the kids. It was formative for me. I knew I didn't want to be caged." Several of his schoolmates had been shot, murdered, or sent to prison. So he studied hard, acing his classes, and, when he reached high school, he earned a place in the International Baccalaureate program at a public school near his home. The mantra that he grew up hearing—

advice given to any young person who showed promise—was that in order to succeed, you had to get out of town as soon as you were able.

Despite the many obstacles he encountered, Michael won a scholarship to a top university. No one in his family and very few people he knew had been to college. College had never seemed like something within the realm of possibilities for a person like him, but his mother and a few other encouraging people had persuaded him to believe that he was headed for success, which meant escape. Michael saw his city crumbling around him—ranking lowest in literacy, the newspapers reported, and highest in crime. By the time he walked in graduation, summa cum laude, home foreclosures were at a historic high. More houses were boarded up; more people living in tents and cardboard boxes in the arroyos. Stockton had become ground zero for the Great Recession. He accepted the scholarship and fled his hometown, determined never to look back.

———

As dissimilar as they are now, the places where Michael and I grew up were once not terribly different.

Stockton, well before it became destitute, started out as a gold rush town. Its seaport on the San Joaquin River—connected to the San Francisco Bay by a deep-water channel—proved useful in shipping goods to support the gold mining industry, and the city built up around that bustling commerce. The University of the Pacific, the oldest chartered university in California, was founded in Stockton in 1851 and included the first medical school on the West Coast. Stockton's location was ideal— the Sierra Nevada mountains and Lake Tahoe were nearby, the Bay Area only an hour's drive, and the fertile soil of the Central Valley, the nation's most productive agricultural region, also positioned Stockton as a vibrant agrarian community.

Orange County also had agricultural origins. As recently as the 1960s, the sheriff often rode his beat on horseback. Many of the towns dotted along the Pacific—soon to become extremely affluent communities— were once inhabited by fruit pickers and farmworkers. As the interstate was built in stages through the 1950s, the citrus groves for which the county was named began to vanish, along with the cow pastures and avocado farms. The highway invited the arrival of new corporate headquarters and shopping malls and hordes of tourists—Disneyland opened in Anaheim in 1955. Stretching down forty miles of the Pacific Coast and well inland, covering an area of nearly a thousand square miles, Orange County shed its agricultural identity and reinvented itself as a bedroom community of Los Angeles. The population swelled from 200,000 in 1950 to more than 3 million today. Along the way, it became one of the wealthiest counties in the nation.

Stockton's massive US naval supply depot, which had provided the area with industry and jobs since World War II, was phased out in the mid-1990s. With its gold rush and naval days behind it, and most of the residents struggling, Stockton needed its own reinvention. The city managers eyed the highways that crested the brown hills and glided down to the glittering prosperity of the Bay Area. They wanted to lure some of that glitter eastward. So they rebranded Stockton a bedroom community as well, a more affordable option for people who were being priced out of San Francisco and Silicon Valley, and they started to build new housing at a breakneck pace.

In time, Stockton and Orange County both tumbled into historic bankruptcies. The events were similar in cause—poor leadership, a myopic and unreasonably optimistic vision of the future, and vulnerability to the dangerous greed of Wall Street—but the damage that the bankruptcies exacted on their communities, one being poor and one wealthy, was quite different.

———

In December 1994, while crossing the office floor at Salomon Brothers, I heard murmurs of a big bankruptcy, and I spotted several newspaper headlines. The words ORANGE COUNTY were emblazoned on the front pages of the *New York Times* and *Wall Street Journal*, but I figured it couldn't be *my* Orange County, in California. There was no way that a place with so much wealth could go bankrupt. I knew there was an Orange County in Florida and another just up the Hudson from Manhattan. Maybe, like

Springfields, every state had one. But I got to my desk, dug out my own copy of the paper, and there it was—my home turf, gone bust.

Salomon had just been hired by Orange County to assess the financial damage. A team would be flying out in the morning to determine the degree of the problem. I'd been freshly promoted to VP, and my supervisors knew I was from there, so they asked if I'd be willing to take on the job. The whole thing would probably last a few days.

The next morning, I flew back to my county with a light bag to see what kind of mess they'd gotten themselves into. It would be a year and a half before I returned to New York.

———

The mess had been many years in the making, all centered on what people had assumed to be the Midas touch of longtime Orange County treasurer and tax collector Robert Citron. Salomon's first encounter with Citron was many years earlier, when our head of interest rate derivative sales, Michael Corbat, flew out for a meeting. The flamboyant Citron arrived wearing a loose-fitting, canary-yellow suit. Corbat (who would become CEO of Citigroup in 2012) was less than impressed with Citron's understanding of the investments he'd made. Corbat dialed back to the New York office from a pay phone to report that Bob Citron had no idea what he was doing and that Salomon would not be pursuing business with the county. If one had wanted to heed the warning signs, they were there to see.

The people of Orange County chose not to. They loved Bob Citron. In this Republican and Libertarian stronghold, the ostentatious Democrat Citron was adored for his quirks, a sort of unofficial county mascot. Here's how the *Orange County Register* portrayed him: "Robert L. Citron was an eccentric man. He had a strong affinity for Navajo jewelry; a zeal for USC football so intense his car horn played the Trojan fight song; and a license plate declaring LOV-USC, even though he didn't graduate from the school. The former treasurer–tax collector consulted psychics and astrologers on the movements of the markets. He amassed a collection of 300 ties that he rarely wore, composed 14-page odes to the virtues of

Chrysler automobiles, sported a calculator watch to precisely tally restaurant tabs, and got away with it all because people believed he was a genius."

Born in Los Angeles in 1925, Bob Citron got his start in a junior position in the Orange County Tax Collector's office in 1960, and ten years later he was elected to the top role, which the county then combined with the job of treasurer, giving Citron control over the assets of Orange County, even though he had zero experience in investing and finance. In turn, he relied on Wall Street firms for guidance—most of all, Merrill Lynch—and began making investments for the county in the early 1970s. The money he invested came from property taxes, and the process for collecting those funds was entirely abnormal—when homeowners in Orange County paid their property taxes, they were required to make out their checks to Robert Citron, rather than to Orange County, which would have been customary. In retrospect, this offered yet another sign that Citron approached the job of treasurer–tax collector as an opportunity to build a personal reputation rather than to perform a selfless and efficient public service. As an elected official, he'd found an effective way to burn his name into the consciousness of voters, since they had to write a check directly to him twice per year.

Citron's Wall Street investments focused on derivatives—financial instruments of which few people had heard, which made him seem like even more of a financial wizard. Derivatives are notoriously risky and difficult to understand; they were once described by Warren Buffett as "financial weapons of mass destruction, carrying dangers that, while now latent, are potentially lethal." A derivative is a contract between two parties, and its value is derived by its relationship with an underlying asset. In the case of Orange County, Citron wasn't buying the underlying bonds but rather bond derivatives whose values were tied to the movement of market interest rates. In almost every case, Citron was betting that the rates would continue to decline, which would positively affect the value of the derivatives—if interest rates went down, the value of the county's assets went up, and vice versa. But to believe that he actually knew what would happen with interest rates is pure hubris. There are

too many factors that are entirely out of anyone's ability to predict—
such as inflation, employment, GDP growth, manufacturing capacity,
and foreign exchange rates, to name just a few—for this to be a prudent
investment strategy. In fact, it would be fair to call it a blatant guess,
like making a wager on the Super Bowl—not on the actual game, because one team would be favored over the other, but instead betting on
whether the next commercial would feature humans or animals. How
could anyone, sitting in a living room over a platter of nachos, presume
to know?

Yet Citron thought he'd solved the puzzle. Beginning during the
presidency of Reagan—who was an Orange County icon—interest rates
had been falling. That trend continued for so long that it made Citron
look wickedly smart, and public confidence in his abilities soared. He
started by investing millions of dollars, then tens of millions, hundreds
of millions, and eventually billions. With these sorts of bets, and at the
level that Citron was investing, interest rates didn't need to move much
for him to make or lose a great deal of money. An interest rate movement
in long-term government bonds of just one basis point, which is a hun-
dredth of 1 percent, could shift the county's fortunes by many millions of
dollars. Other municipalities, cities, school districts, and public agencies
noticed Citron's success and wanted a piece, so he agreed to form a pool,
accepting their capital and investing it alongside the county's money. For
the investors' contributions to the pool, Citron offered them a high rate
of return and allowed them to withdraw money throughout the year to
cover their civic operations.

Besides the motivation to be a good government official and help
as many citizens as possible, there was no particular advantage for the
county in Citron agreeing to invest outside money; he didn't earn a fee
for running the pool. His motivation was driven more by pride, ego,
and a love of the spotlight—the same impetus that moved him to wear
flashy jewelry and bright suits, and the same reason he instructed Orange
County residents to write their property tax checks directly to him. He
wanted to be noticed and remembered.

While not explicitly illegal, it was highly unusual for a county to invest in the markets in such a fashion, since property tax dollars were intended to be used for day-to-day expenses, public services, and payroll for public employees, including teachers, police officers, and firemen. The appropriate investment behavior with such money is to place it into a simple, safe financial vehicle, similar to a checking account, from which these expenses would be covered. The same is true for the outside investors in the pool who were risking their essential working capital—if Citron wasn't the genius they thought he was, they were making an enormous and potentially catastrophic misjudgment.

The public seemed not to have noticed what Citron was doing, even though if one were to look back over the annual reports leading up to the county's financial collapse, there was clear evidence that something was amiss. Orange County's annual reports, which were publicly available, included information detailing sources of revenue. Simple pie charts on the first couple of pages, for example, showed that interest income had catapulted from basically 0 to 40 percent of the county's discretionary revenue in only a decade. No one thought to ask where that money was coming from. When someone is raking in profits, there isn't much incentive to look closely at how and why.

The sorts of derivatives that Citron purchased, and the depths of risk he reached, were unprecedented. He took $7.6 billion in public funds and leveraged that into an investment pool that hit $20.6 billion at its peak. He was borrowing against the pool to increase his bets, thereby multiplying his exposure to interest rate movements even further. By the early '90s—twenty years into his run as county treasurer—Merrill Lynch had convinced Citron to sink his resources into increasingly exotic securities, with names like "step-up double inverse floaters," which carried massive risk but could yield impressive profits. For a while, things went well—one year, the derivative investments yielded $344 million for the county alone. "I don't know how Citron does it," a member of the board of supervisors remarked, "but thank god he can." The investment pool was making a bundle.

And then, quite suddenly, it wasn't. In February 1994, interest rates tilted upward, wiping out a chunk of the pool's assets, yet Citron—again advised by Merrill Lynch—doubled down. Interest rates continued to move against him, but still Citron increased his bets, naïvely confident that rates would resume their long downward trend. The pool was hemorrhaging money.

When Citron had first begun to purchase his derivatives, Merrill Lynch and many other Wall Street firms had provided him with loans so that he could leverage up his investments—essentially, if Citron wanted to bet one dollar, Wall Street lent him an additional two dollars, so his bets were tripled with the borrowed capital. And his gamble was even scarier than that, since the securities he purchased were often already several times leveraged. Now, with the bottom falling out, those Wall Street firms grew nervous. They gauged Citron's losses and wanted repayment of the loans, thereby forcing liquidation of a big chunk of the pool at distressed prices. Finally, on December 4, 1994, county officials decided it was time to take the dice away from Citron. They drove out to his home, rang the doorbell, and handed Citron his letter of resignation, which he signed before bursting into tears. Two days later, the county filed for bankruptcy. No one saw it coming—except, perhaps, the bankers who were selling him the derivatives.

Merrill Lynch had circulated internal memos about the risks in Citron's portfolio as early as 1992, but those warnings didn't stir action, let alone caution. Clearly, many senior people within the bank knew that what they were doing was wrong, yet they let it continue, selling him riskier and riskier derivatives and collecting their fees and commissions each time. Orange County had become one of Merrill's top-five clients, as well as one of the largest purchasers of derivative securities in the world. The bank wasn't willing to jeopardize the loss of that business, no matter how precarious and unsuitable Citron's investments were.

His own lawyer later argued that the sixty-nine-year-old Citron tested at a seventh-grade level in math, had a severe learning disability, and had long been suffering from dementia. Citron himself admitted that he lacked a basic understanding of what he had done and that he had simply been following the advice of his bankers. They'd held his hand and led him to the slaughter.

———

Stockton also fell victim to Wall Street's skill for selling a vision, even if that vision was certain to prove unsustainable and disastrous in time.

Starting during the recession of the 1970s, Stockton fell into disrepair. The downtown all but emptied out, and the city was overcome by the crack epidemic of the '80s, along with its attendant crime. Gang activity surged, and Stockton was recast as a city of drugs and violence.

By 1997, when Gary Podesto became mayor—he would serve two terms—the economy was looking up, even while most of the community still lived in some degree of squalor. Podesto wanted a legacy project, and he thought that rebuilding the decrepit downtown area could be just the thing. A real estate boom also arrived, and that upswing inspired both the mayor's office and the city council to move forward on revitalizing Stockton through big development projects. Podesto and the council hired an aggressive city manager, Mark Lewis, and paid him handsomely at nearly $200,000 annually. Lewis took it upon himself to convince the city council that they deserved nicer things and that their time was now. He declared at a 2005 council meeting: "Stockton is the place, I mean, I think, uh, really the gem of all California." Even the most faithful Stockton enthusiast would smell bullshit on such a meandering yet hyperbolic statement.

Podesto and Lewis proposed massive new development projects that would restore to the city the kind of cachet that might attract Bay Area transplants and convince the world to take Stockton seriously once again as a place of commerce, resources, and entertainment. They rolled out plans for the San Joaquin River waterfront, adjacent to downtown—this was the port on which Stockton was founded a century and a half earlier. It would be a complete revamp: new buildings and events centers, an arena, and supporting infrastructure. Projects of this size are, of course, beyond any city's operating budget. That's where Wall Street came in, offering Stockton a way to realize the dream all at once by issuing bonds to cover the cost. The city council voted enthusiastically to support the plan, with only one of its seven members expressing concern and dissent. When the first $47 million of municipal bonds were issued, they sold easily and quickly.

The city broke ground on the Stockton Arena, a vast twelve-thousand-seat venue for concerts and sports, which would include a hotel and outdoor ballpark. Plans also moved forward for new parking garages and an expensive overhaul of the marina, complete with condos priced at seven figures. The cost for the arena project was estimated to be as high as $150 million. Construction was completed in less than a year, and the city booked Neil Diamond to perform at the opening party on January 15, 2006.

Stockton is a working-class town that is nearly half Hispanic. Caucasians, who comprise the majority of Diamond's fan base, make up only about 20 percent of Stockton's citizenry. As such, Diamond was a questionable choice to open the new arena, and, unsurprisingly, the show didn't sell out. The fee for Diamond's performance was paid for with public money, and the city refused to disclose the amount. Finally, after a barrage of pressure from the media, they admitted that the cost of booking the sequined crooner to play Stockton had been a million dollars.

Mark Lewis, the celebrated city manager brought in by Mayor Podesto, had been given discretionary spending powers, including the decision to pay Neil Diamond his hefty fee. The week before the concert, Lewis admitted that the event was expected to lose money, ultimately costing taxpayers an estimated $396,650. To make matters worse, the charity tapped to receive proceeds from the concert, the Stockton Parks and Recreation Foundation, would come away empty-handed. Two days after the concert, the city council voted to fire Mark Lewis, after nearly five wild years on the job.

Spending a million dollars on Neil Diamond—love him or hate him—is the perfect example of how out of touch the city managers were with their constituency. The marina project revealed a similar failure to understand how to serve the general population of Stockton. Not many residents, in a city crushed under poverty, would ever be looking for a place to park a yacht.

"For city leaders at the time," said later councilmember Michael Tubbs, "there was a pressure. You want to have a legacy. You want to have things to point to. But you can't have a great city where 22 percent of the people live in poverty, where your kids aren't reading, where half the jobs are minimum wage. You will never have a tax base to support all these expensive capital projects. Let's do first things first. I think our investment philosophy as a city organization was just off—we'll put lipstick on a pig and make a marina and an arena and hope they'll bring in all this revenue. And they *will*, one day, but never until folks have pockets of disposable income to make use of these amenities."

———

During the early 2000s, when Northern California was beginning to recover from the dotcom bust, the housing market began its rise to historic levels. All across Stockton, residential construction exploded in hopes of attracting Bay Area commuters. In most local economies, residential housing is a small percentage of overall growth and value creation, but in Stockton, an extremely large percentage of expansion was funded by mortgage debt, since the city had basically shifted its central industry to home construction. Eager to cash in on its proximity to the center of tech and culture, Stockton was soon rolling in property tax revenue. Median home prices quadrupled in just six years.

Leading up to this moment, Stockton also overcommitted on future pensions, offering retirement at age fifty to the city's underpaid police- and firemen, while boosting their pensions and benefits, including medical coverage for life. Depending on assumptions, offering pension and health-care benefits to a single fifty-year-old retiree creates a future obligation with a present value in the neighborhood of $1.5 million. While no one would argue that these essential members of society need to be taken care of, Stockton did so irresponsibly. In those market boom times at the turn of the millennium, overcommitting on pensions may not have seemed terribly risky. Yet the city managers were making the same mistake they made with their massive bond-funded development projects—they expected that the good times would never end. "There were a lot of commitments made during the good years that were ongoing," said Councilmember Tubbs, "but the presumption was that the rate of growth in terms of our tax revenue would continue to increase at these astronomical numbers in perpetuity. Folks did voodoo math to make things work out."

Everyone remembers what happened next. Beginning in 2007, the bottom fell out of the markets. Over the following few years of what would become known as the Great Recession, nearly 9 million jobs were lost across the country, many trillions in household wealth evaporated, and roughly 4 million homes were foreclosed upon each year. The Dow Jones lost more than a third of its total value during 2008 alone. While the damage spread globally—affecting individuals along with mortgage lenders, investment banks, insurance companies, automobile makers, and commercial banks, who quickly shrank away from the risk of issuing small business loans (leading to the closure of 2.5 million businesses)—there may have been no community harder hit than Stockton, which led the nation in foreclosures per capita.

This meant that property tax revenue evaporated, and soon the arena and other major development projects proved reckless, as Stockton was unable to make its debt payments. The city managers found themselves facing significant budget shortages. With widespread unemployment, Stocktonians struggled to stay afloat, let alone spend money in the local economy, and many businesses shuttered. It was a vicious cycle—the closures, along with the cessation of construction projects, put even more people out of work, who in turn sank deeper into poverty and, in many cases, lost their own homes.

Seemingly overnight, the Stockton resurgence was crushed, and the city transformed from a place of pride, optimism, and construction cranes to one of resentment, despair, and homeless encampments.

———

In late 1994, just days after Orange County filed for bankruptcy, I flew out with a small Salomon team, hired by the county to assess the loss. We were prepared to liquidate the pool and reinvest the assets, if it came to that. We set up shop in the Hall of Administration, and our phone rang off the hook during that first week—senior officials from the Federal Reserve; Arthur Levitt, chairman of the SEC; George Stephanopoulos, senior advisor to President Clinton; Bob Denham, Salomon's chairman and Warren Buffett's consigliere—all of them calling to find out what was happening and to offer up advice.

Orange County had become the largest municipal bankruptcy in US history, and, as such, it made for a major international news story. The press swarmed, and tensions ran high on all sides. We quickly learned that we would be attacked for everything we did. No matter what it was, someone was cued up to shout in opposition. Even though we were not to blame—as Salomon hadn't been involved with Orange County in any way prior to the bankruptcy filing—we were the only people they had to shout at. The board of supervisors basically went into hiding, leaving us on the front lines to answer questions, provide updates, and formulate solutions.

The level of financial illiteracy on the part of the elected officials and the board of supervisors shocked us. None of them understood what Citron had done to bankrupt the county; none of them had even an elementary grasp of derivatives. And it was their job to oversee his activities. But then again, every crisis seemed to arrive with a new species of monster. The bankruptcy stirred a lot of anxiety and debate around derivatives in general—if they had been so harmful in Orange County, should they be regulated or even banned? Or had the county simply been making investments beyond an appropriate level of risk and sophistication for a municipality? These were all new questions swirling around the staid world of municipal finance. For us, the questions were of secondary importance; I assumed they would be debated by others after the county had been extricated from its mess.

By the end of the month, we had assessed and liquidated the pool. Even though Citron's investments had plunged the county into financial chaos, our team, led by Michael Corbat, was able to sell the assets at market prices, but that still left Orange County with a loss of $1.64 billion, a staggering number at the time. And now that the county couldn't depend on revenue from the investment pool, there was a 40 percent hole in the discretionary budget, not to mention the county lacked the funds to satisfy its maturing debt obligations, and big payments were coming due quickly. So there were major income statement and balance sheet problems, which would require completely restructuring the county's finances, while it was on the precipice of defaulting on its debt.

The job for which we had initially been hired was complete, yet despite several convincing reasons to head back to New York—and against the advice of everyone at Salomon, who insisted that continuing to work on the project would be career suicide—I decided to stay and lead the efforts to steer the county out of bankruptcy. This was my home turf, and the crisis promised to offer a different sort of challenge than any I'd known.

We converted the top-floor conference room into our war room and started working on potential solutions. Someone brought donuts each day to kick-start our marathon strategy sessions.

Tom Hayes, the former California state treasurer and director of finance, often joined us. He'd been asked by Governor Pete Wilson to join the team as the senior county employee to help liquidate the pool and get the recovery process under way.

We noticed that Hayes never took a donut. "What's the problem?" our investment banking analyst, Tom Purcell, asked him. "You don't like donuts?"

"As a county employee, I'm forbidden from accepting gifts."

"It's not a gift; it's a fucking donut."

"I didn't create the ethics rules," Hayes said.

But we kept hounding him.

"All right," he finally said. "How much is it?"

"A donut? Uh, how about eighty-two cents," Purcell said with a grin. We set up a cup for Hayes to drop in his money each morning so he could eat a donut. We'd watch him sort change in his palm, toss it into the cup, and then we'd sit down to discuss how the county had leveraged up their pool by three times and lost nearly $2 billion investing in risky derivatives. But heaven forbid a government official were to accept a donut.

In April 1995, Bob Citron surrendered to the police and pled guilty to six counts of securities fraud and misappropriation of public funds, which meant he was facing up to fourteen years in prison. A trial was set for November. The most damning discovery was that Citron had secretly kept a second set of books for the other municipalities participating in the investment pool. He wasn't skimming money for himself but rather for Orange County—illegally redirecting $89 million into the county's accounts under the justification that, since the pool had been making such high profits because of his financial brilliance, the county deserved a higher rate of return than the other investors.

———

Our first major effort in solving the bankruptcy was to propose a modest sales tax increase of half a percent, which would provide the revenue necessary to restructure and repay a substantial portion of the county's debt. While waiting for it to be put to a public vote, my team worked diligently researching other sources of funds. The most memorable and telling question I received during the quest to find new revenue streams was in a public discussion over whether the landfills could perhaps take in garbage from outside the county. A concerned citizen earnestly asked: "Would it be possible to take in the *cleaner* forms of garbage and avoid the dirtier and smellier stuff?"

We kept working at it, hunting for potential revenue from every possible source, including some as minor as parking tickets, or investigating whether there was land to sell, or if we could offer up the rights to erect cell phone towers throughout the county, which hadn't yet been done. We looked into whether we could privatize the parks and even the John Wayne Airport (which ultimately had little value, since it was controlled by the airlines). We turned over every stone, but there just weren't enough dollars.

One afternoon, a few blocks from the Hall of Administration, I was waiting at a crosswalk with Orange County sheriff Brad Gates and Dale Horowitz, Salomon's godfather of municipal finance, who was in for one of his regular visits from New York. We'd been discussing the political intricacies of each county agency, and we'd continued our conversation over lunch. The streets were empty, and the light wasn't changing. After looking both ways, Dale started to cross.

"No, no, no," the sheriff said. "Hold up there, Mr. Horowitz, and wait for the signal."

"Are you kidding me?" Dale said. "There aren't any cars."

"I am not kidding you," the sheriff said. "You jaywalk and I'm gonna bust your ass."

Dale, the New Yorker, silently fumed.

We knew that Sheriff Gates was the most important person in the county to have on our side. A man of impressive height and imposing stature, Gates embodied the old Orange County—rugged men on horseback, farms and orchards and cattle. He was by far the most popular elected county official, often described as a real-life John Wayne character. And in fact, the sheriff had developed a friendship with Wayne over the years, even snagging an election endorsement from the silver-screen cowboy: "Brad Gates has what I like in a man for a tough job—he's got true grit." (One highlight of Sheriff Gates's résumé was having directed the Bronco chase of O. J. Simpson.) As Gates was universally respected, admired, and often feared, we were relieved when he supported the sales tax increase, for which he took substantial heat from his conservative constituency. It was ironic that in order to get buy-in from the community, we needed the sheriff, who, admittedly, didn't know a lot about finance. But he did know about integrity and honoring one's commitments.

The county's other elected officials were reluctant to back our tax increase, fearful of the political damage that such a position would inflict. The five supervisors debated which two of them could come out against the measure to save face.

"Wait," we said, "all five of you have to support this."

"Why?" they asked. "We only need three yes votes to get this on the ballot."

"But it's not just about getting it on the ballot," we pleaded, "it's about winning it, and you've all got to be behind this to make it happen."

The public seemed similarly unconcerned or ignorant of the dire consequences of defaulting on the debt. At countless public and private meetings, we explained and debated the issue, and no one cared.

"You need to pay your debt obligations," we'd say.

And they'd say, "Why? What's the downside?"

"For one, a higher interest expense."

"Okay, we'll pay a higher interest expense. Or we won't borrow."

"But you need to borrow," we'd say.

"Why do we need to borrow?" they'd ask.

And we'd explain that the county couldn't be run without access to the markets, since the markets provided the ability to finance growth and infrastructure, schools and roads, and so on. If the county defaulted on its debt, it could be ostracized and cut off.

Still, they had a hard time appreciating the extent of the potential damage or why it should concern them. So we'd start the discussion all over again, but we never seemed to make any progress.

The citizens had become disconnected from the finances and operations of the county. They didn't understand it, and they didn't feel involved in it, so they didn't consider themselves responsible for fixing it. The system had become too complicated and obscure, involving abstruse municipal finance issuances like TRANS (tax and revenue anticipation notes) and COPS (certificates of participation), debt instruments of which no one had heard.

Our broader disconnection from government finance coincided with the economic expansion over the previous few decades. Central bankers and treasury secretaries across the globe laid claim to having created that positive growth, and we took them at their word. For the first time, we started to believe that the puppet masters at the top needed only to pull a few strings in order to make the world a better and more productive place. For example, if a central banker were to raise or lower interest rates by as little as a quarter of a percent, that could grow the economy or protect it from overheating in the face of rising inflation.

To fill our void in understanding what was happening in government finance, we developed a dangerous blind faith in macroeconomic decision making, such as federal spending and interest rate policies. This led us to soften our demands for prudence and oversight in most other matters of government finance. Local policies no longer seemed to matter. All that was needed was a slight tweak to interest rates or increased federal spending, we were made to believe, and all of our economic ills would be cured. Macroeconomic policy floated in like a vast bank of ocean fog, obscuring our view and comprehension of government finance, and we seemed content to surrender our responsibility and involvement to the higher powers. We came to accept borrowing and spending at potentially untenable levels, while growing numb to the meaning of huge numbers.

The one number that matters more than any other in attempting to assess the viability of our financial system is, to put it very simply, the difference between what we've promised versus what we have. That difference represents the burden on our financial system; it's a negative number, since our future obligations far exceed our existing assets. For the sake of this discussion, let's call that negative number our *net financial burden*. To draw out the concept a bit more, our financial obligations and promises include all government pensions and retirement benefits, as well as Social Security, Medicare, Medicaid, and of course the national debt (which most experts calculate at $22 trillion, and growing to levels approximating our annual GDP). Those obligations and promises compose the amount we owe. Subtract that amount from what we have, which includes the cash that has been accumulated to meet those promises, plus the investment returns on that cash, as well as expected future contributions, and the difference would give us our net financial burden.

The problem is that the numbers are unfathomably large, and there's a lot of disagreement over the figures that would allow us to calculate a true net financial burden. For example, is our unfunded pension deficit $4 trillion or $20 trillion? It depends on whom you ask. The difficulty of nailing down real figures only contributes to our inability to appreciate the magnitude of these numbers. When dealing with numbers this high, magnitude is a very difficult concept to grasp. To a normal person, *trillion* feels as abstract and imaginary as *bazillion*, and yet these deficits and shortfalls are very real, and very dangerous.

What we do know is the amount we owe is much more than the amount we have. Our net financial burden has reached many tens and possibly hundreds of trillions of dollars, which is more than sufficient to place a massive strain on the future viability of our financial and economic systems. There's no way to know if and when the strain will be too much, but the laws of physics have never been avoided. Everything has a breaking point. Which can only make one wonder, why have we not assessed this danger with more concern and diligence?

To the contrary, there seem to be growing voices arguing for the expansion of borrowing and government spending to achieve various policy objectives. Nobel Prize winners and politicians alike have put forth theories including the revival of a century-old idea called Modern Monetary Theory (MMT), which argues that government's monopoly control over money allows, if not requires, that any and all fiscal policies be undertaken to ensure full employment—for example, printing as much currency as desired, without cause for worry that such an action would lead to inflation or possibly the loss of systemic financial integrity. Regardless of its potential for success—and it should be noted that it has not yet been executed successfully—support for MMT does seem to provide evidence of the limited concern for our growing debt burden.

This lack of concern was first made evident by the behavior of the citizens of Orange County. When the sales tax increase was brought to a public vote on June 27, 1995, the measure was murdered at the polls. The message delivered by voters was that they didn't care or feel responsible for the county's financial situation. The county leadership had gotten itself into this mess, and therefore it was not the citizens' responsibility to get it out.

After the failure of the tax measure, Orange County's debt was trading at a steep discount. At one point, there wasn't even a market for the debt; we couldn't get a quote for it. It was a perverse realization, but finally it became clear that, with a few exceptions on the county level, we outsiders—the Salomon team and our fellow advisors—were the only ones who truly cared about solving the bankruptcy. Everyone told us they wanted the problem to go away, but no one—not the municipal government agencies, nor the elected and appointed officials, nor, it seemed, the citizens—was willing to be inconvenienced in the slightest. Fix it, they said, but don't bother me. Not my circus, not my monkeys.

———

The results of our sales tax referendum highlighted that it is often necessary to fail before there can be the possibility of success—and that people often won't try new ideas until the traditional approaches are exhausted. While it was unsurprising that this famously Libertarian county had voted down a tax increase, we had to try it first, since raising revenue in such a manner is the way most financial crises or shortfalls are solved. In Orange County, that tactic bombed terribly, yet it gave us a license to move forward with new ideas.

One of our core partners who led the legal team was Bruce Bennett, a brilliant and articulate bankruptcy attorney. Anticipating our defeat, Bruce had come up with an alternate plan, a legal solution in which all three key constituencies would deal with their share of the pain—cut back on services for the citizens, haircut the amount due to the bondholders, and trim future pension obligations.

Simultaneously, my colleague Justin Bailes and I had quietly started formulating our own backup plan, which we kept confidential for the time being. We wanted to let the desperation build, to let all parties absorb the likelihood that the county would default on its debt obligations. A few weeks after the sales tax defeat, we were optimistic that everyone would not only be open to a new proposal, but hungry for one. Our plan, Project Robin Hood, would strategically divert revenue to the main county treasury from the wealthiest and less essential agencies, such as the water districts, the transportation authority, the cities, parks and rec, beaches and harbors, making sure not to affect the budgets of school districts, law enforcement, fire, and health services. Despite the name, Robin Hood, there was no theft involved—the plan utilized the existing tax base to pay off the debt coming due, while not significantly impairing the county's ability to provide services to its citizens.

To structure Project Robin Hood, we had to find the money. We began researching the agencies that seemed flush with cash, and Justin was tasked with gathering their financial information. He would get someone on the phone and then often drive out to their headquarters to pick up physical copies of their financial statements. "I was probably one of the only people that had ever requested these damn things. They had to issue them by law, but they didn't have to distribute them, and they weren't available anywhere." This was before such documents could be stored online and easily accessed.

"The California system had created a ton of different silos of funds," Justin recalled. "There must've been thirty water districts in Orange County, and each one had a property tax allocation, each had its own revenue sources. The Irvine Water District, for example, owned golf courses and hotels and had a giant reserve fund, and so we basically were finding pockets of hidden money. Some of it seemed like slush funds for property developers. There was a lot of money, but none of it was accessible to the county because under state law, property tax was directed to each of these water districts, and so much went to the sanitation district, and so much went to the Orange County Transit Authority. Our idea was: Let's go to where this money's been siloed off, and if they have the resources, then let's redirect the money."

Basically our plan was to break down the silo walls and shift the capital around. Mathematically the plan worked, but we knew it would get pushback from the government representatives running the agencies from which we wanted to take the money. We presented our plan to the board of supervisors on July 30, 1995, and they voted to approve it, even while everyone else hated it. The agency heads prioritized their own interests over that of the county. Even the creditors who were among the primary beneficiaries despised the plan—one of their advisors, Jon Schotz, was quoted in the *Los Angeles Times* saying, "Did they pass out an air-sickness bag with this thing?" They thought it was a pipe dream, and since they doubted that the plan had any chance, they didn't want to waste time and energy on something they were sure would fail.

———

A procession of wheelchairs snaked between the packed aisles, ending at a podium and microphone, each person waiting for a turn to shout at the Orange County Board of Supervisors and the bankers sitting at the tables up front. The citizen currently on the clock explained that he had diabetes, poor healthcare, and no job. "If you think you can come up in here and stop the buses, *my buses*, you got another think coming!" The crowd behind him cheered, which seemed to add a squirt of gasoline to his indignation. "That's right!" he said. "Another think coming! Without the number-59 bus, I can't get to my doctor."

Chairman Gaddi Vasquez leaned toward his own microphone to notify the speaker that his three minutes were up.

"What?" the citizen shouted. The room teetered again on the edge of chaos.

Sitting beside my Salomon team, I glanced at Vasquez, who looked like a man in bad need of a gavel, but all he had was a ballpoint pen and a small microphone mounted on the counter in front of him. "Thank you," Vasquez said, his voice growing louder against the noise. He sounded as though he were responding to a standing ovation from an adoring audience, rather than the roar of an angry crowd. "Thank you, ladies and gentlemen. All right, thank you, thank you." Once the room had quieted enough for him to be heard, he repeated his original instructions: "Please, ladies and gentlemen, keep your remarks to three minutes or shorter. We have a lot of people to hear from tonight."

The next speaker stepped to the microphone. She was an anomaly in this emotionally charged room—a quiet, composed, polite woman who began by thanking the supervisors for allowing her to speak, then described the dominoes that would fall across her life if public transportation were to be cut. "I take the bus to go to a job. I go to the job to get the money I need to rent my own apartment. I need to rent an apartment so I can leave my abusive husband. If you take away the buses, I will lose my job at the restaurant, and I won't be able to get an apartment, and I will be trapped. Please don't take away the buses."

As she sat down, a man dressed in women's clothing jumped to his feet and lifted into the air a small cage in which a pair of crude statues of bankers was affixed. "Criminals! Put 'em all in jail!" He shook the cage and rattled the banker statuettes. One broke free from its mooring and bounced against the bars. Typically dressed in fishnet stockings and a miniskirt, Will B. King was a well-known local character who frequented the county board meetings and any other public government sessions that he could fit into his schedule. He'd staged one spectacle or another at many of our board meetings—waving a toilet plunger and shouting that the county was going down the drain, or pulling oranges from his stuffed brassiere as he addressed the supervisors—but the caged bankers was definitely his magnum opus. He rattled his art project and yelled, "Lock 'em up! Put the bankers in jail!"

Chairman Vasquez thanked Will B. King for his contribution, and the next citizen came to the mic.

For hours, the procession continued. While the concerns of Orange County's less affluent citizenry were real and urgent, the protest itself seemed to have been orchestrated by Stan Oftelie, the head of the Orange County Transportation Authority (OCTA), who sat nearby in solemn appreciation of the testimonies of his constituency. Stan didn't want his transportation budget cut, and he knew his only hope was to argue that the cuts would impact the less fortunate. He later insisted that these scores of people had shown up of their own volition. I liked and respected Stan, even though we found ourselves on opposite sides of this sudden drama, and I found the board meeting protest a pretty deft political maneuver, especially since the cuts wouldn't likely impact bus service unless he and the OCTA's board made that decision—the buses were only one small expenditure in his agency's vast budget.

Most of the world knew Orange County, this coastal stretch of Southern California, as one of the richest and most conservative communities in the nation. "No one rides the buses in Orange County." That's what we'd been told, time and again, as we worked toward a solution for the county's monumental budget crisis. But here they were, one after another, the bus riders of the OCTA, offering valid reasons why we had to find other sources to solve the county's bankruptcy. Finally, late into the night, they made for the exit—almost all at once, as if to catch the last bus—and the special public session of the board of supervisors meeting was adjourned.

Our plan to deal with the bankruptcy brought increased scrutiny on the entirety of county operations, which provoked the municipal agencies to soften their stance. They quite suddenly started to cooperate. "If you were the head of the Orange County Transit Authority or the Irvine Ranch Water District," Justin said, "you did not want to highlight how well funded you were. That was my take. They lived in shadows. They had these cushy, appointed jobs that they got because they knew the county commissioners or people who influenced the county commissioners, and they did not want to have a lot of light shone on the little recesses of their world."

After eighteen months of grueling work in Orange County, living out of suitcases and battling with the citizens, supervisors, media, attorneys, and creditors, we finally broke the dam and found a way to solve the bankruptcy by redirecting the existing tax base. Sure, the solution may sound simple in retrospect, but the reason such situations are uniquely difficult is that they often have more to do with a disconnected populace, the self-interested motives of politicians, and the greed of Wall Street than with the actual financial and economic fundamentals.

In 2007, Stockton's mounting pension crisis arrived. During the previous years, when allocations for public employees were set at untenable levels, the city hadn't reserved enough cash to cover those payments. Now the bill had come due, and the city owed CalPERS—California Public Employees' Retirement System, the state's pension and retirement fund—tens of millions of dollars that it couldn't pay.

Wall Street was drawn like a shark to blood in the water. Executives from Lehman Brothers rushed to Stockton with a PowerPoint for the city council, pitching a funding vehicle called pension obligation bonds. With these borrowings, the city would have capital to cover its current pension balances and could defer facing the larger crisis until new people were elected to deal with it. That's exactly what it did. The pension obligation bonds were inherently risky: The city's general fund served as their backstop, which meant that if anything were to go wrong, not only would Stockton go deeper into debt, but the city's operating budget would be at risk—including the retirement savings and healthcare for its current and former employees, as well as public services for citizens.

The council voted unanimously to approve the issuance of the pension obligation bonds, with Lehman being paid to underwrite the offering. Very soon after, on September 15, 2008, Lehman Brothers went out of business. The markets collapsed; Stockton defaulted on its payments; and the city's general fund was plundered. Over the next few years, Stockton descended into a hell of poverty and foreclosures.

A special council meeting was called on June 26, 2012, after the city council decided in a closed-door session to file for bankruptcy under Chapter 9 of the US Bankruptcy Code. Reminiscent of the Orange County Board of Supervisors meeting years before, residents and public employees lined up to take their turns at the microphone, decrying the city for slashing benefits. But in this case, the stakes were much higher, as healthcare and pensions were on the chopping block.

"The decisions that you are making tonight are effectively throwing a grenade in my life, destroying everything that I've worked for." This was the testimony of Kristina Pendergrass, who had worked as a 911 dispatcher in Stockton for seventeen years. Pendergrass lost her health benefits and was at risk of losing her retirement savings, as the lawyers for the bondholders were threatening to invade those purses.

"I'd like to say to the councilmembers and the city manager that your smirks . . . and your lack of concern for us does not go unnoticed," another man said, barely able to keep his emotions in check. "The world is watching, thank god, so that they can see that we are victims of a society that is failing us."

Another speaker, Gary Jones, a former SWAT team leader for the police force, was battling a brain tumor. Stockton's bankruptcy meant that he wouldn't be able to afford to continue the treatment that was keeping him alive. "If I lose this medical," he told the council, "for me, it might as well be a life sentence." Jones's tumor was in his speech center, so he struggled as he addressed the council, taking time to form his words, fighting back tears. "You get a phone call, something like this changes your life, instantly—"

A timer started beeping in the room.

"Mr. Jones," a councilmember said, "thank you. Your time is up."

The effect of the cuts extended well beyond the public employees who watched their retirements go up in smoke. In the four years after the mortgage crisis, the city saw an exodus of police officers—losing a net average of a hundred per year—who moved to communities where their pensions and benefits would be less at risk of getting slashed. Shrinking the police force led to a marked increase in murders and violent crimes. Unemployment rose to levels among the highest in the nation. And the city leaders who had written and produced this tragedy would soon exit stage left and melt into the crowd.

———

Well beyond Stockton, there is a colossal, looming pension crisis in this country. Stockton may be a warning, a look into our nation's potential future. The current failures are on many levels, each contributing to a vicious circle that is quietly sinking us further and further into a pit. In short, here's how pensions work and why the system is dangerously broken.

Public employees—a population that numbers in the millions nationwide—receive pension and other retirement benefits as part of their compensation. This is the support upon which they will depend when they retire. Whether they work for the federal government, or for a state, county, or city, their employers pay into a retirement account. That money is typically invested in a central fund, usually referred to as a retirement system, which then invests the contributions from each municipality, promising a certain investment return. The municipalities then set pension allocations for their employees based on those anticipated returns. The higher the projected returns, the lower the cash contributions the municipalities need to make and the lower the demands placed on their annual budgets.

Things go wrong in two main ways. First, municipalities are not making sufficient payments to fund future obligations, which creates an immediate shortfall. For example, both the Illinois and New Jersey state pension systems are conservatively estimated to be less than 40 percent funded, with pension shortfalls in the neighborhood of $150 billion. Second, many retirement systems have been promising their constituents—the municipalities that hand over pension capital to invest—an annual return of 7 percent or even higher on their investment pools. But experts now project closer to a 5 percent long-term expected return, and when the markets shifted, these retirement systems didn't adjust accordingly. That 2 percent discrepancy might not sound like much, but when you're dealing with such large pools of capital, the estimated national shortfall in these pension funds has been calculated to be somewhere between $4 trillion and $20 trillion—and growing—a looming financial calamity of epic proportions.

The obvious question is: Why don't Illinois and New Jersey and other retirement systems simply increase the funding requirements to match future obligations and adjust their expected returns from 7 percent down to 5 percent? The answer: politics. The oversight boards for most of these retirement systems are populated by elected officials and union leaders. If those board members adjust the expected returns downward, that would put a bigger cash burden on the municipalities to make up the gap, and the board members would be blamed. Therefore they keep their return assumptions high in order to lessen the cash burden on their constituents. No one has the political will to take the political heat for making the prudent and required changes, so everyone looks the other way, knowing, or at least hoping, that the day of reckoning will not arrive until after their term on the board has finished.

The problem doesn't end there. Municipalities—many of the same not fully funding their pension obligations to begin with—exacerbate the problem by utilizing the aggressive investment return assumptions of their respective retirement systems to justify the promise of even more retirement benefits. In the face of budgetary pressures, politicians often bridge the gap of a cash shortfall by offering government employees more retirement and health benefits rather than an increase in wages or salaries. By doing so, cash demands on the current-year budget are mitigated, as these benefits represent a future burden, whose impact is no doubt deemed manageable, or at least not as onerous, when using aggressive investment return assumptions. This completes the vicious circle: Underfunding leads to the need to overstate investment returns, which in turn encourages the promise of more benefits.

The circle will be difficult to break, as the pension boards don't have a vested interest in tackling the problem by making the painful but necessary changes in oversight and stewardship. Their horizon of responsibility doesn't match the challenge. Bruce Bennett once told me: "To a politician, 60 percent funded is as good as 100 percent funded, since the day of reckoning won't arrive until after they leave office." The only statistic most politicians care about, other than their polling numbers, is whether they have the cash to fund operations during their term in office. Pension math is something politicians either don't understand or choose not to understand; it's politically expedient to do so, and it requires the acknowledgment of a problem too difficult to solve. And all of this is happening right in front of our eyes, but nobody is doing anything to stop it. The complexity and opportunity for abuse provided by public finance has clearly overtaken the structure of an outdated government not designed to operate in the modern financial world.

———

Michael—that gifted boy who'd grown up in the rough Stockton neighborhood—was finishing high school when the financial markets collapsed in 2008. "The recession didn't really hurt my family that much because we've lived in a perpetual recession. It was just normal; we were always struggling." He'd been more or less aware that something dark was brewing—he noticed changes in the industry while in the summer program at Wharton after his junior year at Franklin High School, as well as a couple of years later, when he did an internship at Credit Suisse.

Michael escaped Stockton with a scholarship to Stanford, and he figured he would never return to his home city, except for the occasional family visit. He was smart and ambitious, a young black man from a poor neighborhood making his way through one of the top universities in the country. He became president of Stanford's NAACP chapter and landed a summer internship at Google, followed by an internship in Obama's White House. He had come to Stanford as a political science major—the human side of politics had long intrigued him.

Obama provided an inspiring model. Michael thought he might want to return to the White House as a staffer after Stanford, or maybe join Teach for America. He could have done anything at that point. He would soon graduate with honors, and lucrative offers had already been floated to work on Wall Street or internationally, in management consulting or private equity.

But then, while he was still interning at the White House, the direction of Michael's life changed when his phone rang one day with news that his cousin, just one year older than he was, had been shot and killed in South Stockton at a Halloween party.

Michael felt not only pain over the loss of his cousin but also an overbearing sense of guilt, a recognition that he had abandoned the city that had formed him and, in doing so, had turned away from an important part of himself. "Made me really think about what was the point of going to a school like Stanford," he told *Forbes*, "if it wasn't for doing something to make my community better."

In the wake of his cousin's death, Michael knew he had to return to his hometown and give whatever he could. While finishing his studies at Stanford, he decided to run for a seat on the Stockton city council. Oprah Winfrey met Michael on a visit to campus and was so impressed by him that she donated to his campaign. The only political candidates Oprah had ever financially supported were Obama and Cory Booker. The rap star MC Hammer soon threw his own support behind Michael, and these endorsements gave him a nice boost with his community. Yet he was still an undergraduate college student pitted against an entrenched incumbent who was much better funded.

"I didn't want him to come back to Stockton," Michael's mother, Racole, said during his campaign in the documentary *True Son*. "You know, maybe when you get older, then come back and try to help Stockton. . . . I wanted my son to graduate and go make some money. But we didn't have a choice. If he goes to do what *I* want him to do, I'm pretty sure he would not be happy. This is a calling for Michael."

Running for a council seat was a grueling process, and there were times when Michael nearly gave up, but he kept walking the streets of Stockton, talking to residents, describing his plan to help reinvent the city and curb its plague of gang violence. "I was twenty-one years old," he said in a conversation at City Arts & Lectures in San Francisco. "I had no beard. I had two very shabby, ill-fitting suits, one pair of dress shoes. And then knocking on doors was actually very scary. I think part of it was that it was a time that the city had a record number of homicides, so folks weren't just opening their doors, much less for young black guys." But the people who did open their doors bought into Michael's message. "I remember the first door I ever knocked on, it was a guy named Eric. He came out and was telling me how he had all these hopes and aspirations and dreams for his daughter, and that when he saw me as a young person from Stanford coming back, he wanted that for his daughter. If I could help make that happen, I had his support."

The League of Women Voters arranged a televised debate in the days leading up to the election, and Michael's charisma and passion outshone his opponent. The exposure from the debate was the final push Michael's campaign needed. In November 2012, at age twenty-two, Michael D. Tubbs was elected to the city council, the youngest member in Stockton's history. "We can change Stockton," Tubbs told the press at the time. "I never said I was going to do it by myself. But I can be the catalyst. . . . I have a sense of hope."

It must have been difficult, at first, to retain that sense of hope. Only six months prior to Tubbs's election, Stockton had filed for bankruptcy—the largest municipal bankruptcy in US history up to that point, taking over the top spot from Orange County, yet soon to be eclipsed by Detroit. Tubbs's council was tasked with cleaning up the mess and making tough decisions to get the city back on track. "You talk about we're making tough decisions," Tubbs said in the documentary *Who Took Down Stockton?*, "and I keep saying that nothing's tougher than cutting someone's healthcare that they thought they were gonna get for the rest of their life, and they planned accordingly, and they retired accordingly."

Pensions and retirement benefits are a good and necessary thing. The higher the amount, the better, as they will provide for people in their retirement. But most of us don't want to think about the fact that large shortfalls exist and will be devastating in time. Instead, we expect that those shortfalls will be dealt with by someone else, fixed before substantial payouts need to be made. When the inevitable financial reckoning comes, the collateral damage will most certainly hit the people relying on those pensions, but it will also impact the rest of us, putting in jeopardy, as it did in Stockton, the safety and welfare of everyone in our communities, regardless of their place or station.

———

The Orange County bankruptcy was the harbinger of a new national perspective and belief system. Due to the affluence of most residents, the populace of the county didn't care about the threat of debt default or services being cut, because they didn't believe it would affect them. Those things were for the less fortunate, the poor, the bus riders, the homeless—the people without power. In fact, the wealthy majority of the county didn't care about much of anything related to the bankruptcy, other than not being bothered by it.

And indeed, by the end of our year-and-a-half-long battle in Orange County, we found a way to solve the bankruptcy at no real inconvenience to the residents. The bondholders were paid a hundred cents on the dollar with full interest. Pensions were not cut. Services were barely touched. This was an entirely unique outcome for such a massive financial catastrophe, and the county's unwillingness to assume responsibility for its debt rewrote the rules of municipal finance. The citizens probably felt it didn't matter, since we were able to solve the issue with negligible inconvenience.

Sheriff Gates believed otherwise: "It was an embarrassment. When you've got an obligation, you pay for it. You don't walk away from it. When you do that, how can anybody respect you? I think the citizens of the county never really felt involved in the process because they didn't get hurt personally. The smart people paid attention to the government and what was going on in the world. The balance of the public had no idea. They didn't really care one way or the other." The sheriff was clearly in the minority. Most seemed to feel no shame or accountability for the financial mess.

Should the citizens of Orange County have been responsible for fixing the bankruptcy? Were they to blame, since they had elected Bob Citron to office, term after term, for twenty-two years, without taking issue with his lack of a finance or investing background? Or was the board of supervisors to blame, for not providing the proper oversight and recognizing the problem before it was too late? Or should the blame have fallen on Citron, for making billions of dollars of risky investments he didn't understand? Or was it the rating agencies, who should have recognized the mess the county was in, rather than giving it a double-A rating? Or was Merrill Lynch to blame for selling inappropriate financial products to Citron, for allowing their knowledgeable people to take advantage of the county's naïveté, all in the pursuit of profit? The answer to all of these questions is yes—each of the contributing parties deserved a share of the blame.

But placing blame was secondary to the new, more important, and troubling questions that Orange County triggered: Why are we no longer connected to government finance, and why do we no longer feel responsible for the financial viability of our system? What are the implications from that loss of connection and responsibility? Regardless of whether

Orange County was just the canary in the coal mine or in part the cause of a new worldview, we simply didn't care to be bothered by the financial workings of government.

———

Citron died in 2013, at age eighty-seven. He had been facing up to fourteen years in prison and a $10 million fine for his guilty plea on six felony counts, but he was sentenced to only a year, with five years of probation and a fine of $100,000. During his incarceration, if you could call it that, he was given a job in the jail commissary, "processing orders for toothpaste and candy bars that came in from the inmates," according to the *O.C. Register*, while he was allowed to return home every night to sleep in his own bed. He continued to collect his pension: $92,900 per year. CNN reported: "Citron's crimes were not directly related to the bankruptcy nor did he profit personally from them. They occurred during 1993 and early 1994, and involved illegally transferring interest payments from the Orange County investment pool, which included schools, cities, and other government agencies, into an Orange County account. The intent was to hide the pool's soaring returns so as not to spook investors about Citron's risky strategies."

Merrill Lynch was sued many times for its role, and the firm reluctantly shelled out $400 million to settle Orange County's claim. This was a considerable penalty in those times, a quarter of Merrill's annual earnings. Merrill also paid $30 million to settle its criminal charges.

And yet, in the big picture, the largest municipal bankruptcy in American history up to that point resulted in no lasting punishment for those responsible—no real jail time, no restrictions or regulations, just empty gestures. So what lessons were learned, and what will keep this sort of thing from happening again?

As we were wrapping up our work in 1996, Justin found that the county's new finance team was starting to pursue another risky strategy, pension obligation bonds—the same instrument that Lehman Brothers would later push on Stockton right before the market collapse of 2008. This was a similar sort of financial engineering to what Citron had done with the county's money in the first place, and it was one of only two legal loopholes that would allow the county to borrow money without a public vote, funds that could then be used once again to make large, inappropriate investments.

"The county had an underfunded pension system," Justin said, "so basically they borrowed money, and then that money was invested to pay the pension obligations. The whole concept was that they'd borrow at 5 percent, and then they'd invest that money into the stock market and get 8 or 9 percent returns, and, boy, wouldn't that be great? I would go to these meetings, and the three or four guys that had been tasked with doing this would say, 'We really need to do these pension obligation bonds. It's super important.' And I'd say, 'You just lost billions of dollars by trying to run a county hedge fund. You're in bankruptcy today because you borrowed money and then invested it to try to make a higher return, and you're telling me that you think it's a good idea to issue these pension obligation bonds and then use that money to go bet on the stock market?' And they did. They all thought it was a great idea."

Justin argued bitterly with them over this, telling them that Orange County was the last municipality on the planet that should be involved in this sort of risky strategy, but his pleas fell on deaf ears. They were determined. In the end, I had to convince Justin to let it go. We were no longer in charge, soon to be off to our next challenge once the final bow was tied on the financial restructuring we'd been hired to do, and the reins of leadership were returned to the new politicians elected to lead the county postbankruptcy. Even as we exited, it was clear the county had learned no lessons. The pension bonds were issued and in the end proved a successful strategy, given the positive performance of the equity markets in the years that followed the bankruptcy. But a happy ending doesn't make a decision prudent. Instead, it only reinforced the belief that the risks were minimal. Memory of Citron's recklessly ignorant investment strategies was already beginning to fade from the history books. Not too many years later, Merrill Lynch was hired as an underwriter for the county.

———

Through Stockton's troubles, the city had a plague of terrible leadership—both in the mayor's office and on the city council. Stockton earned the top spot on the *Forbes* annual list of "Most Miserable Cities in America" in 2009 and 2011, taking home second place in 2008 and 2010. When the list came out in 2012, Stockton had fallen out of the top ten. Mayor Ann Johnston issued this unironic statement: "This is a fabulous piece of good news, something to enjoy and gloat about." Encouraging citizens to gloat about being only the eleventh most miserable city in America seemed to indicate that Stockton's leadership didn't have the loftiest goals for its revival. In the following year, it was back in the top ten on the *Forbes* list.

Anthony Silva, who served as Stockton's mayor from 2013 to 2017—during much of the bankruptcy recovery process—is a prime example of failed leadership. He held a ceremony in 2015 to reward god with a key to the city, for which he faced fervent protest. He also proposed a legal ordinance to punish residents who wore their pants in a way that exposed their "boxers and briefs." Another initiative he championed was to import endangered Florida manatees to be inserted in Stockton's waterways, so they could dine on the rising water hyacinth population. When scientists explained that the manatees would quickly perish in Stockton's much colder waters, Silva was undeterred. Fortunately for the manatees, the plan never came to fruition.

Late in his term as mayor, Silva was charged on multiple felony counts of grand theft, embezzlement, money laundering, and misappropriation of public funds. These particular charges stemmed from when he had a leadership role in a nonprofit called the Stockton Boys and Girls Club. He allegedly skimmed hundreds of thousands of dollars from the organization's finances to pay for personal travel, retail purchases, and a Filipino online dating site. Another scandal occurred halfway through his time as mayor, when a .40 caliber handgun used in the murder of a thirteen-year-old boy was found to be registered to Silva. He claimed that the weapon had been stolen from his house, and he hadn't gotten around to reporting the theft.

The FBI invaded Silva's residence in 2017, investigating felony charges that two years prior—while he was mayor of Stockton—he invited teenage summer counselors into his camp bedroom for a strip poker game at the Boys and Girls Club. The charges stated that he had provided alcohol to underage counselors in attendance while secretly recording the kids playing strip poker over a six-day period. Silva reached a plea deal with prosecutors and was sentenced only to community service.

When these are our elected officials, what hope can a city like Stockton have that things will ever improve?

———

Fortunately for Stockton, that hope was soon to arrive. In 2016, Councilmember Michael D. Tubbs decided to run against Mayor Anthony Silva. Between the excitement around his run and Silva's mounting scandals, Tubbs won in a landslide, beating the incumbent by 40 points. Tubbs was the first black mayor in Stockton's history, and—at age twenty-six—the youngest ever elected in an American city of more than 100,000 people. His ascendency to the mayor's office has already begun to transform the city, but he's clear-eyed about the tough road that still lies ahead.

One new initiative Tubbs has launched to help address these challenges is Stockton Scholars, which promises a scholarship to every student who enrolls in college after high school. The program began in 2019 with a $20 million donation from the California Community Foundation. Tubbs explained that his impetus for creating the program came from the advantages he reaped from having attended Stanford. "If one person going to an elite institution could come back and be mayor, what if we did that at scale for every kid in our city? What would that mean for the future of Stockton? . . . As the first in my family to go to college—and for free—it's personal, but for the city, it's our best economic development tool. Of the top 100 metro areas, we're number 99 currently in college attainment, and the goal is to triple the number of college graduates in Stockton in the next decade."

Princess Vongchanh is one of the inaugural Stockton Scholars. Her

parents are Thai refugees who came to California as teenagers and settled in a low-income neighborhood in Stockton's Southeast Asian community, which is a sizeable local demographic and one plagued with
violence. "There are definitely gang members in my family," she said in
our interview. "My sisters and I try not to associate with that part of the
family. Because of that, we've had to avoid certain parts of the city or
make sure we don't talk to certain people. Just growing up in that kind
of atmosphere, knowing that I'm so close to being on the wrong path, is
hard. I've tried to focus a lot of my life around education." Princess has
beaten the long odds. She was offered scholarships to Yale and Harvard,
and she ultimately accepted a scholarship to Stanford. The money from
her Stockton Scholars award will cover the cost of books and incidentals.
Princess plans to study computer science and astro engineering, and her
intention is to return to her hometown after she graduates. Her story is
indicative of one of the most promising signs of the Tubbs effect and
echoes a statement I heard many times while visiting—that Stockton's
smart and talented young people want to go get an education and then
come back.

Stockton emerged from bankruptcy in 2015. But its problems are far
from solved. It remains one of the poorest communities in the country. As
of 2018, there were 1,403 homeless children attending the public schools,
and that doesn't account for the hundreds of others who don't attend
school at all. Many live in the arroyos along the riverbeds. Every school
in the district is on the free-lunch program, and nearly all of them serve
three hot meals per day, since otherwise many children wouldn't eat.

Tubbs sees poverty as the root of all Stockton's challenges; revers-
ing this longtime crisis is at the top of his goals as mayor. "Homelessness,
trash, housing, violence, crime, third-grade reading—the real crux of
all those problems is poverty. In a community where 25 percent of the
people are in poverty, where the average median income is $46,000 for a
household—not even for an individual, but for a family—where almost
half the jobs in this county are minimum-wage jobs, all our issues make
sense. They're almost a byproduct."

One of Tubbs's staffers suggested the concept of Universal Basic

Income (UBI). The idea was as straightforward as it was radical. Martin Luther King Jr. had explored it in his final book, *Where Do We Go from Here: Chaos or Community?*: "In addition to the absence of coordination and sufficiency, the programs of the past all have another common failing—they are indirect. Each seeks to solve poverty by first solving something else. I'm now convinced that the simplest approach will prove to be the most effective—the solution to poverty is to abolish it directly by a now widely discussed measure: the guaranteed income. . . . We must create full employment or we must create incomes. People must be made consumers by one method or the other."

Half a century later, Mayor Tubbs committed to testing UBI on his struggling community, launching a small trial—130 families were selected to receive $500 per month for eighteen months, beginning in early 2019. Eligible residents must reside in a neighborhood where the median income is less than $46,033, and there are no strings attached to how the money is used. "Poverty's not caused by a lack of character but a lack of cash," Tubbs said to a small gathering of educators and residents in Stockton. "People aren't poor because they're bad people, because they're different than us, or because they don't know how to manage money. Lots of times they just don't have money to manage. In the conversations I've had with people, I've heard things like, '$500 a month is enough for me to afford child care'; '$500 a month is enough for me to work less so I could spend time with my family'; '$500 a month is enough for me to go back to school.' I've heard a million other ways why $500 a month might make a difference. And I realize what it's really about: In this nation that prides itself on the idea of life, liberty, and the pursuit of happiness, do we trust people to have agency?"

Tubbs doesn't feel that the extra income will keep people from working. "In fact, I think it will make people work better and smarter and harder and also be able to do things like spend time with their families," he told NPR's *All Things Considered*. "Because we're not robots; we're not designed just to work all day and run a rat race. We're designed to be in a community, to volunteer, to vote, to raise our kids. And I think the more inputs and investments we can give people to do those things, the better off we are as a community." The city has partnered with researchers at the Universities of Pennsylvania and Tennessee to evaluate the impact of the UBI experiment.

Tubbs likes to call the program "a hand-up, rather than a hand-out." The funding was raised through a large grant from the Economic Security Project and other outside sources, which deflates the argument that Stockton's UBI experiment is an irresponsible welfare program. "It doesn't cost taxpayers anything. It's paid for from $1.2 million in philanthropic funding. So the idea is that in the next couple of years, we'll have some data that will tell us whether this is a solution that is viable or not." The national response has been electric—both for and against the program. Tubbs has fielded calls from many other leaders wanting to ask him about UBI, and he's often been invited to speak about it on national platforms. "It's incredibly exciting that this community that's majority minority," Tubbs said, "this community where the median age is twenty-six years old, this community that has always been written off as backwards or where you'd look for problems, folks are now looking to this community for solutions."

The job of mayor is often considered the toughest of all elected positions. "I came in very sober minded," Tubbs said in our interview, "in terms of the actual trappings of the office. Being mayor of Stockton is not a glamorous gig. You're trying to pull rabbits out of hats, all day long." When Tubbs first served on the city council and then as mayor, it quickly became evident that no one had been willing to be the bad guy and insist on fiscal responsibility. "The past six years I've been in office, I've said no to things more than I've said yes. I think that's what leadership is: *We can't afford that. Great idea. Love it. How do you pay for it?* There was not a willingness to do that. And if you're not going to be around in five, ten years, let the other guy deal with it, right?"

Tubbs recalls a battle he had as a councilmember over a public library that had closed during the bankruptcy. You'd be hard-pressed to find a bigger advocate of libraries, since they'd been such an important part of Tubbs's life, but he fought against efforts by Mayor Silva to reopen it. "I said, 'Look, I'm all good with libraries. How do we pay for it? Where do we cut? Let's cut [our public spending on] golf courses and pay for the library. I'm good with that.' No one wanted to do that. And it became this big political issue. I voted no eight times in one year—during an election year, and I was running for mayor—because we couldn't find an ongoing revenue source. But at the same time I was voting no, I was working with community members to put an initiative on the ballot to create a funding source that would then pay for the library. The council voted to open the library without having a funding source, but luckily that November, the city voted for the revenue source to pay for it. . . . I saw how, oftentimes, the political answers differ from what the resources at the time ask for."

As a result of Tubbs's fiscal responsibility, Stockton is beginning to turn around. Not only do its revenues exceed its debt payments, but it has also built up a meaningful reserve, which Stockton didn't previously have, socking away three months of working capital to help mitigate future budget shortfalls. Another promising new city leader is John Deasy, who arrived in 2018 and committed to serve for ten years as superintendent of the Stockton Unified School District. After his tenure as the head of the nation's largest school district in Los Angeles, Deasy was attracted by the challenge of reforming Stockton's schools and helping to combat the community's endemic poverty.

"I think we're in a very special time in this city," Tubbs said. "Healthy reserves. Surpluses every year in the budget. You have the whole nation looking at Stockton. This is a special opportunity to do some things that will change the trajectory of this community for the next thirty years."

———

The Orange County and Stockton bankruptcies are case studies in what goes wrong when citizens are no longer connected to government finance; when careless, ignorant, self-serving people are elected to office; when Wall Street operates with inadequate restraints on greedy, unethical conduct and takes advantage of inept politicians.

Before Orange County, there had been other financial catastrophes in other places in which the needed funds were simply not available. In fact, up until Orange County, the typical definition of bankruptcy was that spending exceeded revenue, jeopardizing a government entity's ability to provide services or meet debt and interest obligations. But Orange County was a whole different animal. In Citron we had a rogue treasurer who'd been misguided by a Wall Street bank, which didn't care what happened if its client invested irresponsibly, as long as the firm was making money. Combine this unique set of causes with the deep-rooted apathy of the county residents, and public accountability was changed forever—not just in Orange County, but everywhere. The fact that the bankruptcy was solved without spreading any real pain reinforced people's comfort with being disconnected from government. They were vindicated in believing that someone else would deal with the issue and so came away feeling even less compelled to be involved or to understand. This was the first time in modern financial history in which people woke up one day, found that their municipality had gone bust, and said, "I'm simply not paying. This is not my problem."

While this had never happened before Orange County, now that reaction has become terrifyingly common. It used to be the case, as our English teachers taught us, that nothing rhymed with orange. Now all public financial challenges, to some extent, mimic the abandonment of shame and shirking of responsibility that characterized the citizens and officials of Orange County. Now everything rhymes with orange.

Stockton, for example, picked up right where Orange County left off, deferring pension responsibility, overspending on vanity projects, borrowing at dangerous levels, and very few people sounded the alarm bells until it was too late. One can only hope that Stockton's new, strong, visionary leadership and fiscal responsibility in Mayor Tubbs will turn the city around. The early signs are promising.

But Tubbs is only one man in one city. Without wholesale change in federal, state, county, and city finance, none of us will escape the coming pension blowup. It's easy to play armchair quarterback and make suggestions on how we might avert this disaster—revise the incentive structure for public employees; create oversight boards with the necessary financial expertise to manage how pensions are issued; change the way politicians run cities and limit their ability to spend recklessly while adopting new municipal bylaws to determine what can be built or promised; impose restrictions on what Wall Street can sell to cities and counties. But until we, the people, reignite our level of concern and involvement, none of these things can or will be done. Until we once again feel connected to government and understand how it all works, until we begin electing officials who come into office to solve problems rather than to further their own careers, until we hold them accountable, our future will only become more bleak.

In mid-2018, the US Social Security system went cash-flow negative for the first time since the 1980s, which means more cash is being distributed to retirees than is being taken in. People frequently say that they don't expect Social Security to be there for them when they retire. They're right to be concerned. Large public plans currently have just 70 percent of what they need to pay future benefits to their retirees, according to 2016 figures from Wilshire Consulting, and some states were as low as 35 percent funded. Puerto Rico, at the time of its reorganization, reported that its nonuniform government pension plan was less than 1 percent funded.

There will come a time when the money simply doesn't exist to provide for pensioners. People who worked their entire careers toward collecting their retirement may get nothing, or a lot less than promised.

And here's the thing: Although the pension bubble might be the most perilous financial situation in the modern day, and we are all complicit in allowing the problem to fester and grow, no one pays it much attention, for three key reasons. First, it's not an exciting topic. Not many people want to discuss pension shortfalls and possible solutions—and that includes most politicians and others who are largely responsible for helping solve the problem. Second, the coming collapse feels like an abstract future event, so it's difficult to know how or why we should act on it in the present day. The system is complicated enough that most of us feel that there's nothing that we can do to help fix it. Finally, and most important, there's no accountability, since pension math uses longer time frames than the political terms of those with the power to fix the system. There's no clear way to prevent elected officials from overpromising and, as such, contributing to this dangerous bubble.

Even if you're not relying on a pension for your retirement and you never expect to, this issue should still scare you. Nobody will dodge the fallout from an entire portion of the population being forsaken. Eventually the pain will spread to all of us. At a minimum, it'll have implications on growth and stability. At its worst, given the size of the problem, it may lead to widespread chaos and rebellion, a broader breakdown of our communities and societal structures.

And so the pension bubble remains ignored as it continues to grow, as the demographics of an aging population collide with our poorly constructed entitlement system. This is a conversation that we must have. What will happen to those people who are building a future based on receiving their pensions and retirement benefits? Who will take care of them? What will we do when Stockton starts to happen everywhere, when that 911 dispatcher and that former SWAT team leader battling brain cancer lose what they've worked for, when this problem begins ruining the lives of millions of people around the country? For now, we're all speeding along that road, windows down, music loud, unwilling to look ahead to see that there's a dark storm coming.

EPILOGUE: A SURVIVAL GUIDE

Everything ends badly. Otherwise it wouldn't end.
—TOM CRUISE AS BRIAN FLANAGAN, *COCKTAIL*

Amasked man swings a bat at a police officer in riot gear, whose armor takes the blow. The man is tackled, zip-tied, and added to the others corralled against the outer wall of the bank, awaiting the paddy wagon. Even in the intensity of the moment, he briefly recognizes the doorway across the street from a newscast he saw back in September, sitting in his living room, just before he lost his house in a spate of foreclosures. In the news report, bewildered bank employees wandered onto the sidewalk with their personal effects in cardboard boxes. He'd felt some sympathy for them then—he himself had lost his job when his former employer moved production overseas and closed his plant—but any shred of compassion he'd felt had burned off over the past several months of living in a city park with other demonstrators and unhoused people. Later that night, gathered in their encampment, they trade battle stories and dress their wounds. Some have slept here for months. The skyscrapers and city lights block out the stars as the haggard masses simmer food over small fires and ladle steaming broth into bowls. Scattered around their tents are homemade banners and signs, bandannas and tattered flags—the tools of protest lying in repose, emblems of anger retired for the night.

Elsewhere, a line of exhausted people wraps around the block. Shuffling foot to foot, they wait for their chance to withdraw as much money as possible from the ATM, but only a very small amount is permitted. New austerity measures have been put in place as the nation plunges toward financial collapse. The daily withdrawal limit was instituted to protect against a run on the banks, but this has only encouraged such a run. The people in line calculate what comforts this pittance might allow them—if they are among the lucky ones to get anything at all from the machine. Surely not enough for gasoline, nor rent, nor any luxuries like a doctor's visit or going to the movies. Simply procuring groceries to feed their children would be a victory. They construct and revise small ledgers in their minds to keep themselves alert and busy until the line starts to creep forward. Tomorrow they'll do it all again.

Elsewhere, a bar is filled with soccer fans watching the national team play in an important match. Tensions run high. Most of the patrons can hardly afford the drink they nurse through the game, but without televisions of their own, they've come together to shout for a common cause. In the eighty-second minute, down a goal, the room blacks out—lights extinguished, TV dead. The power has been cut. A latent violence whirls through the darkened room, becoming palpable as voices rise, fists pound on tabletops, and a full-scale revolt seems possible. Somewhere a glass shatters. The bar owner scrambles for his mobile phone. With a few taps, he pays the utility bill, and just before his country registers a 3–1 loss, the power cranks back on. His customers leave in a foul temper, but this sort of thing is nothing new to them. Their wallets are empty, with the exception of identification and family photos. When the national currency tanked the previous year, whatever the people had saved lost much of its value. Out of that chaos, a new currency was born—mobile phone minutes. That's how people pay for goods and services—from bread to taxi fares to utility bills—by sending one another phone minutes.

Elsewhere, a crowd of people wades into the pale blue sea toward a fishing boat coming in with its meager catch of sardines. They clamber aboard and fight over the fish. Not far away, farms are similarly plundered, as hungry mobs capture and slaughter the cattle and horses for meat. Supermarket shelves sit empty. It's not uncommon to scavenge a meal from the trash. Children and adults, dead from starvation, are buried in devastating numbers. Despite having the world's largest oil reserves, the federal government took on historic levels of debt, which led to hyperinflation, medicine shortages, power outages, and mass famine. Many people believe that it's safer to be locked in prison than to fight for survival on the streets. Millions have fled to neighboring countries while many others have been stopped at the border with roadblocks and the fear and anger of the unwelcoming citizens.

Elsewhere, the police are using live bullets against demonstrators, whose wrath is fueled by the president's announcement that workers will soon be required to contribute an extra percentage point of payroll tax to help fund the depleted pension and Social Security systems. Before the president's announcement, this was a peaceful land, one of the safest in the world. Now protesters march, hurl rocks, set fires. While reporting on the crisis, a journalist is shot in the head, viewed live online across the globe. By the time the president walks back the proposed measures—less than a week after his initial announcement—more than two dozen citizens lie dead and scores of others have been injured.

Surely these scenes of violence and chaos must be fiction, hyperbole, a grim vision of a future that we can avoid. If only that were the case. These are actual recent events on the world stage—United States, Greece, Kenya, Venezuela, Nicaragua—and are among an increasing number of such clashes sparked by financial unrest and collapse. In fact, much of today's civil violence is the result of decisions and events related to finance. The world of money has become so dangerous and damaging, so complicated and divisive, that it drives us more and more to anger, instability, protest, and conflict. All of these events might happen again, at any time, in any place. Whether triggered by a pension system that runs dry or a financial system that falls apart, the snapshots above are very plausible portraits of our own near future.

Or perhaps our fate will be a slower, subtler, but no less devastating decline, where elderly citizens die alone in small, bare quarters, with no support, little money for heat or food, no disposable income, abandoned by an entitlement system that has failed them. Or it may be the young who find themselves isolated, unable to procure a meaningful job that will support a lifestyle beyond borderline subsistence, having to pay for the last selfish grab of the baby boomers demanding a comfortable retirement, even while they were to blame for the irresponsible decisions that created the problem. While I'm hopeful that the probability of a breakdown of our society similar to that of Venezuela and Nicaragua is low, should there be any less urgency if our own dark future is one of slow decline, stifling a generation of youth that doesn't have the opportunity to pursue a productive and fruitful life?

Bit by bit, year by year, with each burst of growth, each technological advancement, each new financial instrument, the world of money becomes more convoluted, enigmatic, and impersonal. When I started out as a B. of A. loan officer in the LA jewelry district in the mid-1980s, people used to know their bankers, and bankers used to know their clients. That's now rarely the case, neither in the commercial nor consumer realms. These days, most financial transactions—whether on a trading floor, paying a bill from your computer, purchasing an engagement ring, buying a book—are done online, electronically, without person-to-person interaction. The human element has ebbed toward a vanishing point, and with it, so has the importance placed on character and personal integrity. In only thirty-plus years, these incremental changes have moved the financial industry from a critical tool for mankind to one without stewardship, an industry that doesn't seem to be working for the good of humanity. Many of us now feel that the industry is pitted against us. We are wary, if not afraid, of the financial system. More and more of us have become ambivalent and disconnected. Whatever our feelings are toward the world of money, they are not warm and fuzzy.

Yet all of us—if we have a bank account, credit card, student loan, auto loan, mortgage, life insurance, retirement account, healthcare plan—rely on the financial services industry to enhance our lives and efficiently provide access to things we otherwise couldn't attain. If we agree that money is a central component in our lives, then how can we remain disengaged from the industry? We see growing deficits, increasingly underfunded pension plans, rising debt levels, and there seems to be nothing we can do to stop these threats. Our survival as individuals, as communities, and as a nation depends on coming to understand modern money and finding ways to make the system work better for us.

There's an increasingly common saying about the United States: that we're going to end up being one big retirement system with an army. Our pension and healthcare obligations will crowd out everything else government is intended to do—we'll be forced to cut spending on infrastructure, essential public services, education, police, and fire departments. Taxes will need to be raised; government borrowing will increase, which in turn will limit growth and potentially put us in a vicious downward cycle. This is the existential crisis we're going to face within the next twenty years.

HOW DID WE GET HERE?

How, in only a few decades, did our relationship with modern money become so dysfunctional? What can we do, as members of society, to feel safe and grounded and to navigate a way forward? The first step is to understand what led us to this point.

The majority of the big changes in the financial world over the past thirty-plus years were initially made with good intentions and, for a time, resulted in the betterment of society. There's an industry saying: "Every bad idea on Wall Street started as a good idea." Those changes were ultimately pushed too far until, in the end, each change became a manifestation of both good and bad forces, both beneficial and destructive. Recognizing these contradictions is key to our finding a positive and effective path forward. Here's what we've seen throughout the course of this book about how each evolution of our financial system achieved great progress while also leading to undesired behaviors and outcomes:

Chapter 1, "Fool's Gold": The introduction of the computer spreadsheet unleashed the creative energy of the financial industry, while helping to eliminate human subjectivity and biases.

And yet . . .

The computer spreadsheet led to the erosion of analytical integrity and the loss of character.

Chapter 2, "Welcome to the Jungle": Wall Street partnerships went public, allowing them to obtain the capital required to achieve the scale necessary to offer the products and services demanded by increasingly large corporations and clients.

And yet . . .

The separation of risk from accountability led to the diminution of oversight, which in turn led to destructive behaviors, including the ability to make dangerously large bets with other people's money.

Chapter 3, "Milk and Balloons": Corporate raiders and activist investors recharged American and global business by holding management teams accountable for their performance.

And yet . . .

When corporations were forced to pursue shareholder value over all else, that allowed for rationalizing management decisions that inappropriately prioritized profit over people and product.

Chapter 4, "Conquistadors of the Sky": Speed and precision have enabled the creation of new products and made markets more efficient, increasing access and lowering costs.

And yet . . .

Speed, efficiency, and perceived precision have supplanted thoughtful, careful analysis in all areas of finance, including those best served by analytical reflection.

Chapter 5, "Modern Art": Public company reporting requirements have increased transparency in the financial system, making progress toward leveling the playing field for all investors.
 And yet . . .
Those same reporting requirements have further compressed the measurement period of financial performance used by public investors and management teams, all at the expense of long-term investment and vision.

Chapter 6, "Shooting an Elephant": The construction of financial supermarkets created platforms capable of efficiently delivering the breadth and depth of products demanded by increasingly vast and complex international businesses and markets in a globalizing world.
 And yet . . .
The advent of financial supermarkets led to the creation of financial institutions that are unwieldy and challenging to manage, as well as to the deterioration of the corporate culture needed to foster and sustain desired behaviors.

Chapter 7, "Reach Out and Touch Someone": Commerce moving to the cloud facilitated the creation of new products and markets at prices that made them widely accessible to the general public.
 And yet . . .
The move of commerce to the cloud has contributed to the loss of community and personal connectivity.

Chapter 8, "Diamond Dogs": Increased compensation transparency has shifted negotiation leverage to employees, empowering individuals with the data to support demands for fair market compensation.
 And yet . . .

That same transparency has led to the shortening of investment horizons and an unhealthy focus on compensation as the primary determinant of one's worth in society.

Chapter 9, "The Other Line": The market economy's takeover of the social order has empowered the amateur, democratized advertising and media, and opened up a larger world to people who may not otherwise have had access.

And yet . . .

The market economy's takeover of the social order has replaced meritocracy and community with an unhealthy pursuit of exclusive access and special privilege.

Chapter 10, "Everything Rhymes with Orange": The disconnection of the populace from public finance has allowed for elected officials to manage more efficiently the complexities of funding government operations, for which the public does not have the time, background, or desire to provide input or oversight.

And yet . . .

That same disconnection has created a vacuum of accountability and oversight in public finance, often leading to irresponsible decisions that prove destructive.

The tradeoffs inherent in each evolutionary change help explain why reaching a consensus on the way forward is so difficult. Where some see only an industry serving important needs, others see only hazard. Both viewpoints, to a certain degree, are correct. Yet rather than work to appreciate the dichotomies of modern money, our public discourse has failed us, and so we're in a standoff between those who believe the financial industry to be vital to a functioning world, and those who believe it to be a dangerous beast that must be contained or euthanized if we are to avoid repeated crises.

This tendency toward extremes has yielded an industry without leadership or oversight that is producing large financial and social bubbles, which continue to swell to potentially catastrophic levels. Ultimately, each bubble will burst, with a tipping point impossible to predict. These cycles will inflict their damage time and again, with increasing intensity, as long as we lack the leadership needed to tackle these intractable challenges and as long as we remain detached from the workings of the financial world.

The truth is that these cycles of boom and bust are a necessity if we are to have the freedom to innovate, create, and compete. And our system has usually proven resilient, bouncing back after most challenges, but the challenges highlighted here possess the potential to push bubbles to a point where the center does not hold and the system breaks. How do we achieve a healthier balance in which the swings from prosperity to crash are less extreme and destructive? There are no easy solutions, and no one person, entity, or action is going to fix these problems for us.

WHAT CAN WE DO TO CHANGE COURSE?

We will not survive the status quo. It is imperative that we act. The priority should be that of increasing accountability in the system or in some cases reshaping the accountability mechanics that lead to undesired behaviors. Each chapter in this book provides a story of how a change for good ended up perverting incentives and leading to undesired outcomes. The one overarching lesson that I've learned in all of my years in finance is that accountability comes down to incentives—and I don't necessarily mean monetary incentives. In order to inspire positive behaviors, we must create incentives that will encourage them. Conversely, if we want to discourage unsavory or harmful behaviors, the solution is probably to understand the incentives, usually unintended, or the lack of incentives that inspired those behaviors and change them. If this proves ineffective or not possible, then some form of independent oversight must be put into place to ensure the needed accountability.

There are scores of ways that the financial system could and should be reformed—too many to list, and too many to tackle all at once. We need to begin with urgent, attainable goals and build from there. To help set us on a more stable and productive path forward, here are nine action items—three for each of the important players in the financial system, including you:

THREE ACTION ITEMS FOR THE BANKING SYSTEM AND INVESTMENT MANAGEMENT

1. Change compensation structures to align incentives with investment horizons.

In order to capture the returns provided by longer investment time horizons, wealth advisors and public fund managers need to be evaluated and compensated over a longer period than a quarter or a year. Compensation structures have become too wired to the annual cycle. Why should a majority of compensation bonus cycles be based on the time it takes for the Earth to revolve around the Sun? To restructure the compensation system, the large institutional investors—which include pension funds, endowments, and sovereign funds—must band together to demand managers' bonus compensation be tied to a minimum of three but ideally as many as seven to ten years of return performance. These same institutional investors will have to give up the rights to access the invested capital in order to allow for fund managers to invest long-term and not worry about being judged quarterly or even annually. Extending investment horizons would also ease pressure on public company quarterly results, since they would be less meaningful in the determination of compensation. The bigger ask is for a few entrepreneurial fund managers and wealth advisors to unilaterally establish new incentive structures with these same guidelines. This change would seem both to benefit society as well as create a business opportunity, offering a long-term investment strategy that can yield higher returns through an alignment of firm and investor interests.

2. Create an internal independent review process at each financial services firm to assess the suitability of every product and service for the firm's clients, as well as how and to whom they are marketed.

In the aftermath of every financial crisis, the cause seems obvious, with plenty of clues that things were not right. As noted in the previous chapter, one had only to look at the second page of the Orange County annual report to conclude that the county was engaging in inappropriate investment practices. IPO spinning, unchecked vendor financing, imprudent mortgage lending practices, the opening of unauthorized accounts, the selling of complex derivatives to unsophisticated clients—all were obviously inappropriate, yet large numbers of finance professionals were complicit in allowing, if not encouraging, such practices. We can't assume that government regulators will provide the necessary oversight, or that corporate cultures or hiring practices at the larger firms can ensure that finance professionals do the right thing when nobody is watching. A review process or oversight committee with unconflicted board level authority must be put in place at every firm to assess the suitability of every product and service offered. All financial firms of note have a risk and compliance function tasked with ensuring that the institution itself doesn't take on trading positions or underwrite offerings that will lead to inappropriate risk levels for the firm. That same function must be created at each firm to assess risks to clients and customers. Additionally, it isn't enough to assess the product risk; the review process should also scrutinize the incentive systems and marketing plan to sell or distribute each product. The Wells Fargo scandal, in which lending officers opened unwanted checking accounts, for example, wouldn't have been avoided by a review system focused solely on the suitability of products offered. In that case, the bad conduct stemmed from incentives within the firm.

3. Form a culture or values committee at each financial services firm that enacts mission-driven codes of conduct to encourage positive contributions and penalize undesired behaviors from within.

When Citi formed a committee focused on culture in 2004 and appointed me the first culture czar, the most impactful change we put in place was to tie 25 percent of employees' bonuses to their culture scores, to how they operated within the firm's community. Each employee received a 360-degree review by his or her co-workers and was rewarded or penalized for contributions outside of pure revenue generation. This not only discouraged bad conduct, but it also improved morale by acknowledging and reinforcing positive behavior. Many firms currently have culture committees, but they are often tasked only with making the job more appealing to employees (for example, protecting work-life balance), rather than creating and enforcing rules that will inspire a meaningful shift in behavior. It isn't enough to focus solely on work environment. Each firm, as well as the industry as a whole, must make greater efforts to define its values and model the behavior that would best align with those values. This action item would need to be implemented from the top down at each firm, with senior management forming a culture review process for each major business sector, then appointing leaders who will work for real change. Furthermore, the entire industry needs to place a higher priority on making the case as to why a functional financial system matters to a good society. That's a critical first step toward creating a healthy dialogue on the best path forward.

THREE ACTION ITEMS FOR GOVERNMENT

1. Create a federal-level oversight or review board to assess the management and viability of state and local pension systems.

In the private sector, there's an oversight function that sets minimum standards for retirement and healthcare programs. By most accounts, corporate pension plans are sound and healthy. But for state and local government employee pension systems, a similar oversight mechanism does not exist to ensure that programs are prudently structured and that the funds are properly managed. A federal oversight and review board should be assembled and tasked with monitoring and assessing state and local pension systems. This board would suggest guidelines and standards in areas of governance, performance management, accounting, and plan design. By suggesting prudent and objective standards, the oversight and review board would provide the necessary pressure or cover, depending on the relevant political challenge, for pension boards to take the actions required to improve their funds' financial viability. For example, if the oversight board recommended long-term underwriting assumptions based solely on expected market returns, then that would shine a light on those pension and retirement systems that irresponsibly continue to assume much higher future returns.

2. Require that any person running for election as a treasurer or other financial officer actually has a background in finance.

Pilots can't obtain a commercial license without at least 250 flight hours. Doctors are required to complete an extensive education and residencies and to pass board exams. Massage therapists can't even give certified massages without hundreds of hours of hands-on training. Yet Bob Citron, with zero financial experience, could become treasurer of Orange County and gamble with billions of dollars of public money. The same lack of requirements exists throughout our political system. Many state treasurers, for example, act as chief investment officer, banker, and financier of their state's government, manage the state's pooled investment account, and sit on the board of the state's employee pension funds. Yet under the current rules of many states, any registered voter can run for this office, regardless of relevant experience or background. To qualify as a candidate for a political office involving finance or treasury, office-specific requirements should be put in place, including degrees in business and accounting, together with relevant experience.

3. All financial regulations should be balanced and simple, with the requirements for compliance easy to understand and follow.

Since all financial activity includes the opportunity for good as well as bad behaviors, financial regulations must aim to limit excesses without negating the freedom to innovate, extend access, or increase inclusiveness. Achieving this balance typically requires setting limits as opposed to micromanaging every action through an army of compliance officers enforcing rules that lose sight of the big picture. We can't be focused on donuts while the investment pool is being leveraged three times over and invested in inappropriate securities. Simplicity is key for multiple reasons. Complex regulations get ignored. (How many disclosure documents or notices have you actually read when taking out a loan or signing up for a financial product?) Even worse, complex regulations may be more easily manipulated, which creates unintended negative consequences. Furthermore, complex regulations build barriers to entry for those firms without the financial or personnel resources to comply, effectively giving the larger firms control over that regulated market or sector. Penalties should be clear and consistent, with accountability evaluated at both the individual and firm level and the fines assessed specifically to either or both, depending on who is deemed responsible.

THREE ACTION ITEMS FOR EACH OF US

1. Dedicate time and resources to educate your children and yourself in matters of basic finance and economics.

Although money has become a bigger part of our personal lives and political debate, we know so little about how that world works. Our education system offers no guidance on how to function effectively in the modern financial world. Inclusion of basic finance within our school curriculum would be a prudent first step. For those of us who have completed our education, you can still learn and engage: Select a company and follow it with the same fervor reserved for your favorite sports team or celebrity. The company could be your employer or that of a family member, or perhaps it makes a product or provides a service that you find interesting. If it's a local business or retailer, engage on a personal level. Learn all you can about the business; become a champion of that store, telling neighbors and friends why its offerings are superior to mass-produced alternatives. If it's a public company, sign up for news alerts and monitor financial results. If you buy stock, own, don't rent—take a long-term view, understanding the company's challenges and, if appropriate, sticking with it through ups and downs. Connecting with companies in this way will offer you the advantage of valuable investment knowledge, as well as a deeper understanding of how the wider financial world works.

2. Hold public officials accountable, asking pointed questions about the pension funds falling within their political jurisdiction.

This issue is about more than public employees losing their retirement savings and benefits—which in itself is a tragedy. Gross mismanagement of these pension funds can lead to broad budget shortages and even bankruptcy, and that sort of collapse will affect us all. There needs to be oversight and accountability, and that begins with each of us having a more active role in asking the right questions every time we encounter a politician with any influence over a pension or retirement system. "How funded is our pension plan? How are the funds invested? What exactly are you doing to mitigate the coming pension crisis?" Until we commit to addressing this issue, we can't expect the same of our politicians—they will not prioritize challenges beyond their term of office unless we force them to be accountable.

3. Engage with your local community in a personal way.

Join a local cause or group, a recreation club or philanthropic endeavor. Mentor others; coach a sports team. You're likely to gain proximity to people you otherwise wouldn't have, and you'll learn more about your community, your neighbors, and yourself. Shop locally. Engage in the arts, whether that means regularly visiting museums, attending theater or literary readings, or supporting symphonies, concert halls, and dance companies, in your city, town, or school. These organizations are among the cornerstones of a thriving community. Question why you aspire to the other line—wanting a better life is a natural desire, but luxury is the enemy of experience. Be more invested in the experiences and people around you, particularly those you consider different from yourself. This action item may seem obvious or clichéd, but engagement creates vibrant local communities, and that success will spread nationally and improve our society, our discourse, and ourselves. Unless we break out of our personal bubbles, we will have no hope of preventing the large financial and social bubbles from forming. And when they burst, you will undoubtedly think that you should have been aware of something in the community that you might have seen if you had only taken the time to engage with the world outside of your curated existence.

DEVELOPING SOLUTIONS IS EASY; ACTING ON THEM IS DIFFICULT

There are countless reasons not to act. We're busy. We're tired. We're comfortable. We have a limited understanding of the problems and how they could be solved. We feel powerless.

The larger financial picture is often lost in the glare of the surface concerns that obsess our daily lives. Who has the capacity to worry about understanding modern finance when we're worried about paying bills, achieving the lifestyle we want, saving enough for retirement, and, if we're lucky, leaving something for our children? A recent report by the Federal Reserve found that fewer than 40 percent of working Americans feel that they are adequately saving for retirement, and 25 percent have nothing saved. If faced with an emergency, nearly half the people in our country can't come up with four hundred dollars within thirty days.

The trends in the modern financial world—toward increases in risk and complexity and a decrease in human interaction and connection—should scream out for immediate action. What will motivate us to act and to demand action of others? How can we get out ahead of the biggest dangers and make crucial, fundamental improvements before we're reeling from the next major crisis? Collectively we have the power to effectuate real progress, but proactive collective change is not possible without strong leadership. Who in the industry has the standing or the desire to be a thought leader, to gather the support required to make necessary changes?

There is a leadership vacuum in the financial world. There aren't enough role models like Sheriff Gates and Mayor Tubbs. The industry is so embattled that it has a hard time attracting or keeping the people who could be effective leaders. If good leaders do exist in finance, they are likely in a defensive posture, due to the vilification of the industry, and it's hard to make bold changes when you're playing defense. This has created an unfortunate cycle: The industry often fails because it lacks leadership; when it fails, it is attacked; because of the barrage of attacks, great leaders go elsewhere; and this dearth of strong leadership allows for further failures.

One of the few efforts to attract and develop enlightened leaders is at the Aspen Institute, with which I've been involved for a number of years as a co-founder of their Finance Leaders Fellowship program. Each year we select a class of twenty industry professionals from around the world who have demonstrated the potential for enlightened leadership, and we lead them through a part-time, two-year program of intensive seminars. We have selected four classes thus far, and I have no doubt that this group will make a significant collective impact on the financial services industry. Every time I meet with one or a group of them, my optimism for the future of the industry grows. These leaders will not only be great stewards of the institutions they run but will also work to bend the arc of stewardship for the whole industry in a positive direction.

Money connects with nearly every aspect of our lives, so it's essential to our survival and contentment that we work together toward setting the industry on a positive path. All of us agree that we'd rather live in a world where we can enjoy the benefits provided by a home mortgage, a car loan, a student loan, life insurance, a checking account, a retirement account, and so on. We need the financial system, but it must be reformed. Action must be undertaken by each of the major players in modern money— big banks, small banks, other financial firms, government at the federal, state, and local levels, and we the people—if we are to reclaim the financial industry as a tool that works for the benefit of us all.

———

I recently met with an Aspen Finance Fellow, Brian, who helps run one of the biggest asset managers on the planet. I was visiting family in Stamford, Connecticut, so Brian and I caught up over dinner at a classic white-tablecloth Greenwich restaurant. As we ate, I told him about the encounter I'd had with my uncle earlier that day.

Uncle John is a handsome, charismatic Spartan from my mother's side. After having emigrated from Greece without a dime or a word of

English, he arrived in America and worked hard enough to acquire some real estate just prior to the housing boom that hit Stamford soon thereafter. With those profits, he founded Patriot Bank in 1994 with a mission, he said, to "treat people like people, and not like numbers, the way they do at the big banks."

At the time of this visit, Uncle John was eighty-one and semiretired, still coming in to work each day but often only for half days. When I arrived at Patriot's headquarters at nine o'clock to take him to breakfast, I took the elevator upstairs to the executive suites, only to be told that he was in the retail branch down on the ground level.

It seemed odd that the bank's founder and former CEO and chairman would be down in the public branch, since the scope of his work—which still included handling loans and lines of credit for longtime corporate clients—would take place upstairs in the executive suite. There's usually no contact between retail customers and a bank's top executives. Perhaps, I surmised as I descended to the first floor, John was down there waiting for me. The elevator doors opened, and I wandered into the lobby where the early sun slanted through the windows. A line of people waited for open tellers, as others filled out slips at the counters. I looked beyond the teller windows, scanning for Uncle John, but no luck. And then I spotted him, sitting at a desk beside the entrance. It was a shocking sight, as I couldn't understand why someone of his stature would be stationed in the lobby by the front door.

I walked over and spoke his name, and he stood to hug me, then stepped back to size me up, as he's done since I was a little kid. "You're still growing," he said with a laugh.

"What are you doing down here in the lobby?" I asked.

"This is where I want to be."

"I don't understand. Doing what exactly?"

"I'm the greeter." He smiled.

"The greeter? But this is your bank."

"I'm old now, Chris. I'm nearly retired. They asked me what job I wanted, and I said, 'I want to go back to the beginning.' When people come into the bank, I welcome them."

I looked down at his wooden desk, on which stood a nameplate with FOUNDER inscribed on it.

Right then a customer came in, and Uncle John said, "Welcome to Patriot Bank."

"Hiya, John," the man said, and they shook hands.

"You know that guy?" I asked when the man walked away.

"Sure I do," Uncle John said. "I know everybody." He tapped the desk. "This is what I want to do. I want it to feel personal."

Later that day, sitting at dinner with Brian, I recounted the story. My uncle was an amiable guy, but I still couldn't get over how uncommon it was to have a founder and former CEO of a bank greeting customers in the lobby. Things hadn't been done that way for decades. Brian was taken with the story too. He asked a lot of questions, getting me to set the scene.

Weeks later, Brian called me about some business, but before we got to it, he said, "You know, I can't stop thinking about your uncle. I've told that story to so many people."

"I hear you," I said. "I think about it a lot."

"The story's sweet at first, but then it's something else. I don't quite know why it's stuck with me the way it has."

"I don't, either. But it makes me feel . . ." I searched for the word "optimistic."

"That's exactly it," Brian said. "Optimistic. It's not even nostalgia really. It just makes me feel good."

There was something about the image of the top guy in the bank breaking down all the barriers between him and the general public, dragging a desk to the front door, looking people in the eye, and striving to connect with his customers and community. Brian and I both knew why the story was so affecting. We recognized that the emotions the story stirred in us revealed that something human and elemental had been lost in the world. There was no easy way to articulate it; it was an instinct, like whatever tells us to be kind to our neighbors, to share on the playground, to hold a door for a stranger. The financial world has lost that common humanity. Uncle John showed us a small step toward reclaiming it.

ACKNOWLEDGMENTS

Any book about finance would seem to require the author to settle his own debts, which, in my case, are many. The first and biggest debt is to my mother, Athanasia, my father, Nicholas, Uncle John, and my teachers, professors, and mentors who trained and encouraged me to seek experience without concern for outcome.

Thanks to David Albert and Anand Giridharadas for lighting the spark that ignited this book. David, claiming to see potential in me for storytelling and observation, told me almost three decades ago that I should chronicle my experiences. Fast-forwarding a quarter century, Anand advised me to write, as he put it, "the book the world needs." This advice was my constant North Star in guiding the focus and trajectory of the book. Anand also suggested I collaborate with another writer to ensure that it would be a great book.

My search for a co-writer was short, thanks to my good friend Tamsin Smith, who introduced me to Dan Stone, the best co-writer I could have ever hoped to find. My favorite part of this whole process has been working with Dan, debating the strategy, discussing the concepts, exchanging drafts of the stories that would most efficiently and effectively convey the ideas explored in *How Money Became Dangerous*. Dan is a wonderful person in so many ways and gives me hope that we can live in an intellectually challenging world without cynicism and judgment. Dan deserves significant credit for making this an entertaining and—I hope you agree—impactful read.

Writing a book is one thing; selling it is quite another. Thank you to my dear friend Michelle Kydd Lee at Creative Artists Agency for believing in this book, providing me with immediate encouragement and setting us up with our agent, David Larabell. Thanks to David for great guidance throughout this process, especially the introduction to Denise Oswald at Ecco. Of all the editors with whom we spoke, Denise was the one with whom Dan and I felt a connection. We have no doubt that her intellect, encouragement, and attention have made this a much better book—and she was such a pleasure to work with. Thanks too to the rest of the fine people at Ecco and HarperCollins for their contributions.

It would be too much to thank the hundreds of people interviewed for the book, but I'd like to highlight those central to each chapter.

For chapter 1, "Fool's Gold," a big thanks to my first two friends in the business world, Barry Kagasoff and George Elmassian. I did reach out to Nazareth Andonian in prison on multiple occasions, but he didn't respond.

For chapter 2, "Welcome to the Jungle," I'd like to thank the godfather of municipal finance, who has more than sixty years of Wall Street experience, Gedale Horowitz, as well as my dear friend Laurence Borde.

For chapter 3, "Milk and Balloons," thanks to Mark Albert, the brother of David and proof that this is a small world. Thanks to my many Disney and Wharton friends who contributed countless details and insights, and to my former business school roommate, the inimitable Paul Hynek.

For chapter 4, "Conquistadors of the Sky," thanks to Eduardo Mestre both for his contributions and for teaching me long ago to try to make every meeting provocative and meaningful. Thanks to Michael Soenen, who has a knack for effortlessly making life fun and entertaining, as well as my fellow Greek Petros Kitsos, and my courageous and lovely sister, Lea Medow.

For chapter 5, "Modern Art," the U.S. Filter team was wonderfully supportive. The incomparable Dick Heckmann, Andrew Seidel, Damian Georgino, and Nick Memmo couldn't have been more generous.

For chapter 6, "Shooting an Elephant," a hearty thanks to my business partner and close friend Tom Smach, to my longtime friends and co-workers, Stuart Goldstein and Greg Dalvito, and to Bill Viqueira, for their constant bravery in the face of Wall Street's line of fire.

For chapter 7, "Reach Out and Touch Someone," thanks to the truly special Danni Ashe for trusting us to tell her story, and to my very good friends at Equinix for also trusting us to portray their incredible journey. Peter Van Camp, Andrew Rigoli, Jay Adelson, and John Knuff were a real pleasure to engage. I'd also like to thank longtime friends Will Fleming and Mark Davis for their contributions.

For chapter 8, "Diamond Dogs," thanks to my always-entertaining longtime friend and co-worker Kevin Tice for sharing his journey in, through, and out of Wall Street.

For chapter 9, "The Other Line," a big thanks to longtime friend Michael Tedesco for his insights and clarity on a new and evolving trend. His thoughts on any topic are always unique and provocative.

Chapter 10, "Everything Rhymes with Orange," was a true collaboration of Orange County and Stockton friends. From the Orange County side, thanks to Justin Bailes, Tom Beckett, Bruce Bennett, Michael Corbat, Sheriff Brad Gates, Thomas Hayes, Gedale Horowitz, Stan Oftelie, and Tom Purcell; from Stockton, a sincere thanks for the openness and hospitality you provided to Dan and me, particularly my friend John Deasy, Mayor Michael Tubbs, Lange Luntao, and Princess Vongchanh. What you are doing in Stockton is truly remarkable and a light of hope for all of us.

There are so many who have provided input for the epilogue that I can list only a few, but thanks so much to all who offered ideas and a willingness to debate what the future of finance should look like and how we get there from here: Peter Chung, Mike Dutton, Sarah Friar, Brian Kreiter, Bryan Lewis, Ian McKinnon, Bob Peck, and Jennifer Simpson.

I was told by an author of six books that the best part of writing a book is after publication, when the real learning begins through debate with others about what you've written. I thought it would be a fun, illuminating exercise to begin that process during the actual writing of the book, sharing chapters with those who I believed would provide a unique perspective on the topic in question. The following trusted readers, along with those acknowledged above, are responsible for the insights in this book more than anyone. I enjoyed every minute of our conversation and debate, and I hope this is just the beginning: Mohamad Afshar, David Albert, Gideon Argov, Sara Aviel, Skip Battle, Harish Belur, Tom Bentley, Dennis Berman, Michael Christenson, Stephen DeBerry, Diego de Sola, Bob Druskin, Patrick Fitzgerald, Dan and Nina Goggins, Kristen Grimm, Alan Heslop, Samuel Hodges, Augustin Hong, Bryan Hoyos, Leif Isaksen, Nadeem Jeddy, Stace Lindsay, Siobhan MacDermott, Ranji Nagaswami, Priya Parker, Peter Reiling, Barry Rosenbloom, Laurie and Carl Saxe, Kurt Schacht, Jenny Seyfried, Alexandra Shockey, Gabrielle Simon, Shamina Singh, Shivani Siroya, Gary Skraba, Trina Spear, Diane Strand, Jonathan Veitch, Kirsten Wandschneider, Adam Wasserman, James Whitney, and Class III of the Aspen Finance Fellows/ The Third Way.

A huge thank you to my longtime executive assistant and friend, Angela Murray, for typing what must have been thousands of pages, most of which ended up in the trash; for her many corrections of my grammar; and for the positive reinforcement of every new draft, regardless of how rough and off-message it may have been. Thanks too to Don Walerstein for his legal advice, and to Tom Colligan for his diligent fact-checking.

I'd also like to thank the Aspen Institute's Finance Leaders Fellowship. All of my proceeds from this book will be donated to the worthy and needed cause of creating and nourishing values-based leadership in the financial services industry.

Dan and I would like to thank our brilliant wives, Kim Gooden and Jessica Varelas. As insightful readers and thoughtful editors, they improved the book immeasurably through their hard work and dedication.

Deepest appreciation to Kim, who provided selfless, unwavering support to Dan during this whole process, keeping their family afloat through the waves of deadlines, while gracefully handling her own full-time job that was no less demanding, stressful, or important.

Dan dedicates his years of effort on this book to his father, Dan Sr., who served as a guiding light and special inspiration for Dan in exploring this subject matter.

I must thank my wonderful daughter, Athanacia, for her constant support, patience, and encouragement. No words can properly thank my beautiful wife and best friend, Jessica, for being the editor of my life, making each day better in so many ways while always giving me a reason and a purpose for everything I do. I love both you and Cia so much that it cannot be measured, which, of course, is true of all the important things in life.

INDEX